# Mapping the Legal Boundaries
of Belonging

RELIGION AND GLOBAL POLITICS

SERIES EDITOR
John L. Esposito
University Professor and Director
Prince Alwaleed Bin Talal Center for Muslim-Christian Understanding
Georgetown University

ISLAMIC LEVIATHAN
*Islam and the Making of State Power*
Seyyed Vali Reza Nasr

RACHID GHANNOUCHI
*A Democrat Within Islamism*
Azzam S. Tamimi

BALKAN IDOLS
*Religion and Nationalism in Yugoslav States*
Vjekoslav Perica

ISLAMIC POLITICAL IDENTITY IN TURKEY
M. Hakan Yavuz

RELIGION AND POLITICS IN POST-COMMUNIST ROMANIA
Lavinia Stan and Lucian Turcescu

PIETY AND POLITICS
*Islamism in Contemporary Malaysia*
Joseph Chinyong Liow

TERROR IN THE LAND OF THE HOLY SPIRIT
*Guatemala under General Efrain Rios Montt, 1982–1983*
Virginia Garrard-Burnett

IN THE HOUSE OF WAR
*Dutch Islam Observed*
Sam Cherribi

BEING YOUNG AND MUSLIM
*New Cultural Politics in the Global South and North*
Asef Bayat and Linda Herrera

CHURCH, STATE, AND DEMOCRACY IN EXPANDING EUROPE
Lavinia Stan and Lucian Turcescu

THE HEADSCARF CONTROVERSY
*Secularism and Freedom of Religion*
Hilal Elver

THE HOUSE OF SERVICE
*The Gülen Movement and Islam's Third Way*
David Tittensor

MAPPING THE LEGAL BOUNDARIES OF BELONGING
*Religion and Multiculturalism from Israel to Canada*
Edited by René Provost

# Mapping the Legal Boundaries of Belonging

*Religion and Multiculturalism from Israel to Canada*

EDITED BY RENÉ PROVOST

OXFORD
UNIVERSITY PRESS

# OXFORD
UNIVERSITY PRESS

Oxford University Press is a department of the University of Oxford.
It furthers the University's objective of excellence in research, scholarship,
and education by publishing worldwide.

Oxford  New York
Auckland  Cape Town  Dar es Salaam  Hong Kong  Karachi
Kuala Lumpur  Madrid  Melbourne  Mexico City  Nairobi
New Delhi  Shanghai  Taipei  Toronto

With offices in
Argentina  Austria  Brazil  Chile  Czech Republic  France  Greece
Guatemala  Hungary  Italy  Japan  Poland  Portugal  Singapore
South Korea  Switzerland  Thailand  Turkey  Ukraine  Vietnam

Oxford is a registered trade mark of Oxford University Press
in the UK and certain other countries.

Published in the United States of America by
Oxford University Press
198 Madison Avenue, New York, NY 10016

© Oxford University Press 2014

All rights reserved. No part of this publication may be reproduced,
stored in a retrieval system, or transmitted, in any form or by any means,
without the prior permission in writing of Oxford University Press,
or as expressly permitted by law, by license, or under terms agreed with the
appropriate reproduction rights organization. Inquiries concerning reproduction
outside the scope of the above should be sent to the Rights Department,
Oxford University Press, at the address above.

You must not circulate this work in any other form
and you must impose this same condition on any acquirer.

Cataloging-in-Publication data is on file with the Library of Congress

9780199383009 (hbk.)
9780199383016 (pbk.)

1  3  5  7  9  8  6  4  2

Printed in the United States of America on acid-free paper

# CONTENTS

*Preface* vii
*Contributors* ix

Introduction: Let Us Compare Mythologies 1
CAYLEE HONG AND RENÉ PROVOST

PART ONE  MULTICULTURALISM AND WESTERN SECULARISM

1. The Christian Roots of the Secular State 25
SILVIO FERRARI

2. Conflicting Visions of Political Space 41
SUZANNE LAST STONE

3. Human Rights and Secularism: Arendt, Asad, and Milbank as Critics of the Secular Foundations of Human Rights 56
SHAI LAVI

PART TWO  MULTICULTURALISM AND RELIGIOUS FREEDOM AS SWORDS OR SHIELDS

4. Religious Freedom as "Reflexive Law" 81
INO AUGSBERG

5. The Distinctiveness of Religious Liberty 99
VÍCTOR M. MUÑIZ-FRATICELLI

PART THREE   NEGOTIATING IDENTITY BETWEEN STATE
AND RELIGION

6. "Inside Out/Outside In": Coexistence and Cross-Pollination
of Religion and State   121
SHAUNA VAN PRAAGH

7. Who Is a Jew and the Law: Between London and Jerusalem   143
DAPHNE BARAK-EREZ


PART FOUR   WHOSE VOICE? WHICH TRUTH? ONE OR MANY?

8. A Dialogue between a Liberal and an Ultra-Orthodox on the Exclusion
of Women from Torah Study   155
MENACHEM MAUTNER

9. Religious Claims as Public Reason? Polygamy as a Case Study   192
ANGELA CAMPBELL


PART FIVE   MULTICULTURALISM, RELIGION,
AND THE GEOGRAPHY OF POWER

10. The Acute Multicultural Entrapment of the Palestinian-Arab
Religious Minorities in Israel and the Feeble Measures
Required to Relieve It   225
MICHAEL M. KARAYANNI

11. Localizing Religion in a Jewish State   252
YISHAI BLANK

*Bibliography*   289
*Index*   317

# PREFACE

The essays in this collection are the outcome of a joint research initiative between the Centre for Human Rights and Legal Pluralism at McGill University (then headed by René Provost) and the Minerva Center for Human Rights at Tel Aviv University (then headed by Shai Lavi). The authors first met near Jerusalem for a series of closed round table discussions of the broad theme of religious revival and the turn away from multiculturalist policies as well as the specific topics identified by each participant. A second phase took place nine months later in Montreal, where full drafts of the essays were presented and commented upon at a public conference. In addition to the authors included in this volume, thanks are due to others whose contribution at the conference in Montreal helped improve the papers: Beverley Baines (Queen's University), Alison Dundes Renteln (University of Southern California), Anver Emon (University of Toronto), Christopher McRudden (University of Oxford), Richard Moon (University of Windsor), Vrinda Narain (McGill University), Colleen Sheppard (McGill University), and Laura Underkuffler (Cornell University). Financial support from both McGill and Tel Aviv Universities is gratefully acknowledged.

René Provost
McGill University

# CONTRIBUTORS

INO AUGSBERG is Professor of Legal Philosophy and Public Law and Co-Director of the Hermann Kantorowicz-Institute for Fundamental Research in Law at the Christian-Albrechts-University Kiel. He previously studied at the universities of Freiburg and Heidelberg, and was a Research Associate at the Faculty of Law of Ludwig-Maximilians Universität in Munich. He received a PhD in philosophy from Freiburg University (2001), a PhD in jurisprudence from Hamburg University (2008), and completed his Habilitation in public law and theory in 2013. He is the author or coauthor of five books and editor or coeditor of two volumes. Recent publications in English include "The Myth of the Neutral State," 8 *German Law Journal* 143 (2007), with K.-H. Ladeur; "The Relevance of Network Models Within the Juridic Discourse," 10 *German Law Journal* 383 (2009); and "Religion and the Secular State" in J. Basedow et al. (eds.), *German National Reports to the 18th International Congress of Comparative Law*, Washington (2010), 1, with S. Korioth. His most recent article, "Reading Law: On Law as a Textual Phenomenon," was published in *Law & Literature* (vol. 22, no. 3) in fall 2010.

DAPHNE BARAK-EREZ is a judge on the Israeli Supreme Court. Until 2012, she was a Professor of Law and dean of the Faculty of Law of Tel-Aviv University, where she held the Stewart and Judy Colton Chair of Law and Security. She served as the Director of the Cegla Center for Interdisciplinary Research of the Law and a member of the Council of Higher Education in Israel, a member of the American Law Institute, and a member of the International Academy of Comparative Law. Her main research and teaching areas are administrative and constitutional law. In addition, she taught courses in the areas of feminist jurisprudence, contracts, and payment systems. She is a three time graduate of Tel-Aviv University: LL.B. (summa cum laude) 1988; LL.M. (summa cum laude) 1991, and J.S.D., 1993 (recipient of the Colton Fellowship). She acted as the Director of the Minerva

Center for Human Rights (2000–2001), as the chairperson of the Israeli Association of Public Law, and as the Deputy Dean of the faculty (2000–2002). She was awarded several prizes, including the Rector's Prize for Excellence in Teaching, the Zeltner Prize, the Woman of the City Award (by the City of Tel-Aviv) and the Women in Law Award (by the Israeli Bar). She is the author and editor of several books and of many articles in Israel, England, Canada, and the United States, including *Outlawed Pigs: Law, Religion and Culture in Israel* (2007).

YISHAI BLANK is an Associate Professor of Law at Tel-Aviv University Faculty of Law, and the Faculty's Vice Dean (Academic Affairs). His areas of research and teaching include local government law, administrative law, legal theory, global cities, and urban legal policy. Professor Blank obtained his LL.B. (magna cum laude) and an additional B.A. in Philosophy (magna cum laude) from Tel-Aviv University. He clerked for the Chief Justice of the Israeli Supreme Court, Aharon Barak. He received his S.J.D. in June 2002 from Harvard Law School, where he was a Byse Fellow. He was a member of the Young Scholars in the Humanities and Social Sciences Forum of the Israeli Academy of Science and Humanities and holder of a fellowship from the Israeli Science Foundation (ISF). Professor Blank was a visiting professor at Cornell Law School, Brown University, and the Oñati International Institute for the Sociology of Law. Some of his recent publications include: "The Geography of Sexuality," 90 *North Carolina Law Review* (2012); "The Re-enchantment of Law," 96 *Cornell Law Review* 633 (2011); "Localism in the New Global Legal Order," 47 *Harvard Journal of International Law* 263 (2006); and "The City and the World," 44 *Columbia Journal of Transnational Law* 875 (2006).

ANGELA CAMPBELL is a professor at the Faculty of Law at McGill University, currently serving as the Associate Dean of Graduate Studies. Previously she has served as Director of the McGill Institute of Comparative Law and a convener of the McGill Research Group on Health and Law. Professor Campbell earned her B.A. (Hons), B.C.L. and LL.B. degrees from McGill University. She completed her LL.M. at Harvard Law School as a Frank Knox fellow and Langdon H. Gammon fellow. Prior to joining the Faculty of Law at McGill, she clerked for The Honourable Mr. Justice Frank Iacobucci at the Supreme Court of Canada, and taught at the University of Ottawa's Faculty of Law (Common Law). Professor Campbell researches and teaches in the areas of family law, health law, criminal law, successions law, and feminist legal studies. She is the author of *Sister Wives, Sex Workers and Surrogates: Outlaws by Choice?* (2013).

SILVIO FERRARI is Professor of Law and Religion, University of Milan and Catholic University of Leuven. He has been a visiting professor at the

University of California (Berkeley, 1994 and 2001), the Institute for Advanced Legal Studies (London, 1998–99) and the Ecole Pratique des Hautes Etudes (Paris, Sorbonne, 2004). His publications in English include *Islam and European Legal Systems* (2000, edited with A. Bradney) and *Law and Religion in Post-Communist Europe*, (2003, edited with W. Cole Durham, Jr. and E. A. Sewell). He has recently completed, together with Felice Dassetto, a report on *The Legal Status of Islam in Europe* for the European Parliament (2007). His main fields of interest are law and religion in Europe, comparative law of religions (particularly Jewish law, canon law, and Islamic law) and the Vatican policy in the Middle East. He is president of ICLARS (International Consortium for Law and Religion Studies), member of the Advisory Council on Freedom of Religion and Belief of the OSCE-ODIHR and of the Scientific Committee of the Institut européen en sciences des religions (EPHE, Paris).

CAYLEE HONG is a recent LL.B/B.C.L. graduate from McGill University (2013). Her research focuses on the intersections between religion, culture, and gender as well as their implications for the governance and management of natural resources. She holds an LL.M. from the University of London, School of Oriental and African Studies (2008) and clerked at the Federal Court of Canada in 2013.

MICHAEL M. KARAYANNI is an Associate Professor, Faculty of Law, at the Hebrew University of Jerusalem. He holds the Silver Chair in Civil Procedure and is the Director of the Harry and Michael Sacher Institute for Legislative Research and Comparative Law. He is a member of the Forum of Young Scholars at the Israel Academy of Sciences and Humanities and a past recipient of the Rothschild Prize and of a Fulbright. His research focuses on private international law and interreligious law, civil procedures, and multiculturalism. Professor Karayanni holds an LL.D from the Hebrew University (2000) as well as an S.J.D. from the University of Pennsylvania (2003).

SHAI LAVI is a senior lecturer and the director of the Minerva Center for Human Rights at Tel Aviv University's Faculty of Law. He received his Ph.D. from the Jurisprudence and Social Policy Program, University of California–Berkeley. His book *The Modern Art of Dying: A History of Euthanasia in the United States* won the 2006 Distinguished Book Award in sociology of law from the American Sociological Association. He was a Fulbright fellow at the University of California–Berkeley, a visiting professor at Toronto University, and a Humboldt fellow at the Dubnow Institute for Jewish History and Culture in Leipzig.

MENACHEM MAUTNER is the Danielle Rubinstein Professor of Comparative Civil Law and Jurisprudence at the Tel Aviv University, Faculty of Law, and a former dean of the Faculty. Mautner received his LL.B., *magna cum laude*, and LL.M., *summa cum laude*, from Tel Aviv University. He obtained another LL.M. and a J.S.D. from Yale Law School. Mautner was visiting professor at Michigan Law School (twice); visiting professor at NYU Law School (twice); visiting professor at Cardiff Law School; visiting scholar at Harvard Law School; visiting professor at Venice International University; visiting professor at Columbia Law School. Mautner is the author of five books, the editor of six books, and the author of over 80 articles published in Israel, the United States and Britain. His book *Law and the Culture of Israel* was published in 2011.

VÍCTOR M. MUÑIZ-FRATICELLI is an Assistant Professor of Law and Political Science at McGill University. He clerked for Justices Negrón García and Hernández Denton of the Supreme Court of Puerto Rico and has been a visiting professor at the University of Puerto Rico School of Law. He is the author of *The Structure of Pluralism* (2014), which marshals the British pluralist tradition to reconsider the idea of sovereignty, the sources of political authority, and the relationship between associations and the state. He is currently working on the relationship between religious and state legal systems and on the implications of political pluralism for contemporary theories of justice, with special emphasis on the work of John Rawls.

RENÉ PROVOST was the founding Director of the McGill Centre for Human Rights and Legal Pluralism from its creation in 2005 until the summer of 2010. He previously served as Associate Dean (Academics) of the Faculty of Law. He teaches several courses in the area of human rights and social diversity, including International Law of Human Rights, International Humanitarian Law, Public International Law, Theoretical Approaches to Law, Foundations of Law, and Legal Anthropology. Professor Provost is the author of *International Human Rights and Humanitarian Law* (2002), the editor of *State Responsibility in International Law* (2002), and co-editor of *Public International Law Chiefly as Applied and Interpreted in Canada* (2006), *Confronting Genocide* (2010), and *Dialogues on Human Rights and Legal Pluralism* (2012). He is currently completing a book on the cultural pluralization of international humanitarian law and is the principal investigator for the Centaur Jurisprudence Project, a SSHRC interdisciplinary team project looking at the transformation of the notion of culture before legal institutions.

SHAUNA VAN PRAAGH is an Associate Professor at the Faculty of Law and a member of the Institute of Comparative Law at McGill University and the McGill Centre for Human Rights and Legal Pluralism. She served as Associate Dean of Graduate Studies from 2007 to 2010. She teaches Extracontractual Obligations/Torts, Advanced Common Law Obligations, Graduate

Legal Methodology, and Social Diversity and Law. Professor Van Praagh studied at the University of Toronto (B.Sc. 1986, LL.B. 1989) and Columbia University (LL.M. 1992, J.S.D. 2000), and clerked for the Right Honourable Brian Dickson, Chief Justice of Canada, in 1989–1990. Recent publications include « Troubles de voisinage: Droit, égalité et religion » in J-F Gaudreault-DesBiens (dir.), *La religion, le droit et le "raisonnable"* (2009); "View from the Sukkah: Religion and Neighbourly Relations" in Richard Moon (ed.), *Law and Religious Pluralism in Canada* (2008); "Civil Law and Religion in the Supreme Court of Canada: What should we get out of Bruker v. Marcovitz?" (2008) 43 *Supreme Court Law Review* (2d) 381–411 (with Rosalie Jukier); co-editor, *Stateless Law: Evolving Boundaries of a Discipline* (2014).

SUZANNE LAST STONE is a Professor of Jewish Law and Contemporary Civilization, Professor of Law, and Director of the Center for Jewish Law and Contemporary Civilization, at the Benjamin N. Cardozo School of Law of Yeshiva University. She has held the Gruss Visiting Chair in Talmudic Civil Law at both the Harvard and University of Pennsylvania Law Schools, and also has visited at Princeton, Columbia Law, Hebrew University Law, and Tel Aviv Law. She is a graduate of Princeton University and Columbia University Law School and was a Danforth Fellow in 1974 in Jewish History and Classical Religions at Yale University. Before joining the Cardozo faculty, Stone clerked for Judge John Minor Wisdom of the Fifth Circuit Court of Appeals and then practiced litigation at Paul, Weiss, Rifkind, Wharton and Garrison. In addition to teaching courses in Jewish Law and Political Thought and Jewish Law and American Legal Theory, she currently teaches Federal Courts and Law, Religion and the State. Professor Stone writes and lectures on the intersection of Jewish thought, legal theory, and the humanities. Her publications include: "In Pursuit of the Counter-text: The Turn to the Jewish Legal Model in Contemporary American Legal Theory," (*Harvard Law Review*); "The Jewish Conception of Civil Society," in *Alternative Conceptions of Civil Society*; "Feminism and the Rabbinic Conception of Justice" in *Women and Gender in Jewish Philosophy*; and "Rabbinic Legal Magic" (*Yale Journal of Law & Humanities*).

# Mapping the Legal Boundaries of Belonging

# Introduction

## Let Us Compare Mythologies

CAYLEE HONG AND RENÉ PROVOST

> The glittering and hurting days are almost done
> Then let us compare mythologies
> I have learned my elaborate lie
> of soaring crosses and poisoned thorns.
> —Leonard Cohen, *Let Us Compare Mythologies*[1]

Every community is plural, but each defines its plurality along particular lines that project a certain mythological construction of its own identity. This speaks to a—mostly imagined—moment of creation, in which a group of individuals overcome some of their differences by deeming them inconsequential, to proclaim instead that certain shared attributes can cement a bond and create a foundation upon which a community can be built. The process of constructing any community thus involves a mapping of identities, the delineation of the boundaries of belonging that will at once enclose and exclude. In this sense, the concept of a community is necessarily relational, projecting a claim to specificity that constructs its own other. As such, the figure of the stranger is the necessary shadow of the edification of our sense of self.[2] What shape that stranger takes—the African slave, the wandering Jew, the exotic Oriental, the effeminate gay man, and so on—is as infinitely variable as there are versions of any given community. Viewed in this light, the mapping of identities does not refer to a static mythology that imposes a finite and fully defined list of attributes upon which individuals are included and excluded. Quite the opposite: the boundaries of belonging to a community are ineluctably and perpetually contested terrain, a process of mythological construction that is necessarily collective, continuous, and unstable. Perhaps even more than the image of the self or the projection of the other, the space in between captures the encounter for which diversity stands. Religious revival and multicultural policies each challenge, in their own ways, this image of plurality.

As perceptively noted by James Boyd White, it is difficult to talk about religion because it speaks to a way of experiencing life that affirms ineffable or mysterious links between self and others, truth and uncertainty, real and occult.[3] Any conversation that straddles across religious boundaries engages competing and at times mutually inconsistent cosmologies that often reduce the other to sheer irrationality or obscurity. This poses a particular challenge when we attempt to speak to a reality that spans religious beliefs, linking individuals to form a national community superimposed upon the religious ones; there is a real risk that the common language forged to speak in terms of categories like citizenship or nationality will silence aspects of religious beliefs considered fundamental to its adherents, a silent erasure of difference that may be taken as the marker of a coherence that is in fact more apparent than real. Lawyers, for whom the erection of such intellectual scaffoldings presents a largely irresistible urge, may be more at risk than most of falling prey to this illusion of coherence in the process of creating and interpreting legal norms meant to regulate diversity in our societies. Creating political communities where difference can exist, including where people can faithfully live out their religious beliefs, has been a consistent challenge for states professing their acceptance of diversity.

As Brenna Bhandar remarks, one technique of managing difference is multiculturalism.[4] It reputedly defies undifferentiated models of citizenship not only by acknowledging that individuals are abstract members of a political community but also by recognizing difference as a key part of integration.[5] Joseph Raz sees multiculturalism as a "normative precept motivated by concern for the dignity and well-being of all human beings," which helps groups coexist in the same political society while maintaining their distinct identity.[6] These lofty aims involve practical policies that provide for group representation in government authorities, promote pluralistic public services, allot resources to encourage traditions and identities of society's different groups, and permit accommodations, including legal exemptions.[7]

Yet it is very difficult to trace a linear progression of multiculturalism as a coherent policy because each variant of the doctrine in a given country is a projection of that particular community's sense of self. Thus multiculturalism has been implemented, revised, and in some cases retracted in different ways in Australia, Canada, the United States, the United Kingdom, Sweden, the Netherlands, and arguably Israel as well.[8] Canada and Israel, in particular, can be taken as two models of the incorporation of multicultural policies within liberal democratic states that have diverse populations and significant minority groups.

Canadian multiculturalism is unique in several ways. To begin with, the existence of aboriginal groups has resulted in multiculturalism policies that are markedly different from those in Europe and Israel.[9] In addition, according to Christian Joppke, multiculturalism in Canada is "entrenched as an identity option for society as a whole [while] European multiculturalism has always been for immigrants only."[10] Will Kymlicka makes a parallel argument in Citizenship and Immigration Canada's Report where he states that "[m]ulticulturalism serves as a link for native-born citizens from national identity to solidarity with immigrants and minorities. And conversely, multiculturalism provides a link through which immigrants and minorities come to identify with, and feel pride in, Canada."[11] In this way, multiculturalism can also be intrinsically linked to national identity. This offers an alternative to Raz's articulation of multiculturalism as a *replacement* of nationalism as the "common bond of society."[12] In places like Canada, multiculturalism is not exterior to nationalism, but rather a significant form of it.

Within the Canadian context, Québec also offers a distinct translation of the multicultural model, labeled "interculturalism." According to the 2008 Report of the Consultation Commission on Accommodation Practices Related to Cultural Differences, known as the Bouchard–Taylor Commission, the Canadian multiculturalism model is not well suited to Québec because the latter is "constantly concerned about its future as a cultural minority."[13] Within this context, interculturalism "seeks to reconcile ethnocultural diversity with the continuity of the French-speaking core and the preservation of the social link."[14] While it emphasizes exchanges between citizens and recognizes difference, interculturalism demands a "reciprocal willingness to compromise based on core values such as gender equality, freedom of conscience, fairness, secularism and so on."[15] Nonetheless, scholars caution against overstating the differences between the two approaches. Joseph Garcea, for example, challenges the assumption that multiculturalism causes segregation whereas interculturalism promotes integration.[16]

Québec's interculturalism highlights how national minorities regulate diversity amid their own concerns over identity and security. In particular, debates over accommodation and the differences between Canadian and Québécois approaches to integration reveal how anti/post/multi/intra/-culturalism are themselves sources of negotiations over power and autonomy. The Bouchard-Taylor Commission argued that Québec's integration debates are linked to a general crisis of perception resulting from the unease of "Quebecers of French-Canadian ancestry ... with their twofold status as a majority in Québec and a minority in Canada and North America."[17] In this way, Québec's policy cannot be fully understood outside of its broader political grievances with Canada.

If Canada is one ideal-type in the discussion of multiculturalism, embodying multiculturalism as a tool of nation-building, Israel is another ideal-type, a state defined by its alignment with one specific religion. Eliezer Ben-Rafael and Yochanan Peres note that Israel's Declaration of Independence at once defines the country as a democracy, bestowing equality and liberty on all, and as Jewish, creating an exclusive link with a specified segment of its population.[18] This exclusion is also reinforced by state symbols such as the state flag, the official emblem, and the national anthem, as well as citizenship laws.[19] A basic but tangible example is the Ministry of Immigrant Absorption's slogan, "coming home to Israel." While the ministry seems to also cater to non-Jewish immigrants, it unmistakably projects the image that Israel is Jewish and for Jewish newcomers.

Whether Israel's approach is seen as contrary to multiculturalism depends on how multiculturalism itself is understood. If multiculturalism is inherently rooted in recognition, it is difficult to square Israel's formal definition of itself as Jewish with the principles of multiculturalism. According to Keith Banting and Will Kymlicka, multiculturalism requires "extend[ing] some level of public recognition and support for ethnocultural minorities to maintain and express their distinct identities and practices."[20] Under this view, if the self-definition negatively affects other groups' claims for recognition and legitimacy, it would seem contrary to multiculturalism. An extreme example is the controversial loyalty-oath legislation, which would require new immigrants, including non-Jewish ones, to pledge loyalty to Israel as a Jewish and democratic state.[21] This contravenes the underlying basis of multiculturalism, as understood for example by Michael Karayanni who argues that:

> what seems to be unique in current studies on multiculturalism is not merely the observation and presentation of societies that happen to be diverse in terms of the religious, cultural, national and ethnic affiliation of their members, rather, it is the central argument that such divergence is legitimate and should be accommodated.[22]

It is also hard to see how Israel's approach aligns with the view that multiculturalism should promote an inclusive national identity. Hanna Lerner points out that in Israel, for example, "the non-Jewish sectors in the population have been by and large excluded from the discussions over the constitution, which centered around the definition of the identity of the state."[23]

Given Israel's self-definition and the historical exclusion of other groups from discussions of that definition, is it possible to imagine an inclusive identity for non-Jewish Israelis according to a multicultural model? How can they be included within Israeli nationhood when it is understood in terms of "the Jewish people"?[24] The definition of the state as Jewish also inspires extensive debate among Israeli Jews in the public arena given the contested meanings of Judaism and Jewishness.[25] While Avi Sagi and Ohad Nachtomy argue that a pluralistic politics of recognition is central to contemporary Israel, how meaningful is it where the state's basic self-conception is based on the majority religion?[26] This in turn begs the question of the mythical nature of the representation of places like Canada, Québec, and the United Kingdom as secular. While the crucifix in the Québec National Assembly and the role of Queen Elizabeth II as the titular head of the Church of England project a very minimal religious presence compared to the symbolic and practical role of Judaism in Israel, they may nonetheless highlight how Israel as "Jewish" is more visible, and seen as more problematic to inclusive citizenship, because Christianity is still the neutral marker of normalcy. The Queen's role is explained as "tradition" while the Québec Court of Appeal recently held that Catholic prayers before city council meetings are "heritage."[27]

Just as multiculturalism has different meanings and modes of operation, so too does "difference." It was suggested at the outset that every community confronts its plurality in different ways, and this includes the very vectors along which difference is measured. Thus multiculturalism's perceived insistence on culture as a central marker of difference has generated skepticism in some quarters, despite the famously fungible nature of the concept of culture. In some places, language has been taken as the factor of commonality of choice (e.g., in Québec), whereas religion is identified in many other places as a key element marking membership in the community (e.g., in Israel). Thus, even in places in which multiculturalism is embraced as a desirable policy, what it stands for has been highly variable.

Yet, multiculturalism has increasingly been identified with religious diversity. Debates over multiculturalism's successes and failures are often linked to views that, on the one hand, multicultural policies still privilege the beliefs and practices of the majority, or on the other hand, that religious accommodation goes "too far," especially in regard to minority religions.

The so-called post-multiculturalism discourses, cropping up since the mid-1990s across Europe and even Canada, highlight multiculturalism's disappointments while calling for revised public philosophies, policies, and programs that promote "nation-building," "social cohesion," "common values and identity," and "unitary citizenship."[28] According to Joseph Garcea, multiculturalism faces criticism because it allegedly segregates, exacerbates conflicts between and within groups, hinders social and economic equality, and, with particular reference to Canada, poses problems for minorities like Québec and aboriginal identities.[29] The "fragmentation critique" has had particularly strong resonance in both Canada and Europe. According to Lloyd Wong, the theory holds that "multiculturalism policy and the reality of cultural pluralism contribute to a fragmentation of society and make social cohesion difficult if not impossible."[30] While multiculturalism has been critiqued by both the political left and right in Europe since the 1970s, Tariq Madood and Will

Kymlicka point out that post-9/11 critiques emerge from the "pluralistic centre-left" and "social-democratic discourse."[31] Thus groups that reject polarizing models of race and class and who argue for an inclusive national identity are now also calling for post-multicultural approaches.[32]

In both Europe and Canada, this so-called retreat from multiculturalism is explained by changes to factors like population demographics and security. Steven Vertovec suggests that "super-diversity" is a factor that has "propelled us all into an era of postmulticulturalism."[33] States are experiencing a new level and kind of complexity in their population given a dynamic interplay of different variables in the state such as ethnicity, language, religion, cultural values, legal status, migration channels, and transnationalism.[34] Other scholars, however, point to "specific situations of ethnic and religious antagonism and terrorist events in Europe in the mid-2000s" as spurring the retreat.[35] In particular, the murder of Theo Van Gogh in Amsterdam, the Danish cartoons, the Madrid and London train bombings, and urban riots in France and Northern England linked security and ethnic, cultural, and especially religious diversity to multiculturalism's failure. For example, Madood sees the race riots of 2001 in Britain as "[throwing] an altogether different light on Britain's multicultural reality."[36] Following the riots, the Home Office's report on community cohesion, known as the Cantle Report, marked a key shift away from multiculturalism to the need to enhance a "greater sense of citizenship," strengthen the "use of the English language," and "agree on some common elements of nationhood."[37]

Furthermore, concerns over terrorism have exacerbated what Abbas sees as "the recasting of citizenship laws according to security considerations."[38] Multiculturalism policies have been seen as creating spaces for radical religious and political movements.[39] This feeds back into concerns about fragmentation and inequality whereby socioeconomic exclusions and the breakdown of social relations are seen as grounds for extremism.[40] For example, Vertovec points out how the characterization of the 2005 London bombers as "home grown terrorists" exemplified public fears about separateness and exclusion.[41] In many places, security takes on a dialectical meaning, referring to both national security/public safety and the maintenance of identity.

In this climate of terrorism and securitization, attacks on multiculturalism are often attacks on religion, especially Muslims and Islam.[42] As Modood notes, the terrorist attacks in London were the platforms from which to criticize multiculturalism.[43] Less obviously in Québec, the longstanding debates over the role and relevance of multiculturalism in the province have focused on religious symbols, public space, and security. For example, several legislative initiatives have sought to require people to show their faces during the delivery of government services and have proposed denying accommodation if warranted by reasons of security, communication, or identification.[44] Ingrained in debates over these policies is the rejection of multiculturalism. While the claim that there is no room for multiculturalism in Québec is linked to its perceived imposition by Canada and the unique emphasis on secularism as a result of the Quiet Revolution in the 1960s, the denunciation of multiculturalism is, certainly nowadays, frequently connected to threats of religious difference.

In this climate, the relationship between multiculturalism and other tenets of the democratic state, like equality, also sits uneasy. Multiculturalism is placed in relation to, and often in opposition to, equality. Multicultural policies including accommodation are often viewed as potentially enabling inequality. For example, across Canada and Europe there are persisting debates as to whether religion (and its adherents) perpetuates discrimination against women, sexual or religious minorities. Multiculturalism is thus characterized as being hijacked by groups who reject the basic values of the liberal democracy. However, like elsewhere in Europe and North America, such concerns are based on exclusionary notions of acceptable and unacceptable difference.

The innocuous displays of diversity in municipal parks on Canada Day are not the same type of multiculturalism dismissed as fragmentary or dangerous. This is contrasted with, for example, debates within the National Assembly of Quéebec, most recently with the proposed Charter of Values, where freedom of religion is seen as inherently conflicting with gender equality.[45] In these discussions, religious or ethnocultural difference of some sorts (like Islam and Sikhism) is considered a threat to Québec's fundamental values.

However, multiculturalism is seen not only as hindering equality because it may recognize radical, dangerous difference, but also as enabling and concealing power relations. Talal Asad suggests that multiculturalism normalizes, regulates, and contains. It constitutes an integral aspect of the "process of administrative normalization" whereby "fundamentally different traditions are described as necessarily contradictory (and therefore in need of regulation), state power extends itself by treating them as norms to be incorporated and coordinated."[46] Consequently, the contradictions of multiculturalism—whereby its discourse and practice may endorse a view of "equal and identical rights of universal citizenship" while buffering inequalities and discrimination—are explicable by the persisting fear that unassimilated immigrants are a threat to the social body. Ironically, this fear both justifies multiculturalism policies and fuels critiques of multiculturalism.

Yet even amid these critiques, multiculturalism continues to be a critical way in which difference is understood, negotiated, and governed. The intersection between religion, nationalism, and other vectors of difference in both Canada and Israel offers a revealing laboratory in which to examine multiculturalism in particular, and the governance of diversity in general. While we expressly focus on religion, Bhandar points out that the difference multiculturalism governs is at once cultural, gendered, religious, and historically situated.[47] Language is also crucial. In the case of Israel and Canada, language is intertwined with multiculturalism and religion.

The importance of recognizing a linguistic minority's right to their language has been extensively theorized by Kymlicka, for whom national minorities like French Canadians and Israeli Arabs should be accorded language rights to allow them to maintain their distinct cultures.[48] However, the accommodation of immigrant minorities is limited to providing language training to promote their linguistic integration while not requiring them to abandon their language.[49] The connection between language, culture, religion, and identity is especially useful in Israel to decode multicultural policies. As Meital Pinto argues, "[t]he issue of language rights illustrates, and sometimes takes to the extreme, the complexity of the multicultural existence in Israel."[50] For example, Michal Tannenbaum shows how Hebrew and the "melting pot ideology" combined to assimilate migrants: "the Israeli discourse on language policy is closely related to the revival of Hebrew as a spoken language as a key element of Zionist ideology. This discourse is essentially based on the idea that one language, namely Hebrew, is necessary for national unity, and multilingualism is therefore perceived as divisive."[51] On the other hand, as Hostovsky Brandes notes, Arabic is seen as central to the "cultural identity of Arabs in Israel."[52] Pinto points out that fears about providing equal status to both Arabic and Hebrew relates to the fear that publicly visible Arabic threatens the status of Hebrew and the "Jewish character of Israel."[53] Thus the accommodation of Arabic highlights how multiculturalism disputes capture a complex interaction between nationalism, identity, religion, and language. As Asad argues, the discourse and politics of multiculturalism are linked to the fears of the unassimilated migrant, which in the context of Israel includes national minorities. In this way, defining and assessing multiculturalism in Israel cannot be pursued without understanding questions of national identity and minority relations in general. While Russian language rights are also a major issue in Israel, the issue is far less politicized given that Russian is less intertwined with questions of nationalism and religion. This can be related to the Bouchard-Taylor Commission in Québec, initially established by the provincial government to investigate appropriate policies of cultural accommodation, but in which language issues soon came to occupy a central place.

The intensity of the debate about multiculturalism policies in Canada, Europe, and Israel suggests that the death of multiculturalism has been greatly exaggerated. While multiculturalism as a policy does not offer easy and universal responses to the complexities of contemporary diversity within modern states, neither does its formal abandonment by some governments signal a refusal to acknowledge social diversity. Multiculturalism policies may have been eschewed in some states, but the challenge of multiculturalism as a social reality remains, calling for continued scholarly engagement of the kind offered by contributions to this volume. The essays tackle in turn five current fundamental issues about religion and multiculturalism.

*MULTICULTURALISM AND WESTERN SECULARISM.* Secularism is a hallmark of liberalism: the separation of religion and politics, and of the private and the public, are critical, defining distinctions for the western liberal state. Yet, secularism is criticized for failing to reflect, and have significance for, other traditions. In this collection, Silvio Ferrari (Chapter 1, "The Christian Roots of the Secular State"), Suzanne Last Stone (Chapter 2, "Conflicting Visions of Political Space"), and Shai Lavi (Chapter 3, "Human Rights and Secularism: Arendt, Asad, and Milbank as Critics of the Secular Foundations of Human Rights") critically examine the basic assumptions about secularism. In particular, they interrogate secularism's relationship with religion, multiculturalism, and rights and examine the opportunities and limits of secularism in today's societies, often defined by a radical plurality of religions and cultures.

Ferrari and Stone challenge the view that religion and secularism are polar opposites by showing how secularism is rooted in a Christian legal tradition. Ferrari examines the different conceptions of what he terms "God's law" in Jewish, Christian, and Islamic legal systems. He shows how their different interpretations of the nature and scope of God's law have an impact on the acceptance or rejection of the secular state. While the Christian legal tradition "paved the way to the secular state," Ferrari argues that "the Islamic and Jewish traditions did not provide a congenial habitat for the development of a similar type of state." Stone likewise contends that "keeping religion and politics apart is an idea with a history and that history is primarily a Christian one."

Lavi also challenges the assumption that "the secular" is "the universal opposite of religious particularism." In asking about secularism's relationship with human rights, he seeks to examine "the nature of secularism and its place within modernity." This inquiry reframes the typical question—"what is religion's relationship to human rights?"—thereby unsettling the assumptions (and unease) about religion's place in modernity. This also underscores how secularism and human rights, according to Lavi, are "taken for granted as fundamental characteristics of the modern age" while "religion is interrogated, favorably or unfavorably, as the 'odd man out.'" In reformulating the question as "what is the relationship between secularism and human rights?" Lavi, like Stone and Ferrari, studies secularism "for its highly particular set of dispositions, practices, beliefs, and arrays of knowledge and experience."

All three authors are also concerned with difference, especially in light of their shared observation that religion is a growing, not dwindling, presence in the public sphere. If secularism is grounded in Christianity as Stone and Ferrari contend, is it still a relevant, meaningful, and useful way of organizing the state and recognizing others?[54] As an extension, if human rights are a secular project with secularist presuppositions, as Lavi argues, can they keep their universalist aspirations? Stone and Ferrari explore the extent to which secularism is a concept that can travel from one tradition to others, relying on Alan Watson's idea of "legal transplants."[55] In particular, Ferrari argues that it is futile to "export the model of the secular state to religious and legal traditions that do not meet the conditions for accepting it." Instead, "each civilization [must] look within its own religious and cultural tradition," for example, by finding tools to address issues that secularism has historically dealt with, such as the status of the other. Partly answering Ferrari's call, Stone also recognizes secularism's Christian roots and similarly suggests examining whether "there are counterparts within their respective traditions to liberal notions of the political sphere and of public space." She turns to a specific issue—Jewish thought about political space—to show similarities and differences with Christian/western liberal constructions and conceptions. In particular, she underscores that the Hebrew Bible distinguishes between sacred and profane space, but not between public and private space.

Lavi also looks at difference in examining how human rights are "commonly grounded in a sense of empathy": rights protect people on the basis of human beings' common ability to feel compassion and sympathize with those in radically different positions. The belief that "rights that are owed to all human being as such, regardless of their membership in a particular political community" is rooted in empathy and "in a commitment to the anguish and suffering of others." Lavi, however, argues that "defenders of empathy-based rights"—which includes some of the biggest names in human rights scholarship—"cannot take for granted empathy as a means for promoting religious tolerance, without questioning the way in which empathy itself is a secularist sentiment." John Milbank, for example, argues that despite secularism being rooted in a distorted medieval Christian theology, its manifestation in secular human rights—which has rejected God—reduces "sympathetic imagination" to, as Hannah Arendt also fears, "animal instinct that regards purely the other, or else to a rationally reflexive projection of my own self-interest." Asad similarly exposes the exclusionary formulation and operation of human rights by showing how they recognize only particular forms of suffering, often to the detriment of non-Christian traditions.

In highlighting the need for finding internal tools comparable to secularism and freedom of religion rather than transplanting Western/Christian-centric models, Stone and Ferrari also acknowledge the challenges to which their propositions give rise. Stone is thus "very wary of the attempt to reposition liberal political arrangements as exclusively Christian" since this implies that the Christian approach to the separation of religion and state is the only "natural path." She also warns that defining secularism as Christian casts other religions as "premodern" if they have not became more secularized. It also ignores historical or theological reasons that make secularism more compatible with Christianity. Stone's and Ferrari's observations underscore the problematic nature of a straight transplant of secularism and freedom of religion, without falling into radical relativism. Although they engage relativism by arguing that secularism is neither universal nor neutral, the authors seek to contextualize the concept to avoid exoticization, Eurocentricism or absolutisms. In particular, by recognizing the capacity of each civilization to find its own tools, they embrace difference without reifying traditions as monolithic, static, or apolitical.

Relying on history, theology, and politics, Stone and Ferrari suggest that disputes over values such as freedom of religion or models such as secularism are not rooted in irreconcilable, inherent differences. For example, they show how friction between traditions' differences may be related to power disputes: as Stone argues, "the tension between resurgent religion and the liberal state seems less over secularism per se, but, rather, over the re-enchantment of the secular state." She points out that it is secular liberalism's claim to be a "competing transnational, universal, sacred, and transcendent realm" that primarily causes friction. Ferrari's recognition and acceptance of difference is likewise not absolute: he acknowledges that there are different roads but that their acceptability depends on whether "they converge on the common goal of ensuring religious freedom, which is a fundamental right of every human person." Yet if a tradition does not recognize religious freedom, is it futile or illegitimate to appeal to outside models or values, of which Ferrari and Stone are wary? The controversial dispute within Islam over the permissibility of apostasy, for example, highlights the potential difficulties of assuming that religious freedom is a common goal with a fixed meaning. However, it also emphasizes the plurality of internal views and voices whose diversity provides opportunities for religious freedom or a secular-like model, even though external or internal consensus is likely impossible.

Lavi also shows how human rights, more generally, are neither neutral nor static. While the controversy over the modern, universalizing brand of human rights is frequently articulated as whether it conflicts or is compatible with religion, Lavi shows the inherent limits or biases of human rights as a secularist project. Thus the preoccupation with "irreconcilable differences" between different religions (as well as cultures)—and their views of rights and secularism—fails to take into account human rights' own biases. Thus freedom of religion does not have a fixed meaning, either within a particular faith or even within the discourse of human rights itself. Rather, it is the outcome of specific views on faith, authority, and community.

MULTICULTURALISM AND RELIGIOUS FREEDOM AS SWORDS OR SHIELDS. The perceived increase of religious fundamentalism in western liberal states has been met with concern, often fear, and sometimes violent opposition. Many of the volume's chapters speak to these apprehensions. Ino Augsberg (Chapter 4, "Religious Freedom as 'Reflexive Law'") highlights an anxiety around religious revival, and in particular concerns about the establishment of Islam in the West. Besides associations of Islam with religious extremism and terrorism, the faith is often seen as opposing the fundamental values of the liberal western state. Similar to Stone and Ferrari, Augsberg contends that Islam challenges state neutrality—the "classical western mechanism of coping with religious pluralism"—by rejecting the separation of religion and state and the view that religion is a private matter. While the earlier chapters specifically analyze secularism, Augsberg and Victor Muñiz-Fraticelli (Chapter 5, "The Distinctiveness of Religious Liberty") examine how other legal strategies and concepts—multiculturalism and freedom of religion—accommodate diversity. In particular, they outline how multiculturalism and religious freedom are limited tools for managing difference, especially if we recognize religion not only as an individual personal conviction, but also as an important site of governance for groups of people.

Muñiz-Fraticelli critiques both the failure to recognize that religion and culture are not conceptual analogues and the ensuing narrow conceptualization of religious freedom, including its collapse into multiculturalism. He argues that freedom of religion and multiculturalism stand apart on the basis of their distinct grounding principles: while the latter is based on individual freedom and autonomy, religious claims are indifferent to these. Consequently, "attempt[s] to address issues of religious liberty with reference to multicultural categories ultimately creates an incomplete account." Moreover, this indifference means that religious claims are also "potentially incompatible with the formal state legal system, even if they coexist peaceably with it." While Augsberg specifically asks whether Islam is able to adapt to the modern secularized state given its Judeo-Christian roots, Muñiz-Fraticelli considers religious claims more generally.

Augsberg and Muñiz-Fraticelli both critically examine freedom of religion, especially in terms of its impacts on followers or believers. However, they problematize the conception and treatment of religious freedom in different ways. On the one hand, Muñiz-Fraticelli discusses how religious freedom has been reduced to only "one of its strains"—freedom of conscience—to the exclusion of the "freedom of the Church." Augsberg, on the other hand, argues that religious freedom "has to be regarded in a more complex sense": it must also be seen as society's freedom *from religion* and therefore also functions to protect society from religious claims that infiltrate the public sphere. Muñiz-Fraticelli sees the development of religious freedom as a way of protecting religious authorities' autonomy *from the state* and not the other way around. He is critical of the conception of religious freedom that ignores the "other strain," the "concern for institutional autonomy of religious organizations." Muñiz-Fraticelli's historical approach, which identifies how the articulation of religious freedom by the liberal western state has changed over time, differs from Augsberg's policy-centric approach, which sees the freedom of religion as also safeguarding society from religious claims.

Both authors consider the negative impact of the freedom of religion on religions in a secular, liberal state. Augsberg argues that "religion has to pay" for upholding a secular society. He points out that the view of religion as "just one among many other social functions" is "intolerable to religionists." Augsberg is conscious of the need to balance or coordinate modern society's view of religion, especially as private and individualistic, with religion's resistance to being "part of the game." A suggested solution is the reconstruction of religious freedom as reflexive law that takes this resistance into account, to a degree. A reflexive approach focuses on "creating structural arrangements that enable or support self-regulating mechanisms within the different subsystems." This echoes Ferrari and Stone's call for internal tools in that it demands the state to let religious groups establish their own arrangements, boundaries, and norms. Augsberg operationalizes the concept through tolerant reflexivity, which "affirms the other's otherness" without enforcing its own structure. In particular, tolerant reflexivity calls on the law to account for religion's distinctiveness but requires religions to also tolerate "that they may not take over other social functions."

Augsberg and Muñiz-Fraticelli identify the need to take religion seriously from the viewpoint of believers and not only as a way to protect the individual's right to freedom of conscience. However, both present religious freedom differently: Muñiz-Fraticelli focuses on "the reduction of religious freedom" to only the post-Enlightenment liberal strain and its impact for institutional autonomy and "collective proper group rights"; Augsberg recognizes the collective aspect of freedom of religion, but still focuses on religion as individualistic and private. Consequently, Augsberg more easily identifies a limit to religious freedom, seen, for example, in "tolerant reflexivity." Muñiz-Fraticelli challenges this sort of normative individualism, which persistently defines freedom of religion to the exclusion of its historical counterpart.

*NEGOTIATING IDENTITY BETWEEN STATE AND RELIGION.* States manage their relationships with religion, including religious groups and individuals, through laws and policies that, for the most part, function without controversy. For example, as the Bouchard-Taylor Commission found in Québec, public institutions provide religious and cultural accommodations that very rarely end up before courts or even feature in the news.[56] Yet the legal judgments and policies analyzed by Shauna Van Praagh (Chapter 6, "'Inside Out/Outside In': Coexistence and Cross-Pollination of Religion and State") and Daphne Barak-Erez (Chapter 7, "Who Is a Jew and the Law—Between London and Jerusalem") show that some clashes ineluctably do occur between state and religion, particularly over religious identity and membership.

Van Praagh in her chapter analyzes two legal controversies, a judicial decision in the United Kingdom and a ministerial directive in Canada. First, the United Kingdom Supreme Court's 2009 *Jewish Free School* decision held that a religious school's definition of religious identity for admissions constituted discrimination on grounds of ethnic origins; and, second, Québec's Religion in Daycare Directive banned the "teaching" of religion to preschoolers in publicly funded daycares. Both examples highlight how the state defines the ways people live out or demonstrate their identities: the first, a legal judgment outlining the permissible internal boundaries that a religious community can construct, and the second, a policy delineating the external manifestation of faith. Through legal tools like multiculturalism and human rights, the state manages its relationships with religion by defining how and where religion can be expressed. As Van Praagh argues, these examples show "how state and religion compete and coexist in their messages for, and images of, the individuals who belong to both." As citizens, believers, and members of a religious community, people retain multiple, potentially competing, identities.

Van Praagh and Barak-Erez show how the state, in negotiating its relationship with religion, affects religious identities. Barak-Erez specifically looks at membership debates in Jewish communities: first, in Israel's Law of Return, and second in the United Kingdom's *Jewish Free School* decision. Barak-Erez shows how recognition in Israeli law and admittance to the Jewish Free School in London present similar challenges in determining "Who Is a Jew." Both Barak-Erez and Van Praagh reveal that membership debates have enormous importance not only for their practical consequences but also for symbolic reasons. In Israel, as Barak-Erez notes, the issue arises not merely from claims to legal rights like citizenship, "but rather from the desire to be registered as Jews, and thus receive public recognition as members of the Jewish nation." Similarly, Van Praagh points out how the decision of the United Kingdom Supreme Court does not change the definition of being Jewish save in one narrow context. Yet she points out that the decision "contribute[s] to the ongoing shaping of the relationship between state and religious norms." Limiting the power of religious institutions to define their own membership affects the autonomy of religious communities vis-à-vis the state and, more generally, defines the legal and legitimate actions a religion can take. The chapters therefore speak to the interaction between the state and religious authorities and communities, emphasizing the internal diversities within religions and the difficulty of the state unwittingly acting as a mediator between different views and voices inside a given faith.

Both chapters illustrate the complexity of religious identity, as defined internally by the community and externally by the state. A community can never entirely escape its situatedness within one or several states, even in practices that are purely internal. The London Jewish Free School, a private institution, is a case in point. The chapters further illuminate the individual as a central site of religious beliefs, again in a manner that cannot escape the web of relations that connect an individual to other individuals, to multiple communities, and to the state. Even for religious identity, the genuine nature of spiritual commitment must often be complemented by other factors such as ancestry or broadly held beliefs within the community. No monopoly is granted—to the individual, the community, or the state—in shaping identity. Rather, all interact in a fluid dialogical process that is difficult to reduce to the categories of legal discourse.

*WHOSE VOICE? WHICH TRUTH? ONE OR MANY?* Controversial debates over multiculturalism and freedom of religion frequently relate to the position of internal minorities or vulnerable members.[57] Extensive scholarship has examined how states, religious communities, and women belonging to these communities negotiate the potential tensions between rights. Liberal feminists in particular have forcefully voiced the limits of tolerance and accommodation of some religious and cultural practices, arguing that there may be a tension between gender equality and the multicultural commitment to group rights for minority cultures. In a seminal article first published in 1999, Susan Moller Okin asked whether multiculturalism was bad for women.[58] Okin cited the wearing of headscarves by Muslim schoolchildren, polygamy, clitoridectomy, forced marriages and "honor killings" to demonstrate the potential for a "clash of cultures" and to show that feminism and multiculturalism are not easily reconcilable. These practices were framed with static meanings and presented as clashing rights. By defining women as either independent agents or victims, women's own perspectives were also excluded. The terms of this initial debate came to be seen as flawed in its failure to account for the diverse ways that women negotiate their roles, beliefs, and the expectations of their communities.

Deepening this discussion, Menachem Mautner (Chapter 8, "A Dialogue Between a Liberal and an Ultra-Orthodox on the Exclusion of Women from Torah Study") and Angela Campbell (Chapter 9, "Religious Claims as Public Reason? Polygamy as a Case Study") explore controversial practices justified by religious convictions that are seen as incompatible with the liberal view of equality. Mautner constructs a discussion between an Ultra-Orthodox Jew and a Liberal about women's exclusion from Torah study while Campbell examines polygamy in Bountiful, British Columbia, as practiced by followers of the Fundamentalist Church of Jesus Christ of Latter Day Saints. Mautner and Campbell do not juxtapose competing rights or make overbroad assumptions about modernity and backwardness, an approach often criticized by third world feminists and postcolonial scholars.[59] Rather, both authors center the debate around followers or believers themselves to identify precise tensions between different perspectives and possible opportunities for understanding. Through fieldwork in Bountiful—including interviews with 22 women—Campbell aims to "learn about how [women in Bountiful] understand formal state-made rules regarding polygamy, and how these intersect with community norms about this form of marriage." Although the methodology of each author differs, one proceeding from conversations with group members and the other imagining a dialogue in which internal viewpoints are directly exchanged, both seek to give a central place to the voices of religious individuals that are rarely heard directly in scholarly research.

Mautner's dialogue looks at a controversial issue within Judaism, demonstrating the diversity of views within the faith, including from women themselves, and highlighting specific points of disagreement rather than a vague incompatibility with liberal secularism. While the exchange examines the specific issue of women's exclusion from Torah study, it reflects controversies that span across many religions: the bases of distinction between men and women; the unacceptability of this distinction from a liberal standpoint; as well as the challenges (and possible injustices) of "understanding" or "translating" other cultures and undertaking intercultural communication.

Mautner and Campbell also challenge a dichotomous view of freedom of religion on the one hand and multiculturalism and equality on the other. They show how the polarization of rights fails to account for the intersections between religion, culture, and politics. Campbell questions the value of conceptualizing claims over controversial issues exclusively in terms of religion. She shows how the Bountiful polygamy debate is largely defended as a religious practice protected by religious freedom. In asking whether this approach "enhances or stunts effective discussion and understanding across cultures, perspectives, beliefs, and traditions," she argues that religious claims on their own—although potentially valuable to public discussion—"do not provide an adequate structure for assessing politically and socially controversial practices." Like research on veiling, Campbell shows how women in Bountiful practice polygamy for numerous reasons, which are not limited to religious convictions.[60] Mautner likewise reveals the slippage between religion and culture in discussing the difficulties of "translating" meanings from one culture to another. His Ultra-Orthodox narrator examines veiling in Islam and clitoridectomy to show how women engage in these practices for many reasons and thus challenges blanket assumptions about modernity or agency.

MULTICULTURALISM, RELIGION, AND THE GEOGRAPHY OF POWER. As earlier noted, multiculturalism policies have been criticized since the mid-1990s for exacerbating conflicts between and within groups, segregating populations, and hindering equality. Leading scholars on multiculturalism like Kymlicka have pointed to "a worldwide retreat from multiculturalism"[61] in which there is a greater emphasis on social cohesion.[62] While Vertovec argues that "post-multicultural agendas certainly do not mean that multiculturalism is dead,"[63] the critiques challenge multiculturalism's basic assumptions and claimed successes. Michael Karayanni (Chapter 10, "The Acute Multicultural Entrapment of the Palestinian-Arab Religious Minorities in Israel and the Feeble Measures Required to Relieve It") and Yishai Blank (Chapter 11, "Localizing Religion in a Jewish State") tackle this critique to show how even proponents of multiculturalism are thinking more critically about it.

Karayanni looks at a controversial aspect of multiculturalism in a particularly controversial setting—the accommodation of "illiberal" minorities in Israel—and asks what it can offer to western legal systems. His starting point is the "multicultural predicament"—the real concern that accommodating minority groups may adversely affect the rights and well-being of some individuals within the group. Karayanni challenges the broad, generalized readings of multiculturalism by demonstrating how challenges with accommodations in the constitutional context of a nation-state, like Israel, become more acute than those made in western liberal democracies. In particular, discussions of the multicultural predicament have taken for granted "the political and constitutional order" where "one can at least imagine a common civic institution of citizenship inclusive and egalitarian in substance." Nation-states, however, by promoting the interests of the hegemonic group, may aggravate the multicultural predicament: there may be especially strong pressures from both the state and the minority group for maintaining respective identities, and to compound the tension, the state lacks a common concept of citizenship that would motivate (or legitimize) state interventions into intra-illiberal practices.

Karayanni's approach challenges basic assumptions about multiculturalism and highlights the internal and external power issues. By looking at the jurisdictional authority granted to different religious communities in Israel, including Palestinian-Arab Muslims and Orthodox Jews, he shows the distinct challenges of state-led efforts to mitigate the effects of illiberal practices, especially in the context of family law regimes. He also shows how what constitutes multiculturalism is dependent upon its political context: for example, the religious authority granted to Palestinian-Arab religious communities has traditionally been seen as multicultural accommodation while the accommodations accorded to Orthodox Jewish religious institutions are "anchored in the established nature of Judaism in Israel" and not seen as accommodations.

Blank also critically examines the underlying assumptions made about multiculturalism by focusing on the role of local governments in structuring and regulating religious-secular tensions in Israel. He shows the critical, although often ignored, role of place and locality in multiculturalism. While the central government and national politics are seen as the sites for debates over multiculturalism, Blank points to the "localization of religious liberty in Israel." He argues that "conflicts between religious and secular groups, as well as among different religious groups often take place in smaller polities, in the form of a battle over the shape and content of local public spaces, controlled and regulated by local governments." This echoes more recent multiculturalism literature, which designates the local as the privileged site in which the grand idea of multiculturalism is given formal shape, down to the issue of sharing sidewalks in a particular neighborhood.[64]

Thus both Karayanni and Blank question *who* controls, and who *should* control, multicultural processes, including accommodations. They highlight that power may not reside where it is traditionally assumed to be and understanding such internal and external power dynamics is needed to developing effective multicultural policies. Karayanni focuses on the relations between and within different groups while Blank considers how location and space structure these group interactions.

Multiculturalism may also be seen as the balancing of competing interests, crossing different relationships and different localities. Karayanni's and Blank's examinations of Israel expose these tensions especially given the extensive diversity within Jewish groups, the significant population of non-Jewish Israelis, and the presence of over a quarter of a million foreign workers in Israel. For example, Blank shows the difficulties of balancing the need to "benefit from the advantages of the localization of religion without, however, deteriorating into an all out war of factions, and without jeopardizing the individual liberty of persons who wish to live side by side despite their belonging to different religious communities." Blank studies the regulation of pork selling to reveal how Israeli courts try to balance the different interests emerging at local levels. The cases show that on the one hand, courts must balance the freedom of occupation of pork sellers and right of consumers of pork to eat what they want, and on the other hand, the role of local governments to protect the religious beliefs of people who oppose pork consumption. More generally,

Karayanni shows the competing interests between the external protections desired by a minority group such as independent religious courts, the impact those protections may have on group members, and how multicultural policies themselves are politically and legally situated.

## Notes

1. (Montreal: Contact Press, 1956).
2. See generally: E. Lévinas, *Entre Nous: Thinking-of-the-Other*, trans. M. Smith and B. Harshav (New York: Columbia University Press, 1998); C. Taylor, *Sources of the Self—The Making of Modern Identity* (Cambridge: Cambridge University Press, 1989).
3. See J. Boyd White, "How Should We Talk About Religion?," in J. Boyd White ed, *How Should Talk About Religion? Perspectives, Context, Particularities* (Notre-Dame: University of Notre-Dame, 2006) 1, at 2–5.
4. "The Ties that Bind: Multiculturalism and Secularism Reconsidered" (2009) 36:3 Journal of Law and Society 301 at 304.
5. T. Soutphommasane, "Grounding Multicultural Citizenship: From Minority Rights to Civic Pluralism" (2005) 26: 4 Journal of Intercultural Studies 401 at 403.
6. J. Raz, "Multiculturalism" (1998) 11:3 Ratio Juris 193 at 197.
7. S. Vertovec, "Towards Post-multiculturalism? Changing Communities, Conditions and Contexts of Diversity" (2010) 61:199 International Social Science Journal 83 at 84.
8. Ibid.
9. T. Abbas, "Recent Developments in British Multicultural Theory, Policy, and Practice: The Case of British Muslims" (2005) 9: 2 Citizenship Studies 153 at 162.
10. C. Joppke, "The Retreat of Multiculturalism in the Liberal State: Theory and Policy" (2004) 55: 2 British Journal of Sociology 237 at 247.
11. W. Kymlicka, "The Current State of Multiculturalism in Canada and Research Themes on Canadian Multiculturalism 2008–2010" Citizenship and Immigration Canada (Minister of Public Works and Government Services Canada (2010) at 9–10.
12. Raz, *supra* note 6 at 202.
13. See G. Bouchard & C. Taylor, "Building the Future: A Time for Reconciliation," online: <http://www.accommodements-quebec.ca/documentation/rapports/rapport-final-integral-en.pdf/> at 19 [Bouchard-Taylor Commission Report].
14. Ibid.
15. Ibid. at 82. See also G. Bouchard, *L'Interculturalisme* (Montréal: Boréal, 2012).
16. J. Garcea, "Postulations on the Fragmentary Effects of Multiculturalism in Canada" (2008) 40:1 Canadian Ethnic Studies 141 at 157. See also Micheline Labelle, who observes that both models face the common obstacle of "la consolidation d'un sentiment d'appartenance à la société québécoise et à l'implantation d'une citoyenneté québécoise territoriale et pluraliste," in "Les intellectuels québécois face au multiculturalisme: hétérogénéité des approches et des projets politiques" (2008) 40:1 Canadian Ethnic Studies 33 at 38.
17. Bouchard-Taylor Commission Report, *supra* note 13 at 18.
18. E. Ben-Rafael & Y. Peres, *Is Israel One? Religion, Nationalism, and Multiculturalism Confounded* (Leiden: Brill, 2005) at 38.
19. M. Karayanni, "Multiculture Me No More! On Multicultural Qualifications and the P.alestinian-Arab Minority of Israel" (2007) 54: 3 Diogenes 39 at 51.
20. K. Banting & W. Kymlicka, "Introduction: Multiculturalism and the Welfare State: Setting the Context," in K. Banting & W. Kymlicka, eds, *Multiculturalism and the Welfare State*, (Oxford: Oxford University Press, 2006) at 1.
21. "Israeli Cabinet Approves Loyalty Oath for Non-Jews," (11 October 2010) *The Independent* online: <http://www.independent.co.uk/news/world/middle-east/israeli-cabinet-approves-loyalty-oath-for-nonjews-2103194.html>.

22. Karayanni, "Multiculture Me No More!," *supra* note 19 at 39.
23. H. Lerner, "Constitutional Incrementalism and Material Entrenchment" in Avi Sagi & Ohad Nachtomy, eds, *The Multicultural Challenge in Israel* (Boston: Academic Studies Press, 2009) at 4.
24. Ibid. at 4.
25. Ben-Rafael & Peres, supre note 18 at 43.
26. "Introduction" in A. Sagi & O. Nachtomy, eds, *The Multicultural Challenge in Israel* (Boston: Academic Studies Press, 2009).
27. Saguenay (Ville de) c. Mouvement laïque québécois, 2013 QCCA 936.
28. See W. Kymlicka, "The Rise and Fall of Multiculturalism? New Debates on Inclusion and Accommodation in Diverse Societies" (2010) 61:199 International Social Science Journal 97 at 98; see also J. Garcea, A. Kirova & L. Wong, "Introduction: Multiculturalism Discourses in Canada" (2008) 40: 1 Canadian Ethnic Studies 1 at 1.
29. Garcea, *supra* note 16 at 141.
30. L. Wong, "Multiculturalism and Ethnic Pluralism in Sociology: An Analysis of the Fragmentation Position Discourse" (2008) 40: 1 Canadian Ethnic Studies 11 at 13; see also Garcea, *supra* note 16 (stating that "[o]ne of the central questions in such debates has been whether multiculturalism contributes either to harmony and integration or conflict and fragmentation within the Canadian polity" at 142).
31. T. Madood, "Remaking Multiculturalism after 7/7" (2005), Open Democracy online: <http://www.opendemocracy.net/conflict-terrorism/multiculturalism_2879.jsp>; see also Kymlicka, *supra* note 29 at 98.
32. Madood, ibid.
33. Vertovec, *supra* note 7 at 90.
34. Ibid. at 89.
35. Wong, *supra* note 30 at 25.
36. Joppke, *supra* note 10 at 250.
37. "Community Cohesion: A Report of the Independent Review Team" (2001), Coventry University online: <http://image.guardian.co.uk/sys-files/Guardian/documents/2001/12/11/communitycohesionreport.pdf>, at Chapter 5: Our Themes and Proposals.
38. Abbas, *supra* note 9 at 159.
39. Banting & Kymlicka, *supra* note 20 at 3.
40. Vertovec, *supra* note 7 at 86.
41. Ibid..
42. C. Allen, "Down with Multiculturalism, Book-burning and Fatwas" (2007) 8: 2 Culture and Religion 125 at 132.
43. Madood, *supra* note 31; see also Allen, *supra* note 42.
44. See Bill 94, *An Act to Establish Guidelines Governing Accommodation Requests within the Administration and Certain Institutions*, 1st Sess, 39th Legisl., Québec, 2010 (re-instated during the 39th Legislature, 2nd Session le February 24, 2011) at section 6, available online: <http://www.assnat.qc.ca/en/travaux-parlementaires/projets-loi/projet-loi-94-39-1.html>; Bill 60, *Charter Affirming the Values of State Secularism and Religious Neutrality and of Equality Between Women and Men, and Providing a Framework for Accommodation Requests*, 1st Sess, 40th Legisl., Québec, 2013, at sections 6–7, available online: <http://www.assnat.qc.ca/en/travaux-parlementaires/projets-loi/projet-loi-60-40-1.html> [Charter of Values].
45. Ibid.
46. "Multiculturalism and British Identity in the Wake of the Rushdie Affair" (1990) 18 Politics & Society 455 at 471.
47. Bhandar, *supra* note 4 at 304.
48. See, for example, *Multicultural Citizenship: A Liberal Theory of Minority Rights* (Oxford: Clarendon Press, 1995).
49. For example, Bouchard and Taylor document requests in Québec related to linguistic diversity, *supra* note 13 at 80.
50. M. Pinto, "Who is Afraid of Language Rights in Israel" in A. Sagi & O. Nachtomy, eds, *The Multicultural Challenge in Israel* (Boston: Academic Studies Press, 2009) at 26; see

also M. Karayanni, "Separate and Different: Religious Accommodations for the Palestinian-Arab Minority in Israel" (2006) 5 Northwestern University Journal of International Human Rights 41.
51. M. Tannenbaum, "Multiculturalism in Israel: A Linguistic Perspective" in A. Sagi & O. Nachtomy, eds, *The Multicultural Challenge in Israel* (Boston: Academic Studies Press, 2009) at 310. See also T. Hostovsky Brandes's discussion of the "centrality of Hebrew to Israeli nationalism" in "The Hand in Hand Bilingual Education Model: Vision and Challenges" in A. Sagi & O. Nachtomy, eds, *The Multicultural Challenge in Israel* (Boston: Academic Studies Press, 2009) at 59.
52. Hostovsky Brandes, ibid. at 62.
53. Pinto, *supra* note 50 at 43–44.
54. See C. Calhoun et al., eds, *Rethinking Secularism* (Oxford: Oxford University Press, 2011).
55. A. Watson, *Legal Transplants: An Approach to Comparative Law*, 2nd edn (Athens: University of Georgia Press, 1993). See also P. Legrand, "The Impossibility of 'Legal Transplants'" (1997) 4 Maastricht Journal of European & Comparative Law 111.
56. Bouchard-Taylor Commission Report, *supra* note 13 at 18.
57. A. Eisenberg and J. Spinner-Halev, eds, *Minorities within Minorities: Equality, Rights and Diversity* (Cambridge: Cambridge University Press, 2005).
58. S. M. Okin, in J. Cohen, M. Howard, M. C. Nussbaum, eds, *Is Multiculturalism Bad for Women?* (Princeton: Princeton University Press, 1999). The article was first published in the *Boston Review* but was republished in a book under the same title that included numerous responses by prominent scholars; see also L. Volpp, "Feminism versus Multiculturalism" (2001) 101:5 Columbia Law Review 1181.
59. S. Mahmood, *Politics of Piety: The Islamic Revival and the Feminist Subject* (Princeton: Princeton University Press, 2005); M. L. Fernando, "Reconfiguring Freedom: Muslim Piety and the Limits of Secular Law and Public Discourse in France" (2010) 37: 1 American Ethnologist 19; O. Avishai, "'Doing Religion' in a Secular World: Women in Conservative Religions and the Question of Agency" (2008) 22: 4 Gender & Society 409.
60. H. Hoodfar, "More Than Clothing: Veiling as an Adaptive Strategy" in S. Alvi, H. Hoodfar and S. McDonough, eds, *The Muslim Veil in North America: Issues and Debates* (Toronto: Women's Press, 2003) 3.
61. See Kymlicka, "The Current State of Multiculturalism in Canada and Research Themes on Canadian Multiculturalism 2008–2010," *supra* note 11 at 5.
62. See Kymlicka, "The Rise and Fall of Multiculturalism?," *supra* note 29 at 98; see also Garcea, Kirova & Wong, *supra* note 29 at 1.
63. Vertovec, *supra* note 7 at 92.
64. See S. Van Praagh, "Sharing the Sidewalk" (2010) 8:3 Canadian Diversity 6.

# PART ONE

# MULTICULTURALISM AND WESTERN SECULARISM

# 1

# The Christian Roots of the Secular State

SILVIO FERRARI

## 1. Introduction

In this chapter I would like to test the following thesis: that the different fortunes of the secular state in the predominantly Jewish, Christian, and Muslim countries depend significantly (although not exclusively) on their different religious backgrounds and, in particular, on the conception of God's law that developed in the theological and legal traditions of these three religions. I am not denying the importance of historical events and cultural processes in the formation of the secular state. But, on the one hand, history alone cannot explain the whole picture, as historical facts take place within a reference framework provided, in our case, by the sacred texts and the interpretive tradition of each religion. Historical processes do not develop in a vacuum, and believing that they are completely disconnected from the religious and cultural context in which they take shape is as naïve as believing that they are totally dependent on it. On the other hand, it is true that the secular state constitutes a model of organizing the relations between citizens and public institutions that does not concern exclusively religion nor is it produced only by religion: it presupposes a certain way to conceive politics, law, economics, and so on; in other words, it is the outcome of a complex process of which religion is just one component. But the analysis of a single element—if performed keeping in mind the context in which it is included—is a way to better understand the whole picture.

After a short description of what God's law means in the Jewish, Christian, and Islamic legal systems, I shall focus on the different interpretations of the nature and scope of God's law in these religious traditions. The impact that these differences have on the acceptance (or rejection) of the secular state in Israel and in the Christian and Muslim countries[1] will be examined in the last part of this chapter.

Before starting this examination, two preliminary remarks are required. First, my analysis will focus primarily on Sunni Islam, Orthodox Judaism, and

Roman Catholic Christianity: the legal traditions of other currents of Islam, Judaism, and Christianity will not be considered in this chapter. Second, my intent is purely descriptive. I want to explain why the Christian legal tradition (and particularly the Roman Catholic one), based on divine natural law, paved the way to the secular state and why the Islamic and Jewish traditions did not provide a congenial habitat for the development of a similar type of state. However, I am in no way implying that one tradition is better than the other, nor that the secular state is preferable to other political models.

## 2. God's Law in the Legal Systems of Judaism, Christianity, and Islam

The legal systems of the Jewish, Christian, and Muslim religions have in common the fact of deriving their legitimacy from divine will: they are systems of law based on rules that were laid down by God himself. God's law occupies a very central place in these legal systems. The validity of all the provisions contained in each of them depends on their conformity (or at least nonopposition) to the rules of divine law[2] that constitute their foundation: that is, it depends on the will of God and not on the will of humans as is normal in all legal systems with a nonreligious foundation.[3] The ability to dictate new rules and to change the legal system in adherence to the transformation and the needs of the religious community meets a limit in the impossibility for divine rules to undergo any change that is not attributable to the will of God himself.[4] The superiority that each of these three religious legal systems claims over the secular ones hinges on the concept of divine law that, as it is dictated by a higher authority than any human one, demands absolute obedience and respect even when it conflicts with the rules set out by human powers: *magis oportet obedire Deo quam hominibus.*

These brief remarks are sufficient to understand the importance that divine law has in the three legal systems that are the subject of this chapter. To understand their relationship with the secular legal systems it is therefore necessary to examine the concept of divine law that prevailed in each of them in more detail.

The main element of affinity between the legal systems of Judaism, Christianity, and Islam is that God's law is known by us through revelation. It is (in whole or in part) a "revealed" law: not in the sense that it "reveals" itself as we gains the ability to discover and to know it (as may happen in other religious experiences), but because it is made known through the initiative of God, without whose intervention we would not have been able to learn the content of divine law. This element that is common to all three legal systems must not, however, lead to neglecting the importance of the difference implicit in the parenthesis "in whole or in part" that has been employed to qualify the source of divine law: while for the legal systems of the Christian Churches divine law is not all revealed law, for the Islamic and (though in different form) the Jewish legal systems divine law and revealed law coincide. The importance of this difference, which at first glance could seem minor, is great, and so it is appropriate to address this issue more in detail.

## 3. Divine Law and Natural Law in the Legal Traditions of Orthodox Judaism, Roman Catholic Christianity, and Sunni Islam

Every cultural tradition[5]—defined as the set of principles and values that are shared by a stable community of people and that grant it social cohesion—must face the problem of the "other," that is, the person who does not identify himself with the fundamental assumptions on which community life is based. Defining the legal status of the "other" is a problem shared by all communities, be they political, religious, ethnic, linguistic, and so on. Today, more than ever, no community can realistically think of living in perfect isolation; therefore there is no doubt about the need to establish an appropriate catalogue of rights and obligations that apply to the "other."

The manner in which the problem of the "other" is addressed depends on the different religious and cultural traditions. In the Roman Catholic legal tradition, the main instrument for tackling this problem has been the notion of divine natural law.[6] The clearest explanation of the divine natural law theory dates back to Thomas Aquinas, who has the merit of having drawn with great lucidity the distinction between divine revealed law and divine natural law.[7] The first is given by God through revelation and cannot be known outside of it (i.e., it cannot be learned by humans only through reason). The second is also given by God, but through the creation: it is inscribed in the conscience of everyone, as we are created in the image and likeness of God, and it is knowable through the proper use of the rational faculties which every human being has.[8] Both laws are immutable, binding, and superior to human law, but the divine revealed law rules over the lives of the faithful (that is, those who received the baptism), while the divine natural law governs the lives of all.[9]

The idea that, at the time of creation, God gives every human being the ability to distinguish right from wrong through the correct use of reason makes it possible to establish an element of commonality among people of different religions.[10] The "other" is not a "lawless" person or a person who has a law that is totally and irretrievably different from mine: on the contrary the other is, like me, able to perceive what is right and wrong even if, without the aid of revelation and divine grace, she may not be able to live up to this perception. There is therefore an area of rights and duties that are common to everyone, and all of us, through the proper use of our rational faculties, may recognize the universal value of these rights and duties.

This mode of addressing the problem of the "other" is not universal. Other religious traditions lack the concept of divine natural law or articulate it differently. In Orthodox Judaism (in the Reform and Conservative currents the approach is different), the concept of natural law is controversial[11] and the issue of the legal status of the "other" is set in terms that differ from those presented above. According to the Jewish doctrine, the whole of humankind was governed—before the law of God was revealed to Moses on Mount Sinai—by the Noahide commandments, given by God to Adam and Noah: these commandments prohibit blasphemy, idolatry, murder, theft and robbery, sexual misconduct and eating a limb taken from a live animal; a seventh precept orders the establishment of courts to administer justice.[12] On Mount Sinai, God gave Moses the law that, henceforth, would rule the Jews: non-Jews should instead continue to live in accordance with the Noahide laws, reaffirmed on the occasion of the Sinaitic revelation.

So since the revelation to Moses two legal systems have coexisted, the one reserved to the Chosen People and the other for everyone else: the analogy between this pattern and the Roman Catholic one is quite obvious. Both are based on two regulatory complexes, respectively addressed to the faithful (divine revealed law and Sinaitic revelation) and to all humankind (divine natural law and Noahide law). But there are also some significant differences: the seven Noahide commandments are revealed by God and not inscribed in the conscience of every human being at the time of his creation. Though this point is the subject of endless discussions, the majority position of Orthodox Judaism affirms that the Noahide laws rest more on the revelation than on conscience or reason. Consequently it is debated whether all the Noahide commandments could have been understood by reason only, without the help of divine revelation,[13] and the idea that Noahide law is a kind of natural law is far from being shared by the majority of Orthodox Jewish law scholars, among whom "natural law theories never have been popular."[14] In this framework, the universal scope of human rights is founded on a special revealed law for non-Jews, rather than on a rationally knowable law common to all humans: the commandments given by God to Noah allow people to recognize full legitimacy to the presence of the "other" but do not cancel the fundamental difference with God's Chosen People (that not all people are chosen to be part of).[15] This difference is not negligible, and it reappears in the Jewish legal tradition more than once, for example in the debate about the eternal life of the non-Jew.[16] But it did not have a paralyzing effect on the ability to develop a theory of the universality of human rights: the existence of the Noahide precepts, that is a (rudimentary but basically good) law that governs the behavior of non-Jews and allows them to lead a righteous life, provides a sufficiently strong basis to assert the existence of a cluster of rights and duties that pertain to all human beings.[17]

The Sunni Islamic doctrine and jurisprudence address the problem of the legal status of the "other" in a way that is different both from the Jewish and from the Christian ones. In its legal tradition, the notion of divine natural law seems to be absorbed and exhausted in that of divine revealed law to the point that Chafik Chéhata could write that "the orthodox Islamic theology does not admit the existence of a natural law, that is a law that is born from nature and, as such, is independent of revelation and religious dogma."[18] This statement is disputed by some scholars[19] who refer to the notion of *fitra* as a form of "prerevelatory, natural guidance . . . ingrained in the human personality"[20] that enables one to distinguish good and evil, but this notion has had scarce development in the legal speculation. However, to avoid misunderstandings, it should be immediately made clear that the Catholic doctrine does not accept the idea of a law that is born from nature and is completely independent of religious norms either: the Thomist conception that distinguishes between divine revealed law and divine natural law emphasizes the derivation of both from God and therefore concludes that the second cannot be in contradiction with the first. But Thomas Aquinas, assuming that human rationality is a reflection of divine rationality, says that good and evil, right and wrong are objective categories that can be learned through human reason, even without the intervention of divine revelation. This same conclusion is alien to the Sunni legal tradition that is strongly imbued with the Ash'arite philosophy according to which right and wrong have their only foundation in God's will.[21]

To better understand the differences between these two conceptions of law and justice it is helpful to recall briefly the story of the Mu'tazilite theological school, which flourished between the eighth and ninth centuries in connection with the establishment of the Abbasid dynasty and the shift of the political center of gravity of Islam from Damascus to Baghdad.[22] It was a time of religious pluralism. Islam, following its rapid expansion, ruled over areas where the majority of the population followed other religions: the problem of the "other," the non-Muslim, and his legal status within a community politically and militarily dominated by Islam, was more pressing than ever. It was also the time when Islam entered more deeply in touch with Greek thought, through the Arabic translations of the works of Aristotle and Plato, encouraged by the new caliphs: "a wind of rationalism blows in the Muslim world" and encourages the "use [of] the Greek reason for the defense and explanation of the revelation" contained in the Quran.[23] In this context of rapid change Mu'tazilites affirmed two very important principles: the ability to rationally prove the existence of

God and the ontological character of good and evil. Believing that an act is good or bad in itself (and not because God has commanded or forbidden it) opens the way to the idea that there can be universal moral principles, knowable through the proper use of reason. These theories, which have some similarity with those of Thomas Aquinas, laid the foundation for the development of the notion of natural law but, after an ephemeral success, they were crushed by the reaction of the Hanbali traditionalists and by the success of the voluntaristic doctrines of al-Ash'ari. A former follower of the Mu'tazilite doctrines, al-Ash'ari detaches himself from them and adopts a middle course between these and the traditionalist views of the Hanbali school. Al-Ash'ari does not oppose a moderate use of reason in interpreting the sacred scriptures but, to combat Mu'tazilite rationalism, he affirms the absolute freedom of divine will: "good and evil"—al-Ash'ari writes—"are so because God has declared that a certain act was good and another bad, but [God] could have stated the opposite, for example, that killing and stealing were well and then these acts would have been good."[24] Al-Ash'ari's ideas prevailed, bringing about the decline (in Sunni Islam) of the Mu'tazilite doctrines and inspiring the work of a great jurist of the eleventh century, al-Ghazali. In a work significantly entitled in the Latin translation "Destructio philosophorum," al-Ghazali discusses the causal link between two events (such as the rising of the sun and light, decapitation and death) and writes that "if one follows the other, it is because He [God] has created them in that fashion, not because the connection in itself is necessary and indissoluble. He has the power to create the satisfaction of hunger without eating, or death without the severance of the head, or even the survival of life when the head has been cut off."[25] These statements leave little room for natural law: if it all comes down to divine will, it is pointless to seek in this world a rationality that is intelligible to humans. So it is better to rely fully on revealed law and try to build a relationship with the "other" through paths that do not require a (nonexistent) law of nature.

Obviously the whole picture is much more complex, both because al-Ash'ari and al-Ghazali doctrine cannot be reduced to these statements alone and because, even after the Mu'tazilites' defeat, there are Muslim philosophers and lawyers who rejected a voluntaristic approach to the definition of the relation between divine revelation and human reason.[26] Apart from these remarks, however, it is important to underline that the al-Ash'ari and al-Ghazali voluntaristic theories are not foreign to Western and Christian thought. In the fourteenth century, Duns Scotus and William of Occam argued that, if God really is omnipotent, he cannot be bound by anything, including his own creation. God's transcendence overcomes all human categories, and investigating nature to know God is a pointless exercise, because human reason is unable to understand God, who can be known only through revelation.[27] The similarity between these ideas and those supported a few centuries earlier by al-Ash'ari and al-Ghazali is striking,[28] but in Christian thought they never acquired a role comparable to that which the theories of al-Ash'ari have gained in Muslim thought: the "rationalist" Thomas Aquinas won the day in the West, while the "rationalist" Mu'tazilites were the losers in the East.

From these events it is wise not to draw hasty conclusions about the irrationality of Islamic law:[29] the defeat of the Mu'tazilites—which until very recently marked the character of Sunni Islamic law[30]—does not mean the exclusion of the rational analysis of law nor the use of reason as a tool of interpretation of the rules. But this defeat led to excluding that human reason can be the foundation of the legal order and therefore constitutes a barrier to the development of an organic conception of natural law.[31]

To sum up, one does not have the impression of being in the presence of elements that are completely absent in the philosophical and legal tradition of Islam and present only in the Christian one (or vice versa): it is instead a matter of potentialities that have been more fully developed in one system and less in another. The terms of the legal and philosophical debate are similar; what is different is the result. The philosophy of Thomas Aquinas is still part of the official teaching of the Roman Catholic Church, and it is no coincidence that Thomas (and not Duns Scotus or William of Occam) was made a saint and proclaimed a Doctor of the Church. In the Muslim world an equally important role was instead played by the philosophy of al-Ash'ari. This helps to explain the weakness of the concept of natural law that makes it difficult for Islamic legal thought to address the problem of the "other" in the same way it is dealt with in the "Christian" West. It is not accidental that in the Islamic tradition the legal treatment of the "other" still remains largely grounded not on the notion of equality but on that of diversity and separateness. The "other"—the Jew and the Christian, for example—is different and is entitled to maintain this diversity through a legal framework that gives him the right to enjoy the Christian or Jewish rules concerning personal status law, family law, inheritance, and so on. This is the best sense of the notion of *dhimma*[32] and of its Ottoman institutional projection, the *millet*.[33] In the Western countries, where the influence of Christianity has been stronger, the concept of natural law (once it had been thoroughly secularized)[34] paved the way for the affirmation of the equality of citizens regardless of their religion, which has become irrelevant with reference to the enjoyment of civil and political rights. In this perspective the "other" (the Jew and the Muslim, for example) could be included in the national community in terms of substantive equality exactly because religious membership had become irrelevant.[35] On this point the Jewish legal tradition is closer to the Islamic than to the Christian one. A couple of examples may be useful here. For instance, it is significant that Israel has maintained the *millet* system—albeit much reduced in scope—that it inherited (through the British Mandate) from the Ottoman Empire. And in Israeli law there is no civil marriage, another element that brings Israel closer to the countries with an Islamic legal background and distances it from the European countries with a legal tradition influenced by Christianity. Paradoxically, a growing number of Europeans deem that the Islamic and Jewish approach is more suitable to dealing with the cultural and religious transformations of the Old Continent than the Christian one, but that is another matter.

## 4. God's Law and the Secular State

As we have seen, Judaism, Christianity, and Islam share the notion of God's law, but conceive it in different terms. The impact of this difference emerges clearly when examining the different fortunes of the notion of secular state in the countries with a predominant Jewish, Christian, or Muslim population.[36] My argument is that, all historical conditions being equal, a secular state is more likely to take shape in countries with a Christian religious background because their legal tradition has been deeply influenced by the concept of natural law.

A good starting point for testing this argument is provided by the state constitutions: each constitution contains a few provisions devoted to defining the principles and values on which the state is based and the presence or absence of religion among them can provide some helpful indications.[37]

European countries have a population that, at least nominally, is largely Christian: therefore one would expect to find some references to Christianity in their constitutions. On the contrary, they are largely silent. A few constitutions contain some general references to God or religion in their preambles,[38] but none of them define the state as a Christian state. There are some constitutions (again a minority) that recognize a church of state or a dominant religion,[39] but these provisions regard the relations between church and state more than the nature of the state. England has an established church, but this does not mean that England can be defined an Anglican state.

The constitutions of the states where Muslims are the majority of the citizens are much more explicit. One third of them define the state as an Islamic state[40] and more than half include sharia among the sources of state law[41] (another thing that is completely extraneous to the constitutions of the European countries, which make no reference to religious laws when they list the sources of the state law).

Israel has no constitution, but two fundamental laws define the state as "Jewish and democratic,"[42] and the law on the foundations of law affirms that when a court finds no answer to a legal question in statute law, case law or by analogy, it shall decide it in the light of the principles of freedom, justice, equity, and peace of Israel's heritage.[43] According to some lawyers this statement contains an implicit reference to Jewish law.[44]

These different ways of defining the relation between state and religion in the constitutions are linked to the conceptions of divine law that have been described in the previous paragraphs.

To understand the connection between the notion of the secular state prevailing in Europe and the doctrine of divine natural law, it is necessary to take into consideration what happened in the Old Continent in the sixteenth and seventeenth centuries. After the Lutheran Reformation, large regions of Europe were plagued by wars of religion that set Catholics and Protestants against each other for over a century. Wars of religion were a novelty in Europe, and they could not find a suitable place in the theoretical framework into which war had been considered up to then. The Protestant Reformation had shattered the common religious horizon of the medieval period, when most Western Europeans believed in the same God and recognized the same religious authority, the Pope. Wars of religion were fought by each opponent in the name of a different God, and the pope was no longer a *super partes* referee but had become the head of one of the conflicting parties. Therefore these wars could not be ended by appealing to the judgment of the pope, which had been possible (at least in principle) during the Middle Ages. A new way out had to be found to put an end to wars that seemed endless. Two solutions were found for this problem: one short-term and political in nature, the other long-term and philosophically oriented. The first consisted of the application of the principle *cuius regio, eius et religio*, which, through the forced emigration of religious minorities, led to the creation of religiously homogeneous confessional states: although it cost considerable "religious cleansing," it had the merit of putting an end to civil wars. The second solution was found by Grotius and expressed with the famous saying *etsi Deus non daretur*. It took almost two centuries to transfer Grotius's intuition from the world of philosophical speculation to that of political action, but in the end this principle inspired the (never completed) secularization of the public institutions that took place in much of Europe during the nineteenth century. Grotius's proposal therefore requires more detailed examination.

The problem Grotius had to solve was a religiously motivated conflict: if a peaceful society had to be rebuilt, the starting point could no longer be religion, which had to be confined to one's private life. A new starting point was required, and it was found in a natural law integrally founded on God's rationality and therefore fully accessible to human reason. In other words, to make peaceful coexistence possible between Catholics and Protestants, politics, the law, the economy, and the other areas of public life had to be secularized, placing them under the exclusive control of reason and philosophy and freeing them from the control of religion and theology: that is, they had to be conceived and regulated *etsi Deus non daretur*. The center of gravity of religion shifted from the public to the private life, and at the same time the center of gravity of public law moved from divine law to natural law based on reason. Alberico Gentili's *silete theologi in munere alieno*—the admonition addressed to theologians to keep silent in matters which concern others—finds in Grotius's *etsi Deus non daretur* its most convincing justification.[45]

This development was possible only because of the central place the doctrine of divine natural law had gained in Europe during the Middle Ages. As underlined by Catherine Larrière, Grotius's *etsi Deus non daretur* does not imply the negation of God; it presupposes only God's rationality: in perfect opposition to al-Ash'ari's voluntarism, Grotius writes that "just as even God cannot cause that two times two should not make four, so He cannot cause that which is intrinsically evil be not evil."[46] In this way Grotius does not need to deny the divine origin of natural law: it is enough to affirm its accessibility "to all humankind, Christian or not."[47] It is obvious that Grotius's theory constitutes a major departure from the traditional Roman Catholic doctrine that affirms the human inability to grasp with certainty and in fullness the content of natural law (because of original sin) and in this way justifies the need for the Church's guidance in interpreting divine natural law. But Grotius does not alter the structure of the Roman Catholic philosophical and legal discourse on natural law: the philosopher takes the place of the theologian, but this is more a substitution than a revolution.[48]

In the countries with a Jewish or Muslim religious background the weakness of the concept of divine natural law helps to explain why the search for an appropriate legal status of the other followed routes different from the creation of a secular state.

Differently from divine natural law in Christian thought, in the Orthodox Jewish legal tradition the Noahide law is part of the revealed law, and it is debated whether all its principles can be discovered through rational investigation. Although Selden and Spinoza tried to follow a path similar to Grotius's, this background made the rationalization of the Noahide law and its reduction to natural law difficult, and after 1948 it prevented the creation of a secular state in Israel. The double-revelation theory—one universal (to the whole of humankind, the Noahide revelation) and one particular (to a specific people, the Sinaitic revelation)—provided the intellectual background for a different solution to the problem of the "other": a state with a double root, one universal (the will of the citizens) and one particular (the cultural and religious heritage of the Jewish people). Of course the definition of the State of

Israel as a democratic and Jewish state is primarily the outcome of a political compromise between the secular and religious currents of Zionism, but this compromise was possible because its content was coherent with the theological and legal background made available by the Jewish tradition to the founding fathers of the State of Israel.

The Islamic approach to the secular state is even more problematic. Due to the weakness of the notion of divine natural law in this tradition, the Christian route is blocked; the Jewish route is impassable too, as it requires a universal revelation that is unknown to Islam.[49] That leaves a very narrow passage based on the interpretation of the sacred texts: secularization of the state has to find its legitimacy directly in the Quran and the Sunna. This attempt was made in the twentieth century by a group of modernist Muslim thinkers, largely under the influence of the Western thought that had spread in their countries under the colonial powers, but their conclusions have been accepted only by a fraction of Muslim public opinion and religious authorities. As a consequence, the notion of the secular state remains extraneous to many Islamic countries[50] where the state is clearly founded on Islamic principles and non-Muslims (in particular Christians and Jews) have the right to live according to their personal law, provided they accept the supremacy of the Muslim ruler.

## 5. Conclusion

What are the consequences that can be deduced from the analysis carried out in the preceding pages? The first and most important of them is that it is futile to attempt to export the model of the secular state to religious and legal traditions that do not meet the conditions for accepting it. This model is not culturally neutral: it is connected to Christian theological concepts.[51] So it is not universal, and it is pointless to think that, born in the Christian West, it can easily take root in the Muslim East. A second conclusion follows on naturally from the first: rather than trying risky legal transplants, it is preferable for each civilization to look within its own religious and cultural tradition for the suitable tools to address the problem of the "other" in terms that are appropriate to contemporary society. All the models considered in the preceding pages— including the Western and Christian secular state—show evident limits in governing the tensions induced by the process of religious pluralization that is developing in many parts of the world, but each of them has in itself the potential to meet this challenge. In the West the solution is not to jettison the concept of the secular state; rather, it is to initiate a reflection that allows its application in a way that is not hostile to religion. In the Muslim countries the problem is not to give up the Islamic state but within it to guarantee freedom and equality to non-Muslim people and communities. They are different roads, but all are acceptable if they converge on the common goal of ensuring religious freedom, which is a fundamental right of every human being.

Scholars of law and religion can contribute to this strategy by indicating the connection between the legal and the theological categories and showing the importance of knowing different religious legal traditions in order to understand contemporary political transformations. A sound knowledge of the theological background of political categories helps in deciphering not only their roots but also their potentialities, as shown by the examination of the notion of the secular state. Paying due attention to the dangers of essentialism and determinism, a better understanding of the connections between religion and politics is the precondition to providing convincing answers to questions posed by the growing presence of religion in the public space.

# Notes

1. By "Christian and Muslim countries," I indicate the countries where the majority of the population professes that faith: even though it is just a numerical datum, incapable of revealing the effective vitality of a religion, the fact that over half of the population of a country follows the same religion normally indicates that some cultural categories that may be traced to the religion of the majority have had (and can have) a significant importance in establishing the legal tradition of that country. The data on the religious membership of the population have been taken from the Association of Religion Data Archives (ARDA), available online: <www.thearda.com>.
2. Divine in the sense that it is promulgated by God. Greek philosophers had a different notion of the divinity of law: for them law had a divine character that was, however, independent from its promulgation by God. See R. Brague, *The Law of God* (Chicago: University of Chicago Press, 2007) at 28.
3. On the distinction between religious and nonreligious (or secular) legal systems see S. Ferrari, "Canon Law as a Religious Legal System," in A. Huxley, ed, *Religion, Law and Tradition: Comparative Studies in Religious Law* (London: RoutledgeCurzon, 2002) 49–60, at 101–3.
4. History shows that also the religious-based legal systems are subject to change: interpretation and second level provisions are the most common instruments to change a law that is assumed to be unchangeable. See S. Ferrari, "Adapting Divine Law to Change: The Experience of the Roman Catholic Church (With Some Reference to Jewish and Islamic Law)" (October 2006) 28:1 Cardozo Law Review 53–66.
5. On the notion of tradition and, in particular, of legal tradition see H. P. Glenn, *Legal Traditions of the World: Sustainable Diversity in Law* (Oxford: Oxford University Press, 2010).
6. See J. Stone, *Human Law and Human Justice* (Stanford: Stanford University Press, 1968). The scriptural foundation of divine natural law theory is to be found in Paul's Letter to the Romans (2:14–16): "For when Gentiles who don't have the law do by nature the things of the law, these, not having the law, are a law to themselves, in that they show the work of the law written in their hearts, their conscience testifying with them."
7. See D. J. Klassen, *Le Droit naturel dans le pensée de Thomas d'Aquin*, in Louis-Léon Christians et al., dir, *Droit naturel: relancer l'histoire?* (Bruxelles: Bruylant, 2008) 257–92.
8. Although, according to the Catholic doctrine, this knowledge is imperfect due to the natural sin that clouded the human ability to recognize inerrably the principles of natural law (see *Catechism of the Catholic Church* [Città del Vaticano: Libreria Editrice Vaticana,

1993] at n. 1960): as a consequence their definition by the Church authority has become a necessity (and this is the most questionable profile of the whole theory, as the declarations of the Church in this field are valid *erga omnes*). However this definition, although formulated in the light of divine revelation, must be based on human reason.

9. On the problem, much discussed among the canonists, of the subjection of infidels to the precepts of divine revealed law see P. Maroto, *Institutiones iuris canonici ad normam novi codicis* (Rome: Commentarioum pro Religiosis, 1921) at 21–22; R. Naz, *Infidèles*, in *Dictionnaire de droit canonique*, vol. 5, (Paris: Letouzey et Ané, 1953) c. 1360; Giuseppe Dalla Torre, *Infedeli*, in *Enciclopedia del diritto*, vol. 21 (Milano: Giuffrè, 1971) at 418.

10. "The natural law, present in the heart of each man and established by reason, is universal in its precepts and its authority extends to all men. It expresses the dignity of the person and determines the basis for his fundamental rights and duties.... It also provides the indispensable moral foundation for building the human community. Finally, it provides the necessary basis for the civil law": *Catechism of the Catholic Church*, supra note 8, at n. 1956 and 1959.

11. For a general overview of the debate on natural law see D. Novak, *Natural Law in Judaism* (Cambridge: Cambridge University Press, 1998) (according to whom "Noahide law is the Jewish way of thinking natural law" at 191); see also the review to this book published by B. Jackson, "The Jewish View of Natural Law" (Spring 2001) 52:1 Journal of Jewish Studies 136–45; J. I. Dienstag, "Natural Law in Maimonidean Thought and Scholarship" (1987) 6 Jewish Law Annual 64–77. Novak's opinion is shared by N. Lamm and A. Kirschenbaum, "Freedom and Constraint in the Jewish Judicial Process" (1979) 1 Cardozo Law Review 105–20; A. Lichtenstein, "Does Jewish Tradition Recognize an Ethic Independent of Halakha?," in Marvin Fox, ed, *Modern Jewish Ethics: Theory and Practice* (Columbus: Ohio State University Press, 1975) 62–65; see contra M. Fox, "Maimonides and Aquinas on Natural Law," (1972) 3 Diné Israel 5–36; J. Faur, *Understanding the Covenant*, in 9 Tradition, Spring 1968 at 41; S.L. Stone, "Sinaitic and Noahide Law: Legal Pluralism in Jewish Law" (1991) 12 Cardozo Law Review 1157–214; J. D. Bleich "Judaism and Natural Law" (1988) 7 Jewish Law Annual 5. advocates a very limited notion of natural law.

12. On these commandments see D. Novak, *The Image of the Non-Jew in Judaism: An Historical and Constructive Study of the Noahide Laws* (New York and Toronto: Edwin Mellen Press, 1983); N. Rakover, *Law and the Noahides: Law as a Universal Value* (Jerusalem: The Library of Jewish Law, 1998).

13. While most scholars agree that some of Noah's commandments can be known through reason, it is debated whether all of them could have been known without God's revelation. See N. Rakover, "Jewish Law and the Noahide Obligation to Preserve the Social Order" (1991) 12 Cardozo Law Review 1076–86.

14. E. Dorff, "Judaism as a Religious Legal System" (1977–78) 29 Hastings Law Journal 1331–360 ("Because Judaism is basically a positivistic legal system based upon the Covenant at Sinai" at 1352).

15. The diversity between this approach and the one prevailing in the Christian legal tradition emerges, for example, when examining the question of the prohibition of usury. This prohibition is based on a passage from Deuteronomy that says: "do not charge a fellow Israelite interest, whether on money or food or anything else that may earn interest. You may charge a foreigner interest, but not a fellow Israelite, so that the Lord your God may bless you in everything you put your hand to in the land you are entering to possess" (Deut. 23:19–20; see also Deut. 15:2–3). This passage clearly shows the existence of two laws: one that governs the relations among Jews, based on brotherhood, and another that governs the relations between Jews and non-Jews, based on justice. The two laws are not inconsistent or contradictory, but they are different: those closest to me (in this case those who share my religion) are entitled to something more than all other people. Christianity inherited from Judaism the prohibition of usury, but from the beginning understood it as a principle of divine natural law: therefore this prohibition was extended to all people, applying the principle that—outside the divine revealed law—there is just one law (the divine natural law) that is common to Christians and non-Christians. On the

different way to conceive the prohibition of usury in Judaism and Christianity see B. Nelson, *The Idea of Usury. From Tribal Brotherhood to Universal Otherhood* (Princeton, NJ: Princeton University Press, 1969) at 3–28; see also A. Dumas, "Intérêt et usure," in *Dictionnaire de droit canonique*, vol. 5 (Paris : Letouzey & Anè, 1953), c. 1476.

16. Can a righteous gentile, who lives according to the Noahide law, reach the eternal life? The Tosefta answers in the affirmative (Sanhedrin 13:2) and this is the position of most contemporary Jewish law scholars (see for example Rakover, *supra* note 13, at 1073–1136). But Maimonides writes it is not enough to respect the Noahide precepts because they are rational, it is necessary to respect them as the revealed law of God, that is by faith: only in this case will a gentile have a share in the world to come (see J. E. David, "Maïmonide, la nature et le droit: un vieux problem revisité," Christians et al., *Droit naturel*, *supra* note 7, at 237–41). Interestingly the Catholic answer to the same question is different: human beings who live according to divine natural law can reach eternal salvation even if they do not know the Christian revelation or reject it "bona fide." The grounds on the basis of which the law is observed (because it is rational or because it has been revealed) is not decisive. For an overview of the Roman Catholic doctrine see M. Ruokkannen, *The Catholic Doctrine of Non-Christian Religions According to the Second Vatican Council* (Leiden and New: York-Köln, Brill, 1992).

17. On human rights in the Jewish legal traditions see M. Konvitz ed, *Judaism and Human Rights* (London: Rutgers, 2001); A. Maoz, "Can Judaism Serve as a Source of Human Rights?" (2004) 64 Zeitschrift für Ausländisches öffentliches Recht und Völkerrecht n. 3, at 677

18. C. Chéhata, "La religion et les fondements du droit en Islam" (1973) 18 Archives de philosophie du droit at 17. See also C. G. Weeramantry, *Islamic Jurisprudence: An International Perspective* (London: Macmillan, 1988) at 65; M. Khadduri, "Nature and Sources of Islamic Law," in I. Edge, ed, *Islamic Law and Legal Theory* (Aldershot: Dartmouth, 1996) 87–107 at 90–92.

19. The existence of a conception of natural law in the Islamic legal philosophy is affirmed by A. Ezzati, *Islam and Natural Law* (London: Icas Press, 2002) at 60–92, while A. E. Emon, *Islamic Natural Law Theories* (Oxford: Oxford University Press, 2010) makes a distinction between hard and soft conceptions of natural law; for a more nuanced position see Y. B. Achour, "L'idea di giustizia naturale nel pensiero giuridico sunnita" (2004) 4 *Daimon. Annuario di diritto comparato delle religioni*, 225–42. On the peculiar approach of Islamist theology to natural law see F. Griffel, "The Harmony of Natural Law and Shari'a in Islamist Theology," in A. Amanat and F. Griffel, eds, *Shari'a: Islamic Law in the Contemporary Context* (Stanford: Stanford University Press, 2007) 38–61.

20. A. Sachedina, *The Islamic Roots of Democratic Pluralism* (Oxford: Oxford University Press, 2001) at 85; see also Y. Mohamed, *Fitra: The Islamic Conception of Human Nature* (London: Ta-Ha, 1996); A. Ezzati, *Islam*, ibid., at 93–109.

21. See M. Khadduri, *The Islamic Conception of Justice* (Baltimore: Johns Hopkins University Press, 1984) at 94–95; M. H. Kamali, "Methodological Issues in Islamic Jurisprudence" (1996) 11:1 Arab Law Quarterly 3–33, at 15; W. B. Hallaq, *A History of Islamic Legal Theories* (Cambridge: Cambridge University Press, 1997) at 135.

22. See R. C. Martin, M. R. Woodward and D. S. Atmaja, *Defenders of Reason in Islam: Mu'tazilism from Medieval School to Modern Symbol* (Oxford: Oneworld, 1997); A. K. Reinhart, *Before Revelation: The Boundaries of Muslim Moral Thought* (Albany: State University of New York Press, 1995); A. W. Nader, *Le système philosophique des Mu'tazila: premiers penseurs de l'Islam* (Beyrouth: Les Lettres Orientales, 1956); T. Nagel, *The History of Islamic Theology: From Muhammad to the Present* (Princeton: Wiener, 2000) 93–170.

23. R. Caspar, *Traité de théologie musulmane* (Roma: Pontificio Istituto di Studi Arabi e d'Islamistica, 1996) at 148.

24. Ibid., at 181.

25. *Tahafut al-falasifah* [*Incoherence of the philosophers*] (Lahore: Pakistan Philosophical Congress, 1963) at 185.

26. See for example T.-A. Druart, "Al-Fârâbi (870-950): une éthique universelle fondée sur les intelligibles premiers," in L.-L. Christians et al., dir, *Droit naturel*, *supra*, note 7, at 215–32.

27. See J. Stone, *Human Law, supra* note 6 at 55–60; G. Makdisi, "Ethics in Islamic Traditionalist Doctrine," in *Religion, Law and Learning in Classical Islam* (Hampshire: Variorum, 1991) at 50–51.
28. For example Ockham writes that, if God had so willed, stealing, lying, and committing adultery would have been virtuous (see *Opera Theologica*, vol. 5 (New York: Franciscan Institute Press, 1967-1986), at 352); al-Ash'ari used the same examples to support his thesis. Correctly Brian Tierney underlines that according to Ockham (and again we are not far from al-Ashari), although God could have created a different universe, "in the existing world that God had actually chosen to make, human reason could provide a guide to human moral conduct" ("Natural Law and Natural Rights," in J. Witte, Jr. and F. S. Alexander, eds, *Christianity and Law*, (Cambridge: Cambridge University Press, 2008) 89–104 at 96): but the possibility of a different universe, where stealing is good and giving to the poor is bad, undermines the ontological nature of good and bad.
29. The irrationality of Islamic law (albeit "within circumscribed limits") is affirmed by J. Schacht, *An Introduction to Islamic Law* (Oxford: Clarendon Press, 1982) at 202.
30. It affected to a lesser extent the Shiite Islamic law and, within Sunni Islam, the Hanafi school, where the voluntaristic trend of al-Ashari had less influence: see B. G. Weiss, *The Spirit of Islamic Law* (Athens and London: University of Georgia Press, 1998) at 35–38.
31. See Y. B. Achour, "Nature, raison et révélation dans la philosophie du droit des auteurs sunnites," in E. E. Dais et al., eds, *Consequences of Modernity in Contemporary Legal Theory* (Berlin: Duncker & Humblot, 1998) 3–20.
32. See K. Hashemi, *Religious Legal Tradition, International Human Rights Law and Muslim States* (Leiden and Boston: Nijhoff, 2008) at 135–212.
33. See G. M. Quer, "Pluralismo e diritti delle minoranze. Il sistema del «millet»," (2010) 1 Quaderni di diritto e politica ecclesiastica 257–308.
34. See *infra*, para 4.
35. This does not mean that the practical application of this model has been satisfactory. Jews were persecuted in the secular and Christian Europe much more heavily than in Muslim countries where, at least until 1948, the *millet* system ensured them a safe habitat.
36. "Secular state" is an expression that can have many different meanings. I make use of it to indicate a state where the same civil and political rights are enjoyed by citizens independently from the religion they profess (or do not profess).
37. This part is based on S. Ferrari, "Religion et constitution," in M. Troper and D. Chagnollaud eds, *Traité international de droit constitutionnel*, vol.3: *Suprématie de la Constitution* (Paris: Dalloz, 2013), 437–478.
38. See the constitutional preambles of Germany, Liechtenstein, Poland, Sweden, and Switzerland.
39. It is the case of the constitutions of Armenia (article 8,1), Denmark (article 4), Greece (article 3), Iceland (article 62), Liechtenstein (article 37), Malta (article 2), Monaco (article 9), Norway (article 16); in England, where there is no written constitution, the Church of England is the established Church. This provision is much more frequent in the constitutions of Muslim states: 23 of them (that is, more than half of the 44 States where Muslims are the majority) declare Islam to be the religion of the state.
40. Ten countries have a constitution that defines the State as Islamic: Afghanistan (article 1), Bahrein (article 1), Iran (article 1), Maldives (article 1), Mauritania (article 1), Morocco (preamble), Oman (article 1), Pakistan (article 1), Saudi Arabia (article 1), Yemen (article 1).
41. Seventeen constitutions of Muslim States list sharia among the sources of State law: Afghanistan (article 130), Bahrain (article 2), Egypt (article 2), Iran (article 4), Iraq (article 2), Kuwait (article 2), Libya (article 1 of the Constitutional Declaration 2011), Maldives (article 43), Mauritania (preamble), Oman (article 2), Pakistan (articles 227–30), Qatar (article 1), Saudi Arabia (article 1), Sudan (article 5), Syria (article 3), United Arab Emirates (article 7), and Yemen (article 3).
42. See the basic laws on Human Dignity and Liberty (1992, art. 1) and on Freedom of Occupation (1994, article 2). Moreover the fundamental law on the Knesset (1958, article 7A) defines Israel as the State of the Jewish people. The debates on the meaning of the

word "Jewish" in the basic laws are endless but this word, along with a reference to the Jewish nation, includes also a reference to the Jewish religion. See A. Maoz, "Constitutional Law," in I. Zamir and S. Colombo, eds, *The Law of Israel: General Survey* (Jerusalem: Hebrew University of Jerusalem, 1995) 5–49 at 33–36.
43. See article 1.
44. See A. Maoz, "Constitutional Law," *supra* note 42 at 35. See also I. Zamir and A. Zysblat, *Public Law in Israel* (Oxford: Clarendon Press, 1996) at 152.
45. On the relations between Grotius and Gentili see K. R. Simmonds, "Hugo Grotius and Alberico Gentili" (1959) 8 Jahrbuch für Internationales Recht at 85–100.
46. *The Law of War and Peace*, I, I, 10, 5, Lonang Institute 2005, available online: <www.lonang.com/exlibris/grotius/gro-001.htm>.
47. C. Larrière, "Grotius: droit naturel et sociabilité," in Christians et al., dir, *Droit naturel*, *supra* note 7, at 314.
48. Thus confirming the exactness of C. Schmitt's intuition that "all significant concepts of the modern theory of the state are secularized theological concepts" (*Political Theology: Four Chapters on the Concept of Sovereignty* [Chicago: University of Chicago Press, 2005] at 36).
49. Islam recognizes a number of revelations to specific people—the Jews and the Christians, for example—but the only revelation that is addressed to all humankind is the Quranic one.
50. Not to all, however. Twelve Muslim countries have constitutions that affirm the secular character of the State. All of them (with one exception: Lebanon) are non-Arab States. Keeping in mind that the majority of the States that define themselves as Islamic are Arab States, these data seem to bring to light a significant difference between Arab and non-Arab Islam. See S. Ferrari, "Religion et constitution," *supra* note 37.
51. See I. Augsberg, "Religious Freedom as 'Reflexive Law'" and S. Last Stone, "Conflicting Visions of Political Space," in this book.

# 2

# Conflicting Visions of Political Space

SUZANNE LAST STONE

## 1. Introduction

Liberalism, as Michael Walzer points out, is built on the art of separation: the separation of religion and politics and the separation of the private and public spheres. In each sphere, "institutions are responsive to their own internal logic, even while they are also responsive to systemic determination."[1] Keeping religion and politics apart is an idea with a history, and that history is primarily a Christian one, rooted in the experience of European Christendom and made possible because Christians, virtually from the beginning, viewed church and state as conceptually separate entities, with different jurisdictions and powers, and even a different logic. Thus, Silvio Ferrari, in the first chapter of this volume, argues that the secular state was made possible by the Roman Catholic legal tradition, which conceptualized God's law as divine natural law, in contrast to Jewish and Islamic conceptions. A crucial turning point, he contends, was the rise of religious wars between Catholics and Protestants in Europe. The solution to such wars could no longer lie in the pope or religion; rather, it was found in "a natural law integrally founded on God's rationality." Philosophers thus took the place of theologians. The "center of gravity" of public life shifted from divine law to natural law based on reason even as the "center of gravity" of religion shifted to the private sphere. With the ascendance of Protestantism, the foundation was further laid for the privatization of religion. The Enlightenment discourse also took place against the backdrop of attempts to emancipate society from clerical rule. It relied heavily on the Protestant notion of religious internality—that religion is basically a matter of belief and conscience—to free society of an institutionalized church.

Genealogical accounts of the Christian roots of the liberal state are hardly new. What is new, however, is the increased call on liberal societies in a post-Christian world to acknowledge these roots and to recognize that the art of separation—and, with it, the privatizing of religion—is nothing but an imposition of secular liberalism's Christian cultural heritage on non-Christian religions whose basic terms of reference are entirely different. Thus, Ferrari states forthrightly: "This model [the secular state] is not culturally neutral: it is connected to Christian theological concepts." The argument that secularism is a cultural artifact of Christianity, a "universal parochialism" to use Shlomo Avineri's term or a "particularism masquerading as a universal," to use that of Charles Taylor, is usually invoked to encourage greater accommodation and sensitivity by the Western liberal state to "way of life" claims made by adherents of non-Christian religions.[2] As such, the argument is a very welcome corrective to the Western liberal tendency to judge claims through the distorting lens of the Christian experience.

For example, Western liberalism's very definition of religion as being about belief and not custom or law has a distinctly Protestant cast that does not suit religions such as Judaism or Islam. The Jewish Free School case seems to exemplify this issue, and certainly the veil controversies in Europe are emblematic of this problem. Much ink has been spilled on whether the veil is a symbol of subordination and oppression, an ironic feminist gesture, or an expression of conscience. The terms of the debate, which insist on seeing external manifestations and ritual behavior such as dress as symbols with inherent meaning—as pointing to some inner truth—betrays a Christian trope that Adam Seligman has called the "sincere mode."[3] For the veil is not a symbol, it is a practice, as is wearing a kippah. Such practices may signify diverse things to diverse people, or they may not signify anything at all. This does not reduce the practices to "culture" as opposed to "religion." Here, claims of conscience are not rooted in discrete dogmas or propositions, but in loyalty to a way of life, much of which is ritualized or rooted in custom, to which the person feels conscientiously bound as a whole. In short, the liberal art of separation, of differentiating between constructs such as religion, culture, politics, and law, while well suited to the Western Christian cultural heritage from which it sprang, encounters difficulties when extended to law-based religions or more comprehensive religious cultures, such as Islam and Judaism.

At the same time, we should be very wary of the attempt to reposition liberal political arrangements as exclusively Christian. In the first place, the argument seems to imply that there is only one natural path—the Christian one—to the separation of religion and state. Yet, motivations for separation can be exceedingly complex. Historians still debate which was primary in the early American experience: the Enlightenment embrace of reason and consent as the exclusive legitimate basis for politics or the wish to protect the purity of the "garden of religion" by segregating it from politics and mundane affairs. Similarly, secular space may emerge out of a certain conception of the deity rather than from external critique or opposition to clerical rule. Thus, Marcel Gauchet traces the rise of secularism on the world historical stage to the increasing disenchantment of religion: gods were vanquished from the world and the divine became increasingly transcendent and removed from this-worldly affairs.[4] Furthermore, Mark Lilla has recently argued that the complex picture of the Christian triune God is inextricably caught up in this story because divided sovereignty is more compatible with a picture of a divided god than a unified one.[5]

In the case of religions framed around legal traditions, shifting pictures of the divine law are as important as pictures of God. Ferrari focuses on the varying pictures of God's law as discovered through reason versus revelation. But other pictures of law can—and should—be examined. Is the religious law imagined as a comprehensive system uniting all aspects of life under a single sacred framework, thus leaving no room for a separate political domain? Or is the law conceived as plural, consisting of different jurisdictions with distinctive logics? Alternatively, is the religious law imagined as primarily political, a blueprint for a divine government, or is it imagined as exquisitely ethical, taking into account only the rights of individuals and not societal needs or a collective such as the state? If the latter, what law regulates social need: the ideal law of an ideal society or a real law adjusted for a real society? Shifting pictures of God and most especially of the nature of Jewish law, as well as Jewish historical experience, all played roles at various times in shaping counterpart doctrines to liberal separation.

Second, since modernity itself is characterized by increasing differentiation and the splintering of social life into multiple domains, the argument that liberal separation is thoroughly Christian implies that non-Christian religions, unless they have gone through a process of reform, are quintessentially premodern: they simply have not gone through the modern process of secularization in the sense of differentiation of realms. We should be suspicious of such claims, too. After all, resurgent religion is itself a modern phenomenon and, as such, one of its chief characteristics is the reconstruction of a tradition far more traditional than the original ever was. True, both Islam and Judaism, for example, begin with strong original visions of a unified religious polity in which the political authority is both subject to and enforces the divine law. Yet, over time, both developed doctrines and practices that reflected and could further sustain an increased differentiation of spheres. Both developed conceptual predicates for treating political order differently from religious order and for treating public space differently from private space. The original vision of unity was retained as an ideal, however, and often assumed mythic proportion, especially in the popular imagination. Today this dynamic is proving a potent obstacle to forging models more congenial to separation from the resources existing within Islam and Judaism. And it is hardly accidental. Political religion, which aims to recover an original ideal vision of a unified religious polity, or of a comprehensive religio-legal system united under a single sacral framework, is in no small way an attempt to overcome the fragmentation of modernity by imagining a unity that is depicted as a return to origins.

It is against this backdrop that Muslim and Jewish thinkers are looking back today on a wide variety of legal doctrines and theories, as well as historical experiences, in order to engage the question of whether there are counterparts within their respective traditions to liberal notions of the political sphere and of public space. In what follows I wish to present a summary sketch of the Jewish religious perspective on the political sphere and public space in the hopes that an engagement with the internal perspective of one non-Christian religion will allow us to identify points of tension and thus better understand—and even manage—contemporary contestations over political and public space.[6]

## 2. Visions of Political Space Within Traditional Judaism
### 2.1. Political Space as a Site of Order in the Service of Religion

Within Judaism, there are a variety of doctrines that roughly correspond to a division between religious and political spheres. Indeed, several of these doctrines were developed in tandem with Islam and Christianity in the twelfth and thirteenth centuries along with the emergence of criminal law as public rather than religious law. Across traditions, a new perception of an individual who could be deterred and a "public sphere" having both powers and need for new social regulation came into being. Biblical evidentiary restrictions on conviction were jettisoned by all three religions, and there developed in this period of intellectual cross-fertilization between Islam and Judaism essentially a two-tier system of law, which viewed revealed law as ideal law for an ideal society. Real law, on the other hand, derived its authority from the revealed law, but its actual content was devised to ensure social order for a real society. This served to justify the assignment of certain extra-legal powers to political authorities who were not restrained by religious law. In short, far from positing a total, unified halakhic society, medieval Jewish jurisprudence imagined Halakha as composed of different jurisdictions generating law in accordance with different principles. Thus, the political realm emerges as a space with its own distinct logic and laws.

The medieval Jewish discussion centers on the rights of monarchs, including the prerogatives of the "Jewish king," and is revived in modern halakhic discussions of the legitimacy of the law of the state, including a Jewish State. This discussion compresses a long tradition of legal and political discourse about the universal dimension of kingship, which begins in the Hebrew Bible.

In Deuteronomy 17, the king has only one positive duty: to write out a scroll of the law, read it every day of his life, and obey its commands. At the same time, the king is described as a monarch "like all the other nations." The text thus immediately sets up a tension between a model of kingship that is particular and culturally specific and one that is universal. That tension is fully exploited in the medieval discussion, which begins with Maimonides.

Maimonides's views on kingship cannot be separated from his philosophy of the law. The Torah in its entirety is a divine political structure because all of its laws have a purpose: the perfection of the body or the soul. The Torah's commandments addressed to governmental structures are part of the perfection of the body because they aim at securing social order, which is a necessary condition for achieving perfection of the soul.[7] Accordingly, the Jewish king has so-called emergency powers to depart from Torah law in order to maintain social order.[8] These emergency powers are only theoretically temporary, and they entail the power to punish free of the biblical procedural restrictions of two witnesses and forewarning.[9]

Kingship is not precisely a realm of politics, discretion, or wisdom, however; it is a realm of law. As Gerald Blidstein points out, Maimonides transferred over to the Jewish king a separate body of Talmudic law about the universal so-called Noahide laws that bind non-Jewish societies.[10] In addition to six substantive commands—exemplifying the minimal demands of a civilized political community, such as prohibitions on murder, theft, and the like—Noahide law includes a seventh command of justice known as *dinin*.[11] For Maimonides, *dinin* is nothing but the requirement to establish governmental structures capable of preserving order by punishing violations of the other Noahide laws. The Talmud had already noted that "Noahides" punish in accordance with the testimony of one witness and without forewarning.[12] In Maimonides's Code, the Jewish king, like the non-Jewish government, is authorized to punish on the basis of the testimony of one witness and without forewarning. "Maimonides's entire edifice of monarchic powers identified Jewish and gentile governance as a single structure possessing similar goals and utilizing similar instruments."[13] The biblical language to appoint a king "like all the other nations" thus becomes a warrant for resorting to conventional norms of governance to define the powers of the Jewish king. Of course, these "non-Jewish" norms of governance are themselves offshoots of Talmudic jurisprudence.[14] Nevertheless, from the Jewish point of view, they are universal and not particular norms.

The most far-reaching articulation of this view is that of Rabbi Nissim Gerondi in his Eleventh Homily. Gerondi posits a central gap in the Halakha—the lack of conventional modes of governance able to preserve social order. Torah law, with its requirements of judging in accordance with the testimony of two witnesses and forewarning, cannot accomplish this end. Thus, it is deficient by comparison to other political systems. Yet, the Torah itself provides the means for correcting this deficiency. The king, who is concerned only with guilt or innocence, may punish without resort to the Torah's method of criminal adjudication. Like Maimonides, Gerondi links the king's authority to a general religious command to preserve social order. Gerondi goes far beyond Maimonides, however. First, power, not institution, is key for him. Thus the religious command is not to appoint a monarch per se but, rather, always to embed "monarchical" power somewhere in the Jewish polity.[15] Indeed, the monarch is merely the site of social order historically chosen by the people who may consent to another institutional form if they so desire. Second, the language about the need for public order and social welfare is so broad that it is virtually impossible to confine the "power" Gerondi is describing to punishment.[16] Third, Gerondi does not place the king's powers within the more conventional emergency jurisdiction model, although he cites the phrase once or twice. Moreover, the political domain is stripped of any aura of the religious. Although there is a vague bow to the Jewish king upholding the religion, there is no attempt to integrate the king within the rest of the system, as Maimonides labored to do, nor is there any attempt to coordinate state power with religious law and institutions. This is a separate, actually and theoretically permanent jurisdiction legitimately operating under its own rules. Although Gerondi is largely silent on what these rules are and whether there are any inherent limits to them, I believe we must read him against the background of the prior discussion as implicitly incorporating any rules permitted to non-Jewish societies.

The medieval discussion of the rights of kings also intersects with a more familiar Talmudic principle: *dina de-malkhuta dina* (DDM) ("the law of the land is the [legitimate] law"), which is first articulated in the context of the power of foreign rulers to tax and expropriate land and which eventually became a cornerstone for the successful integration of the formerly legally autonomous Jewish communities into the legal systems of the nation-state. Paradoxically, the principle originally served to make the Halakha fully functional in exile, but then the postulate took on a life of its own as the jurists begin to theorize in the Middle Ages about its conceptual basis. The Talmud already hints at a close association between the principle and the custom of the people,[17] and many of the medieval theories revolve around one or another form of popular consent or social contract theory. These conceptual bases began to undermine the conception of Halakha as an all-encompassing system. Portions of Halakha become theoretically optional and not mandatory as the principle was extended through a series of logical progressions and in tandem with the extension of the rights of kings in Europe far beyond the concrete context from which it sprang—taxes and land—and far beyond what is necessary to resolve actual, rather than theoretical, cases. Rather than continuing to make the Halakha fully functional in exile, the sphere of Halakha became more and more contracted.

One of these conceptual bases, proffered by the medieval commentator Rashi, connects the principle to the self-same principle underlying the powers of the Jewish monarch. Rashi focuses on the one instance in the Babylonian Talmud where DDM functions not as a duty-imposing rule but as a power-conferring rule to Jewish litigants in an intra-Jewish dispute to take advantage of non-Jewish validation of deeds even though the signatories are non-Jews and the method contrary to Jewish law.[18] Here, DDM is allowing non-Jewish law to penetrate Jewish law as an alternative norm. Rashi draws on the familiar Jewish legal principle that only one who is himself under a divine obligation to perform an action can be an effective legal agent for others. He explains the Talmudic permission as resting on the notion that non-Jews are commanded to "institute justice," citing the Noahide norm of *dinim*. Accordingly, they can be effective agents for all matters subsumed under that command. Recall that, from the internal perspective of rabbinic Judaism, this command obligates humanity to preserve social order by enacting systems of law. The kingdom's law is rooted ultimately in divine command and therefore has legal and moral legitimacy equal to that of Jewish law. Accordingly, non-Jewish legal activity can serve here as an alternative norm even for Jews and even when it is at variance with Jewish law. Conversely, he notes, with respect to matters not subsumed under the command of *dinim*—Jewish marriage and divorce bills—DDM cannot be invoked as a power-conferring rule to utilize alternative norms. The implication of Rashi's rationale is that large portions of the Halakha are in fact replaceable by the law of other civilizations, thus shrinking the scope of Halakha to matters of ritual and religious prohibition.[19]

Already in the medieval period, Me'iri had observed that the doctrine of the Jewish king and that of "the law of the kingdom" are merely two facets of a single concept: conventional political institutions or governments "like all the other nations." Both doctrines, then, ultimately can be traced back to the coexistence within Judaism of two normative systems, the one consisting of universal obligations binding all humanity and the other of commandments particular to Jews. The Bible first launched this complex internal structure by describing the pre-Sinai world as one filled with law given to humanity, including Israel's forefathers. This account is transformed in the Talmud into a full-fledged description of two normative orders. The Talmud primarily focused on the universal law as an explanatory model for the law that existed before "the law"—the law given at Sinai—and used the model as a contrasting image of a conventional society, unlike the covenantal one forged at Sinai, in order to explore the differences between the two and construct identity. Although it left open the relationship between the two legal orders, it largely presented that relationship as a historic progression, with the universal law superseded for Jews by the particular obligations revealed at Sinai. It was left to the medieval period to construct a far more complex relationship between the two, with the universal law serving in the eyes of some jurists essentially as an alternative source of norms even in a national Jewish context.

In short, the universal Noahide obligation to institute good government and the laws of Jewish kingship are merely two faces of the same coin: both authorize a jurisdiction that operates outside some of the strictures of the religious law for the sake of effective government. And despite the fact that the initial notion of a universal law within Judaism is intricately tied to divine command—it is an outgrowth of the idea that humanity was given a universal law before Sinai—the actual norms that govern this space are for the most part conventional or consensual, consisting of the practices and agreements of general society aimed at producing social order. These practices are available for use even in a purely internal Jewish context. The Jewish king, and modern successors constituting the political realm, operates in accordance with Noahide law and not the particulars of Sinai law. Still, from both a jurisprudential and philosophic perspective—recall, for example, Maimonides's postulate about the welfare of the body politic as a precondition for the welfare of the soul—the universal political realm is perceived as in the service of the particular, making it possible.

## 2.2. Political Space as Profane

The very existence of a "universal" legal system within a particular legal system opened a deep fissure in Jewish thought. From an internal perspective, the Noahide system is the law humanity was commanded to follow, including Israel's forebears, and is binding on everyone. The giving of the Torah at Sinai imposed additional obligations only on Jews. But if the universal Noahide law is God-sanctioned and a reflection of the moral and political law, what precisely is the point of the particular laws given later at Sinai? Various nineteenth-century reformers sought to solve this question by reconstituting Judaism into the Noahide, moral, universal religion, in which ritual is secondary, at best. Conversely, one could view the particularist obligations added at Sinai as the essence, and the universal, political law as necessary but insignificant.

Indeed, Gerondi's sermon, which forms a critical background text for the license of the modern Jewish state to govern pursuant to conventional norms of social order, explicitly deals with the question "why Sinai?" For, in the course of outlining the Jewish king's powers, he reconceives the purpose of the

Halakha as well. For Gerondi the sphere of Sinai law is the sacred and the numinous and the sphere of true justice. Thus, certain biblical laws, such as judging in accordance with two witnesses, were never intended as a practical means to govern society. Rather, they are intended to bring on the divine effluence. In addition, they are truly just precisely because they focus solely on the rights of the individual and do not take into account the needs of society. If we speak of Christian influences, by far the most important here is the Gelasian doctrine of two powers—pope and king. Yet, Gerondi is certainly working off earlier rabbinic sources as well as extending the doctrine of Noahide law to one logical conclusion. He is following, as Gerald Blidstein pointed out, Yehuda Halevi, who wrote about "the social-ethical law given to humanity (Noahide law) to which the spiritual-ceremonial law is added at Sinai," and decisively splitting the two into the realm of the sacred and particular, where true justice is possible, as opposed to the realm of the profane and universal, where the needs of society are irreconcilable with the rights of individuals.[20]

Thus, in the case of Judaism, the coexistence of universal and particular elements in one tradition led to an internal splitting of the tradition along lines more or less analogous to the modern differentiation of realms. Increasingly, the particular laws given exclusively for Jews at Sinai becomes seen, even from an internal standpoint and not only from the standpoint of the host nation-states in which Judaism later was set, as religion or ethics. They are sacred and mysterious norms or norms for an ideal society in which the interests of the individual are not compromised by collective goals.

Modern separation or differentiation of realms not only allows different realms of human experience to proceed in accordance with different conceptual logics. It also provides a means for one realm or activity to critique the other. This is the most powerful claim of modern positivism's separation thesis: by differentiating between law and morality, strong moral critique of modern law is made possible. One of the more interesting questions for those observing the Jewish religious tradition today revolves around this issue of critique. What resources should or could the tradition call on in order to critique the organization of the contemporary political sphere? Keen observers of the tradition will note that, outside the State of Israel (which presents a unique set of problems),[21] the standards used to judge the political sphere are not, by and large, the particular religious or ethical aspirational norms of the Jewish tradition but, rather, draw on the large body of Jewish sources that develop the universal Noahide Code. That body of law is in itself an ongoing project that develops in tandem with developments in the larger political sphere. For example, while the original markers of good government in the service of religion from the Talmudic period through the medieval period cite the Noahide ban on idolatry and blasphemy, over time, these criteria are reinterpreted to fit a secular age. Thus, the ban on idolatry is in the process of reinterpretation in terms of commitment to the rule of law. In short, the tradition continues to provide a standpoint from which to judge the very space it authorizes. In doing so, we can catch glimpse of what—in the eyes of Judaism—is a well-ordered political space and what is, instead, seen as inimical to the common project of government.

## 2.3. Public Space as Expressive

While the Hebrew Bible only seems to know the distinction between profane and sacred space and not the distinction between public and private space, the Talmudic rabbis were exquisitely sensitive to the differentiation of space. In addition to cataloguing a variety of forms of actual physical space—from the private to the public and ambiguous spaces in between—the rabbis also seem to recognize the conceptual and constructed aspect of space.

Public space is a human construct, the attempt by humans to shape the place and thus the nature of their interactions. In their introduction to *Public Space and Democracy*, Marcel Henaff and Tracy Strong differentiate four kinds of spaces organized by ancient Greeks: private, sacred, common, and public.[22] Common space is open to all in the same way and admits of no criteria, but it is not a space in which one goes to speak to others. Public space, by contrast, is a human construct aimed at interaction, communication, and expression. It is theatrical, in that it is a place in which one is seen and shows oneself to others. In contemporary France, as Patrick Weil points out, the Greek common space has become public space, such as the market or the mall, while the Greek public space has become political.[23] It is the space where citizens interact and shape, under French *laïcité*, a space that must be stripped of any markers of identity other than that common to all citizens.

In my preliminary investigation, Talmudic Judaism, too, seems to differentiate between common space, such as the market and the bathhouse, which members of all religions can enjoy,[24] but it is not a space in which one goes to speak to others. By contrast, public space is known as the *pharhessia*, from the Greek "frank speech," and it is a legal construct rather than a descriptive term. If under French *laïcité*, public space is about citizen interaction stripped of markers of identity, in the religious mentality public space is precisely that space where religion is glorified or shamed. It is the sphere of communicative action, where the worth of religion is communicated.[25]

We can catch a glimpse of this art of dividing space in the wonderful, albeit perplexing, Talmudic story about Rabban Gamliel's visit to the Roman bathhouse of Aphrodite, whose statue adorned the bath.[26] The philosopher Proklos asks how he could bathe, given the presence of the statue. Rabban Gamliel first puts him off—"One does not respond in the bathhouse"—and then explains once outside: "I did not enter into her domain, she entered into mine." Treating the statute as mere decoration rather than idolatry, and the bath as a preexisting common space,[27] creates a space that pagans and Jews can share and enjoy.[28] At the same time, this is not political space, the space of genuine interaction and frank, communicative speech. Rabban Gamliel refuses to speak Torah in the bathhouse.

## 3. Conflicting Visions of Transcendence

I have focused on three crucial elements in Jewish thought about political space: first, the function of political space is to preserve order, an order that is, in turn, in the larger service of religion. Second, political space is profane and not to be confused with sacred space in which ultimate values are expressed. Third, public space, as a sphere of communication, is where religion is glorified or shamed. In the contemporary moment, however, liberal political space seems to pose special challenges to the religious viewpoint.

It may well be that, in conditions of postmodernity, it is no longer possible to perceive political space as in the service of religion, in contrast to an earlier time, when secularism was less pervasive. Yet, the tension between resurgent religion and the liberal state seems less over secularism per se, but, rather, over the re-enchantment of the secular state. Whereas before, under thinner conceptions of liberalism, political space was secular in the strict sense—profane, or not holy—and holiness resided in the private sphere, increasingly, with the rise of universal human rights, for better or worse secular liberalism presents itself (and is certainly perceived by many religious adherents) as a competing transnational, universal, sacred, and transcendent realm.

It may be that the Christian roots of the secular state and the public-private divide have long been obscured from view; yet the Christian heritage of the West is, in fact, re-emerging in full force with the rise of the human rights movement. I have detailed at greater length elsewhere how rooted human rights discourse is today in Christian imagery.[29] For one thing, the incontrovertible or absolute character of human rights blurs the division between secular morality based on unaided reason and the realm of the sacrosanct, inviolable, or the sacred occupied by religion. Moreover, at the heart of the discursive tradition of human rights is the growing contention that its moral logic, and universalism, is ultimately conceptually incoherent apart from religious presuppositions. Thus, Michael Perry,[30] Max Stackhouse,[31] and Nicholas Wolterstorff,[32]—drawing on diverse Christian themes and history in varying ways—all assert that the foundation of human rights is essentially theological.

Certainly, the language of sacredness permeates the discourse; indeed, bare statements are common about the inviolate nature of humans and their sacredness, decoupled from secular justifications for treating humans as sacred (i.e., of ultimate value). Thus, the discourse has shifted from a Western political conception that flourished in a Christian setting; to a secular political and then moral tradition that claimed to have been made possible only by Christianity; and now to a discursive tradition whose key insights are validated by Christianity and by moral intuitions preserved primarily in Christianized readings of the Bible and other religious traditions and narratives.

In a sense, the modern political always relied on a certain "immanent transcendence,"[33] much as it may have disavowed it. Both Spinoza and Rousseau recognized the need for religion—or religion under the guidance of the state—to bolster democracy. In modern politics, nationalism, civic religion, and totalitarian political ideologies all took the structure of religion and contributed to a kind of re-enchantment.[34] Whether this process is unconscious or a logical necessity, it is persistent and recurrent—and the human rights movement follows this pattern. Within the Jewish religious worldview, however, imputing sacredness to the wrong place is the equivalent of idolatry.

To be sure, this does not mean, as Ferrari also points out, that Judaism (and Islam) lack a means of organizing life together with others in a just fashion. But these doctrines may well proceed along lines quite different from that of contemporary human rights discourse, which has grown out of the natural law tradition taken up by the West from Christianity. Indeed, those thinkers within the halakhic tradition who have most advanced a discourse of human rights, such as Rabbi Hayyim David HaLevi, draw on a distinct tradition within Jewish legal thought that formulates duties owed to others around the idea of reciprocity.[35] This approach avoids both the language of sacredness and ontological arguments; instead, it refocuses attention on human rights as a more limited political project intended to achieve political justice. Human rights, after all, as Adam Seligman writes, are a theory: "Though often treated as sacrosanct, they are but means to a further end ... They are one way to live together based on some commonly acceptable notions of fairness and justice."[36]

In sum, the contemporary Western state may be the long product of Christianity, but many of its central features—a political realm distinct from the religious realm and a robust concept of citizenship that transcends religious identity and guarantees religious freedom—can be found within the rich resources of Jewish law. It is the task of the legal historian and theorist not only to identify these points of convergence but also to pinpoint the sometimes radically divergent assumptions behind seemingly similar structural arrangements.

# Notes

1. M. Walzer, "Liberalism and the Art of Separation," (1984) 12 Political Theory 315, 315–30.
2. S. Avineri, "The Paradox of Religion and the Universality of Human Rights", in A. Sajo, *Human Rights with Modesty: the Problem of Universality* (Dordrecht: Springer, 2004) 317; C. Taylor, *Multiculturalism* (Princeton: Princeton University Press, 1994) 44.
3. See A. B. Seligman, R. P. Waller, M. J. Puett, and B. Simon, *Ritual and Its Consequences: An Essay on the Limits of Sincerity* (Oxford: Oxford University Press, 2008) 103–30.
4. M. Gauchet, *The Disenchantment of the World: A Political History of Religion*, trans. Oscar Burge (Princeton, NJ: Princeton University Press, 1999).
5. M. Lilla, *The Stillborn God: Religion, Politics and the Modern West* (New York: Knopf, 2007).
6. See generally S. Last Stone, "Religion and State: Models of Separation from Within Jewish Law" (2008) 6 International Journal of Constitutional Law 631, 631–61.
7. See Maimonides, The Guide of the Perplexed 3:31; 26–27.
8. Maimonides, *Mishneh Torah*, Laws of Kings 3:11.
9. There are scattered statements in the Talmud reporting a tradition that the court meted out punishments not according to law "in order to safeguard the law." Babylonian Talmud, Sanhedrin 46a and parallels. The two cases attached to the statement tell of impositions of the death penalty by the court for highly public violations of the law. See G. J. Blidstein, "'Ideal' and 'Real' in Classical Jewish Political Theory" (1990) 2 Jewish Political Studies Review 43, 43–66. But see H. Ben-Menahem, *Judicial Deviation From Talmudic Law: Governed by Men, Not by Rules*, 1 Jewish Law in Context (New York: Hardwood Academic Publishers, 1991) (arguing that Talmudic judges had power to disregard norms and exercised broad judicial discretion. The Talmud also depicts the court as authorized to "correct" the law, by relaxing or tightening it, through rabbinic legislation addressing social needs, applicable to everyone. Maimonides conflates these two depictions and reinterprets the talmudic tradition about a few judges exercising discretion in the sphere of punishment as a power-conferring rule authorizing judges to exercise discretion when sitting in so-called emergency jurisdiction. This transformation of the Talmudic materials can be explained by Maimonides's near-Hobbesian predilection for centralized order and for severity toward murderers (above any other category of sinner) and by his rationalist assessment of the biblical procedural protections of two corroborating witnesses and forewarning as not any sort of truth-guarding mechanism necessary to protect the innocent).
10. Id. Blidstein, *supra* note 8 at 58–60. Traditional jurists commenting on Maimonides note this connection. See Meir Simcah Hakohen of Dvinsk, *Ohr Somayach*, Laws of Kings 3:1.
11. *See* S. Last Stone, "Sinaitic and Noahide Law: Legal Pluralism in Jewish Law" (1991) 12 Cardozo Law Review 1157, 1157–214.
12. Babylonian Talmud, Sanhedrin 56a–58b.
13. Blidstein, *supra* note 9 at 58.
14. Indeed, as an historical matter, their real origin may well lie in talmudic observation of Roman practice just as much as in legal dissection of the Genesis narratives "attesting" to the universal law God commanded. For Maimonides, surely, it didn't matter. He most likely thought the whole topic of universal Noahide law was based on natural law thinking on the part of the jurists from the beginning.
15. G. J. Blidstein, "On Political Structures—Four Medieval Comments" (1980) 22 Jewish Journal of Sociology 47–58.
16. *See* G. J. Blidstein, "On Lay Legislation in Halakha: The King as Instance," in S. Last Stone, ed, *Rabbinic and Lay Communal Authority* (New York: Yeshiva University Press, 2006) 1–18.
17. The Talmud notes that Jews are consistently using the bridges without paying the owners. This practice is taken as evidence of a pre-existing halakhic norm known to the populace, later given legal expression by the Talmudic jurists as DDM. One of the more radical

extensions of this mode of reasoning is in a contemporary responsum on the authority of the State of Israel. It begins with the observation that Jews are granting legitimacy to the legislation of the State and then seeks a rationale for this practice in DDM. Ovadiah Hedaya; cf. the contemporary responsum of Rabbi Moses Feinstein on the permissibility of using secular wills. He cites the familiar expression: "If the children of Israel are not prophets, they are the sons of prophets." The instinct of the people must be given weight and it is the task of the rabbinic decisor to comb the sources to ascertain the legal basis that underlies Jewish customary practice. See J. I. Roth, "Crossing the Bridge to Secular Law: Three Models of Incorporation" (1991) 12 Cardozo Law Review 753, 753–64. But see S. Shiloh, "Equity as a Bridge between Jewish and Secular Law" (1991) 12 Cardozo Law Review 737, 737–52.
18. Babylonian Talmud, Gittin 9b.
19. Jewish law maintains that with respect to financial matters, as opposed to religious matters, it is possible for parties to contract out of the law in any event, despite the fact that these norms originate in divine law. But the rationale that links the validity of Gentile law to the Noahide command of *dinim* would suggest that it could extend to all laws subsumed under the Noahide command, including criminal law and punishment, traditionally categorized as "religious." Rashi elsewhere assumes that it is permissible to hand Jews over to the criminal processes of the non-Jewish government, despite bypassing of Jewish evidentiary and penal law. Babylonian Talmud, Tractate Niddah 61a. Rashi's theory has very few internal limits, except that subjects unique to Jewish law cannot be displaced.
20. Halevi also speculated whether certain social laws were really religious commands with no social function except to bring on the divine overflow.
21. I address this issue in "Law Without Nation? The Ongoing Jewish Discussion," in A. Sarat, L. Douglas, and M. Merrill Umphrey, eds, *Law Without Nations* (Stanford: Stanford University Press, 2011) 101–37.
22. M. Henaff and T. B. Strong, "Introduction: The Conditions of Public Space: Vision, Speech and Theatricality," in M. Henaff and T. B. Strong, eds, *Public Space and Democracy* (Minneapolis: University of Minnesota Press, 2001) 1–33.
23. P. Weil, "Why the French Laïcié Is Liberal" (2009) 30 Cardozo Law Review 2699, 2699–715.
24. On the Talmudic development of a "public services" rationale, associated with the traditions of Rabbi Yohanan, who consistently negated the suspicion of idolatry in common spaces of general utility, see G. Blidstein, "Rabbi Yohanan, Idolatry, and Public Privilege" (1974) 5:2 Journal for the Study of Judaism 154–61.
25. For the relationship between religion, ritual, and space see C. E. Fonrobert, "Neighborhood as Ritual Space: The Case of the Rabbinic Eruv" (2008) 10 Archiv für Religionsgeschichte 239–58. See also C. E. Fonrobert, "Gender Politics in the Rabbinic Neighborhood: Tractate Eruvin," in Introduction to the Feminist Talmud Commentary—Seder Moed 43–59 (Tubingen: Mohr Siebeck, 2007) (A feminist commentary on the Babylonian Talmud).
26. See generally A. Yadin, "Rabban Gamliel, Aphrodite's Bath, and the Question of Pagan Monotheism" (2006) 96:2 Jewish Quarterly Review 149, 149–79.
27. Later Amoraim codified this notion as follows: "That which is public, cannot be forbidden." See Blidstein, *supra* note 23.
28. See M. Halbertal, "Co-existing with the Enemy: Jews and Pagans in the Mishnah," in G. N. Stanton and G. G. Stroumsa, eds, *Tolerance and Intolerance in Early Judaism and Christianity* (Cambridge: Cambridge University Press, 1998) 159–73.
29. See S. L. Stone, "Religion and Human Rights: Babel or Translation, Conflict or Convergence?" in *Proceedings of the Israel Democracy Institute* (forthcoming)
30. M. Perry, *Toward a Theory of Human Rights* (Cambridge: Cambridge University Press, 2007).
31. M. Stackhouse, "Why Human Rights Need God: A Christian Perspective," in B. Barnett and E. M. Bucar, eds, *Does Human Rights Need God* (Grand Rapids: Wm. B. Eerdmans Publishing Company, 2005).
32. N. Wolterstorff, *Justice: Rights and Wrongs* (Princeton, NJ: Princeton University Press, 2008).

33. The term is Emile Durkheim's. See S. Trigano, "The Rediscovery of Biblical Politics" (2009) 4:3 Hebraic Political Studies 306–307.
34. Ibid., at 204–318.
35. For a more detailed analysis of possible paths of convergence between Judaism and the idea of human rights, that do not rely on the natural law tradition, see Stone, *supra* note 33.
36. Seligman, "Introduction," 12 in A. Seligman ed, *Religion and Human Rights: Conflict or Convergence* (Hollis, NH: Hollis Publishing Company, 2005), 12.

# 3

# Human Rights and Secularism: Arendt, Asad, and Milbank as Critics of the Secular Foundations of Human Rights

SHAI LAVI

## 1. Introduction

In this chapter I wish to discuss the relationship between religion and human rights.[1] Before we plunge into the matter, we may wish to reconsider the question and its premises more carefully. There are, essentially, two different ways to broach the issue. The first takes human rights as its starting point and poses questions to religion. Can religion be reconciled with human rights? Is religion inherently antagonistic to human rights, or quite to the contrary, could it be redeemed as the origins of human rights? Can religious wars and religious intolerance be moderated and contained through human rights? In posing these questions, human rights and—somewhat more implicitly—secularism are taken for granted as fundamental characteristics of the modern age, and religion is interrogated, favorably or unfavorably, as the "odd man out."

In what follows, I wish to approach the question from a different angle. Rather than interrogate religion about its relationship to human rights, I propose we focus our attention on the secular and its relationship with human rights. Recent scholarship in the social sciences has drawn attention to a prevalent bias within the field (including law), which has turned religion into its subject matter while taking for granted the secular.[2] While sociology of religion and anthropology of religion have established themselves as respectable subdisciplines, and while the problematic issue of state and religion has played a central role in political science and law, little has been written before the 1990s about the sociology and anthropology of the secular, or about the role of secularism in law and politics, other than in the negative sense as freedom from religion. To the extent that "the secular" has been thematized, it has been understood on its own terms—as a process of growing rationality, disenchantment, and the disintegration of the life world into separate spheres of autonomous rationality (economy, politics, law, morality, science, etc.).[3]

More recently, with the growing presence of religion in the public sphere and the emerging understanding that, far from declining, religion is in fact fortifying its place within the modern world, scholars have begun turning their attention to the secular, no longer taking for granted its place within modernity.[4] By the same token that a scholarly account of religion should not accept uncritically religion's self-understanding, so too the new scholarly accounts of secularism do not accept the secularist understanding of the modern age (but nor do they revert to a religious perspective). Rather, they reject any attempt to understand the secular as the universal opposite of religious particularism and wish to study secularism for its highly particular set of dispositions, practices, beliefs, and arrays of knowledge and experience.

Human rights as a deeply secular set of ideations, practices, and sensibilities is a good candidate for such an inquiry. To be sure, viewing human rights as a secular ethics is by no means uncontroversial. Current scholarship on the relationship between human rights and religion has pointed out, quite the contrary, the religious origins of human rights.[5] Setting aside the complex relationship between religion and human rights, this essay takes as its point of departure a different set of concerns. It asks: what can we learn about human rights by exploring its relationship with secularism, and what can we learn about the secular age by highlighting the particular characteristics of human rights as a dominant ethics?

There is a further, less critical, but equally pressing reason to consider the secular dimension of human rights. In recent years, the language of human rights has gained surprising popularity outside the secular-liberal West and has become, in the international political arena, synonymous with justice. The growing universality of human rights discourse may be read as a clear sign of its success, but may equally suggest that the concept has been watered down and that its unique historic origins and philosophical commitments have been forgotten. The growing prevalence of human rights discourse among mainstream religious leaders as well as so-called fundamentalists may be taken as further evidence of this development. If "human" in human rights stands for an all-encompassing humanity, and "rights" stands for an all-encompassing sense of justice, who—but for the most parochial—would object to it? But then, what can be gained from such abstract and undisputable truisms? What is required is a critical analysis of the specific sense in which both "human" and "rights" are employed in this combination. Critique here is first and foremost an attempt to understand the phenomenon in its distinctness, and only secondarily to single out its promises as well as its shortcomings.

There are two aspects of the following critique of human rights that distinguish it from more familiar ones. First, the critique focuses on the secular nature of human rights and brings to the study of human rights insights from the critique of secularism. Striving to understand human rights, the chapter turns to religious traditions as a counterpoint reference. Second, the critique here does not follow the well-trodden path of condemning human rights for its focus on the atomistic individual and its commitment to negative rights. Quite to the contrary, I wish to focus on the ways in which human rights are commonly grounded in a sense of empathy, which give rise to duties that reach beyond the limits of negative rights. Consequently, I will focus on the line of critique of human rights that takes seriously its commitment to duties of care and gives heed to empathy as the ground for human rights.

Human rights is an expansive and opened-ended concept that has multiple definitions. Defined in a broad manner, human rights include all forms of liberal rights—civil, political, social, and cultural.[6] Broadly understood, human rights becomes synonymous with the notion of rights per se. There is, however, another more restricted sense of human rights, which will be the main focus of the following discussion. In its restricted sense, human rights is a specific notion of rights that is distinguishable from other notions of rights—such as civil and political rights. Whereas social, civil, and political rights are the rights of humans as citizens, human rights are the rights of humans as such, whether or not they are citizens of any given state. This explains the centrality of the category of human rights in international law, and specifically in international humanitarian law. These commitments extend to human beings as such, even if they are citizens of an enemy country or lack citizenship altogether. In what follows and up to a point, I will maintain the distinction between the two, and use the term "human rights" to discuss the more limited terrain of legal protection. Nevertheless, it would be a mistake to overlook the close connection between human rights and rights in general, and I will return to examine this affinity below.

Human rights *sensu stricto* has a distinct claim to universality. Its premise is not simply that all human beings have rights (Christian morality would be equally universal in this sense), but more forcefully that the only reason why humans deserve such rights is their being human (rather than, for example, because they were created by God). Human rights' universalism is also manifest in its rapid spread across the globe. If there is today a lingua franca of morality, human rights is no doubt its most common idiom.

To be sure, civil rights likewise aspire to be universal, and are often designated as "natural law." But ultimately the validity of civil rights is bound to the state and depends on the preexistence of a civil and political order. Not so with human rights, in the strict sense, which aims to guarantee fundamental rights beyond the limitations of civil and political society. This distinction is often blurred when the two are discussed in one breath, as with the French Declaration of the Rights of Man and the Citizen.

Human rights' claim to universality should not, however, blur its particularism. If human rights is not to become an empty signifier, the idea needs to be clarified and its roots laid bare. A good way to clarify the concept and its uses is to turn to history, and specifically to the rise of human rights along with a secularist ethics. To be sure, historicizing human rights does not undermine human rights' claim to moral validity. As a matter of principle, no claim to a rationally grounded morality can be undermined simply by pointing to historical origins. Rather, the turn to history aims to draw attention to some of the underlying presuppositions of human rights not merely as an abstract system of thought, but as a practical ethics—grounded in sentiment as much as in reason. The question, therefore, is not whether human rights is universally binding, but rather what universality means in this context, and what were the conditions of possibility that have allowed human rights to emerge as universally binding.

It is in this vein that the chapter will discuss the critique of human rights offered by three scholars. Hannah Arendt, the German-Jewish political theorist, who offers a careful study of the inherent contradictions of human rights in her *Origins of Totalitarianism*; Talal Asad, who has launched a powerful critique of secularism and the human rights discourse, taking his cue from the Western confrontation with Islam; and finally, John Milbank, a Christian theologian, who turns to medieval writings to think through modern legal concepts. Though coming from different intellectual traditions and scholarly disciplines—political theory, anthropology, and theology—the three seek to understand and consequently criticize human rights as a secular project, and turn to history in order to shed light on its significance in contemporary law and politics. All three reject the simplistic understanding of human rights as grounded in the alienated and atomistic individual and take seriously the role of empathy as its foundation; yet, each arrives at a different understanding of the phenomenon—its promises and shortcomings.

With the help of Arendt, Asad, and Milbank, the chapter seeks to lay out the secularist presuppositions of human rights. One may raise the objection that, in contrast to religion, "secularism" is not a valid analytic category, because there is very little if anything that links together different "secularist" positions other than the negative and trivial fact that they are not religious. To this challenge two responses are in place. First, to the extent that it makes sense to speak of religion and human rights, there is a fortiori reason to speak of secularism and human rights. After all, secularism is a relatively new phenomenon, and compared to the great variety of religions and religious history, secularism has a much shorter and distinctly modern career. Second, as we shall see, secularism is here understood less as matter of belief (or its absence), and more as a set of practices, less as concerning the divine and supernatural (or its absence), and more as a social and political attunement.

## 2. Human Rights' Critique: Beyond Negative Rights and the Atomistic Individual

The most common critique of human rights—posed both by right-leaning communitarians and left-leaning Marxists, feminists, and other critics—focuses on the negative freedom of human rights and its inherent individualism.[7] Rights within a liberal paradigm, so goes the critique, guarantee freedom only in the negative sense, namely, freedom from state coercion. The atomistic individual is both the theoretical and methodological premise of liberal theory and liberal rights, and liberal rights offer nothing more than the right to be left alone. If, nevertheless, individuals have obligations toward fellow individuals, as both classic and modern theories of the social contract claim, this is only because and only to the extent to which such duties can be justified from the point of view of the isolated individual. Liberals, to be sure, do not assume that individuals are self-centered, greedy, or egotistic, only that they have a right to be so. This is the basis of the liberal rights discourse, and the target of most critical accounts of the classic liberal notion of rights. Critics claim that individuals are always part of larger communities and that duties, responsibilities, and solidarity lie at the foundations of any just polity and legal system.

There is, no doubt, some truth to this line of critique, especially when directed against classic theories of rights from Locke to Kant. In recent years, however, rights discourse has evolved dramatically—so much so, that older critiques seem to have lost much of their original bite. With the growing concern with social rights, and the rise of humanitarian protections on the international level, these critics seem to be directed against a human rights scarecrow.

Furthermore, and more tellingly, the image of the detached individual misses the mark even when we confine ourselves to classic strands of human rights theory. This become evident if, rather than focusing on Locke and Kant, we turn to the Scottish Enlightenment; alternatively, this also becomes clear if we examine more closely the underlying ethos of the French Revolution. As we shall see, one of the characteristics of these alternative strands of human rights theory and history was a notion of empathy that linked individuals together through an acute awareness and empathy with suffering. There is little coincidence that this commitment was formulated most clearly and unabashedly by the most avid advocate of liberal rights and political economy, Adam Smith. It may be worthwhile quoting at some length a paragraph from "The Theory of Moral Sentiment":

> How selfish soever man may be supposed, there are evidently some principles in his nature, which interest him in the fortunes of others, and render their happiness necessary to him, though he derives nothing from it, except the pleasure of seeing it. Of this kind is pity or compassion, the emotion we feel for the misery of others, when we either see it, or are made to conceive it in a very lively manner. That we often derive sorrow from the sorrows of others, is a matter of fact too obvious to require any instances to prove it; for this sentiment, like all the other original passions of human nature, is by no means confined to the virtuous or the humane, though they perhaps may feel it with the most exquisite sensibility. The greatest ruffian, the most hardened violator of the laws of society, is not altogether without it.[8]

The following inquiry and critique takes as its point of departure precisely this notion of sympathy (or what we call, today, empathy) as essential to any attempt to understand the contemporary challenge of human rights. Liberal thought from Adam Smith, through the French Revolution, to the UN Declaration of Human Rights, and to the most recent humanitarian delegations to catastrophe zones are grounded in a sense of empathy and in a commitment to easing the anguish and suffering of others. It is not about compassion beyond rights, but rather about compassion as the basis of rights. This notion of empathy is especially prevalent in the more restricted sense of human rights, discussed above, namely, as the rights that are owed to all human being as such, regardless of their membership in a particular political community. Some straightforward examples include fundamental human rights such as the right of every human being to food, shelter, safety, and security.[9]

Whereas Adam Smith and thinkers who followed his legacy have characterized empathy as a universal, innate character of human beings, I will follow the lead of Arendt, Asad, and Milbank and suggest that the modern notion of empathy and its role in contemporary law and politics is far less obvious and much more contested than defenders of human rights often presuppose. Though my focus will be on the critique of human rights *sensu stricto*, I will nevertheless argue that, for all three thinkers, the critique has bearing on the more inclusive conception of rights in the liberal tradition.

To briefly recap, the following critique of human rights thus differs from some of the more familiar critiques in three ways. It does not accuse human rights for its individualism, but rather questions the specific way in which community is imagined; it does not blame human rights for its detachment, but rather for the specific ways in which it engages; and it does not attempt to rid legal discourse from metaphysics, as many secularist critics have done, but rather seeks to unveil the metaphysical assumptions that underlie the secularist understanding of humanity inscribed in the history of human rights.

## 3. Human Rights and Empathy: Past and Present

Lynn Hunt's recent *Inventing Human Rights: A History* offers an insightful introduction to the history of human rights. Hunt's history, to be sure, does not search for the first appearance of the term "human rights." Throughout the eighteenth century the more common expression was, in fact, "natural rights." Jefferson, for example, began using the term "rights of man" only after 1789 and "human rights," which was invented by the French in the 1760s (*droits de l'homme*), only became popular thanks to Rousseau's *Social Contract* of 1762.[10] Hunt's book focuses on eighteenth-century France and America and serves, in what follows, as a helpful starting point for excavating not so much the history of the concept, but more importantly its conceptual underpinnings.

The book's main argument is that "imagined empathy" served as the basis of human rights. Imagination does not mean fabrication, but rather the ability to place oneself in the shoes of the other and identify with her suffering. Hunt explains, "As eighteenth-century people pushed for the expansion of self-determination, they ran up against a dilemma: what would provide the source of community in this new order that highlighted the rights of the individual? It was one thing to explain how morality could be derived from human reason rather than Divine Scripture or how autonomy should be preferred to blind obedience. But it was quite another to reconcile this self-directed individual with the greater good . . . The philosophers, like eighteenth-century people more generally, called their answer 'sympathy.'"[11]

What eighteenth-century writers called sympathy (literally, "suffering with"), and what we are accustomed to call empathy,[12] played an important role in the creation of equality. While the notion that all human beings were equal had ancient roots, the development of human rights depended on creating a new basis of equality. Indeed, it was one thing to believe in equality in the Kingdom of Heaven; it was quite another to view all persons in the mundane reality as equal. Empathy allowed one to enter into the body of the other and suffer with her.

Empathy, which had a place of honor in the republic of arts and letters and in the development of the new genre of the novel, played an equally important role in the day-to-day practice of the new notions of human rights. One of the paradigm cases was the prohibition on torture and cruel punishment. In France, punishment was harsh up to the end of the nineteenth century. Capital offenses were highly popular and increased in number; executions were often accompanied by public torture to increase deterrence.[13] Criticism of torture and cruel punishment began two decades before the revolution and was associated with Voltaire and other writers of the Enlightenment. It was, however, only six weeks after passing the Declaration of the Rights of Man and the Citizen that the French deputies abolished all uses of judicial torture as part of a reform of criminal procedure.[14]

On the other side of the Channel, Blackstone, too, believed that criminal law should always be "conformable to the dictates of truth and justice, the feelings of humanity, and the indelible rights of mankind."[15] Compassion and empathy toward the inflicted body in pain, rather than any calculus of utility, seem to have been the main motivation underlying the attack on corporeal punishment. More precisely, empathy toward pain was a necessary condition for developing a universal calculus of pain. "We should not forget that even criminals possess souls and bodies composed of the same materials as those of our friends and relations," exclaimed Benjamin Rush, "they are 'bone of their bone.'"[16] A similar position was voiced, most famously, by Cesare Beccaria in his proposal to reform punishment.

This seemingly "natural" and "reasonable" approach was, however, not self-evident. Not even for Voltaire, who originally decried torture and the death penalty not because of their cruelty, but because they were inflicted on the innocent. A more vocal adherent of the traditionalist approach was Pierre-François Myuart, who offered a point-by-point refutation of Beccaria. "I pride myself on having as much sensibility as anyone else, but no doubt I do not have an organization of fibers [nerve endings] as loose as that of our modern criminalists, for I did not feel that gentle shuddering of which they speak."[17]

Empathy may well be a universal trait, but its emergence as a political drive was strikingly new. Hunt explains, "Under the traditional understanding, the pains of the body did not belong entirely to the individual condemned person. Those pains had the higher religious and political purposes of redemption and reparation of the community. Bodies could be mutilated in the interest of inscribing authority, and broken or burned in the interest of restoring the moral, political, and religious order."[18]

Under Christendom the suffering body could have any number of meanings from punishment to penitence and redemption. Not so in the emerging secular view, in which pain belonged solely to the here and now. "Where pain had served as the symbol of reparation under the old regime, now pain seemed an obstacle to any meaningful quittance."[19]

Torture and punishment are merely one example, albeit one that continued to play a central role in twentieth-century international human law, such as in Article V of the Universal Declaration of Human Rights (1948), stating that "No one shall be subjected to torture or to cruel, inhuman, or degrading treatment or punishment." But there are many other instances. At their center lies the protection of the human body stripped from any social, political, and historical context.[20]

Sympathy and empathy continue to accompany human rights discourse both in practice and in theory. A recent book by Martha Nussbaum is especially worth mentioning in this context, because it brings us closer to the question of religion, secularism, and human rights. In her new book, *The New Religious Intolerance: Overcoming the Politics of Fear in an Anxious Age*,[21] Nussbaum discusses the emerging fear in the United States and Europe of Islam and of other minorities including blacks and gays. The immediate context for her contemplations is the French prohibition of the burqa in public schools, but her argument is broader. Much of the discrimination against minorities, Nussbaum argues, is grounded in deep anxieties about the stranger and foreigner. To overcome the politics of anxieties and to secure a political notion of equality, we must turn to empathy. For Nussbaum, as Hunt has already pointed out, an abstract belief in human rights will not do. What is required is empathy with human experiences that are very different from our own. It is only on the basis of such empathy that true acceptance may emerge.

Nussbaum calls this ability "participatory imagination" or simply "empathy," and explains that "More generally, what the imagination does is to make others real for us. A common human failing is to see the whole world from the point of view of one's own goals, and to see the conduct of others as all about oneself. Thus: 'those veiled women are aggressively defying Frenchness.' ... By imagining other people's way of life, we don't necessarily learn to agree with their goals, but we do see the reality of these goals for them. We learn that other worlds of thought and feeling exist."[22] For Nussbaum, empathy may help us overcome our fears. It is crucial for seeing how people who seem very different than us are in fact not all that different. "In empathy the mind moves outward, occupying many different positions outside the self."[23] The way to occupy these different positions is by imagining ourselves in the place of others. The most immediate way of doing so is through empathy. Specifically, empathy is a condition for religious tolerance and allows us to view otherwise alien traditions and practices as similar to our own. Empathy—putting oneself in the place of another—is a fundamental human capacity, like imagination itself. It has a universalizing effect to the extent that it allows us to bridge the gaps that divide people and see commonality where previously only difference could be seen.

What Nussbaum and other defenders of empathy-based human rights fail to see is that a critique of current political prejudices cannot take for granted empathy as a means for promoting religious tolerance, without questioning the way in which empathy itself is a secularist sentiment. A critique of the secular character of empathy suggests that the failure of human rights is not under-inclusiveness, but rather the way in which it includes. Consequently, the political challenge we face is not how to overcome religious intolerance through a turn to empathy, but rather to acknowledge the secular intolerance that is intimately tied to the practices of empathy and is embedded in human rights. This is precisely the task which Arendt, Asad, and Milbank have taken upon themselves.

## 4. Hannah Arendt and the Politics of Pity

Arendt was one of the first political thinkers to draw critical attention to the interrelationship of human rights, the politics of empathy, and secularism. The problem that Arendt poses in her historically grounded book, *The Origins of Totalitarianism*, is how to explain the fact that precisely in the age of human rights and in the wake of international law, Europe faced the most atrocious violations of human rights. For the German-Jewish political thinker, the answer does not lie in the evil intentions underlying the crimes—those are often present but can hardly explain the systematic violations of rights. Rather, she asks how such crimes became possible and why nothing, or very little, stood in the way of their execution. The ground for these unprecedented atrocities, Arendt claims, lies in the emergence of a new political formation, the totalitarian regime.

One important element in the rise of the totalitarian regime was the failure of the modern liberal nation-state to protect human rights. This observation may sound, at first, as a logical truism. For Arendt, however, the failure of human rights to protect "the rights of man" was not accidental, and though not inevitable, had its seeds planted early on with the rise of the modern nation-state and the promise of human rights. Human rights failed to protect the rights of humans due to an inherent shortcoming of the ideal of human rights present from its early inception.

In the chapter "The Decline of the Nation-State and the End of the Rights of Man,"[24] Arendt traces the internal paradox of human rights back to the bedrock of modern politics, to the French Revolution. The Declaration of the Rights of Man and the Citizen gave birth to a new legal and political order, which aspired to protect all citizens regardless of their religious affiliation or social status. But the modern notion of rights, Arendt argues, hid a fundamental paradox.

The grounding of rights on the foundations of the abstract concept of "humanity" stripped human beings from anything that identified them, historically, culturally, or religiously and left them entirely dependent on the political protection of the modern nation-state. Arendt refers in this context to Edmund Burke, who was famously aware of this danger, when he contrasted the traditional "rights of the English man" with the emerging ideal of universal rights. Burke found the protection of the former much more reliable—because they were grounded in history, tradition, and institutions—than the latter, which relied only on the good will of the revolutionaries and denied human beings their particular history and tradition.

Arendt adds the important insight that the new legal protection of human rights had, in fact, an institutional grounding. Its new basis was the modern nation-state, which emerged alongside the rise of human rights. Put simply, the famous declarations of the rights of man *and* citizen ultimately protected only the rights of man *as* citizen. Humans had their rights guaranteed only if and as long as they were citizens. Stateless people (including citizens of very weak states or citizens whose citizenship was lost or revoked) depended on the good will of the "hosting" state. Though the status of stateless people was not a real question in the nineteenth century, this vulnerability was inscribed into the French idea of human rights.

The problem materialized in the aftermath of the First World War with the growing number of stateless people who roamed the lands of Europe: Russians, Germans, Slovaks, Croats, and, by no means an exception, the Jews. "Once they had left their homeland they remained homeless, once they had left their state they became stateless; and once they had been deprived of their human rights they were rightless, the scum of the earth."[25] Indeed, once one became stateless, there was little protection that "human rights" could offer. The Declaration of the Rights of Man and the Citizen turned out to be a promissory note that had no cover. In her words, "The conception of human rights based upon the assumed existence of a human being as such broke down at the very moment when those who professed to believe in it were for the first time confronted with people who had indeed lost all other qualities and specific relationships—except that they were still human. The world found nothing sacred in the abstract nakedness of being human."[26]

Arendt's critical take on human rights is not limited to her novel account of totalitarian regimes. The latter express in the most extreme way a danger that threatens ordinary liberal politics. To think of human beings only through their humanity has led to what Arendt describes in other parts of her work as the "politics of pity," turning the suffering of human beings into the primary motivation of politics. The problem is not sensitivity to suffering as such, but rather the turning of this sensitivity into the basic motivation and criterion for political action and intervention. Arendt believes that thinking of human beings only through their capacity to suffer is, in the final analysis, the animalization of humanity. This problem is dominant in certain strands of liberal politics and, as scholars following Arendt have argued, becomes most apparent in the politics of (mainstream) humanitarian aid.[27]

Arendt does not condemn the liberal tradition as a whole, but rather distinguishes between two strands of the liberal-democratic tradition—the American and the French. The Europeans, she claims, have suffered from this malaise more than the Americans. Arendt distinguishes, in this context, between compassion and pity on the one hand, and solidarity, on the other. Whereas the former is based on need, the latter is based on political action—which is grounded in freedom rather than need. Solidarity, she writes, "though it may be aroused by suffering, is not guided by it, and it comprehends the strong and the rich no less than the weak and the poor; compared with the sentiment of pity, it may appear cold and abstract, for it remains committed to 'ideas'—to greatness, or honour, or dignity, rather than to any 'love' of men."[28] Arendt further distinguishes between pity and compassion. Whereas compassion is a pre-political sentiment, which has its place in the intimate sphere of private relationships, pity is the translation of that sentiment into politics. "Pity, because it is not stricken in the flesh and keeps its sentimental distance, can succeed where compassion always will fail; it can reach out to the multitude and therefore, like solidarity, enter the marketplace."[29] "But pity," continues Arendt, "in contrast to solidarity, does not look upon both fortune and misfortune, the strong and the weak, with an equal eye; without the presence of misfortune, pity could not exist, and it therefore has just as much vested interest in the existence of the unhappy as thirst for power has a vested interest in the existence of the weak."[30]

Arendt claims that pity was at the heart of the French revolutionaries, who were concerned primarily with the needs of the lower classes and emerged out of compassion to these needs—first and foremost to hunger. In contraposition, "The passion of compassion was singularly absent from the minds of the American revolutionists."[31] Unlike the French Revolution, the American Revolution did not take its cue from the suffering of the masses, but rather from the will to secure the freedom of the financially secured—and thus did not emerge out of necessity and pity, but rather out of freedom and solidarity. Thus, Arendt does not simply criticize the concept of human rights, but rather shows its multiple forms, preferring one legacy over the other.

Arendt's critique of human rights and critique of empathy go along with her deep understanding and critique of the secular age. The Declaration of Human Rights was a turning point in history, because it meant nothing more nor less than "that from then on Man and not God's command or the customs of history, should be the source of Law." Under the new order, fundamental rights, such as the right to life and property, which until then had been outside the political ordered and guaranteed "by social, spiritual, and religious forces," became dependent upon government and constitution.[32] Arendt concludes,

> Since the Rights of Man were proclaimed to be "inalienable," irreducible to and uneducable from other rights or laws, no authority was invoked for their establishment; Man himself was their source as well as their ultimate goal. No special law, moreover, was deemed necessary to protect them because all laws were supposed to rest upon them. Man appeared as the only sovereign in matters of law as the people was proclaimed the only sovereign in matters of government. The people's sovereignty (different from that of the prince) was not proclaimed by the grace of God but in the name of Man, so that it seemed only natural that the "inalienable" rights of man would find their guarantee and become an inalienable part of the right of the people to sovereign self-government.[33]

For Arendt, secularism, like democracy, is simultaneously a promise and a danger. Stripping humanity of the authority of tradition, it leaves a political vacuum that cannot be easily filled. During the French Revolution, "Nature" emerges as a promising candidate, but Arendt points out to the unintended consequences of this choice. The grounding of politics in abstract universal reason goes hand in hand with the reduction of humanity to its natural existence and political justice to pity. In contrast, Arendt claims that only the grounding of politics in concrete institutions and in the artificial (rather than natural) notion of equality can properly protect human freedom. The French Revolutionaries failed to see this, and the Founders of the American Federacy were all too aware of it.

One may question whether Arendt's contraposition of America and Europe, and specifically her attempt to link the European tradition of the nation-state to the rise and fall of human rights and to the emergence of totalitarian regimes, does justice to the historical records. One may further question whether the twentieth-century development of humanitarian law indeed has its roots in the French Revolution, or whether—as some recent scholarship suggests[34]—post–World War II discourse on human rights has a different genealogy and perhaps much more recent origins. For current purposes, the details of the historical account are less important than her claim that underlying the modern and secular notion of human rights lies a politics of empathy and pity.

This latter claim, too, may be challenged: does not the very notion of rights demand equal treatment and respect regardless of any feelings, including empathy? Do human rights—as a demand for dignity and justice—not stand in stark opposition to the politics of pity? Or simply put, do not the rational and universal aspirations of human rights contradict any attempt to reduce humanity to its animal nature?

Here I do not wish to defend Arendt's position, but only to clarify it. Arendt refuses to take the liberal tradition on face value and refuses to treat the above questions as rhetorical. Her main insight is that any attempt to base modern politics on rational secular abstractions of the individual is bound to fail, but not because it ignores the concrete needs of individuals (as leftist critics of liberalism have often suggested), but quite to the contrary—because it is bound to think of individuals only through their most abstract common denominator, that is, their natural needs. Contrary to common secularist wisdom, rational abstraction does not free us from nature, but rather binds us to it.

## 5. Talal Asad and the Critique of the Secular

In a series of articles and public lectures, the renowned anthropologist Talal Asad offers a different set of reflections on the question of human rights and empathy. Asad is well aware of Arendt's critique of human rights and follows certain of her moves, but the general tenor of his critique is quite different.

Asad's primary concern is to expose the very specific, and by no means universal, sense in which the "human rights" idiom is formulated and practiced. Though less historically grounded than Arendt, Asad derives his basic insights from the history of European colonialism and postcolonialism. His observations, however, are not limited to this context and pertain to more general patterns emerging within the West, including the relationship between the secular state and its religious minorities. If, for Arendt, the big historical paradox lay in the emergence of totalitarian regimes in the age of human rights, the big puzzle for Asad is the tension between the missionary enterprise of Western countries to spread humanism, human rights, and democracy to non-Western countries, which is accompanied by the infliction of great devastation and suffering on colonized and occupied populations.

Non-Christian traditions have been especially vulnerable to these dialectics. Specifically, Asad is concerned with the common association of Islam (or fundamentalist Islam) with cruelty and barbarism. He does not wish to defend such practices, but merely to ask why human rights only protect against specific kinds of suffering, corresponding to a particular form of cruelty. Certain forms of cruelty are denounced by the West, whereas others are tolerated or even promulgated. Humanitarian concerns are much less rational and consistent than they claim to be, but they are not entirely arbitrary. In fact, the infliction of suffering has been institutionalized in certain settings such as warfare, sports, scientific experimentation, and the death penalty, so "inflicting physical suffering is actively practiced and also legally condoned."[35]

While this may sound like a simple accusation of hypocrisy and duplicity, Asad shies away from such conclusions and rejects the simple, albeit common, explanation of discrimination against "the other." Rather, he seeks the underlying logic of the articulation of suffering in the West, which has its own logic and its own language. "What is interesting," he writes, "is not merely that some forms of suffering were to be taken more seriously than others, but that 'inhuman' suffering as opposed to 'necessary' or 'inevitable' suffering was regarded as being essentially *gratuitous*, and therefore legally punishable."[36]

One of the many examples Asad uses to demonstrate the liberal calculus of pain is the military practice of strategic bombing. Strategic bombing takes the lives of innocent bystanders and inflicts mass destruction, but is viewed as legal and moral, as long as the collateral damages are not intended and as long as they are outweighed by the pursuant of legitimate ends. Thus, in a polarizing example, Asad compares the denouncement of torture by UN soldiers from Belgian and Canada in Somalia with the destruction of entire city blocks and the killing of a considerable number of civilians by the U.S. military, and concludes that while torture was condemned as a human rights violation per se, the death of civilians through aerial bombardment was regarded not as "a matter of human rights abuse but of *collateral damage*."[37]

One may easily counter that torture is deliberate and thus cruel, whereas strategic bombing is a tragic choice of the lesser evil.[38] But this is precisely Asad's point. Once one takes a critical distance from the moralizing language of the West, in which human rights prefigures dominantly, and observes both practices and justifications anthropologically, one cannot but be struck by the highly particularistic set of presuppositions and customs that characterize secular ethics, and by the heightened attention they give to specific forms of suffering while underplaying others.

Asad discusses, further, more mundane examples of this logic of the "lesser evil." Flogging, for example, is seen as an inhumane and cruel punishment as imprisonment becomes a model of modern secular justice. This distinction cannot be taken for granted. The very possibility of comparing different kinds of pain as a justificatory argument is central to the secular ethics of the modern state. One form of suffering is used as a measuring rod to justify another.

For Asad, this specific concern with cruelty is characteristic of Western societies as secular societies. "A major motive of secularism has clearly been the desire to end cruelties—the deliberate infliction *in this world* of pain to the living body of others, and the causing of distress to their minds that religion has so often initiated and justified."[39] But ultimately, the desire to eliminate pain, a regulatory ideal of secular ethics, can never be attained, and is thus replaced by a proxy—the rational calculus of pain and cruelty. Under this secular ethics, the affliction of pain is no longer justified in the name of a higher and absolute good, but rather in comparison to other forms of cruelty, which are deemed irrational and barbaric.

Unlike Arendt, Asad does not identify empathy with "suffering" in general, but rather with a certain calculus of suffering, which is characteristic of the language and practice of human rights. Cruelty is marked by the excess of pain and its irrationality. As long as pain can be justified and has its place within the chambers of reason, it is not understood as cruel. The ability to undertake such a calculus, and to place a specific form of suffering within a comparative framework, is a mark of rational, secular ethics.

Asad takes a further step and seeks to place in context the very desire of secular ethics and human rights to eradicate suffering as part of progressive politics. Asad's critique is by no means a defense of cruelty, but offers an anthropological account of the very categories that are used to identify cruelty and lump together very different practices: "There is a secular viewpoint held by many (including anthropologists) that would have one accept that in the final analysis there are only two mutually exclusive options available: either an agent (representing and asserting himself or herself) or a victim (the passive object of chance or cruelty)."[40]

When we say that someone is suffering, we usually do not think of him or her as an agent. In contrast, Asad points to non-secular traditions, which think of pain not merely as a passive experience. The experience of childbirth would be an interesting case to begin challenging the secularist conceptualization of pain, and opens a whole series of cases from the suffering of the criminal under corporeal punishment to the most recent debates on child circumcision. In this sense, too, Asad's critique differs from Arendt's. Whereas her account of human rights and empathy depends on a clear distinction between active doing and passive suffering, Asad suggests that the distinction itself is deeply secular.

## 6. John Milbank and the Critique of the Possessive Individual

In a recent article, "Against Human Rights: Liberty in the Western Tradition," John Milbank, a leading critical theorist, approaches the question of human rights from yet another perspective. His work, here and elsewhere, assumes that much of the modern approach to politics, law, and society stems from secularist presuppositions that should be critically examined and ultimately overcome. He turns to medieval Christian theology in search for an Archimedean vantage point from which he critically observes and seeks to overturn these presuppositions. Milbank, however, does not simply contrast the secular present with a medieval past. He claims, rather, that the secularist positions themselves often have their roots in medieval theology, albeit in a distortion of a more genuine Christian approach. Milbank's position can be compared and contrasted with the more familiar formulation of political theology by Carl Schmitt.[41] If, for the latter, all significant concepts of the modern theory of the state are a secularization of theological concepts,[42] then, for the former, they are a secularization of *contorted* theological concepts.

Milbank takes on the liberal conception of human rights for its inherent failure to protect human dignity. He criticizes the liberal assumption that "the notion of human rights is the high mead, the finest distillation of the western tradition—the very point where it fulfills itself by denying its specificity and opening up to the universal."[43] The root of his critique is the subjective ground of human rights. Milbank juxtaposes this modern subjective notion with its medieval counterpart of an objective *jus*, which can be found in the writings of the Fathers of the Church. The battle lines Milbank draws set apart the modern secular notion of individualism, which he deems as "possessive individualism," from the objective medieval concept of a "right order." Whereas the former is based on human will, the latter is grounded in divine order.

The modern view of human rights is most clearly present in Hobbes, but is echoed in Locke and later theorists of the social contract. At its heart is the double notion of sovereignty—both of the individual sovereign and of the state as sovereign. The inalienable and hence absolute rights of the individual are mirrored in the absolute and hence inalienable rights of the sovereign state.

Whereas liberal thinkers view the inalienable rights of the individual as a limitation on the absolute power of the state, Milbank sees the very notion of inalienability, common to both, as the root of the problem of human rights and the liberal state. The danger in absolutism is the lack of any external limitation on its power. It is only from within the logic of sovereignty that boundaries are drawn, but any such attempt at self-restriction that is grounded in notions of self-ownership is bound to give way under pressure, "For if it is only 'self-ownership' that is absolutely inalienable (or ownership of the will itself by itself, as Rousseau and Kant later saw, in an Ockhamist lineage) then this is compatible with more or less any actual bondage—provided there is consent, which may well be taken to be tacit, since this is assumed to be sufficient by all known polities (to some degree absolutely, and in certain circumstances contingently)."[44]

Milbank contrasts the absolutism and subjective notion of the modern sovereign (both state and individual) with the medieval notion of personhood and dominion, which are mediated and relative. The political structure of the Middle Ages was highly decentralized and, perhaps more importantly, had intermediary institutions that mediated between the individual and the ruler and thus allowed for more individual freedom. No worldly power had absolute authority, and all political authorities were limited by an objective order external to them.

Milbank reverses the common opposition between religion and the secular by identifying the former, rather than the latter, with absolute power. His position may be criticized for ignoring the stark differences between modern absolutism and modern democracies. The latter, unlike the former, are ruled by law, not by the absolute power of human beings. Though Milbank does not directly address this problem, he seems to suggest that the rule of law itself has an absolutist character. While for liberals, the rule of law sets apart democracy from absolutist regimes, for Milbank the two share a great deal in common—where one form of absolutism is simply replaced by another. The affinity between seemingly different secular political formations—sovereignty and liberal democracy—becomes clear once the two are compared to medieval political institutions.

Milbank's critique of secular politics as absolutist seems to contrast not only with liberal positions but also with Asad's, who criticized human rights precisely for its balancing and relativizing approach to the calculus of pain. There is no reason to assume that the critics of secularism are reconcilable. And yet, it may be helpful to point out that Asad's main concern is with the content of the norms, whereas Milbank seems to be concerned with their authority, regardless of their specific content.

To emphasize the absolutist nature of modern politics, Milbank turns to an analysis of the modern notions of property rights, which are central both in the liberal and the neo-liberal traditions. "Absolute inalienability and alienability belong together," he argues. "The tyranny of the individual to alienate his property is mirrored in the right of the state to do the same. There is no external order that bounds either the state or the individual."[45] In contrast to the liberal concept of property, for Aquinas *jus* was objective, but not in the modern sense of objectivity as a thing that could only be shared in terms of a literal partition. "Aquinas did not think of the right to buy, sell and manage as material, 'thingy' processes, which the law later legitimizes (after the dualistic, biopolitical manner of modern liberalism), but rather saw these rights (outside any such dualism of nature and culture) as incorporeal relations in which we stand to things which are instrumentally subordinate to a more general and guiding incorporeal relationship of humanity as a whole to corporeal things as a whole."[46] The modern notion, quite to the contrary, places an "excessive stress upon the isolated individual."[47]

The last quotation from Milbank notwithstanding, it is important to distinguish his critique of rights from the more familiar communitarian and Marxist critiques. For Milbank the heart of the problem is not the liberal emphasis on the isolated individual, detached from a broader social and political context. Though problematic, it is not the ground of the problem, but a mere symptom. The real problem lies in the subjective nature of liberal theory and politics.

It is in this context that we can now turn to Milbank's more specific discussion and critique of empathy as an important supplement to the liberal notion of human rights. Like Arendt and Asad, albeit on his own terms, Milbank addresses sympathy as an important ingredient in the liberal world view. Milbank readily admits that, in comparison to the liberal image of the possessive individual, the turn to compassion and empathy can and should be viewed as a potentially redeeming aspect of liberalism. Still, he seeks to distinguish between the modern sense of sympathy (or empathy) and the Christian notion of *agape*, which is significantly different.

Adam Smith and other thinkers of the Scottish Enlightenment relegated sympathy to the sphere of "civil society" that lies outside the economic order: "For Hume as for Adam Smith, however, our sympathy for the distressed is a weaker emotion than our sympathy for those unjustly treated; our sympathetic fear confronted by those punished by the law; and our sympathetic admiration for the lives of the wealthy. Hence society is built mainly upon justice and accumulation—not upon benevolence. This is confined to the margins. Benevolence—as marginal, as unilateral, or as non-festive—is a fake substitute for charity. This is why I argue that the space of charity was abolished."[48]

For Milbank, benevolence cannot find its ground in the human on its own, and empathy based on this kind of evolution is bound to fail just as human rights is to fail:

> Sympathetic charity cannot resolve the aporia of sympathy and imagination. If there is only my-self and the other, and no God, then sympathetic imagination reduces either to animal instinct that regards purely the other, or else to a rationally reflexive projection of my own self-interest. Imagination can only be a discerning recognition of the other for his own sake, and for the sake of his entire set of sensible and intellectual relations, including his relation to myself, if it is an active anticipation (to use a favorite Cambridge Platonic word) of the divine telos for humanity and the cosmos."[49]

This final passage highlights some commonalities between Milbank's critique of human and both Arendt's and Asad's critiques. Milbank, like Arendt, sees the danger that the politics of sympathy (or empathy) will reduce human beings to their animal instinct and, once again like Arendt, points to the close connection between the reduction to animal nature and rational reflection. Finally, and in tune with Asad's critique of the secular opposition between active doing and passive suffering, Milbank proposes the religious attunement of "active anticipation" as an alternative ground for the political ethics of solidarity.

## 7. Conclusion

Each of the three thinkers discussed in the chapter offers a different understanding both of human rights and of secularism and thus constructs differently the relationship between the two. More specifically, they each offer different answers to the following set of questions: What are the inherent limitations of human rights? How do these limitations become clear once human rights is understood as a secularist project? What is the role of empathy in comprehending and consequently in criticizing human rights? Finally, each develops a different relationship to the secular and its place vis-à-vis religion. While it is striking to find three so very different thinkers asking the same set of questions, the differences between their answers is probably as glaring as their affinities.

By way of conclusion, I wish to emphasize the difference between the three thinkers and focus on the way each of them conceptualizes the relationship of secularism and history as part of a critique of human rights. Central to Arendt's position is her radical commitment to secular modernity. With all her critique of human rights as a secular politics, Arendt is well aware of the fact that there is no going back. Religion, tradition, and authority—the Roman trinity of the Ancient World, which survived the Middle Ages, has come to a dramatic end with the rise of the modern age. But to give up on religion, tradition, and authority is not to give up on belief, history, and politics.[50] The question for Arendt is whether and how the latter will take new form in the modern age. Human rights has not been able to meet this challenge, but this is only a reason to strive forward, while constantly reinterpreting the past. Since the future of human rights, as much as its past, is closely tied to the history of the nation-state, it may well be that with the current challenges facing the nation-state, new political forms will emerge that will be more congenial to the legal protection of humans, not in the abstract, but rather as members of new political formations.

Milbank's position on the relationship between secularism and history is radically different. For him, past traditions cannot be left behind, and the secular age cannot free itself from theological thinking. The very attempt to escape theology will not lead to a break with tradition, but only to its distortion. While Milbank is far from being naive and surely does not think that one can simply step back into the Middle Ages, he does believe that the only way to overcome the present limitations of liberal thought is by returning to forgotten possibilities that can be found in ancient institutions and in the writings of classic Christian theology.

Asad's position is perhaps more complex. Like Arendt, he too acknowledges that the secular age is our reality and cannot be replaced by religion. Yet he calls for a much greater modesty in the secular claim to universality. Secularism is as much a tribal tradition with its specific beliefs, practices, and sentiments as any other tradition. Though secular practices cannot be criticized for their unavoidable partiality, "we seculars" would probably do better if we faced and embraced this partiality, rather than glorify human rights as an epitome of progress and perfected reason.

Each of the three thinkers approaches the problem of human rights from a different conception of history and the relationship between secularism and modernity. It would make no sense to try and synthesize their positions into one coherent argument. Such an attempt would necessarily require removing the critiques from their concrete historical and theoretical context and would lead precisely to the kind of abstraction that all three thinkers oppose in their writings. What we are left with is, therefore, not an answer to the question of the relationship of human rights and religion, but rather, and at best, a new way of formulating the question, taking as our point of departure neither human rights nor religion, but rather the question concerning the nature of secularism and its place within modernity.

# Notes

1. This chapter was first presented at the Israel Democracy Institute (IDI) in a conference on "The Role of Religion in Human Rights Discourses." The author is grateful to the conference organizers and participants for their helpful comments and to the IDI for granting permission to republish the piece.
2. See, for example, J. Milbank, *Theology and Social Theory: Beyond Secular Reason* (Oxford: Blackwell, 1993); T. Asad, *Formations of the Secular: Christianity, Islam, Modernity* (Stanford, CA: Stanford University Press, 2003); For a less critical account of secularism, see C. Taylor, *A Secular Age* (Cambridge, MA: Harvard University Press, 2007).
3. See, for example, M. Weber, "Religious Rejections of the World and their Directions," in Bryan S. Turner, ed, *From Max Weber: Essays in Sociology* (London: Routledge, 1991) 323–59.
4. See J. Casanova, *Public Religions in the Modern World* (Chicago: University of Chicago Press, 1994). See also note 1 above.
5. J. Witte, Jr. and F. S. Alexander, eds, *Christianity and Human Rights: An Introduction* (New York: Cambridge University Press, 2010); J. Witte, *The Reformation of Human Rights: Law, Religion, and Human Rights in Early Modern Calvinism* (Cambridge: Cambridge University Press, 2008).
6. T.H. Marshall, *Citizenship and Social Class, and other Essays* (Cambridge: Cambridge University Press, 1950).
7. On the left, the classic text is, no doubt, K. Marx, *On the Jewish Question* (Cincinnati: Hebrew Union College, 1958). On the right, one may think of E. Burke, *Reflections on the Revolution in France* (Stanford, CA: Stanford University Press, 2001). The argument was

picked up by writers on both sides in the 1990s and continues to shape the contemporary discussion. See, for example, M. Glendon, *Rights Talk: The Impoverishment of Political Discourse* (New York: Free Press, 1993/1991); M. Tushnet, "The Critique of Rights" (1993) 47:1 SMU Law Review 32.
8. A. Smith, *The Theory of Moral Sentiment*, 2nd edn (London: A. Millar, 1761) 1–2.
9. See, more generally, I. Brownlie and G. S. Goodwin-Gill, eds, *Basic Documents on Human Rights*, 6th edn (Oxford: Oxford University Press, 2010).
10. L. Hunt, *Inventing Human Rights: A History* (New York: W.W. Norton, 2007) 122.
11. Ibid., 64.
12. The word "empathy" (*Einfühlung*) was coined in the second half of the nineteenth century by the German philosopher Rudolf Lotze to convey the idea that appreciation of art depends on the viewer's ability to project his personality onto the viewed object. The word "sympathy" has older origins and signified an emotional affinity between things, or a community of feeling. In what follows, I will use the term empathy.
13. Hunt, *supra* note 10 at 77.
14. Ibid., 135–36.
15. Ibid., 81.
16. Rush, quoted in ibid., 76.
17. Myuart, quoted in ibid., 93.
18. Hunt, *supra* note 10 at 94.
19. Ibid., 97.
20. Consider the following international law documents: *Standard Minimum Rules for the Treatment of Prisoners*, adopted Aug. 30, 1955 by the First United Nations Congress on Prevention of Crime and the Treatment of Offenders, U.N. Doc. A/CONF/611, annex I; *Declaration on Social Progress and Development* G.A. res. 2542 (XXIV), 24 U.N. GAOR Supp. (No. 30) at 49, U.N. Doc. A/7630 (1969); *Universal Declaration on the Eradication of Hunger and Malnutrition*, adopted on 16 November 1974 by the World Food Conference convened under General Assembly resolution 3180 (XXVIII) of 17 December 1973; and, most recently, *Universal Declaration on Bioethics and Human Rights*, adopted "by acclamation" at the UNESCO General Conference on 19 October 2005.
21. M. C. Nussbaum, *The New Religious Intolerance: Overcoming the Politics of Fear in an Anxious Age* (Cambridge, MA: Harvard University Press, 2012).
22. Ibid., 39.
23. Ibid., 39–40.
24. H. Arendt, "The Decline of the Nation-State and the End of the Rights of Man," in *The Origins of Totalitarianism*, 3rd edn (London: George Allen & Unwin, 1966) 267–302.
25. Ibid., 267.
26. Ibid., 300.
27. G. Agamben, *Homo Sacer: Sovereign Power and Bare Life* (Stanford, CA: Stanford University Press, 1998).
28. H. Arendt, *On Revolution* (New York: Viking Press, 1965) 84.
29. Ibid., 84.
30. Ibid.
31. Ibid., 79.
32. Arendt, *supra* note 24 at 290–91.
33. Ibid., 291.
34. S. Moyn, *The Last Utopia: Human Rights in History* (Cambridge; MA: Harvard University Press, 2012).
35. Asad, *supra* note 2 at 113.
36. Ibid.
37. Ibid., 128.
38. Compare E. Weizman, *The Least of All Possible Evils: Humanitarian Violence from Arendt to Gaza* (London: Verso, 2012).
39. Asad, *supra* note 2 at 100.
40. Ibid., 79.

41. C. Schmitt, *Political Theology: Four Chapters on the Concept of Sovereignty*, ed. George Schwab (Chicago: University of Chicago Press, 2006).
42. Ibid., 36–52.
43. J. Milbank, "Against Human Rights: Liberty in the Western Tradition" (2012) 1:1 Oxford Journal of Law and Religion 7.
44. Ibid., 3.
45. Ibid.
46. Ibid., 12.
47. Ibid., 5.
48. J. Milbank, "The Invocation of Clio: a Response" (2005) 33:1 Journal of Religious Ethics 35.
49. Ibid.
50. H. Arendt, "What is Authority?" *Between Past and Future* (New York: Penguin Classics, 2006) 91.

PART TWO

# MULTICULTURALISM AND RELIGIOUS FREEDOM AS SWORDS OR SHIELDS

# 4

# Religious Freedom as "Reflexive Law"

INO AUGSBERG

## 1. Introduction

When we take a look at current developments in religious affairs from a legal point of view, asking which modifications of traditional legal treatments might be needed, it is worthwhile to analyze the ongoing changes in more detail. Focusing on possible social problems caused by religious "revival," we can see that it is not so much religion in general but the establishment of one specific religion, Islam, within the modern Western world that appears to be problematic. This newly established religion within the region challenges the classical Western mechanism of coping with religious pluralism, the idea of state neutrality. For we can detect that this idea is based on a specific understanding of secularism in the sense of a basic separation between state and religion. This concept of secularism, and the concurring notion of religion as a primarily private issue, may be regarded as specific Judeo-Christian conceptions. At least it presupposes a certain conceptualization of religion. Thus we have to ask whether it is possible or even necessary to maintain these concepts or whether we will have to rearrange things in order to account for the apparent particularities of non-Western religions. In order to answer these questions, the first step is to take a closer look at the function of religious freedom in modern society, therewith outlining the relevance that religion and religious freedom still possess. The second step, then, is to assume that we can adopt the position of religion, therewith demonstrating that, from the religious perspective, the endeavor to reduce religion to one societal sphere among others is an act of total impertinence. The third step is to question how we can construct our legal tools in a way that takes this impertinence duly into account. Two practical examples shall clarify the general idea before I come to a preliminary conclusion.

## 2. The Return of Religion in Western Europe

The ubiquitous talk of religious revival[1] necessitates a fundamental differentiation with regard to different denominations on the one hand and different geographical areas on the other. Whereas the importance of Christianity is increasing in South America, Africa, and Asia,[2] maybe even in North America,[3] in at least continental Europe the story of Christian churches is still one of constant decline. The only remarkable increase that can be observed refers to the number of people leaving the churches. To take the German example:[4] In 1950, more than 96 percent of the population in the Federal Republic of Germany belonged to one of the major Christian confessions. About 50 percent were Protestants; about 46 percent belonged to the Catholic confession. This situation hardly changed until the beginning of the 1960s. Yet from then on the number of persons leaving the churches increased. Nowadays, only about 31 percent of the population still belongs to the Catholic and about 30 percent to the Protestant confession. About one third of the population does not belong to any religious confession at all. Even of those people still belonging to one of the Christian communities only a small percentage actively participates in the parish, attends church services, and so on. And this trend is continuing.[5]

Thus, if we talk of religious revival in Western European states, it is not a "homemade," Christian phenomenon. The revival of religious issues in continental Europe is basically the arrival of Islam. The increase of religious believers is based on the faith of immigrants. If there may be some growing awareness for religious issues on the Christian side, too, it is a reaction to the newly established Islamic confession. In fact, looking at the recent cases regarding religious issues we can observe an interesting double movement: as far as Christian religious issues were concerned, recent cases mostly tell a story of retreat. The famous cases of the crucifix in the classroom[6] is just the most prominent example of a general movement that sees Christian tradition challenged and forced to retreat by a contemporary society no longer firmly based on Christian convictions. By contrast, religiously motivated struggles with regard to Islam are struggles that aim at getting public recognition for the new religion.

Undoubtedly, this new religion causes anxiety and angst among not only autochthonous Christian believers, but also amongst agnostics and atheists. And also undoubtedly, though this fear is to a large degree an irrational, phobic phenomenon,[7] it is not entirely without *fundamentum in re*. In order to demonstrate potential social problems connected with the issue of integrating Islam in modern Western societies,[8] one does not have to point to the extreme cases of terrorists proclaiming to be religiously motivated or of the attacks on the

Danish cartoonist who drew a caricature of the Prophet Mohammed. On a much more everyday level, one can find in contemporary society forms of behavior that in a modern secularized perspective may appear not only uncommon but inappropriate. From this point of view, it seems for instance hard to understand why Muslim girls should not be able to participate in coeducational gym classes or take part in school trips, just as the boys can.[9]

Of course we may doubt whether these issues are genuinely religious. By contrast, one might argue that such forms of behavior are culturally rather than religiously grounded.[10] Thus, some scholars rightly emphasize that within the same region and the same social and cultural environment for instance the so called "honour killings" can be found in Christian communities just as well as in Islamic families.[11] However, one may also ask whether we can really differentiate between culture and religion in such an accurate manner or if we rather have to regard culture as a result of religious practices in a given social environment. The distinction itself is ambivalent. For it could be no more than just the product and effect of a specific culture and a specific religion.[12] Hence the distinction will not help us to come to terms with those phenomena. No more than we can positively call them merely religious,[13] can we attribute them solely to culture. For this reason the concept of "multiculturalism" already includes the idea of religious pluralism, and vice versa. The debate on "post-multiculturalism"[14] thus has to be understood not only as a challenge to previous optimistic concepts of a culturally diverse society, but also as a challenge to religious pluralism. In this perspective, political resistance toward social diversity is no longer a move practiced solely by the very conservative side, aiming at as much social homogeneity as possible. By contrast, deliberate leftists have begun to see religion as a "danger" to individual freedom and thus have identified as one of the "core conflicts" of today's society the conflict between "the universal validity of human rights" on the one side and "cultural difference"—that is, religion—on the other.[15] Consequently, rather than conceiving of religious freedom as a "sword" for religious groups, that is to say as an instrument to protect and bring forward their specific idea of social life against the "imperial" state order,[16] religious freedom, taken as part and parcel of a universalistic concept of human rights, serves as a potential "shield" against particularistic impositions.

## 3. Neutrality and Secularization

The question then is how to handle the seeming discrepancy of a society that on the one side is becoming more and more secularized and on the other side is facing a religious revival in the way of increasing religious pluralization. In modern Western states, one traditional answer to the problem of how to cope with religious pluralism and its effects is the idea of state neutrality. Accordingly, the state is not allowed to identify itself with a certain denomination. Rather, it has to keep equidistance to all religious denominations.[17] Church, that is to say, religion, and state have to be treated as principally separate spheres.[18]

Apparently, this approach to the problem is a reasonable compromise between more one-sided solutions like the French concept of *laïcité* on the one side and state church systems like in Greece on the other.[19] In contrast to these solutions, the concept of state neutrality appears to be universally applicable. If this were the case, then the before-mentioned discrepancy would, from the legal point of view, simply not exist. As the principle forbids privileged treatment of specific religions, no religious group should particularly profit or be negatively affected by this figure. In applying the neutrality principle, there should be no particular religious issues at stake. Hence pluralization of religion would be no problem of religious freedom, but rather a proof of its universalistic validity.

However, a closer look at the principle reveals that the idea of state neutrality includes an important assumption: it presupposes a general difference between the state on the one side and religion on the other.[20] If we take this separation of social spheres as the defensible core meaning of "secularism,"[21] then the neutrality principle presupposes secularization. Thus it is at odds with an understanding of religion that does not accept this basic separation between the religious and the political sphere, but supports—for religious reasons—theocratic concepts. Moreover, it is also at odds with religious concepts that defy the claim that religion forms just one social sphere among others.[22] With reference to such possible religious denominations, the neutrality principle itself is not neutral,[23] as it implies a particular statement on the relationship between state and religion—and therewith also on religion itself. It favors religious positions that accept or have learned to accept, in the course of time, that this difference between politics and religion is the fundament of the modern Western state. In this sense, differentiation and dedifferentiation are the decisive categories for an analysis of modern society's relationship to religion.[24]

The next question is whether the statement in favor of neutrality and thus of differentiation has specific religious roots. Maybe the acceptance of the state–church difference is not merely the result of a historical process in which some religious communities have learned to adapt to the new political demands. Maybe the doctrines of certain religious denominations are in favor of such a difference and therefore can be regarded as the basis for the emerging conception. Arguably, one could point to several theological figures within the Christian tradition—to, for instance, the difference between *imperium* and *sacerdotium*, or, as Gianni Vattimo has repeatedly done, thus presenting secularization as a constitutive element of authentic Christianity, to the figure of *kenosis*[25]—that may support or at least help to accept secularism. One might also refer to the difference between positive and Divine law and the difference between positive and natural law, claiming that the dichotomy established with the first distinction enabled the second one.[26] With regard to the Jewish tradition, one might argue that after the second destruction of the Temple in Jerusalem the disentanglement of religion and state has become one of the fundamental experiences for the Jewish community. While law and religion remained closely intertwined, this intertwined legal-religious regime developed rules of collision in order to cope with the state rules of the diaspora situation.[27] In particular the difference between Noahide and Sinaitic law could provide a basis for a fundamental distinction with regard to universal, secular, and particular, religious law.[28]

Thus, the important differences notwithstanding, both Christianity and Judaism may appear as basically favoring, or at least not openly opposing, the concept of secularization as discussed above. Historical narratives apparently support this premise. Some historians have tried to characterize even the general concept of freedom as a distinctively Christian idea in Western practice.[29] Looking at the development of religious freedom, as the corresponding legal response to a concept of religion that is no longer automatically identical with the state and its people, Georg Jellinek has stated—with reference mainly to the situation in the British colonies in North America in general and the life and work of the Baptist Roger Williams in particular[30]—a distinctive tendency within Christianity itself toward this idea of religion as an individual choice that therefore cannot be enforced by state power.[31] Therewith, Christianity becomes, in a remarkable dialectical movement, the religion that defies its own claim for absolute validity by granting freedom of religion to each individual.[32] Though we may doubt whether Jellinek's historical account in general and his idea of religious freedom as first emanation of the later on developed concept of human rights in particular are correct,[33] one cannot doubt that Christianity has in fact at least subsequently taken this turn. The Second Vatican Council explicitly stated that individual religious freedom was not a mere concession to the worldly sphere that the church could no longer dominate with religious directives, but an internal consequence of religion itself.[34] As Christian faith is based on the figure of human dignity, it follows that the thus dignified individual must be able to make her own choices.[35]

By contrast, one may ask whether Islam is equally able to adapt itself to the figure of secularization. Can we find here functional equivalents to the kind of mechanisms that enabled the other religious denominations to come to terms with secularization? Or will we rather detect remarkable differences?[36] To raise this kind of question does not necessarily imply essentializing statements on the characteristics of Islam, therewith putting aside its undeniable manifoldness. It may well be that a perspective on Islam and Islamic law as a holistic concept is mistaken, and that instead of this we should put much more emphasis on observing, for instance, the close connection of Islamic law and local customs.[37] Yet in any case we must be cautious not to fall back on a Eurocentric perspective by supposing that any religion will necessarily come to terms with the separation between state and church, that is to say, will accept secularism. By contrast, our current idea of religion as a primarily private matter that therefore can fairly easily be adjusted to the concept of the religiously neutral state could be regarded as a historical exception rather than the rule.

Hence the problem cannot be solved by simply assuming that these different forms of religious conceptions—namely Islam—will in due time experience a development that will modify their general attitude toward the state. The factual possibility of such developments notwithstanding—the Catholic Church is an example of how the idea of the state–church relationship can alter in the course of time[38]—such a process of *aggiornamento* cannot be taken for granted.[39] More importantly, though one might doubt with very good reasons that more legal repression, for example with regard to the headscarf cases, will help to create Islamic moderates,[40] to believe in this kind of *aggiornamento* would mean to rely on a concept of religion that may not be as universal as it seemed to be. It is not at all self-evident that secularism is an inevitable historical development that any religious group will sooner or later have to experience and to accept. More likely, it is a distinctive element of the evolution of the modern Western world, and there is a price that has to be paid in order to maintain the concept. According to Talal Asad, "[s]ecularism is not simply an intellectual answer to a question about enduring social peace and toleration. It is an enactment by which a *political medium* (representation of citizenship) redefines and transcends particular and differentiating practices of the self that are articulated through class, gender, and religion."[41] Thus, the question about Islam's ability to adapt itself to the modern secularized world is not so much a positive statement about a specific religion. Rather, the question points to a different, and maybe even more disturbing, direction. It outlines the possibility that, as our current understanding of religion appears to be based on the difference between the secular and the religious,[42] this concept of religion itself might be inadequate in order to do justice to newly emerging phenomena. Maybe we are imposing on Islam categories that only belong to one specifically modern Western tradition.[43] Thus for instance Leora Batnitzky states that the "concept of religion as a sphere separate from politics is a modern construct just as the concept of law as an autonomous realm is a modern construct. Modern concepts of law and religion are born together."[44] In this sense the difficulties with Muslim immigrants forming a religious minority in Europe could be based on the fact that the concepts of "religion," "culture," "majority," "minority," and so on are specifically European ideas.[45]

> However, the current situation is even more complex. For the endeavor to conceptualize religion in this modern way is an operation that even Christian religionists criticize: "The concept of religion is itself an idea that is necessary only if one plans to divide the world into multiple spheres, one of which is somehow related to the life according to a narrative about God, and the other of which is somehow related to . . . well, to something else. Serious religions, however, do not conceive of the world in this way. In particular, the principal western religious traditions, Judaism, Christianity, and Islam, all reject it."[46]

Thus those phenomena that apparently mark the particularities of Islam within our modern western world could also be regarded as an aspect of religion that belonged at least partly to other religious denominations, too, and that, following the early Protestant example, has been suppressed just quite recently.[47]

As lawyers we do not have to respond to these theological, historical, and sociological questions in a positive sense. Even if we wanted to, we could not, as the answer lies well beyond legal competences. Yet what remains to be answered is whether or not our traditional legal concepts, in particular the idea of state neutrality, are flexible enough to take these outlined possibilities duly into account. If the concept of state neutrality is self-contradictory because it undermines its own purpose by possibly neglecting basic assumptions of certain religions while supporting the view of others, do we have to substitute it? Or is the idea of secularism so decisive for our modern society that we have to arrange our concept of religious freedom accordingly?

## 4. The Concept of Functional Differentiation

In order to provide an answer to these questions, the first thing is to elaborate on the meaning of secularism within the context of religious freedom. In the course of history, Western societies have changed their basic internal structures from stratification to functional differentiation.[48] Accordingly, the main differences in society are no longer determined by belonging to a specific class, family, or organization. The most important differences emerge with regard to specific societal functions. These functions are fulfilled by specialized social spheres, for example economy, law, art, or science. Society as a whole has become so complex that its operations can no longer be guaranteed from a central point of observance. Thus, if one wishes to maintain and enlarge society's complexity, that is to say the sheer number of possibilities performed by social operations, political control of all these different types of operations is no longer conceivable. Rather, they follow their own codes and programs directed by the specific function that they fulfill.

So far, functional differentiation is hardly more than a well-known, already Weberian description of modern society. Yet with regard to the normative sphere, we can also speak of legal mechanisms that are specifically adjusted to this kind of differentiation and the problems going along with it. In this respect, Niklas Luhmann has developed the idea of "basic rights as institutions,"[49] in the sense that fundamental rights do not function solely, and not even primarily, as a guarantee of individual freedom against state action. Rather, these rights serve as a barrier against totalitarian tendencies of social subsystems with regard to the other subsystems. As one can observe a noteworthy tendency of social subsystems to colonize their environment, that is to say the other social subsystems, fundamental rights set boundaries to such tendencies. Though Luhmann developed this idea mainly in regard to a classical movement of the political system claiming the competence to control and direct all types of social affairs, the general idea can be transferred to other subsystems too. Hence we may for instance talk of dangers of too much economization or juridification of society. What is more, the idea applies well to certain religious groups supporting a totalizing molding of the entire society according to religious rules, therewith neglecting that there is a general difference between state and society on the one side and religion on the other. If it is the task of fundamental rights to secure an independent sphere of action for each societal subsystem, then the guarantee of religious liberty can only reach as far as the exertion of faith does not encroach upon the activities of other social spheres.[50] Religious freedom thus has to be regarded in a more complex sense: it is no longer merely the freedom of religion, taken as a *genitivus subiectivus*, that is, the freedom of religious groups and individual believers, but also society's freedom from religion. Its function is not only to prevent the state from prohibiting religious activities, but also to safeguard society from religious claims stretching beyond the private sphere into the public realm. Secularization, then, is an effect of a general structural problem—in other words, functional differentiation and its legal guarantee—on religions.[51]

## 5. Taking Religion Seriously

If we describe the function of religious freedom in this way, it should have become clear that there is a price that must be paid for upholding such a concept of society, and apparently it is especially religion that has to pay. In order to explain in more detail the specific costs for religion that go along with the concept of a functionally differentiated society, we should take a look at common self-conceptions of religion. Religionists regard the idea of religion being just one among many other social functions as intolerable: "[a]s any serious student of religion knows, religion has no sphere. It possesses no natural bounds... Rushing past boundaries is what religion does."[52] Religion, one may say, is the social subsystem that defies its own status as being merely a social subsystem.[53] Religious belief opposes the idea that religion has a specific function for society just as for instance economy or education have one too.

There are at least two ways of explaining this religious resistance against its own functional analysis. One way is to describe what functional analysis is all about: it is a way of comparing different possible solutions for a given set of problems, and that is to say, it is a way of conceiving of functional equivalents.[54] To ask for the function of religion is to presuppose that there are, at least theoretically, other possibilities of solving the same problem. Consequently, a functional analysis asks for the possible substitution of religion with something else. Obviously this is a form of questioning religion that can be practiced only from the outside, not from the inside of the religious system.[55] The idea of belief being just one option among many others is characteristic of the secular perspective: only with secularism do alternatives to belief in God became thinkable.[56]

The second way is more important. Most religions rely on the basic difference between immanence and transcendence.[57] Yet this distinction is a difference that at the same time subverts the idea of distinctiveness, for the transcendent is conceived of as in contrast to any form of differentiation.[58] God is, as Nicolas of Cusa states quite paradigmatically, *ante omnia quae differunt*.[59] Thus it is, from the religious point of view, impossible to re-integrate the non-immanent into a plurality of immanent distinctions by stating it to be a social sphere. There is *per definitionem* no point of contact or passage between the immanent and the transcendent. By contrast, access to the transcendent sphere is possible only by religious faith. Of course religion is constituted by intramundane communicative acts. Yet to take religion therefore as a solely worldly phenomenon misses, from the religious point of view, the decisive aspects of belief. As the belief transcends the world, it cannot be reduced to one of its spheres alone. Stephen Carter stresses exactly this basic claim of religion clearly enough: "[f]rom the traditional Christian point of view—and certainly from the point of view of many other faiths—religion is not merely an aspect of life, to be divided from its other parts. Belief in God is a totality."[60] Therefore, religion is also, from the religionist's point of view, not only an individual phenomenon or a personal decision. Rather than being an expression of one's individuality, the religious personality is constituted by the communal belief. "Like a culture or a language," George Lindbeck states, religion is "a communal phenomenon that shapes the subjectivities of the individuals rather than being primarily a manifestation of those subjectivities."[61] Thus, once again, it is opposed to secularization as the socio-structural equivalent to the privatization of religion.[62] Hence a certain tendency to individualize religious freedom that we can find in the judicature of, for example, the German Federal Constitutional Court, indicates a distinctive and, from the religious point of view, non-neutral position.[63]

## 6. Religious Freedom as "Reflexive Law"

The question then is how can we possibly coordinate this basic function of religion and religious freedom in a modern society on the one side with religion's resistance to be a part of the game on the other? How can we construct legal mechanisms that do not simply ignore this resistance, but that take it duly into account?

My suggestion is that we should try to reconstruct religious freedom as a "reflexive law." I take this notion from Gunther Teubner, who therewith tried to characterize a common aspect in both Habermas's as well as Luhmann's (and also Philippe Nonet's and Philip Selnick's)[64] legal theory.[65] Teubner's general idea is that in highly complex societies that can no longer be integrated from a central point of view, the only remaining option of guaranteeing social coherence in the (weak) sense of compatibility between the different subsystems is installing internal mechanisms of reflexion within each subsystem.[66] Against the background of this general assumption—which we can easily recognize as a variation of Luhmann's thesis on functional differentiation—he stresses that under such conditions of increased social complexity the fundamental legal task has to be modified. As the law can no longer directly control the diverse social activities, it has to concentrate on creating structural arrangements that enable or support self-regulating mechanisms within the different subsystems.[67] This newly designed legal task includes not only safeguarding the autonomy of the different social spheres, but also the development of internal reflexive structures that sensitize the subsystems for the environmental effects caused by their respective intent to maximize the system's *eigen* rationality.[68]

Interestingly, a central reference for Teubner in his attempt to develop this new concept of law is a quotation taken from Luhmann's book on the "function of religion."[69] Here, Luhmann states that all systems not only have to fulfill adequately their own specific function, but, moreover, as every social system forms part of the social environment of the other social subsystems, their task also is to establish a sensible relationship of compatibility toward the specific functions and characteristics of the other systems. In order to avoid having processes of optimization within one functional sphere create problems in other subsystems, limitations have to be implemented into the reflexion structure of each social system.[70] Teubner resumes the argument as follows: "It is the task of reflexion structures in any social subsystem to resolve conflicts between function and performance by imposing internal restrictions on given subsystems so that they are suitable as components of the environment of other subsystems."[71] Hence, reflexivity in this sense does not only mean a turn back toward one's own structures, in a self-encapsulating, monadic way. By contrast, the concept describes an excentric movement by which a system looks beyond its own boundaries to the specific requirements of the system's environment. The system must learn to see what it does not and cannot see.[72]

A suitable way to describe how we could operationalize this internal reflexion of environmental needs could be the concept of tolerance. Thus we must distinguish between tolerance and acceptance. Tolerance does not level differences; it affirms the other's otherness by upholding one's own position.[73] Tolerance in this sense implies an attitude that underlines the system's difference from an outer sphere, even in a way that it might regard the otherness of the environment as a potential threat for its own integrity, which motivates it to shut down its borders.[74] Yet it does not try to enforce its own structures and characteristics onto the other. Tolerant reflexivity in this way is a double-bind movement that reflects on the fact that, as the system is constituted by its distinction from an outer environment, this distinction itself establishes a relationship to the environment that cannot be abandoned.

With regard to the relationship between law and religion, the interesting aspect of this concept of tolerant reflexivity is that it runs both ways. It affects both the religious and the legal sphere. Hence, on the one hand, the law has to take into account religion's distinctiveness. In order to acknowledge this distinctiveness, one has to resist any attempt to construct, legally or politically, what religion should be all about. We might call this a "second-order neutrality"[75] that knowingly operates within the boundaries of its own systemic preconditions: reflecting on its separateness from religion, the law can give no encompassing, constitutive definition of religion. By contrast, the legal system has to accept the self-conception of groups of people claiming to be religious communities.[76] Only if there are evident signs indicating that the community in question in fact follows a rationality that clearly belongs to a different social sphere—for instance, if it behaves like a company aiming primarily at economic success—the law may refuse to grant the specific protection of religious liberty.[77] Moreover, it also has to accept the potentially far-reaching claims of religion with regard to the question of which aspects of life can be seen as specifically religiously motivated. If there can be no clear-cut legal definition of religion, there can be no principle boundaries in this respect, too. Once again it is the religious self-conception that sets the stage. Legal control is restricted to a form of plausibility test.[78]

On the other hand, the religions have to tolerate—not necessarily to accept—that they may not take over other social functions. Religious groups may try to influence the operations and decisions in other social systems—in particular with regard to politics—but they may not attempt to substitute the spheres of the political, legal, economic, and so on entirely. That is the meaningful core of the idea that religious ideas have to be "translated" in order to become part of the political process:[79] the idea of translation implies the necessity to uphold the boundaries between religion and politics, for the sake of both of them. Only by keeping religion and politics apart, that is, by preventing a leveling of the distinctions, can society maintain the full complexity of social possibilities enabled by functional differentiation. In this sense Stephen Carter is right in stating that religion may serve society best by resisting the otherwise dominant cultural forces and political convictions, thus offering alternative models for social developments.[80] By contrast, if a religion does not tolerate the basic functional difference, then it is legitimate, in order to safeguard the social order, to discriminate against this religion on the basis of its non-tolerating of this social order. Hence the law has to observe the internal religious processes of reflecting the relationship to its environment and adjust its own legal mechanisms accordingly.[81]

## 7. Two Examples

Two examples might help to illustrate this kind of reflexive tolerance both on the side of society as well as on the side of religious groups within the society. The first example is taken from the German context. According to Article 140 *Grundgesetz* (GG, i.e., German Basic Law) and Article 137 paragraph 5 *Weimarer Reichsverfassung* (WRV, i.e., the constitution of the Weimar Republic), "Religious societies shall remain corporations under public law insofar as they have enjoyed that status in the past. Other religious societies shall be granted the same rights upon application, if their constitution and the number of their members give assurance of their permanency."[82] Despite this status as corporations under public law, the respective religious communities do not become an integral part of state organization.[83] However, this status implies several possibilities that corporations under private law cannot use. The most important of these privileges are stated in Article 137 paragraph 6 WRV: accordingly, religious societies that have achieved this status are entitled to levy taxes on the basis of the civil taxation list. Traditionally, the great Christian churches and also some smaller religious communities already possessed this status. Thus for "new" religions to achieve this legal status is highly attractive not only for pragmatic reasons, but also with regard to their general acceptance in society, as it brings them at par with those traditional religious communities.

In consequence, the community of Jehovah's Witnesses applied to be granted the status of corporation under public law. The German Federal Administrative Court denied the status, claiming that in order to be granted this specific form of legal status, the respective community had to demonstrate some kind of loyalty to the state.[84] The community of Jehovah's Witnesses, however, as it instructs its members not to participate in state elections, would fail to show this loyalty.

This decision was overruled by the German Federal Constitutional Court.[85] The Court explained that it is not an infringement of the constitution if a religious community objects to the state as a secular institution. As long as the religious community does not attempt to overthrow the current legal system in order to install a theocratic regime, that is, as long as it respects the fundamental rights of the citizens and the principle of religious tolerance, its attitude toward the state is an inner religious phenomenon that the state may not criticize.[86] Thus the Court stated that it suffices if a religion tolerates the state and its institutions, even if it does not accept them, and that, if so, then vice versa, the state has to tolerate the religious group—and thus grant it the requested status. Both spheres, the legal system and the religious community, have to reflect on and pay attention to each other's internal regard of the other, and hence to learn to live with each other's distinctiveness.

The second example belongs to the United States. The case in question regards tax exemptions granted under Section 501(c)(3) of the Internal Revenue Code.[87] That section states that qualifying religious or civic public interest organizations need not pay federal taxes. The trade-off for the benefit of this exemption is that no substantial part of the organization's activities may include "carrying on ... propaganda, or otherwise attempting, to influence legislation ... [nor may it] participate in, or intervene in (including the publishing or distributing of statements), any political campaign on behalf of any candidate for public office." In the 1980s, supporters of abortion rights filed a lawsuit against the Catholic Church, arguing that the Catholic Church, because of its advocacy against abortion rights, which it expressed constantly, and in particular at election times, had violated the code.[88] Though the lawsuit was eventually dismissed, as the plaintiffs were said to have no standing,[89] the federal judges on first hearing ordered the Church to turn over internal documents regarding the question of the Church's position toward abortion rights. To quote once again Stephen Carter: "[i]t should at least occasion a bit of comment that the federal government decides which benefits to grant or deny to religions depending on the content of their teaching."[90] In fact, if the religious claim for universal validity of its doctrine is taken seriously, it cannot be confined to aspects regarding merely "spiritual" affairs. To take religion seriously means to understand that its doctrine tends to cover worldly aspects of life, too. In order to safeguard freedom of religion, this tendency must not be ignored. It has to be reflected upon and taken into account.

## 8. Conclusion

Religious pluralization confronts our traditional concepts of the state–church relationship with new challenges. With regard to this emerging new situation, we cannot simply wait and see. There has to be a deliberate answer to the current situation. On the one side, this response has to be clear-cut: for a constitutional state based on individual basic rights and a modern society constituted by functional differentiation, freedom of religion cannot include the possible overthrow of the entire constitutional and social order in favor of religious regimes. Thus individual freedom of belief ends where the societal and political order is at stake. In this sense, secularism is an indispensable part of our legal system. Moreover, by protecting the differentiation of society in functionally diverse social spheres and defying the claim of religion to be more than just a social system, fundamental rights also serve to prevent the potential hegemony of specific religious groups and hence help to guarantee religious pluralism.

On the other side, we have to pay tribute to the idea of minority protection not only with regard to inner-religious tensions, but also with regard to politics. Religious freedom is essentially the freedom not to have to cling to a majoritarian conviction, and therefore especially a freedom to resist political imperatives. Thus though the state may not support religious beliefs that tend to ignore or even to undermine the separation of religion and state, religious freedom compels state authorities not to press the internal development of religious groups toward a certain direction. We may hope for a more liberal "Euro-Islam" more strongly in favor of a secular society.[91] Yet the state is not allowed to support and thus construct such a religious denomination with its own means.

# Notes

1. See, with more references, K.-H. Ladeur and I. Augsberg, *Toleranz—Religion—Recht. Die Herausforderung des „neutralen" Staates durch neue Formen von Religiosität in der postmodernen Gesellschaft* (Tübingen: Mohr Siebeck, 2007) at 1 et sqq.
2. See the reports by J. Casanova et al. in H. Jonas and K. Wiegandt, eds, *Säkularisierung und die Weltreligionen* (Frankfurt/M.: Fischer, 2007).
3. For the situation in the United States see T. W. Smith and S. Kim, "The Vanishing Protestant Majority" (2005) 44:2 Journal for the Scientific Study of Religion 211–23; N. Feldman, *Divided by God: America's Church-State Problem—And What We Should Do About It* (New York: Farrar, 2005) at 51 et sqq.
4. For a closer account on the following see S. Korioth, "Jeder nach seiner Facon," *Kritische Justiz, Beiheft 1* (Baden-Baden, Nomos 2009), 175–85; D. Pollack, *Säkularisierung—ein moderner Mythos?* (Tübingen: Mohr Siebeck, 2003) at 77 et sqq; C. Waldhoff, *Neue Religionskonflikte und staatliche Neutralität—Erfordern weltanschauliche und religiöse Entwicklungen Antworten des Staates?, Gutachten D für den 68. Deutschen Juristentag* (Munich: C.H. Beck, 2010) at 1 et sqq.
5. See Pollack, ibid., at 92–94.
6. See for the German case 93 *Entscheidungen des Bundesverfassungsgerichts* (i.e. the official collection of decisions of the German Federal Constitutional Court) (Tübingen: Mohr Siebeck, 1995) 1–37; for the level of the European Court of Human Rights see *Lautsi v Italy*, Application no 30814/06, ECtHR (Grand Chamber) Judgment, 18 March 2011.
7. For a critique see M. Nussbaum, *The New Religious Intolerance: Overcoming the Politics of Fear in an Anxious Age* (Cambridge, MA: Belknap Press, 2012).
8. On this question see, e.g., J. R. Bowen, *Can Islam Be French? Pluralism and Pragmatism in a Secularist State* (Princeton, NJ: Princeton University Press, 2009).
9. For a short account of the respective German case law see Ladeur and Augsberg, *Toleranz—Religion—Recht, supra* note 1 at 105–8.
10. See Waldhoff, *supra* note 4; M. Rohe, *Das islamische Recht*, 2nd edn (Munich: C. H Beck, 2009) at 338 and 390.
11. See Rohe, ibid., at 270.
12. On this problem see T. Asad, *Formations of the Secular: Christianity, Islam, Modernity* (Stanford: Stanford University Press, 2003) at 159 et sqq.
13. On the difficult process of constructing a religious command see Asad, ibid., at 10.
14. See for an overview on the discussion C. Hong & R. Provost, "Introduction: Let Us Compare Mythologies" in this volume.
15. U. Sacksofsky, "Religiöse Freiheit als Gefahr?" (2009) 68 Veröffentlichungen der Vereinigung der Deutschen Staatsrechtslehrer 38.
16. See R. Cover, "Nomos and Narrative," in M. Minor, M. Ryan, and A. Sarat, eds, *Narrative, Violence, and the Law: The Essays of Robert Cover* (Ann Arbor: University of Michigan Press, 1993) 95.
17. For the German debate see K. Schlaich, *Neutralität als verfassungsrechtliches Prinzip* (Tübingen: Mohr Siebeck, 1972) at 135 et sqq; S. Huster, *Die ethische Neutralität des Staates* (Tübingen: Mohr Siebeck, 2002); Ladeur and Augsberg, *Toleranz—Religion—Recht, supra* note 1. For the development of the American model, see, e.g., M. D. McGarvie, *One Nation Under Law: America's Early National Struggles to Separate Church and State* (DeKalb: Northern Illinois University Press, 2004).
18. For an interesting comparison of theory and practice in the handling of this principle, see J. Fox, "Separation of Church and State in Stable Christian Democracies: Fact or Myth?" (2012) 1 Journal of Law, Religion & State 60–94.
19. For a short overview on the situation in France and Greece, see the reports by B. Chelini-Pont and N. Ferchiche and by C. K. Papastathis in J. Martínez-Torrón and W. Cole Durham, Jr., eds, *Religion and the Secular State/La religion et l'État laïque: Interim National Reports/Rapports Nationaux Intermédiaires*, issued for the occasion of the XVIIIth International Congress of Comparative Law, Washington, D.C.—July 2010 (Provo,

UT: International Center for Law and Religious Studies, Brigham Young University, 2010) 299 and 339. For a comparative approach see W. Brugger and M. Karayanni, eds, *Religion in the Public Sphere: A Comparative Analysis of German, Israeli, American and International Law* (Heidelberg: Springer, 2007); A. von Ungern-Sternberg, *Religionsfreiheit in Europa. Die Freiheit individueller Religionsausübung in Großbritannien, Frankreich und Deutschland—ein Vergleich* (Tübingen: Mohr Siebeck, 2008).

20. See E.-W. Böckenförde, "Die Entstehung des Staates als Vorgang der Säkularisation," in *Der säkularisierte Staat* (Munich: Carl Friedrich von Siemens-Stiftung, 2007) 43–72, at 64 et sqq.; I. Augsberg, "Die Entstehung des neutralen Staates als Vorgang der Säkularisation" (2008) 53 Zeitschrift für evangelisches Kirchenrecht 445–55.

21. See J. Casanova, *Public Religions in the Modern World* (Chicago: University of Chicago Press, 1994).

22. See S. L. Carter, *God's Name in Vain: The Wrongs and Rights of Religion in Politics* (New York: Basic Books, 2000) at 72 et sqq.

23. See generally T. M. Scanlon, *The Difficulty of Tolerance: Essays in Political Philosophy* (Cambridge: Cambridge University Press, 2003) at 195 et sqq.

24. See P. Heelas, "Introduction: On Differentiation and Dedifferentiation," in P. Heelas, ed, *Religion, Modernity and Postmodernity* (Oxford: Blackwell, 1998) 1–18, at 1.

25. See G. Vattimo, *Belief* (Stanford: Stanford University Press, 1999) at 38 et sqq; G. Vattimo, *After Christianity* (New York: Columbia University Press, 2002). Critical of Vattimo's supposedly too idealistic understanding of Christianity's relationship to secularization is F. Depoortere, *Christ in Postmodern Philosophy: Gianni Vattimo, René Girard and Slavoj Žižek* (London and New York: T & T Clark International, 2008) at 3 et sqq, especially at 31.

26. See S. Ferrari, "The Christian Roots of the Secular State," in this volume.

27. See J. von Daniels, *Religiöses Recht als Referenz. Jüdisches Recht im rechtswissenschaftlichen Vergleich* (Tübingen: Mohr Siebeck, 2009) at 104 et sqq.

28. See on this distinction S. Last Stone, "Sinaitic and Noahide Law: Legal Pluralism in Jewish Law" (1991) 12 Cardozo Law Review 1157–214.

29. See O. Patterson, *Freedom in the Making of Western Culture* (New York: Basic Books, 1991).

30. On Williams see also T. L. Hall, *Separating Church and State: Roger Williams and Religious Liberty* (Urbana: University of Illinois Press, 1998).

31. See G. Jellinek, "Die Erklärung der Menschen- und Bürgerrechte," in R. Schnur, ed, *Zur Erklärung der Menschen- und Bürgerrechte* (Darmstadt: Wissenschaftliche Buchgesellschaft, 1964) 1–77.

32. For a parallel interpretation of Christianity see also J.-L. Nancy, *Dis-Enclosure: The Deconstruction of Christianity* (New York: Fordham University Press, 2008).

33. For a critique see Q. Skinner, *Foundations of Modern Political Thought* (Cambridge: Cambridge University Press, 1978) at 323. Interestingly, Jellinek's contemporaries (and colleagues and friends) Max Weber and Ernst Troeltsch supported the general idea; see E. Troeltsch, "Die Bedeutung des Protestantismus für die Entstehung der modernen Welt" (1906) 97 Historische Zeitschrift 1–66, at 39.

34. See the "Declaration on Religious Freedom *Dignitatis Humanae*," English translation available online: <http://www.vatican.va/archive/hist_councils/ii_vatican_council/documents/vat-ii_decl_19651207_dignitatis-humanae_en.html>.

35. See E.-W. Böckenförde, "Der säkularisierte Staat. Sein Charakter, seine Rechtfertigung und seine Probleme im 21. Jahrhundert," in *Der säkularisierte Staat, supra* note 20, 11–41, at 22.

36. See Ferrari, *supra* note 26.

37. See L. Rosen, *Law as Culture: An Invitation* (Princeton, NJ and Oxford: Princeton University Press, 2006) at 37 et sqq.

38. See on this development R. Uertz, *Vom Gottesrecht zum Menschenrecht. Das katholische Staatsdenken in Deutschland von der Französischen Revolution bis zum II. Vatikanischen Konzil (1789–1965)* (Paderborn: Schoeningh, 2005).

39. See J. Casanova, *Europas Angst vor der Religion* (Berlin: Berlin University Press, 2009) at 48 et sqq.

40. See R. A. Kahn, "Are Muslims the New Catholics? Europe's Headscarf Laws in Comparative Historical Perspective" (2011) 21 Duke Journal of Comparative & International Law 567–94.
41. Asad, *supra* note 12 at 5.
42. Ibid., at 1 et sqq.
43. See G. Anidjar, *The Jew, the Arab: A History of the Enemy* (Stanford: Stanford University Press, 2003); G. Anidjar, *Semites: Race, Religion, Literature* (Stanford: Stanford University Press, 2007).
44. L. Batnitzky, "From Politics to Law: Modern Jewish Thought and the Invention of Jewish Law" (2009) 26/27 Diné Israel: Studies in Halakhah and Jewish Law 7–44, at 35, with reference to Friedrich Schleiermacher.
45. See Asad, *supra* note 12 at 159 et sqq.
46. Carter, *supra* note 22 at 73.
47. See for a general critique of such historical narratives about the separation of religion and politics S. Last Stone, "Conflicting Visions of Political Space," in this volume.
48. See N. Luhmann, *Soziale Systeme. Grundriß einer allgemeinen Theorie*, 4th edn (Frankfurt/M.: Suhrkamp, 1994) at 624 et sqq; hereunto W. Rasch, *Niklas Luhmann's Modernity: The Paradoxes of Differentiation* (Stanford: Stanford University Press, 2000).
49. See N. Luhmann, *Grundrechte als Institution. Ein Beitrag zur politischen Soziologie* 2nd edn (Berlin: Duncker & Humblot, 1975); hereunto H. Willke, *Stand und Kritik der neueren Grundrechtstheorie. Schritte zu einer normativen Systemtheorie* (Berlin: Duncker & Humblot, 1975) at 21 et sqq and 157 et sqq.
50. See N. Luhmann, *Die Religion der Gesellschaft* (Frankfurt/M.: Suhrkamp, 2000) at 315; K.-H. Ladeur and I. Augsberg, "The Myth of the Neutral State: The Relationship Between State and Religion in the Face of New Challenges" (2007) 8 German Law Journal 143–52.
51. See N. Luhmann, *Funktion der Religion* (Frankfurt/M.: Suhrkamp, 1977) at 227.
52. Carter, *supra* note 22 at 72 and 74.
53. See N. Bolz, *Das konsumistische Manifest* (Munich: Fink, 2002) at 27.
54. See N. Luhmann, "Funktionale Methode und Systemtheorie," in *Soziologische Aufklärung, Bd. 1*, 4th edn (Opladen: Westdeutscher Verlag, 1970) at 31; N. Luhmann, "Funktionale Methode und juristische Entscheidung," in *Ausdifferenzierung des Rechts* (Frankfurt/M.: Suhrkamp, 1981) 273–307.
55. See Luhmann, *Die Religion der Gesellschaft*, *supra* note 50 at 118.
56. See C. Taylor, *A Secular Age* (Cambridge, MA: Belknap Press, 2007) at 3 and 25.
57. See from a sociological point of view Pollack, *supra* note 4 at 28.
58. See Luhmann, *Die Religion der Gesellschaft*, *supra* note 50 at 91.
59. See N. von Kues, "De venatione sapientiae," in L. Gabriel, ed, *N. von Kues, Philosophisch-Theologische Schriften*, Vol. 1 (Wien: Herder, 1964) at 1, 56.
60. Carter, *supra* note 22 at 25.
61. G. A. Lindbeck, *The Nature of Doctrine: Religion and Theology in a Postliberal Age* (Philadelphia: Westminster Press, 1984) at 33.
62. See Luhmann, *Funktion der Religion*, *supra* note 51 at 232.
63. See K.-H. Ladeur, "The Myth of the Neutral State and the Individualization of Religion: The Relationship Between State and Religion in the Face of Fundamentalism" (2009) 30 Cardozo Law Review 2445–471, at 2445.
64. Teubner refers specifically to their book on *Law and Society in Transition: Toward Responsive Law* (New York: Harper, 1978).
65. G. Teubner, "Reflexives Recht. Entwicklungsmodelle des Rechts in vergleichender Perspektive" (1982) 68 Archiv für Rechts- und Sozialphilosophie 13–59; see the English version "Substantive and Reflexive Elements in Modern Law" (1983) 17 Law & Society 239–85. See also the critique of Teubner's concept by N. Luhmann, "Einige Probleme mit „reflexivem Recht"" (1985) 6 Zeitschrift für Rechtssoziologie 1–18.
66. Teubner, "Reflexives Recht," *supra* note 65 at 47.
67. Ibid., at 49.
68. Ibid., at 55.

69. See Luhmann, *Funktion der Religion*, supra note 51.
70. Ibid., at 243 and 245.
71. Teubner, "Substantive and Reflexive Elements in Modern Law," supra note 65 at 273. The original German version of the article (supra note 61) includes the direct quotations from Luhmann's text at 46.
72. See Luhmann, "Einige Probleme mit „reflexivem Recht"," supra note 65, at 18.
73. See R. Bubner, "Zur Dialektik der Toleranz," in R. Forst, ed, *Toleranz im Konflikt. Geschichte, Gehalt und Gegenwart eines umstrittenen Begriffs* (Frankfurt/M.: Campus, 2003) 45–59, at 59.
74. See with more references Ladeur and Augsberg, *Toleranz—Religion—Recht*, supra note 1, at 15 et sqq.
75. See Augsberg, supra note 20, at 453.
76. See for the German debate M. Morlok, *Selbstverständnis als Rechtskriterium* (Tübingen: Mohr Siebeck, 1993) at 78 et sqq; S. Muckel, *Religiöse Freiheit und staatliche Letztentscheidung* (Berlin: Duncker & Humblot, 1997) at 1 et sqq, 27 et sqq and 121 et sqq; A. Isak, *Das Selbstverständnis der Kirchen und Religionsgemeinschaften und seine Bedeutung für die Auslegung des staatlichen Rechts* (Berlin: Duncker & Humblot, 1994).
77. Muckel, ibid.
78. One might see this as a legal restriction of attempts to force religion to turn its "inside out." See for a detailed description of this movement S. Van Praagh, "'Inside Out/Outside In': Coexistence and Cross-Pollination of Religion and State," in this volume.
79. See, e.g., B. Ackerman, "Why Dialogue?" (1989) 86 Journal of Philosophy 5–22, at 5; T. Nagel, "Moral Conflict and Political Legitimacy" (1987) 16 Philosophy & Public Affairs 215–40, at 215.
80. See Carter, supra note 22, at 171.
81. This could be regarded as another aspect of legal limits to the attempt of turning religions "inside out" and the belief of religious citizens "outside in." See hereunto again Van Praagh, supra note 78
82. Weimar Constitution 1919, Article 137 para. 5 WRV; official translation by Christian Tomuschat & David P. Currie, available at <https://www.btg-bestellservice.de/pdf/80201000.pdf>, at 133.
83. See, e.g., 18 *Entscheidungen des Bundesverfassungsgerichts* (Tübingen: Mohr Siebeck, 1965) 385–88, at 386 et sq.
84. See 105 *Entscheidungen des Bundesverwaltungsgerichts* (i.e., the official collection of decisions of the German Federal Administrative Court) (Berlin: Heymanns, 1998) 117–27.
85. See 102 *Entscheidungen des Bundesverfassungsgerichts* (Tübingen: Mohr Siebeck, 2001) 370–400; S. Korioth, "Loyalität im Staatskirchenrecht?," in W. Erbguth et al., eds, *Gedächtnisschrift Jeand'Heur* (Berlin: Duncker & Humblot, 1999) 221–45.
86. See 102 *Entscheidungen des Bundesverfassungsgerichts* (Tübingen: Mohr Siebeck, 2001) 370–400, at 395.
87. See Carter, supra note 22, at 68 et sqq.
88. See *Abortion Rights Mobilization, Inc v Regan*, 544 F Supp 471 (SDNY 1982).
89. See *United States Catholic Conference v Baker*, 885 F 2d 1020 (2d Cir 1989).
90. Carter, supra note 22, at 69.
91. See B. Tibi, *Political Islam, World Politics and Europe: Democratic Peace and Euro-Islam versus Global Jihad* (Abingdon: Routledge, 2007); with regard to the French Muslim community see Bowen, supra note 8.

# 5

# The Distinctiveness of Religious Liberty

VÍCTOR M. MUÑIZ-FRATICELLI

## 1. Introduction

The model of religious liberty that has become dominant in contemporary political theory borrows increasingly from the multicultural paradigm. Religious liberty is presented as an individual right, a subclass of the right to a free individual conscience, while the privileges and exemptions often enjoyed by religious associations—including recognition of the direct claims of authority that they make upon their members—are justified as a necessary or convenient deprivation of the individual rights of the congregants, either as concessions of the state or as products of voluntary agreement among members. The model corresponds to a conception of religious freedom grounded on normative individualism that emerges from Enlightenment liberalism and displaces the previously dominant model of freedom of religion—*libertas ecclesiae* or freedom of the church—that was prevalent in the medieval period. This research benefited from Nouveaux Chercheurs-Professeurs grant from the Fonds Québécois de Recherche sur la Societé et la Culture. Some material in section 2 draws from the second chapter of *The Structure of Pluralism* (Oxford University Press, 2014). I want to thank Larissa Smith and Tara Mrejen for valuable research assistance.[1]

The Enlightenment strain of religious freedom is an important historical achievement, one that enormously reduced persecution and sectarian violence and allowed individuals to conscientiously and sincerely abide by their deepest commitments.[2] But it is neither correct nor desirable to argue from this historical achievement that a respect for individual conscience is all there is to religious liberty, and thereby to exclude the older strain—the concern for institutional autonomy of religious organizations—from our understanding of freedom of religion. It is not correct, first, because the historical development of religious liberty cannot be adequately explained without reference to its medieval antecedents[3]; and second, the current complex of legal institutions that reference religion cannot be understood from a perspective exclusively concerned with individual practitioners.[4] And it is not desirable first, because an account of religious liberty that references only the individual conscience severely distorts, at best, the self-understanding of religious adherents and, at worst, demands (coercively or not) that religious doctrine conform to the moral standards of the state[5]; and second, because in doing so, an important institutional counterweight to state authority is mollified, a consequence that should concern not only liberals but all opponents of arbitrary power.[6]

I will not dwell on the normative desirability of a complex conception of religious freedom—that is, one that sustains that the importance of institutional autonomy is perhaps not on par with individual conscience, but is certainly not excluded by any concern for it. My intention is twofold: first, to explain that the wholesale incorporation of the religious-liberty paradigm into the multicultural paradigm is an institutional, historical, and conceptual mistake, and that it distorts our understanding of the institutions that enshrine religious liberty and underlie our justification of them. The Western paradigm of religious liberty is a complex product of diverse historical conflicts and political traditions and only contingently overlaps the multicultural argument.[7] The purpose of this essay is to differentiate religious liberty from multiculturalism as theoretical categories and to at least identify some of the consequences of this differentiation.

Religious claims have a different historical origin from multicultural claims, and this historical origin marks both the subjects of religious freedom and the types of claims that it endorses. This origin accounts for the different institutional embodiments of religious freedom and how they differ from those of multicultural accommodation. It also conditions the conceptual or formal structure of the claims made in the name of religious freedom as opposed to those made in the name of multicultural accommodation. No one aspect is necessarily dispositive, but together they show that the western idea of freedom of religion is more nuanced and complex than ordinarily presented, even by its defenders, and lies partly outside the spectrum of multicultural philosophy and policy.

## 2. The Multicultural Paradigm

There is an obvious challenge to the distinction between multiculturalism and religious liberty as paradigms for the accommodation of difference: these concepts are ambiguous and contested, and they depend, moreover, on the even more ambiguous and contested concepts of culture and religion.[8] To make a normative distinction between multiculturalism and religious freedom seems to require that one lay out a theory, or at least a comprehensive definition, of the concepts to which they refer. But this, I suspect, cannot be done with regard to these concepts, except perhaps through stipulation and surely not by philosophical or empirical argument. It would be simple to say that religion and culture are paradigmatic examples of "essentially contested concepts" (and I think they are), but this only points to a broader methodological position: even concepts that are essentially contested in the abstract may be less so when addressed in more concrete discursive contexts or with reference to discrete historical strains.[9] The difficulty of providing comprehensive definitions should not preempt the more modest endeavor of distinguishing between the kinds of claims that are made in the name of culture and religion, and clarifying at least the historical, formal, and institutional differences between them. This exercise necessarily involves some idealization, but I think that it is justified both because the history, conceptual structure, and institutional response to multicultural accommodation and religious freedom bear out a distinction and because the distinction is prospectively useful in articulating legal and political responses to these claims. We may not be able to define culture and religion comprehensively or distinguish between them at an abstract level, but we may be able to distinguish between culture as used in multicultural discourse and religion as used in the discourse of religious freedom, and that more narrow and "situated" or "contextualized" definition is useful for explaining the appropriateness of rendering one concept in terms of the other.

Given the extent and complexity of the literature on multiculturalism, I will draw in broad strokes. Multiculturalism refers, on the one hand, to a wide variety of policies adopted mainly (though not exclusively) by postindustrial liberal-democratic states in the last decades of the twentieth century, as they faced growing immigrant communities that seemed more resistant than previous migrants to cultural assimilation. On the other hand, multiculturalism is also "a body of thought in political philosophy about the proper way to respond to cultural and religious diversity," marked by a rejection of strategies of "mere toleration" and by "recognition and positive accommodation of group differences . . . through 'group-differentiated rights'."[10] The political and philosophical dimensions of multiculturalism are closely related, and have informed each other over the years, even enjoying a parallel wax and wane of popularity. While something recognizable as multiculturalism is an inherent part of any imperial enterprise and can thus be projected over thousands of years of human civilization and conquest,[11] multiculturalism as explicit policy only comes into being in the 1970s and 1980s, and only becomes a major theme of self-conscious political theory in the last decade of the twentieth century.[12] Here, I will limit myself to the philosophical literature on multiculturalism and forgo an analysis of historical antecedents or empirical policy comparisons. The history that I take as subject is the history of ideas, because of what it clarifies about the distinctness of religious liberty.

Two motivations spur the emergence and growth of the multicultural literature: the first, just mentioned, is the pursuit of policies of cultural accommodation by several post-industrial liberal-democratic countries who were important recipients of immigration. The second is the publication and subsequent reaction to John Rawls's *A Theory of Justice*, the touchstone of twentieth-century liberal political philosophy.[13] Theorists like Michael Sandel and Charles Taylor—who are rather sloppily labeled as communitarians, a moniker most of them rejected—object to what they perceive to be an impoverished conception of the person in Rawls's work and take issue especially with the perceived lack of attention to the constitutive commitments that individuals draw from their cultural, religious, and other ethical communities.[14] The definitive response from the Rawlsian camp was Will Kymlicka's *Liberalism, Community, and Culture*—definitive because later endorsed by Rawls as representing his position in the so-called liberal-communitarian debate.[15]

Kymlicka understands the problem of multiculturalism in distinctly liberal terms: "[a] liberal democracy's most basic commitment is to the freedom and equality of its individual citizens."[16] Drawing on the different strains of the liberal tradition, he articulates "a distinctively liberal approach to minority rights"[17] that takes an individual's societal culture—one "which provides its members with meaningful ways of life across a full range of human activities, including social, educational, religious, recreational, and economic life"[18]—to provide an interpretive context that gives meaning to the different choices with which a person is confronted in a diverse liberal society. The exercise of freedom presupposes such a context, which is why minority cultures need protection, as the loss of their context of choice would prove traumatic to their members because of its high cost and the offense to members' self-identity and so disable them from exercising their freedom meaningfully, from cultivating the virtues of citizenship.

Multiculturalism is, then, first and foremost, a subsidiary strategy adopted by liberal-democratic societies in order to further the primary or dominant strategy of individual autonomy, and more specifically the autonomy of the individual as a citizen of the liberal-democratic state. Multicultural policies can be constructive or remedial: constructive when the cultural context that is preserved by multicultural policies then forms the basis for a deeper identification with a liberal and egalitarian public culture, made all the richer because it is sustained through an overlapping consensus of reasonable views, many of which are culturally rooted; or remedial when multicultural policies address and attempt to ameliorate historical or structural injustices that undermine the self-respect of members of disadvantaged cultural communities and thus prevent them from standing as equals in a common condition of citizenship.

## 3. The Limits of Multiculturalism

The concern of liberal multiculturalism is an important one, and I do not question that some accommodation for societal cultures is a requirement that arises from a respect for human decency.[19] Yet the point of departure of liberal multiculturalists—the autonomous individual—skews the perception of the groups that are objects of recognition or accommodation. The nature of religious groups—my concern in this essay—is especially distorted by the choice of examples that are fielded when discussing religious accommodation.

As Sarah Song observes, "[m]ost of Kymlicka's examples [of polyethnic rights][20] involve religious practices."[21] The cases she alludes to are "exemption from Sunday closing or animal slaughtering legislation . . . from motorcycle helmet laws and from the official dress-codes of police forces . . . the right to wear the yarmulka during military service . . . [and] exemption from school dress-codes so they can wear the chador."[22] This is triply troubling: first, because the examples confuse the causal connection between religion and ethnicity by selecting examples where religious and ethnic membership overlap considerably though not completely. Ethnic claims for exemption not couched in religious garb are less likely to receive as much deference.[23] There are sound strategic reasons for this. Many constitutions have express constitutional provisions protecting religious freedom (the First Amendment to the United States Constitution, section 2(a) of the *Canadian Charter of Rights and Freedoms*, etc.) while few dispositions elevate cultural protection to the same level. An interesting case is section 27 of the Canadian Charter, which mandates that the instrument "shall be interpreted in a manner consistent with the preservation and enhancement of the multicultural heritage of Canadians." But the courts have not derived independent rights from section 27; they have only used it to reinforce other rights, among them freedom of religion.[24]

Second, the equivalence of religious and multicultural claims exoticizes demands for religious accommodation by highlighting cases where members of the religious group visibly distinguish themselves in ways the dominant culture finds unusual and conspicuous. These distinctions are often "alien" because of cultural or temporal distance, or both, from the dominant society. Consider Hasidic Jews, whose garb marks temporal more than ethnic distance, or the Amish or Hutterites, whose exoticism is both temporal and ethnic (due to their German origins), and extends also to their aversion to technology. The exoticization of religious claims by those intent on bringing them under the multicultural paradigm obscures many claims that are also religious but not ethnically minoritarian: conscientious objection by members of many Christian denominations in Christian countries, self-government by mainline churches including both Roman Catholic and Protestant, tax exemptions for religious denominations, and so on. The Roman Catholic Church was claiming religious liberty against the Holy Roman Emperor as early as the fifth century, when its membership, with few exceptions, was coextensive with the population of the Empire (I return to this case in the next section).

Third, polyethnic rights are "usually intended to promote integration into the larger society, not self-government."[25] But in many cases involving religious freedom, it is precisely self-government that distinguishes religious claims from mere cultural claims. It is not (as I argue below) that religious freedom is only about corporate autonomy for churches—that would be to ignore four centuries of development of the doctrine of freedom of conscience—but rather to say that there remains, as Perry Dane has put it, a "specter of intractability" over the boundaries of religious freedom.[26] And this is not captured by the multicultural paradigm. Indeed, religious groups consistently fall outside multicultural categories. The distinctively collective claims that religious groups make—group rights proper, as opposed to group-differentiated rights—are seen as an exception to the general category of cultural rights, which are ordinarily bestowed on individuals.[27] Certainly some cultural groups make collective claims as well—claims to self-government, external rules limiting non-members' liberty, internal rules respecting members' conduct, and recognition and enforcement of traditional norms—but these are usually constituted as nations, peoples, or quasi-states; Kymlicka's distinction between multiethnic and polyethnic states speaks to this.[28]

In this classification, religious groups do not easily fit: they are associations in the state, not aspirants to territorial self-government, although they often exercise jurisdiction albeit along personal, not territorial, lines. They provide contexts of choice to their members, but do so through explicit structures and positive norms, which may be more or less hierarchical, more or less restrictive, but distinguish members from non-members in a much more formal way than the ambiguous and porous boundaries of culture. Now, not all religious associations are formal to the degree of the Catholic or the Anglican churches, with their various gradations in episcopacy and elaborate systems of canon law. But, almost by definition, religious associations have discrete boundaries which make them qualitatively different things from other "groups" like cultural minorities.

Moreover, the various strains that form the paradigm of religious freedom in the West take the formal character of the religious association as paradigmatic. This may have a normalizing effect on other religious associations, which conform, through various legal mechanisms, to the structure of more formal denominations, and should not thereby be taken as an endorsement of a certain organizational principle.[29] But neither should it obscure the observation that the development of religious liberty in the West has been shaped by the confrontation of an organized church and an organized state. While confrontation also shaped the development of multiculturalism (consider most civil rights movements) it was generally aimed at the recognition of individual dignity or, at most, group-differentiated rights, not institutional autonomy.

## 4. Libertas Ecclesiae

The historical sources of freedom of religion—especially the Abrahamic religions in the West—are twofold, and while each is well known, the importance of one or another source is usually downplayed by advocates of a particular conception of religious liberty. The older source is ultimately traced to the conflict between secular and religious authority dating to the end of the Roman Empire and extending through the so-called twelfth-century Renaissance. The first important expression of it is in Pope Gelasius's letter to Emperor Anastasius in 494: "Two [elements] there are indeed, Imperatur Augustus, by which this world is principally ruled: the consecrated authority of the priests and the royal power . . . For if, in matters pertaining to the realm of public discipline, the religious dignitaries, recognizing that royal power was given to you by divine disposition, for their part obey your laws, lest they seem to neglect and reject your decree in worldly affairs; then with what fervor, I pray you, ought one to obey those who have been charged with celebrating the holy mysteries?"[30] The later medieval world was characterized by many overlapping jurisdictions, of which the pope and the Holy Roman Empire were the most prominent. Their conflict came to a head during the Investitures Conflict in the eleventh century, which was resolved in the Concordat of Worms in 1122. It recognized as a constitutive element of the political order the existence of the Church as an autonomous authority, independent of the Empire. Harold Berman and others have called this principle—*libertas ecclesiae*—one of the foundations of Western freedom, as it established external limits to state authority, namely the authority of another sovereign body.[31] Richard Garnett and others have explained not only the foundational character of this concept, but also its explanatory potential, as it seems to make sense of the latitude given to churches and other religious authorities in liberal-democratic states, even following widespread secularization.[32] A general attitude not to interfere with the internal deliberation of religious bodies and to defer to their judgments in matters concerning religious doctrine and religious law is prevalent, and extends, more concretely, to exemptions from certain anti-discrimination statutes, differences in the application of some provisions of the tax code, and special consideration during bankruptcy and tort proceedings.[33]

Only during the Reformation does religious freedom take an individualist turn, developing into a defense of freedom of conscience, which in turn becomes one of the central pillars of liberalism and the second source of the idea of religious freedom. This was a welcome turn and, as I have said, a definite civilizational achievement. Yet it obscured (although it did not replace) the previous collective or corporate strain in the tradition of religious freedom—the oppositional nature of pope and emperor, church and state.[34] This strain remained in the discourse of religious bodies, but all but disappeared from liberal theory, especially because it seemed difficult to articulate in neutral or, at least, non-fideistic ways. Consider, for instance, Peter Berger's defense of religious freedom: "Religious liberty is not one of many benefits that the state may choose to bestow on its subjects; rather, religious liberty is rooted in the very nature of man and, when the state recognizes it, the state ipso facto bows before a sovereignty that radically transcends every worldly manifestation of power. For the religious believer, of course, this is the sovereignty of God; for the agnostic it will be the sovereignty of that mystery within man that ever thrives to go beyond the given—the mystery of man's freedom."[35] The language of divine sovereignty is excluded (with good reason) from the liberal justification of rights in diverse polities, but nothing is substituted for it except the language of individual freedom of conscience, an altogether different idea. At one level, the appeal to conscience helps us to make a distinction between culture and religion. As Sarah Song observes,

> [t]here is, however, an important sense in which religious belief and cultural attachments may be different. Both may be central components of people's identities, but the tenets of religion, unlike the demands of cultural affiliation, are matters of conscience and obligation and therefore might be viewed as being of more fundamental importance. One might argue that adherence to a religious belief entails accepting the belief as being of fundamental importance and embracing the commitment to live by its dictates, whereas being a member of a minority cultural group does not necessarily entail accepting one's cultural identity as being of fundamental importance or accepting any commitment to live according to whatever norms are associated with cultural identity.[36]

Claims of conscience, as claims of culture, do not necessarily presuppose duties toward an institutional authority, which facilitates the subsumption of religious claims under cultural claims: they are both deeply held, hard to revise, and central to identity. But in the process the distinctive origin of religious freedom is ignored. The theoretical dismissal of the institutional claims of religious authority, which are as important to the development of religious freedom as the later arguments about individual conscience, naturally leads to a mistake: the peculiar authoritative structure of religious practice is analogized to a more passive, more inert background, which provides individuals "with an intelligible context of choice, and a secure sense of identity and belonging."[37]

There are certain aspects to religious practice that are properly classed as religious culture: rituals, artistic imagery, particularly pungent profanities.[38] But this is not all that religion is, and it is far short of what it has been throughout history. Religion is often more active than a background context of choice would imply, and makes emphatic assertions prescribing and proscribing conduct and belief. And it is also often less pervasive than the notion of culture would suggest, adapting practices to cultural context, as in the case of liturgical music or vernacular prayer. That some of these adaptations are strategic choices by religious associations points to the historical reality that much of religion in the West is *organized* religion and that this historical development affects the institutional concern of freedom of religion as well as the formal or conceptual structure of religious versus cultural claims.

## 5. Religion as Practical Authority

From Berger's assertion that religious authority is "a sovereignty that radically transcends every worldly manifestation of power" we can extract a more formal principle: that religion is a practical authority, in a way that culture is not. Now, culture and religion share in the form of practice, which Michael Oakeshott defines "as a set of considerations, manners, uses, observances, customs, standards, canon's maxims, principles, rules, and offices specifying useful procedures or denoting obligations or duties which relate to human actions and utterances."[39] Like religious practices, cultural norms enable individuals to relate to each other as engaged in a common performance. These symbolic "procedures" ground cultural meaning, enabling the context of choice that Kymlicka identifies, and may be conventional norms for participants in cultural interaction. They can therefore fall within the province of practical reason, and even help constitute the authority of certain actors in a determinate social context, while not *themselves* being practical authorities.

There are several ways to approach this distinction. I will first address the institutional differences between culture and religion, again as the concepts are used in multiculturalism and religious freedom, and later discuss the idea of authority itself from a conceptual perspective.

On one hand, neither a culture nor a religion as such can act as a legal, moral, or political agent. In this claim, I have in mind Hobbes's famous definition of collective or corporate personhood, whereby "[a] multitude of men are made *one* person, when they are by one man, or one person, represented so that it be done with the consent of everyone of that multitude in particular. For it is the *unity* of the representer, not the *unity* of the represented, that maketh the person *one*. And it is the representer that beareth the person, and but one person, and *unity* cannot otherwise be understood in multitude."[40] Hobbes defined "systems" as "any numbers of men joined in one interest or in one business"[41] and divided these into "regular" and "irregular" systems. Regular were those that had a representative (according to the definition given above) and could thus act with a discrete and common agency; irregular were leagues, factions, and alliances, but also individuals not formally organized who concurrently engaged in some activity, such as participating in a market. On this spectrum, both religion and culture fall on the irregular end: whatever else they might be, they involve a group of persons engaged in a common practice and sharing a common set of symbols, beliefs and practices, and perhaps interests. But as much as they may be personified in speech—Christendom, world Jewry, the Umma—cultures and religions are not persons in the sense of having discrete and common agency.

By contrast, formally constituted cultural associations and religious associations are, by definition, capable of acting as agents—of being "represented"—and of communicating to their members and to third parties in a determinate voice. The beliefs and practices advocated by these groups may correspond to a greater or lesser degree with the beliefs and practices of the universe of persons who self-identify (or are identified by others) as "belonging" to the respective culture or religion. Of course, the boundaries of cultures or religions are often contested, and often by associations that claim to embody them. The boundaries of cultural or religious associations are more rarely questioned, if only because the conditions of membership often have a positive and formal quality that is missing in the former: they are set down in by-laws and constitutions, and when they are ambiguous and unclear, an affirmative decision on the part of the association's officials will resolve the question, at least in the immediate case. But the difference between the religion and the religious group does not turn on the degree of inclusiveness of members of a certain class. It is a qualitative difference (one might even say an ontological one) and certainly one with profound institutional consequences. To identify a cultural association with the culture it celebrates or a religious organization with the religion to which it alludes is something like a category-mistake. They are simply not the same kind of institution. In brief, neither cultures nor religions as such are associations, although there are associations that are primarily organized around shared cultural or religious practices or traditions, and sometimes (usually unsuccessfully) claim to represent or police the boundaries of the entire tradition.

This is relevant to the difference between multiculturalism and religion because the history of religious freedom developed by reference to distinct corporate institutional agents, not cultural groups, to "regular," not "irregular" systems; this explains the concern of religious freedom for group-rights as well as group-differentiated rights and the relative dismissal of the former by multiculturalists. The institutional focus of multiculturalism, its "social ontology" as it were, does not contemplate institutionalized groups that exercise an authority similar to that of the state.[42] It is fundamentally individualistic in its institutional approach, even when it considers the importance of the cultural group in framing the individual's identity. This is why the attempt to address issues of religious liberty by reference to multicultural categories ultimately creates an incomplete account.

A particularly interesting example of this is the report of the Québec commission to study the problem of "reasonable accommodation" in the province, authored by Gérard Bouchard and Charles Taylor (the latter, especially, an ardent advocate of a robust multiculturalism).[43] The commission's mandate "instructed the Co-Chairs to take stock of accommodation practices related to cultural differences, analyse the attendant issues bearing in mind the experience of other societies, conduct an extensive consultation on this topic, and formulate recommendations aimed at ensuring that accommodation practices conform to Québec's core values ... The analysis of accommodation practices related to culture, including religious life, and of related questions led us to directly question our society's most fundamental sociocultural dimensions."[44] The inclusion of "religious life" as an aspect of "accommodation practices related to culture" would go on to distort the subsequent analysis, even when the authors explicitly acknowledge the corporate dimension of religious liberty. Thus, they describe the separation of church and state "as a reciprocal autonomy. The State is free of all religious tutelage while religious associations are autonomous in their fields of jurisdiction, although they remain subject to the obligation to respect basic human rights and the legislation in force."[45] But the acknowledgement of the autonomy of religious bodies is not brought up again; instead the commissioners come to rely exclusively on "[t]he subjective interpretation of religion ... according to which freedom of religion must be regarded as an aspect of the broader category of freedom of conscience, which seeks to ensure that individuals are free to adopt the religious, spiritual or secular beliefs or fundamental reasons of their choice and that they are not compelled to act contrary to their convictions of conscience."[46] I suspect that the reason for the reduction of religious freedom to only one of its strains—the individualist one that emerges after the Enlightenment—is, to a great degree, derived from the larger frame in which the question is put: as an aspect of deep-seated individual commitments similar to those of culture, which may be granted protection in group-differentiated rights, but which also make unintelligible a more robust conception of institutional religious autonomy.

Final confirmation comes from Kymlicka, who acknowledges (approvingly) that multiculturalism offers little support for the corporate strain of religious freedom and the institutional accommodations demanded in its name: "the real issue ... is the pre-modern legal doctrine of *libertas ecclesiae*, which gives religious organizations broad exemptions from equality rights, not the post-modern Multiculturalism Act, which firmly endorses the norms and principles of equality."[47] His assessment of the relationship between equality and religious autonomy is not entirely correct—to give just one example, while *libertas ecclesiae* has been raised to insulate churches from complaints of discrimination on the basis of gender and sexual orientation, it has also been used to protect immigrants though the provision of sanctuary[48]—but his identification of a premodern idea of religious liberty not comprehended in multicultural discourse is exact. They are different concepts and often pull in different institutional directions.

## 6. Religion as a Normative System

Some concepts in the philosophy of law may further illustrate the difference. Foremost is H. L. A. Hart's distinction between primitive and fully-developed legal systems or, to use Hart's less prescriptive language, the distinction between social structures composed only of primary rules of obligation and a society that adds to these secondary rules of recognition, change, and adjudication; the difference turns on Hart's famous explanation of primary and secondary rules and of legal orders as the union of both systems of rules. Primary rules are rules by which "human beings are required to do or abstain from certain actions, whether they wish to or not."[49] Secondary rules, by contrast, are rules about rules—rules that "specify the ways in which the primary rules may be conclusively ascertained, introduced, eliminated, varied, and the fact of their violation conclusively determined."[50] It is telling that Hart momentarily analogizes a system of primary rules alone to one of "custom," but steps away from the analogy "because [the term custom] often implies that the customary rules are very old and supported with less social pressure than other rules."[51] But the momentary lapse is illustrative of a formal feature of customary and, by extension, cultural systems: they are normative systems, even authoritative systems, in that they prescribe the right ways of doing things, for instance how to spice food, how to greet a family member or a stranger, how to dress for a funeral or a wedding. But what they lack is a way (or, for that matter, an authoritative agent) to identify a practice as part of the culture and discard another, to modify or abolish a cultural practice, or to identify cultural deviance in any manner that is generally acceptable in any but the most contingent way.

Now, Hart writes that "only a small community closely knit by ties of kinship, common sentiment, and belief, and placed in an environment, could live successfully by such a regime of unofficial rules."[52] This may put a strain on the idea that cultural systems are similar to systems of primary rules, as cultural systems do not usually require such close connection and often operate on a much larger scale. Yet that would be too hasty a conclusion. The purpose of invoking Hart's distinction is not to create a perfect equivalence, but to bring out a significant difference between cultural and religious norms. Nonetheless, some trepidation is warranted. The direction of the causal arrow in the relationship between the "close-knittedness" and the "effectiveness" of cultural systems is ambiguous, as one of the functions of such systems is precisely to create the kinds of shared meanings and commitments that create communal ties. These ties are not only ties of obligation, but often generate semiotic and hermeneutic rather than practically normative contexts, and are therefore not so profoundly affected, perhaps, by problems of enforcement. Lastly, none of this undermines the conclusion that cultural systems have no "prescriptive agent" to determine the validity of cultural rules. We may be able to trace the emergence of cultural norms anthropologically, and even genealogically, but this will have no bearing on their normative status; by contrast, tracing the origins of a rule in a more developed legal system in a way that shows it not to be identified by a rule of recognition or sanctioned by a rule of change will rule it out as a rule of the system.

Religious groups, by contrast, are constituted by secondary rules. This is true, in a sense, not only in their worldly structure but also, by projection or analogy, in the origin and form of divine intervention (even the deity, it seems, follows precise conventions when proclaiming the law). Religious belief often makes reference to creeds or canonical literature. Even noncredal religious movements—such as Unitarian Universalism or Reform Judaism—are, despite their self-assertions, at least passively creedal. To give an example, Reform Jews consider the bindingness of any given *mitzvah* (especially ritual *mitzvot*) to be a matter for the individual conscience to decide in light of the principles of Judaism, but that attitude toward halakha excludes from Reform Judaism anyone who believes that all the 613 *mitzvot* are binding on all Jews irrespective of individual conscience; Reform latitudinarianism does not encompass Orthodoxy. In order to identify these authorities, it must have something like a rule of recognition; in order to admit changes to these authorities (though they be changes at the margins, such as the recognition of a binding custom) or even to deny in principle the possibility of amendment, it must have rules of change;[53] in order to determine the content of religious obligation it must have rules of adjudication. This is especially the case for the Abrahamic religions, all of which, in most of their manifestations, have designated a special class of officials to clarify matters of doctrine and decide on religious disputes, and the secondary rules both constitute and guide the authority of these officials. Cultural systems have no equivalent to this, and multiculturalism is ill-equipped to accommodate it, for reasons I will suggest in the last section.

Another complementary way of describing the difference between cultural and religious norms builds on Joseph Raz's account of the justification of authority.[54] Authoritative reasons, Raz writes, are preemptive in that they replace, rather than add to, the reasons that a person has for acting; they can do this because they are predicated on reasons that apply to the person in any case, and the person is more likely to comply with those first-order reasons if she accepts and tries to follow the directives of the authority rather than trying to follow the reasons that apply to her directly. This, Raz says, is the normal way of justifying authority. Now, both religious and cultural claims may be authoritative in that they prescribe certain directives to participants in a practice, and even indicate that adherence to the authoritative claim is more likely to realize the benefits of membership.

But cultural claims are rarely preemptive in the way that religious claims almost always are. One reason is that the bindingness of an authority is institutionally constituted by power-conferring norms of the kinds that religious groups possess, but cultural groups do not. This line of reasoning was evident in Raz's early work, but later waned in importance.[55] It has, however, been recovered by Andrei Marmor, who emphasizes that authority is always situated in an institutional context:

> [t]he essential feature of any practical authority is that to have authority is to have *power*, in the normative sense of the term. A normative power is the ability to introduce a change in the normative relations (viz. rights, obligations, etc.) that obtain between those who are subject to the power under the relevant circumstances. The existence of power, however, is essentially an institutional matter, or so I shall argue here. Only rules or conventions of an institution, or a well structured social practice, can confer power. And this is why authorities are essentially institutional in nature, and the obligation to comply with their directives are institutional obligations.[56]

It is important to observe that some cultural norms are authority-conferring norms. Norms regarding gender relations, or the relation between parents and children, or elder and younger members of society, are precisely of this sort. In this "religion" and "culture" are similar, when considered as sociological or anthropological phenomena: religious practices create the institutional preconditions that confer the normative powers claimed by religious authorities, much like cultural practices create the conditions for the power of various other social institutions. But when considered as historical phenomena, the difference not between culture and religion, but between multiculturalism and religious freedom bears out the implications of the argument about practical authority. Modern multiculturalism has not been advanced by "cultures" but by individuals burdened by restrictions on their cultural practices; in those cases, when there has been a claim to respect the culturally conditioned authority of male parents or elders or male heads of families, the multicultural argument has been derivative and has taken the form of a group-differentiated claim to respect certain institutional practices because of the benefit they confer to individuals, where this benefit is evaluated from the perspective of the liberal-democratic state. This has, quite justifiably, led to significant restrictions on such claims of authority.

The distinction, then, is not categorical, but more subtle, and explained as much by historical claims as by conceptual analysis. The arguments that lead to claims of religious liberty, as I observed above, are of two streams: the older tradition of freedom of the church and the later tradition of freedom of conscience. Freedom of conscience, despite some caveats, has some similarity with multicultural claims, especially as it placed the individual believer or practitioner at the center of inquiry. The tradition of freedom of the church, however, places the religious authority at the center of inquiry. In this earlier tradition, religious liberty has been advanced by religious organizations for whom the religious community is perfectly coextensive with the formal religious association. *Extra ecclesiam nulla salus*: this historical claim—which is still one of the demands of religious groups—grounds an important dimension to religious freedom that finds little parallel in multicultural claims. Multiculturalism may reference cultural practices that constitute practical authorities, but religious freedom—at least in the tradition of freedom of the church—references those authorities directly. In this way, religion (in the religious-freedom paradigm) is a practical authority, while culture (in the multicultural paradigm) is not.

It seems necessary to concede that, at the margins of culture and religion, there is certainly a blurring of the line between systems of primary rules and those of primary and secondary rules. There is much in religious practice that is culturally derived, not of doctrinal or dogmatic origin, although, except in religious communities that are largely coterminous with ethno-cultural communities, the cultural and religious elements seem to operate at different levels, or at least be recognized as distinct. This is perhaps most evident in the

Abrahamic religions, and especially in the most proselytizing of these: charismatic Roman Catholic practice in rural Latin America is quite distinct from that of Tridentine parishes in Italy, but both claim, with much justification, that this variance is due to cultural elements exogenous to orthodoxy and equally consonant with the Magisterium.[57] Similar observations could be made of the differences in manner of dress, family structures, or modes of worship between Muslims in Jordan, India, and Indonesia. Even among the Jewish population, dietary and ritual divergence between the Ashkenazi and Sephardic communities (as opposed, say, to the difference between Karaite and Rabbinical Judaism) are understood to be exogenous to the religious requirements of halakha.[58]

The equation of religion and culture serves neither well, because it misclassifies both. What we see when we treat cultures as if they possessed secondary rules is the calcification of the boundaries of the cultural group and its capture by official arbiters of culture: in essence, the transformation of a culture into a cultural association. In reverse, what we see when we treat religious groups as if they were social structures composed only of primary rules is that we mischaracterize and even undermine the very religions that we may be inclined to protect.

## 7. Conclusion

To sum up, the survey of multiculturalism and religious liberty suggests a distinction in the institutional implications of an approach grounded on one or another paradigm. Some claims made by religious adherents will be of a kind with the claims made in the name of minority cultures, and a common institutional framework may suffice for both. Other claims made in the name of religion, however, cannot be put in multicultural terms. Religious freedom differs from multiculturalism because the sorts of claims made by religious groups that have followed a certain historical trajectory are necessarily collective, proper group-rights, as opposed to collectively derived yet individual group-differentiated rights. The reason is formal: religious liberty has as its object both individual practitioners and believers who can be analogized to members of cultural communities and religious associations that cannot be so analogized. The reason they cannot is that religious associations are the sort of corporate agent that can exercise a will while cultures are not. Drawing on Hobbes' famous classification of "systems" we can categorize religious groups as "regular" systems and cultures as "irregular," where regularity or its lack depends on the groups having "a sovereign representative," one that can self-consciously form its will and communicate it as the will of a collective.[59] But against

Hobbes, religious groups, to again echo Berger, claim an authority—a sovereignty even—that is external from the state. Multicultural claims are defended as a necessary corollary of respect for individual freedom and autonomy, which are the very values that undergird the legitimacy of the liberal state. But religious claims are, in principle, indifferent to these principles; they are, in principle, foundationally and, in practice, at least potentially incompatible with the state legal system, even if they coexist peaceably with it.[60] No such claim can be made about culture, because it does not have the same kind of institutionally authoritative structure. Cultures may be authoritative in some vague way, but are not equally authoritative, because they are incapable of being practical authorities.

But the distortion cuts both ways. The elision between religion and culture in the theory of multiculturalism has also had the effect of transforming the authoritative claims of cultural groups into the claims of cultural authorities. Anne Philips decries that "[i]n the political theorist's understanding of culture, the cultural group then becomes associated with a quasi-legal entity that has historically enjoyed or is now claiming jurisdiction over its members."[61] Cultural groups are not as formal as that, but many religious groups are. Granted, there are exceptions, especially as one moves away from the Western experience, but I would argue that the formal distinction holds across a comparative analysis. It is not a tidy distinction, and there are various ways in which cultural practices may change more or less consciously in certain circumstances and ways in which religious norms are predicated upon unspoken conventions and (often cultural) assumptions. But as an ideal type, I think it helps to clarify important differences.

## Notes

1. See B. Tierney, "Religious Rights: A Historical Perspective," in N. B. Reynolds and W. Cole Durham, eds, *Religious Liberty in Western Thought* (Atlanta: Scholars Press, 1996) 29–57.
2. So, for that matter, is multiculturalism, as a philosophical and political complement to liberalism that seeks to minimize instances of ethnic "violence, cruelty and humiliation" (J. T. Levy, *The Multiculturalism of Fear* [Oxford: Oxford University Press, 2000] at 38), and even to actively protect cultural identity because of "the role that it plays in enabling meaningful individual choice and in supporting self-identity" (W. Kymlicka, *Multicultural Citizenship* [Oxford: Oxford University Press, 1995] at 105).
3. Tierney's work is a useful antidote to this, as is H. Berman, *Law and Revolution: The Formation of the Western Legal Tradition* (Cambridge, MA: Harvard University Press, 1983).
4. R. Garnett, "Two There Are: Understanding the Separation of Church and State," in M. Hogan and L. Frederking, eds, *The American Experiment in Religious Freedom* (Portland: Garaventa Center, 2008) 319–30 at 325.
5. See part one of N. Rosenblum, *Membership and Morals* (Princeton: Princeton University Press, 1998).

6. A. de Tocqueville's observations on the relative position of churches in J. P. Meyer, ed, *Democracy in America*, trans. G. Lawrence (New York: HarperCollins, 1969) at 287–90 and in F. Furet and F. Mélonio, eds, *The Old Regime and the Revolution*, translated by A. Kahan (Chicago: University of Chicago Press, 1998) at 171–75 are an early testament to this.
7. When referring to the paradigm of religious liberty, I do not make universal claims, but limit my account and my examples to religious liberty as developed in the Western legal tradition. There are problems even with delimiting the boundaries of that tradition, but I think they do not affect the historical narrative or theoretical implications of this essay.
8. While multiculturalism and religious liberty are not *only* paradigms for the accommodation of difference, this is the main role that they play in liberal political theory. The stated liberal multiculturalist concern is to show "equal respect to citizens [by] recognizing and accommodating their cultural differences, insofar as it does not impact adversely on the rights and freedoms of others" (J. Maclure, "Multiculturalism and Political Morality" in D. Ivison, ed, *The Ashgate Research Companion to Multiculturalism* [Farnham: Ashgate, 2010] 39–55, 40). And the liberal concern for religious liberty, even if directly motivated by respect for conscience, centrally involves accommodation (M. Nussbaum, *Liberty of Conscience* [New York: Basic Books, 2010] 21). My contention is that liberal accommodation to individual claims of conscience neither exhausts nor fully justifies religious liberty, but rather that acknowledgement of a distinct (and often corporate) authority is also an inherent part of the Western tradition of freedom of religion.
9. W. B. Gallie, "Essentially Contested Concepts" (1956) 56 Proceedings of the Aristotelian Society, n.s. 167–98. Despite the dilution, through overuse, which Gallie's category of "essentially contested concept" has suffered since its introduction, it seems amply justified to resort to it in the case of religion and culture, not least because the original author referred to religion as one of his examples.
10. S. Song, "Multiculturalism" in E. N. Zalta, ed, *The Stanford Encyclopedia of Philosophy*, (Winter 2010 Edition) available online: <http://plato.stanford.edu/archives/win2010/entries/multiculturalism/>.
11. Susanne Hoeber Rudolph makes the provocative distinction that "[a] nation-state is a restricted territory in which there is a presumption or at least an aspiration of congruence between the state and a nation or people. By contrast, an empire is an extended territory comprising a group of states or peoples under the control or at least the suzerainty of a dominant power." "Presidential Address: State Formation in Asia—Prolegomenon to a Comparative Study" (1987) 46:4 Journal of Asian Studies 731–46 at 736.
    The imperial label intuitively fits what Will Kymlicka calls "multination states" more than it does "polyethnic states" (W. Kymlicka, *Multicultural Citizenship, supra* note 2 at 11–26); but the dynamics of governing difference may be more similar than intuition intimates.
12. W. Kymlicka, *Liberalism, Community, and Culture* (Oxford: Oxford University Press, 1989); C. Taylor et al., *Multiculturalism: Examining the Politics of Recognition* (Princeton: Princeton University Press, 1994). There were antecedents, of course, especially in the cultural pluralism of H. Kallen, *Cultural Pluralism and the American Idea* (Philadelphia: University of Pennsylvania Press, 1956).
13. J. Rawls, *A Theory of Justice* (Cambridge, MA: Belknap Press, 1971).
14. M. Sandel, *Liberalism and the Limits of Justice* (Cambridge: Cambridge University Press, 1982); C. Taylor, *Philosophy and the Human Sciences* (Cambridge: Cambridge University Press, 1985).
15. Kymlicka, *Liberalism, Community, and Culture, supra* note 12; J. Rawls, *Political Liberalism* (New York: Columbia University Press, 1993) at 27 n. 29.
16. W. Kymlicka, *Multicultural Citizenship, supra* note 2 at 34.
17. Ibid. at 75.
18. Ibid. at 76.
19. This is especially evident in Jacob Levy's normatively minimalist defense of multiculturalism, *supra* note 2.

20. These Kymlicka defines as "group-specific measures ... intended to help ethnic groups and religious minorities express their cultural particularity and pride without it hampering their success in the economic and political institutions of the dominant society." *Multicultural Citizenship, supra* note 2 at 31.
21. S. Song, Justice, *Gender, and the Politics of Multiculturalism* (Cambridge: Cambridge University Press, 2007) at 65.
22. Kymlicka, *Multicultural Citizenship, supra* note 2 at 31.
23. See L. Sager, "The Free Exercise of Culture: Some Doubts and Distinctions" (2000) 129:4 Daedalus 193–208 at 196; also cited by Song, *Justice, Gender, and the Politics of Multiculturalism, supra* note 21 at 65, n. 49.
24. Tellingly, however, the same court that used section 27 to reinforce freedom of religion also reduced the latter to "the notion of the centrality of individual conscience and the inappropriateness of governmental intervention to compel or to constrain its manifestation" departing from (and indeed distinguishing from prior jurisprudence that supported) an institutional, corporate dimension to religious freedom. *R v Big M Drug Mart Ltd*, [1985] 1 SCR 295, at 115 and 121.
25. Kymlicka, *Multicultural Citizenship, supra* note 2 at 31.
26. P. Dane, "Constitutional Law and Religion," in D. Patterson, ed, *Blackwell Companion to Philosophy of Law and Legal Theory* (Oxford: Wiley-Blackwell, 1999) 113–25 at 128.
27. Kymlicka, *Multicultural Citizenship, supra* note 2 at 40–43; Levy, *Multiculturalism of Fear, supra* note 2 at 137–38; L. Swaine, *The Liberal Conscience* (New York: Columbia University Press, 2008) at 116–17.
28. Kymlicka, *Multicultural Citizenship, supra* note 2 at 11.
29. There may be normative problems with this tendency, but I currently don't have a formed opinion about their desirability. Neither do I claim to extend my account beyond the development of religious freedom and multiculturalism in the West; the dynamic between the state and religious associations is markedly different in other historical contexts.
30. Pope Gelasius I, "Letter to the Emperor Anastasius" in K. F. Morrison et al., eds, *University of Chicago Readings in Western Civilization: The Church in the Roman Empire*, vol. 3 (Chicago: University of Chicago Press, 1986) 112.
31. Berman, *Law and Revolution, supra* note 3 at 87.
32. R. Garnett, "The Freedom of the Church" (2007) 4 Journal of Catholic Social Thought 59–86; R. Garnett, "Religious Liberty, Church Autonomy, and the Structure of Freedom," in J. Witte, Jr. and F. S. Alexander, eds, *Christianity and Human Rights: An Introduction* (Cambridge: Cambridge University Press, 2010) 267–82.
33. P. Dane, "Constitutional Law and Religion," *supra* note 26 at 129.
34. Kymlicka, for instance, situates the origin of religious tolerance in the Wars of Religion, *Multicultural Citizenship, supra* note 2 at 155.
35. P. Berger, "Afterword," in J. D. Hunter and O. Guinness, eds, *Articles of Faith, Articles of Peace* (Washington, DC: Brookings Institution Press, 1990) 114–21 at 118.
36. Song, *Justice, Gender, and the Politics of Multiculturalism, supra* note 21 at 65.
37. Kymlicka, *Multicultural Citizenship, supra* note 2 at 105.
38. On the interjective use of religious language, see, e.g., C. Legaré and A. Bougaief, *L'Empire du sacre Québécois* (Québec: Presses de l'Université du Québec, 1984).
39. M. Oakeshott, *On Human Conduct* (Oxford: Oxford University Press, 1975) at 55.
40. T. Hobbes, in E. Curley, ed, *Leviathan: With Selected Variants from the Latin Edition of 1668*, (Indianapolis: Hackett, 1994) at 104.
41. Ibid. at 146.
42. I borrow the term from P. Pettit, "Groups with Minds of their Own," in F. Schmitt, eds, *Socializing Metaphysics* (New York: Rowman and Littlefield, 2004) 167–93.
43. G. Bouchard and C. Taylor, "Building the Future: A Time for Reconciliation," available online : http://red.pucp.edu.pe/wp-content/uploads/biblioteca/buildingthefuture-GerardBouchardycharlestaylor.pdf
44. Ibid. at 36.
45. Ibid. at 176.

46. Taylor reiterates this view in J. Maclure and C. Taylor, *Laïcité et liberté de conscience* (Montréal: Boréal, 2010) 103–7. It bears noting that this interpretation is the one sanctioned by the Canadian Supreme Court in *Syndicat Northcrest v Amselem*, [2004] 2 SCR 551. I believe that the SCC also incorrectly ignores the *libertas ecclesiae* strain of religious liberty.
47. W. Kymlicka, "Disentangling the Debate" in *Uneasy Partners: Multiculturalism and Rights in Canada* (Waterloo: Wilfrid Laurier University Press, 2007) 137–56 at 147.
48. R. K. Lippert, *Sanctuary, Sovereignty, Sacrifice* (Vancouver: UBC Press, 2005); L. Heredia, "From Prayer to Protest: The Immigrant Rights Movement and the Catholic Church," in Kim Voss and Irene Bloemraad, eds, *Rallying for Immigrant Rights*, (Berkeley: University of California Press, 2011) 101–22.
49. H. L. A. Hart, *The Concept of Law*, 2nd edn (Oxford: Oxford University Press, 1994) at 81.
50. Ibid. at 94.
51. Ibid. at 91.
52. Hart, *The Concept of Law, supra* note 49 at 92.
53. Even a rule that says that "till heaven and earth pass, one jot or one tittle shall in no wise pass from the law, till all be fulfilled" (Matthew 5:18 KJV) is proclaiming a rule of change, albeit a quite restrictive one.
54. J. Raz, *Practical Reason and Norms* (New York: Oxford University Press, 1999).
55. Ibid. at 136.
56. A. Marmor, "The Dilemma of Authority" (2011) 2 Jurisprudence 121–41 at 129–30, available online at <http://ssrn.com/abstract=1593191> (citations omitted).
57. The status of Eastern Catholic churches is an interesting counterexample, but it is, quite vividly, the exception that proves the rule. The special status of Eastern Catholic churches is as organizational as it is cultural. Its origin is found in the realignment of formal ecclesiastical communities that had historically followed rituals other than the Latin but aligned themselves with the Roman pontiff following various crises, most important among them the Great Schism of the eleventh century. Its continued accommodation within the Roman Catholic communion necessitates a special code of canon law and special declarations during ecumenical councils (viz. *Codex Canonum Ecclesiarum Orientalium*, cc 1–6).
58. The permissibility of rice or nuts during Passover is often cited as an example that is allowed to Sephardim but proscribed to Ashkenazim for cultural, not religious reasons, but the halakhic status of custom makes such a blanket judgment complicated.
59. Hobbes, *Leviathan, supra* note 40, chapter 22.
60. I borrow the language of incompatibility from Raz, who argues that "[a]ll legal systems ... are potentially incompatible at least to a certain extent. Since all legal systems claim to be supreme with respect to their subject community, none can acknowledge any claim to supremacy over the same community which may be made by another legal system." *Practical Reason and Norms, supra* note 54 at 152.
61. A. Philips, *Multiculturalism without Culture* (Princeton: Princeton University Press, 2007) at 19. Philips attributes the quasi-legal view to such diverse theorists as Ayelet Shachar, Will Kymlicka, Charles Taylor, and Jacob Levy.

# PART THREE

# NEGOTIATING IDENTITY BETWEEN STATE AND RELIGION

# 6

# "Inside Out/Outside In": Coexistence and Cross-Pollination of Religion and State

SHAUNA VAN PRAAGH

## 1. Introduction: Images of Religion–State Interactions

In late June 2010, in the same week that participants in the Tel Aviv–McGill Seminar first met to discuss work-in-progress, the Anna Ticho House in Jerusalem presented a jewelry exhibit in its small upstairs museum.[1] Israeli women jewelry artists were featured; each had created—among other pieces— exquisite and unique brooches. Three of the brooches, distinctive in their materials and design, evoked images that serve to introduce this chapter's discussion of the interactions between religion and secular state and the intersections of their structures, symbols and spheres.

The first was a miniature landscape, a brooch illustrating a chosen place from a bird's-eye perspective. With its tiny details of sea and sky, the brooch presented a map, its sites and markers fully captured and perfectly presented as a complete picture. The second was a collage of bits of material, including broken pieces of Jerusalem sidewalks and buildings, brought together into an image marked by texture and depth and varied shades of stone. And the third was in the shape of a snail shell, made from recycled tin, turning in on itself in a spiral of never-ending motion and rhythm. The three artists use distinctive styles to make the same thing: a piece of art to be displayed against the backdrop of someone's clothes and body. One offers a whole picture, its elements held in balance for a moment fixed in time. Another invites reflection on the ways in which fragments, each with a unique past and place, are transformed and recycled. Yet another conveys the dynamism of creation and a strong sense of the infinite. So, too, different methods and approaches exist for shaping and exploring religious identity of individuals, communities, and institutions. Against the background scenery of "post-multicultural" secular liberal states, religious identity might be perceived, like the first artist's work, as self-contained and comprehensive. Thus, for example, we might recognize and respect the ways in which membership in distinct religious communities is reflected through the education of children. Alternatively, it might resemble the second design: a multitextured collage of traditions and practices and stories, assembled from a variety of sources and authorities. In this form, the education of children might be understood to be a prime context for mixing religious identities together and reconstructing shared community. Finally, like the third snail-shell-shaped brooch, religious identity always engages in a necessarily never-ending conversation or interplay with the perspectives and preoccupations with which it coexists.

This chapter probes religious claims in a cosmopolitan liberal and secular context through selected stories of state law's recognition of religious identities. Religious and state norms and authority use distinctive, and yet overlapping, ways to define affiliation and ensure allegiance. Both may articulate rules for membership or for self-presentation that carry real weight and are justified by recognized sources. But those rules, whether or not they conflict, can become unintelligible in translation. Rather than hoping for a calm and complete framework within which "legal recognition" of religious identity can be defined and delineated, it may be more realistic and effective to identify and explore temporary sites of interaction and resolution.

Two contemporary examples of a liberal state's engagement, through law, with religious identity are discussed below. In the first, the United Kingdom Supreme Court was asked to determine whether a religious school's internal definition of religious identity constituted impermissible discrimination.[2] In the second, the government of Québec introduced guidelines insisting on the nonreligious nature of publicly funded early childhood education in daycares across the province, by banning the "teaching" of religion to preschoolers.[3]

Through the first example—the "Who is a Jew?" case—we are reminded that numerous ways exist for asking and answering the question of belonging or membership. I suggest that the approach adopted by the majority of the Court, grounded in its application of human rights law, may point to the impossibility of full recognition by the state of a religion's internal definition of identity. That is, religion may be necessarily turned "inside out" within a liberal, cosmopolitan, secular state.

Through the second example—the "Religion in Daycare Directive"—we are reminded that numerous ways exist for living and demonstrating identity in day-to-day life. Here, I suggest that, while today's liberal cosmopolitan state must think hard about the justification for sending messages or making rules that are meant to reflect shared norms of all members of a society, it inevitably insists on trying to define limits to explicitly religious participation in public life. That is, religious individuals may be expected to turn themselves "outside in" by the state to which they belong.

The two examples, one in the form of a judgment and the other in the form of a particular policy, show how state and religion compete and coexist in their messages for, and images of, the individuals who belong to both. Taken together, they present an apparent paradox. On one hand, the judgment insists that external behavior trump internal "being" as a guide to identity; while the existence of religious public schools isn't explicitly questioned, their power to define who walks through the door is. On the other, the directive suggests that external identification and celebration should be submerged to internal faith; accreditation as public early childhood education implies particular limits on a daycare's programs and pedagogy.

Perhaps, however, this is not a paradox that requires resolution. Rather, as suggested in the conclusion to a closer examination of the two examples, the contrast invites observation of the complex cross-pollination between the liberal secular state and orthodox or traditional religion. The two neither dictate to one another, nor exist in purely parallel spheres. Rather, both learn something and even transform themselves just a little, as a result of their ongoing negotiations, conversations, and individual and institutional interactions.

## 2. "Inside Out"—Religious Self-Preservation and "Human Rights"

In 2009, the UK Supreme Court ruled that a school admissions policy based on Jewish identity, as defined by the Office of the Chief Rabbi of the United Hebrew Congregation of the Commonwealth, constituted racial discrimination. Children found to be Jewish—according to the "Jewish mother" test applied by the school and approved by the Chief Rabbi—were given explicit priority for admission. The case found that policy to be contrary to the Race Relations Act 1976 and, in so doing, illustrated the limits that a cosmopolitan liberal state may place on recognition for internal rules regarding religious identity. That is, the Orthodox definition of "Who is a Jew" did not withstand the human rights scrutiny that the Supreme Court was bound to apply.

The multiple judgments at the Supreme Court level in the *(R)E v JFS* case are a rich source for analyzing the interactions between religious rules and definitions, on one hand, and the expectations and norms of law in the form of the United Kingdom's *Race Relations Act*, on the other. In order to introduce the analysis of *JFS*, however, I turn to a similar case decided over ten years earlier in the context of membership in an aboriginal, or First Nations, community in Canada. Both subject internal identity rules, perceived as significant to self-preservation of a people, to judgment by a court obliged to make a decision at the behest of an individual excluded by the rules.

In 1998, the Canadian Human Rights Tribunal was asked whether the definition of Mohawk identity and membership in the Mohawk Nation, as applied by the Mohawk Council, was contrary to the *Canadian Human Rights Act*.[4] Peter Jacobs, the biological son of Black and Jewish parents, had been adopted as a baby by Mohawk parents on the reserve of Kahnawake. Later married to a Mohawk woman, and raising Mohawk children, he was denied membership status and the attached benefits by the Mohawk Council, according to rules of affiliation based on blood quantum. Peter brought a claim against the community to which he felt he belonged, and the Canadian Human Rights Tribunal determined that the blood-based rules did indeed constitute racial discrimination. Further, found the Tribunal, the inclusion of Peter—who adhered to Mohawk traditions and values, spoke the Mohawk language and was raising Mohawk children—would not threaten the community's distinct Mohawk culture.

At the same time, however, the Tribunal explicitly acknowledged the limits of its authority: "Acceptability within a community is a matter for the mind, the soul and the spirit and is not the subject matter of Orders."[5] The Tribunal thus realized that it could not simply declare Peter Jacobs to be Mohawk. The human rights norms embodied in the *Canadian Human Rights Act*, and applicable to the creation and application of Mohawk Nation rules, left no doubt that exclusion on the basis of blood quantum was impermissible racial discrimination. And yet the power to provide the sought-for remedy of acceptance into the Mohawk "nation" lay solely with the community itself.

The *Jacobs* decision provides a telling example of the particular ways in which law "hears" claims related to identity and "speaks" to those claims. An individual hopes that human rights law can provide the status she wants; in return, the law condemns one way of defining that status and suggests its substitution by another. But the definition internally adopted and applied by the Mohawk Council cannot be dictated by human rights orders. Instead, it will be the ongoing disagreements and discussion within the Mohawk community itself that continue to shape identity and membership.

In *Jacobs*, identity is tied to blood quantum—invisible, biological, and fixed. In *JFS*, identity is tied to lineage—invisible, not necessarily as biological given the possibility of conversion and adoption, but also fixed. The general tone of the Supreme Court in *JFS*, as it arrives at a similar conclusion, echoes that of the Canadian Human Rights Tribunal in *Jacobs*. In both cases, internal community norms fail to meet the standards against which they are judged. Yet both judgments demonstrate an important degree of respect for the history and significance of the community in question, and both decision-making bodies accept that it is not within the scope of their power to redefine Mohawk or Jewish identity.

The principal feature of *JFS* that distinguishes it from *Jacobs* is that of religion. The Supreme Court of the United Kingdom finds itself in the terrain of religious authority, trying to avoid any substantive engagement with an Orthodox definition of Jewishness. The special sensitivity of secular courts to inappropriate interference with matters of faith is succinctly captured by the Court's Canadian counterpart in the 2004 Supreme Court of Canada decision in *Syndicat Northcrest v Amselem* in which the Court explains that "the State is in no position to be, nor should it become, the arbiter of religious dogma. Accordingly, courts should avoid judicially interpreting and thus determining, either explicitly or implicitly, the content of a subjective understanding of religious requirement, "obligation," precept, "commandment," custom or ritual. Secular judicial determinations of theological or religious disputes, or of contentious matters of religious doctrine, unjustifiably entangle the court in the affairs of religion.[6] Yet *JFS* forces the UK Court to assess a religious definition in the context of Jewish school admissions policy, and thus, in effect, to confront a rule firmly located within the jurisdiction of a religion. As all nine judges write individual opinions, despite the fact the court "has not welcomed being required to resolve this dispute" (at para 8), they inevitably find themselves pulled in different ways into the "entanglement" of which *Amselem* warns. A closer look at the judgment illustrates the range of approaches taken and the complex messages that emerge.

In *JFS*, a Jewish family sought admission for a child to a leading Jewish school ("JFS") in London. The child was refused on the basis that his mother's conversion to Judaism had not been overseen by an Orthodox rabbi, and thus that he was not a Jew according to the Office of the Chief Rabbi of the United Hebrew Congregation of the Commonwealth. Following the expected denial of admission, the family claimed that the school's policy constituted impermissible discrimination as defined by the Race Relations Act. In the Act, discrimination is defined to include treating one person less favorably than another on "racial grounds," which are in turn defined to include "ethnic origins."[7] According to the claimant, a definition of identity or membership that depends on matrilineal descent necessarily depends on ethnic origins and cannot be used to determine eligibility for admission to a religious school.

Early in the judgment, the Supreme Court noted that admission for the particular child was no longer a live issue, and indeed that the school had articulated modified policies for admission as it waited for the outcome of the challenge. But the issue remained for resolution: did the test applied by an

Orthodox Jewish school distinguish between individuals on permissible religious grounds or on impermissible grounds of ethnic origin? More generally, could a religious community refer to its own internal definitions of belonging for the purposes of selecting students?

The majority of the Supreme Court found that compliance with the Race Relations Act required modification to the school's admission criteria. Five of the nine judges found direct discrimination, two found indirect discrimination, and two found no breach of the Act. Included in the judgments are extensive analyses of the interpretation of "ethnic origins" in relevant case law interpreting the Act, but the focus of the discussion here is on the principal ways in which the judges articulate their responsibilities and reactions vis-à-vis the Jewish matrilineal descent rule regarding Jewish identity, membership in the Jewish religion, and priority for admission to JFS.

One approach is to acknowledge the "religious" foundation and nature of the test for community membership, but then to characterize that same test as impermissibly discriminatory on ethnic grounds. Thus, we find the lead judgment—that of Lord Phillips, President of the Court—starting off with an excerpt from Deuteronomy 7, cited as the source for the "matrilineal test" in Judaism,[8] the principle that bestows Jewish identity on any child of a Jewish mother. For the judges in the majority, this test underscores an emphasis on race, ancestry, and ethnicity. That is, a Jewish child is "a member of the Jewish family and a member of the Jewish religion"[9] at one and the same time; there is no way to separate religious from "ethnic" status. According to Lady Hale, "[t]here is no doubt that the Jewish people are an ethnic group within the meaning of the Race Relations Act 1976,"[10] and this assertion is confirmed and elaborated upon by Lord Mance as he enumerates the characteristics of an "ethnic group . . . a distinct community by virtue of certain characteristics."[11]

The child in question, Lord Kerr points out in his concurring judgment, has mixed ethnic origins, and the absence of Jewish identity as recognized in Orthodoxy is a "defining characteristic of his ethnicity."[12] That is, "[i]t is because of his lack of the requisite feature of Jewishness that he has received less favourable treatment."[13] Finally, Lord Clarke captures the essence of this approach succinctly: "the ethnic element is an essential feature of the religious ground."[14]

For all of these judges, there is significant acknowledgement and respect for the rules internal to Judaism, particularly in its Orthodox form. Indeed, there is a willingness to accept the biblical source of the matrilineal test, although there is considerable confusion over "Jewish" identity, with a tendency to replace it with "Orthodox Jewish" identity when referring to the school's policy and the directive from the Chief Rabbi. But the fact that the religious rule in question looks only at the fact of birth, and thus defines identity on the basis of ancestry, appears to transform it into a membership rule grounded in ethnicity. Denying someone admission to a Jewish school on the basis of his lack of Jewish identity—as defined and interpreted within the religion and embodied in a matrilineal descent rule—constitutes ethnic discrimination for the majority of the Court. This is the case even if the school is explicitly permitted to favor Jewish students. Being Jewish then cannot depend on the Jewishness of your mother; in terms specific to the case at hand, being Jewish for the purposes of going to JFS cannot depend on whether an Orthodox rabbi would consider the student's mother Jewish or not.

As might be expected, the starting point for the judges who refuse to find direct discrimination is significantly different. This is an approach particularly concerned with appropriate interference by courts with religious matters,[15] and there is no explicit reference to the biblical source for what is recognized as a religious rule. As Lord Hope reminds us, the school's application form is "firmly rooted in Orthodox Jewish religious law," whereby "religious status is not dependent on belief, religious practice or on attendance at a synagogue."[16] From an Orthodox perspective, the only relevant question is whether the child's mother is Jewish—either through her own mother or through Orthodox conversion. That is a question about religion, to be decided by religious law,[17] and basing school admissions policy on it does not constitute direct discrimination on the basis of ethnicity.

Although the content and interpretation of that law is not, and cannot be, changed by the courts, the fact that it governs admission to "an educational establishment whose activities are regulated by the law the civil courts must administer"[18] means its scope and consequences must be scrutinized. This shared governance of religious schools explains the finding of indirect discrimination by Lords Hope and Walker, who worry that the disadvantage experienced by children "not of Jewish ethnic origin in the maternal line" is not necessary to achieving the school's aims of providing Jewish education for Jewish children.[19] Here we find the suggestion that the school should have considered its admissions policy more carefully, with some explicit analysis of the connection between its strict application of Orthodox Jewish law and its institutional objectives and mission.

Finally, the dissenting judges, Lords Rodger and Brown, display yet another way of casting the relationship of religion to state law. JFS is a school with a Jewish character "provid[ing] general education within an Orthodox Jewish religious framework."[20] As such, it aims to serve a student population of children whom it understands to be bound by Jewish law and practices—that is, children recognized as Jews by the Orthodox Chief Rabbi. When a Jewish child like the one in this case is refused as "not Jewish," that decision is clearly a religious one, arrived at solely because his mother—a convert within Masorti (Conservative) Judaism—would not be recognized as a Jew in Orthodox Judaism. Lord Rodger illustrates this perspective by confidently disentangling the ethnic and religious grounds so intertwined in the majority judgment: "Faced with a boy whose mother had converted under Orthodox auspices, the governors would have considered him for admission without pausing for a single second to enquire whether he or his mother came from Rome, Brooklyn, Siberia or Buenos Aires, [or] whether she had once been a Roman Catholic or a Muslim. . . ."[21]

This is an approach that tries to reflect a deep sensibility for the religious framework, and its institutions and reference points, at stake in the case. Lord Brown articulates the principal issue as one of the power of a Jewish faith school to give preference to those who are "members of the Jewish religion under Jewish law."[22] In strongly affirming that power, he acknowledges ongoing debate within the Jewish community regarding identity and affiliation, but warns the Court away from intervening in that discussion. According to the dissenting judges, then, the Court confuses status based on descent with discrimination based on ethnicity, and—in doing so—essentially condemns a rule internal to Judaism and demands a change to "3,500 years of Jewish law and teaching."[23]

This albeit abbreviated distillation of the judgment identifies three approaches taken by the Supreme Court to a religious identity principle alleged to constitute racial discrimination. The first, adopted by the majority of the Court, is as follows: if the test relies on ancestry, then it's about race/ethnicity even if it is labeled religious; as a result, it must be replaced by a different "religious" test. The second is a modified version: even if the test is religious, the fact that it applies in the governance of public education means that it must be flexible and self-reflective, and those using it should test its effectiveness and validity in achieving the aims of the school. Finally, in counterpoint, we find the third: given that the test is religious in essence, and applies to a school governed by a religious community and its institutions, it should not be replaced by a state-imposed and state-preferred definition of religious identity.

A major aspect of the judgment that will no doubt be revisited by commentators and even the Court itself is the confusion over ethnicity. In giving a large meaning to the term, such that Jews are defined as an ethnic group and thus protected from discrimination under the Race Relations Act, the Court drives itself toward the conclusion that distinctions based on religious rules by some Jews between Jews is impermissible. Even the Court appears to admit the counter intuitiveness of labeling Jewish schools discriminatory in the application of their state-approved preference for Jewish students. But an extensive analysis of the jurisprudence and interpretation of the Race Relations Act lies beyond the scope of the discussion at hand. Instead, the focus here is on the Court's message as to the appropriate degree of state interference with a religious community's own principles and precepts.[24] Even as the Court insists that it cannot replace religious leaders and sources in determining religious identity and status, there is a good reason for labeling the judgment the "Who is a Jew?" case. The Court does indeed send a strong message as to the right way to assess affiliation and membership in a religious community; that is, the way that complies with the guarantees embodied in human rights legislation.

The *JFS* decision requires that the test for admission to an Orthodox Jewish school in London shift focus. The school can continue to prefer Jewish students as a way to deal with oversubscription, but the determination of Jewish identity must be grounded in "synagogue attendance, Jewish education and/or family communal activity."[25] In other words, Jewish identity, at least for the purposes of JFS and similar schools, must be grounded in believing rather than being, in behavior rather than birth. The dissenting judges characterize the new test as "concocted" and, more seriously, as foreign to Judaism itself in that it "requires a focus (as Christianity does) on outward acts of religious practice and declarations of faith."[26] In the aftermath of the judgment, the case of a Jewish school refusing a child—Jewish through her mother, but not from an observant family and therefore not Jewish under the new "practice" test—illustrates the awkward consequences of imposing a test for religious identity foreign to the religion in question.[27]

By tying membership in a religious community to indicators of internal belief and external observance, the Court offers strong recognition of the individual person of faith. Such recognition coincides precisely with a commitment to the promise and practice of human rights, and the protection human rights instruments provide to individuals whose beliefs or belief-based practices may be threatened by state rules or regulation.[28] At the same time that the Supreme Court of Canada in the *Amselem* case warned of inappropriate entanglement by courts in matters of religious doctrine, it went on to assert what counts as religion: "In essence, religion is about freely and deeply held personal convictions or beliefs connected to an individual's spiritual faith and integrally links to one's self-definition and spiritual fulfillment, the practices of which allow individuals to foster a connection with the divine or with the subject or object of that spiritual faith."[29] These then are the aspects of religion to be afforded ultimate respect, recognition, and protection. And they are the aspects expressed by individuals of faith, rather than imposed or defined by that faith's governing institutions.

It is in this sense that the *JFS* judgment suggests the turning from "inside out." The religious and now impermissible rule for acceptance to an Orthodox Jewish school is grounded in the invisible and unexpressed; the Court-approved and permitted rule is based on the visible and articulated. From the vantage point of the individual as holder of fundamental human rights, the Court cannot help but be suspicious of a rule—however deeply embedded within religious doctrine—that defines membership in a religious community via ancestry rather than demonstrated belief. Instead it puts its trust in the way in which people present themselves to the world, how they show their membership in a faith community. Religious identity requires both individuals, and their community institutions, to turn themselves inside out, to expose their individual commitment to their community mores.

It is true that the Court cannot impose a new definition within Judaism of what it is to be a Jew. Jewish identity in all its complex variations and permutations is beyond the scope and capacity of any contemporary cosmopolitan institution of governance. But it can and does contribute to the ongoing shaping of the relationship between state and religious norms. For some in the Jewish community, the judgment may be read as welcome help for increased openness to diversity within the religion and defiance of Orthodoxy; for others, it stands for unacceptable substitution by the court for religious authority in a sphere (education of children) absolutely crucial to the meaningful future of any religion. Whatever their characterization and reception, the voices of the judges clearly engage and interact with religious authority and community.

While it was never possible to be truly "left alone" as a religious community in a diverse liberal state, this judgment confirms the interaction that necessarily accompanies coexistence. Further, it embodies a form of interaction substantially shaped by a human rights framework responsive to the claims of individuals. That is, the notions of individual choice, expression, and practice fundamental to a human rights framework may inexorably push religious traditions and legal systems in particular directions—even if those traditions understand themselves to be impermeable and resistant to change. Neither a Chief Rabbi nor a Chief Justice can provide a comprehensive definition of who is a Jew in the twenty-first century. But, in their coexistence and the coexistence of the legal universes in which they take on significant responsibility, they speak with each other—literally or metaphorically—on a daily basis.

## 3. "Outside In": Religious Self-Presentation and "Secular Space"

In the example provided by the *JFS* case, internal religious community norms and exclusionary definitions are rendered problematic when subject to human rights based assessment. The sensitive process of selecting students based on membership in a faith community is adjusted in a way that makes external self-identification, whether through proclamation or practice, crucial to religious identity. But it is precisely explicit signs of religious adherence that perturb even identity-cognizant postmulticultural liberal societies. That is, while human rights frameworks pose one kind of challenge to religion, the very mix of multiculturalism—in its intertwining of communities and placing of value on diversity and interaction—poses a related challenge to religious institutions and norms.

As in the JFS context, the governance of public space, including the education of children, may fall to distinct actors, all subject to human rights requirements. Alternatively, the governance of public space may primarily fall within the purview of the state, albeit subject to consideration of, and participation by, a diverse mélange of actors and contexts.[30] When that public space is characterized as "secular," religious self-presentation may be targeted and limited, effectively turning religious individuals and institutions "outside in."[31]

In late 2010, the Québec government introduced a guide to religion in publicly subsidized daycares, to take effect in June 2011.[32] Central to the new directive is the notion that early childhood education in the province must be devoid of any religious teaching or learning. That is, public daycares must be religion-free spaces; according to the Minister of Family, "[w]e clearly say that our daycare services that are subsidized are not places to teach faith."[33] Periods of prayer are explicitly banned, as are regular blessings, religious songs, and the learning of religious texts. Holidays may still be celebrated, and the Directive gives specific examples of permitted symbols (Christmas trees, Easter egg hunts, sukkah building).[34] But no activity that conveys religious belief, dogma, or practice can find a place in early childhood education supported and subsidized by the province.

In addition to explicitly articulating its objective of shielding pre-school age children from the teaching of any particular religion, the Directive aims to support the "intégration des enfants par l'apprentissage du vivre-ensemble."[35] By learning to live together, to learn about each other's cultures against a backdrop of shared nonparochial space, Québec's children are meant to "integrate"—ostensibly as they prepare for public school. Indeed, in the last section of the brief Directive, entitled "Ouverture à la diversité," daycares are allowed and encouraged to provide a program of activities that reflect the cultural and religious diversity of Québec's youngest members.[36]

Immediate reactions in the aftermath of the introduction of the Directive fell along a broad spectrum. On the one hand, the spokesperson for the Muslim Council of Canada immediately speculated as to the possibility of a constitutional challenge; on the other, the Director of Québec's official association of early childhood education centers called for more extensive rules curtailing the religious environment of home-based daycares.[37] The fact that the Directive brings with it a substantial increase in the number of inspectors charged with the responsibility of ensuring compliance foreshadows ongoing conflicts over interpretation and application.[38] However the reality of post-Directive early childhood education in Québec plays itself out, it is clear that publicly funded daycares that characterize themselves as religious, as well as those characterized by significant diversity, are now confronted with the difficult challenge of disentangling "culture" from "religion" and "seeing" from "learning."

This last concern grounds the present analysis of the message and implications of Québec's attempt to guide and govern the education of its very young children. Implicit in the Directive are two basic assumptions, perhaps not surprising in a society like Québec's, where religion—as an institutional presence, an organizing influence, a site of community-building, or a principal source of right and wrong—has largely been left behind. The first is that individuals choose faith. As they prepare for making that choice, they should be protected—at least in an educational setting—from the pressure of prayer or worship. The second assumption is that participation in a diverse society flourishes when children are made aware of difference but not immersed in any religiously normative upbringing. These assumptions combine a human rights perspective on religious identity with a multicultural perspective on religious community. Neither coincides with a vantage point from within the very religious traditions and teachings that coexist and compete with the state in governing the growing up of religious children.

To illustrate this tension, we can imagine a classroom of three year olds in a diverse neighborhood daycare and compare it to the same classroom in a Greek Orthodox community daycare, both subsidized and subject to the new directive. In the first, educators will spend the coming months reviewing past practices that include inviting parents to share stories and symbols of their religious holidays with the children; creating a repertory of December songs taken from a wide range of religious traditions, cultures, and languages; and inviting children to draw or construct Christmas trees and Hanukah menorahs and dreidls. Worried about the line between openness to diversity and teaching of religion, the daycare will err on the side of eradicating the aspects of their programming that might provoke questions related to religious identity and celebration.[39] In the second classroom, crucifixes and icons will be scrutinized, Christmas crèches stored away, and blessings and songs revisited. Even if the daycare community knows that it shares a faith and that the children are all being raised in that faith, its leaders will need to turn religious commitment into cultural manifestation.

It is not obvious that much will change in a substantial way for the day-to-day caring of children in either daycare setting. But the structure within which both daycares have to reconceive and redefine their mission does shift in a significant way. The first daycare may be committed to the greatest possible openness to learning how and why people believe and organize their life cycles in different ways. The Directive warns that learning about religion may imperceptibly and impermissibly transform into being subjected to "dogma." Diverse daycares thus will no doubt shy away from testing the precise contours of acceptable cultural appreciation of religious holidays and artifacts.

For the second daycare, it may be difficult or indeed impossible to extricate the religious character of the daycare from its quotidian operation. It will probably try to pull references to God or Jesus out of any of the stories or songs in the classroom and then will hope that inspectors do not confuse shared religious identity with transmission of faith from teachers to children. The challenge to this daycare is to its very foundation, that is, to the notion of bringing the very young children of a faith community together to learn and grow into responsible citizens not only of that community but also of the society in which they live.

This Directive cannot and does not change the fact that Québec children grow up within many communities and contexts, and that the values and rules they learn illustrate many different paths to meaningful citizenship. What it does do is suggest that being exposed to multiple traditions as a young child is a good thing in theory, but only if none is actually transmitted as a religion. Religious faith and teaching are thus kept invisible in any meaningful way. When religious symbols are apparent, as in the case of crucifixes and Christmas angels, their meaning and the religious foundations they signify are off-bounds. Religion is to be left either unseen or—if visible—not talked about.

This example, like that of *JFS*, offers a snapshot of interaction between state and religion. Here, a liberal, cosmopolitan society that describes itself as secular and diverse sends a strong message to its religious communities and citizens. At least in space defined as public, religious identity as such is to be kept quiet. It can be recognized and shared as cultural affiliation, but its deeply normative and faith-based character is something to engage with on an individual and internal basis. External manifestations of faith, teaching and learning of religious precepts and prayers, have no place in the shared forum of public education. Instead of turning "inside out," this is turning "outside in." The explanations and stories that sustain faith and combine belief with practice are to be packed away, stored within individuals, and relegated to family homes with their doors shut.

The apparent consequence of the human rights–based approach in the *JFS* example was the introduction of a religious-identity test foreign to religion—or at least to the particular religion in question. The apparent consequence of a "multiculturalism" (or "ouverture à la diversité") approach in the Québec daycare directive example is the introduction of a religious-learning model also foreign to religion—or at least any religion that cannot metaphorically replace a Christmas crèche with Santa Claus. Specifically for religious practice at the orthodox end of the spectrum of any faith, it is probably impossible to separate religious learning from other aspects of early childhood education. Further, for a daycare within such an orthodox religious community, the notion of learning about various religions as reflected in the different cultural backgrounds of children in the classroom holds no resonance. The Directive and its implications thus provide a telling illustration of the potential tensions between the normative expectations, principles, and practices of religious tradition on one hand and liberal secular tradition on the other.

The "outside in" dynamic that marks the Directive's imagined model of multicultural learning is similar to that found in an earlier public policy initiative on the part of the Québec government in 2010, and again in 2013 in a multipronged attempt to underscore the secularism and religious neutrality of state institutions. The earlier initiative took the form of a rule that employees and clients of provincial public institutions and services (educational, health, and administrative) would be expected to interact with each other with faces uncovered.[40] Informally referred to as the "niqab bill," the proposed legislation sent a clear message to Muslim women who cover their faces that they could not remain covered in their interactions with others in the public sphere. Whether in teaching or learning, healing or being treated, providing or claiming documents, specific religious identity—as conveyed via a face covering—must remain invisible or internal.

The Bill did not go so far as to require the visibility of individual faces of all participants in public society at all times; indeed, it anticipated appropriate exceptions to the uncovered face principle in the absence of compelling reasons related to safety, communication, or identification. And yet the policy behind the Bill does assume that individuals can choose beliefs and practices in a way that make external symbols and signs irrelevant and unnecessary. While acknowledging a variety of identities and community affiliations, it refused a diversity model that contemplates the full expression of religious faith in everyday interactions in the shared public sphere.[41] Faith is moved from the "outside in."

That Bill was ultimately unsuccessful, but in 2013 a more extensive set of proposals was introduced in Québec, referred to as the *Charter of Quebec Values*.[42] The "outside in" dynamic was even more apparent in the Charter's absolute prohibition of conspicuous signs of religious identity worn by state employees, a policy ostensibly grounded in societal values of secularism and gender equality. The change of government following the 2014 provincial elections in Québec signalled the demise of this proposed *Charter of Québec Values*.

In all of these policy initiatives, we find pressure on the ways in which religious individuals and communities define and understand their own modes of manifestation. The ways in which this particular liberal, secular, cosmopolitan state envisages public services and early childhood education are at odds with the ways in which religious traditions and their adherents understand self-presentation and learning. They may also be at odds with human rights guarantees of freedom of religion, and with some versions of multiculturalism. But the critique leveled at them on these grounds can and will be met by arguments constructed on precisely the same grounds. That is, the policies themselves have been articulated on the basis of equality and diversity. Regardless of whether Québec's version of those notions is right, wrong, or still in flux, religious communities find themselves engaged with the human rights and multiculturalism frameworks embedded in the society in which they participate.[43]

Thus, as the Orthodox Jewish Council for Community Relations of Québec appeared before the Québec National Assembly to weigh in against the "niqab bill," one spokesperson asserted: "The fact that someone belongs to a religion and wears an outward religious sign should not automatically [prevent him or her] from working in the public service or receiving government services ... Religion is a part of the identity of a person ... And it's not for the state to set out what that person should do. The choice should be the citizen's."[44]

The contribution is telling. In it, we find allegiance between the Orthodox Jewish community and the sector of the Muslim community that understands its faith to require the niqab or burka—unsurprising given that both situate themselves at the conservative or traditional end of the range within their respective religions. And we find outward religious signs characterized as crucial aspects of individual identity, chosen and expressed on that basis. Within the religion itself, the perspective on external manifestations of identity might not be grounded in choice but rather in obligation and community affiliation; before the Québec National Assembly, it turns into an argument firmly anchored in the autonomy of the individual as citizen of faith in a society where personal liberty is part of the collective fabric.

Taken together, the daycare directive, the attempted niqab bill, and the *Charter of Quebec Values* proposed in 2013 envisage "secular space" in a way that denies full religious self-presentation. They all have arisen as consequences of ongoing discussion and disagreement over accommodation of cultural difference in Québec and over the appropriate contours of shared governance.[45] We might say that religious identity, communities, and authority have provoked state institutions to respond and shift—in both form and substance—in line with human rights protections and recognition of diversity. In return, those same institutions are in the process of talking back, and of forcing re-engagement with their religious counterparts. The boundaries and limits for explicitly religious participation in this particular society, and in liberal cosmopolitan societies more generally, become one of the primary sites for interaction.[46] As with the *JFS* example, religion and state remind each other that they cannot exist in purely parallel spheres, but rather negotiate their relationship on an ongoing basis.

## 4. (Re)New(ed) Conversations: Cross-Pollination and Coexistence

> "Law, says the priest with a priestly look,
> ...
> Law is my pulpit and my steeple.
> Law, says the judge as he looks down his nose,
> Speaking clearly and most severely,
> ...
> law is The Law."
>
> —W. H. Auden, "Law, Like Love" (1941)[47]

Auden's poem captures the stance and tone most usually associated with religion, on the one hand, and state law, on the other. Law for the priest is the Church and its teaching: the institutions and words that constitute the normative system governing its subjects. For the judge, there seems no need to identify sources and sites: the law is simply "The Law" writ large, governing all and putting religion in its place.

The excerpt from the poem also provides an illustration of the ways in which religious and state authority appear to speak to each other through the *JFS* judgment in England and the public policy directives in Québec. On the one hand, the Court and legislature state "The Law" and, in doing so, step uninvited into the sphere of pulpit and steeple. On the other, religious communities assert "Law" just as confidently and cast a "priestly look" upon the attempts by the state to impose its version. In the contexts explored above, the "judge" insists on the dichotomy between identity and observance, and between sharing and teaching; the "priest" just as insistently denies those divisions. The model is one of necessary disagreement and conflict, of jealously guarded jurisdiction and power.

The examples discussed in this chapter provide lessons that question that picture. In juxtaposing the judgment on admission to religious school with the directive on the religious content of educational daycares, we find a more complex dynamic than that imagined between traditional priest and judge. Indeed, three lessons in particular, drawn from the discussion above, point in directions for better understanding the conversations, cross-pollination, and coexistence of the "law" of both religion and state.[48] The first lesson questions the pride of the priest, the second the power of the judge, and the third the limited dialogue between them.

The first lesson is that traditional or orthodox, official or authoritative rules are not the only or primary way to define religious identity and its expression. Religious communities, their members, and their modes of practice defy capture by the formal norms that may be articulated by their institutions. In the same year that the UK Supreme Court was directly confronted by intra-community pluralism, a sociologist in Paris published the findings from interviews regarding the transmission of Judaism within mixed-faith families. Her conclusion mirrors the observation of one of her subjects: "Etre juif, c'est plein de choses différentes."[49] It is the same conclusion reached by another sociologist, this time studying identity as revealed through Argentine Jewish fiction and illustrating the complex range of ways in which individuals understand themselves to be Jews.[50] The official rules may be the easiest to identify and recognize, but—even before considering the liberal state's potential intervention—knowing what they are doesn't provide a comprehensive appreciation of the reality they purport to govern.

The second lesson is that the state's form of recognition does not dictate or replace the religious rule. As a consequence of a human rights vantage point, state law may appear to define religious identity in a way that contradicts the definition found within a particular religion. But both state and religion make the same mistake if they take a court decision that emphasizes individual belief and practice as a direct modification of a religious norm. The court simply lacks the power to truly change the internal authoritative definition of who belongs to a particular faith. Similarly, in the pursuit of a particular model of social diversity, the state may adopt policy—such as that embodied in the daycare directive—that implies a particular private/public distinction foreign to some religious traditions. But again it would be a mistake to overstate the power of a legislative assembly to dictate profound change within religion itself. The state's language, whether derived from human rights instruments or varied models of multiculturalism, is necessarily limited and artificial in trying to convey who is a Jew or what it feels like to be a curious three year old keen to join in the celebration of religious holidays. There is no way to detail all examples of permissible and impermissible interaction with religion in a daycare classroom, just as there is no way to capture the full picture of membership in a faith community.[51]

Third, the interaction between religious and state law does have bidirectional impact on institutional definitions and perspectives, as well as on individuals. We have seen that religion may be pushed into self-preservation and self-presentation modes that aren't familiar. As suggested above, an "inside out" or "outside in" dynamic can operate, depending on context. But that dynamic need not be understood as a one-way imposition of "The Law" on religious "law" or a signal to religion that it assert itself as "The Law" in direct competition with its state counterpart. Instead it is a dynamic that reveals as much ongoing flux within liberal, cosmopolitan, "post-multicultural," secular states as within the religious communities that combine, connect, and coexist with them. When religious claims compete with liberalism as alternative, comprehensive ways to order private and public life, then both religion and state engage in constant negotiation of the everyday ways in which they can coexist in a mode of respect if not deference.[52] Further, the individuals for whom identities are necessarily multivalent refer simultaneously to multiple frameworks for their sense of self and their interactions with others.[53]

This third lesson, dependent upon the first two, suggests a shift in the focus of "legal" analysis along the lines proffered by critical legal pluralism. Instead of disputing the application of human rights law to the issue in *JFS* or the interpretation of diversity in the daycare directive, we focus on the implications for dialogue, modification, exchange, and the creation of new norms and practices. So, for example, the *JFS* decision may prompt internal discussion within Judaism itself and within the administrative institutions of religious schools across the United Kingdom. On the other hand, the British Equality and Human Rights Commission, and similar institutions, may be prompted to refine the definition of racial discrimination and the consequences of the decision for shared governance of public education.

In Québec, the Directive will prompt early childhood educators and families across the province to think about the objectives of the programs and pedagogy in place for preschool children. Through the Directive, the building of a sukkah is explicitly placed side-by-side with the decoration of a Christmas tree, and that juxtaposition in itself modifies the collective consciousness of the range of religious faiths and symbols that characterize the province's daycare population. Likewise, controversy over the niqab bill effectively put to rest discussion of the hijab, the head covering at the center of ongoing controversy over the past decade in Québec. At least until the more recent proposed prohibition of all religious head coverings for state employees, the hijab effectively became "invisible" and acceptable, just one of the ways in which Québec girls and women present themselves in public. At the same time, religious leaders and institutions are pushed into a self-reflective mode: including acknowledgment that other faiths might become part of early religious education, and the intensity of internal debates over face covering in Islam might be turned up even further.

These constitute examples of the back-and-forth influence of the assumptions, norms, and practices propagated within the law-making communities and institutions of religion and state, or—more specifically—religious tradition and postmulticultural liberalism. In his reaction to the *JFS* litigation, the Head of the Movement for Reform Judaism in the United Kingdom, Rabbi Dr. Tony Bayfield, decries the deflection and distraction represented by the case. While disagreeing strongly with the admissions criteria implemented by JFS and their impact on Jewish families, Rabbi Bayfield points out that the court-defined faith test does not fit Judaism and may not fit many faiths at all today. But for him, the "real issue is how we develop faith schools ... which model and lead the way so that the mainstream of all faiths can contribute values of respect, understanding and social justice."[54] The same might be said in the Québec daycare context. Instead of getting caught up in disputes over the precise contours of religious training for toddlers, the directive might be turned into an invitation to all to learn from religious diversity. That is, the central project—outside the scope of litigation and legislation—turns schools and daycares themselves into sites of law creation and of the development of meaningful principles and practices.

In conclusion, we return to the images captured by the three brooches described at the outset. The comprehensive landscape, whether of religion or state, can be beautifully rendered, precise in its details, deliberately delineated. We learn much from looking at it, considering the reasons for which it is presented in a particular way, and hearing the tales associated with its construction. But the moment we turn away, it necessarily changes and blurs; the next time we look, the landscape may be different even if only in the tiniest detail. The collage captures the mix of sources and stories and influences that give both religious communities and liberal state their fascinating texture, their always-shifting movement, their ability to build and renovate on a never-ending basis. No analytical model in theory or practice can convey what this brooch does in its exquisite juxtaposition of materials and messages.

Finally, we look again at the smooth spiral design of the third. Without the appreciation of normative community conveyed by the first brooch, combined with the second's insistence on mixing and transgressing defined boundaries, the third brooch might appear overly simplistic. But, as a conclusion to consideration of the first two, this final brooch captures the important intertwining of competing, sometimes conflicting, and always coexisting definitions of individual and collective identity. Religion and liberal state, in all their complex richness, develop and change in response to each other. The spiral represents their ongoing cross-pollination and communication, as it constantly turns itself inside out, and outside in.

# Notes

1. The exhibit, "Women's Tales: Four Leading Israeli Jewelers," is featured on the following website: <http://www.imj.org.il/exhibition/Israeli-Jewelers.html>. Thanks go to Shai Lavi and René Provost for their initiative and investment in the joint venture between Tel Aviv and McGill Universities that this collection embodies; to Anthea Vogl, LL.M. (McGill) 2011, for her insightful research assistance; and to the Social Sciences and Humanities Research Council for funding the team research project, "Nouvelles formes de gouvernance," under the leadership of Pierre Noreau. The opportunity to present and discuss this paper, in the form of a Faculty Seminar at Universidad Torcuato di Tella in Buenos Aires, was greatly helpful and appreciated. This paper is dedicated to the memory of the late Louis Henkin, Professor of Human Rights and International Law, who reminded me—in my time as a doctoral candidate at Columbia Law School—about the crucial complexities within, and the important similarities among, the world's religions.
2. *R (on the application of E) v Governing Body of JFS and the Admissions Appeal Panel of JFS and others (United Synagogue)* [2009] UKSC 15 [*JFS*].
3. Famille et Aînés Québec, "Directive: Activités ayant pour objectif l'apprentissage d'une croyance, d'un dogme ou de la pratique d'une religion spécifique dans un centre de la petite enfance ou une garderie subventionnée" (December 2010) [Famille et Aînés Quebéc].
4. *Jacobs & Jacobs and Canadian Human Rights Commission v Mohawk Council of Kahnawake* [1998] CHRD No. 2. TD 3/98 [*Jacobs*].
5. Ibid., at para 38.
6. *Syndicat Northcrest v Amselem*, [2004] 2 SCR 551 at 759.
7. *Race Relations Act* 1976 (UK), section 1.
8. *JFS*, at para 2.
9. Ibid., at para 43.
10. Ibid., at para 67.
11. Ibid., at para 83.
12. Ibid., at para 110.
13. Ibid., at para 122.
14. Ibid., at para 130.
15. Ibid., at para 157.
16. Ibid., at para 182.
17. Ibid., at para 203.
18. Ibid., at para 160.
19. Ibid., at para 205.
20. Ibid., at para 223.
21. Ibid., at para 230.
22. Ibid., at para 249.
23. Ibid., at para 225.
24. See the contribution by Daphna Barak-Erez to this book collection for a complementary discussion of the case, including focused examination of the assumptions and implications of the judgments for religious practices and duties.
25. *JFS*, at para 50.
26. Ibid., at paras 225 and 258.
27. J. Kalmus, "Jewish Girl's King David Place Goes to Non-Jew" *The Jewish Chronicle* (11 June 2010), available online: <http://www.thejc.com/node/32947>. See further S. Mancini, "To Be or Not To Be Jewish: The UK Supreme Court Answers the Question; Judgment of 16 December 2009, *R v The Governing Body of JFS*, 2009 UKSC15" (2010) 6 European Constitutional Law Review 481–502.
28. Further discussions of "religious freedom" within a human rights narrative are provided in this collection by, in particular, Ino Augsberg, Christopher McCrudden, and Daphna Barak-Erez.
29. *Syndicat Northcrest v Amselem* [2004] 2 SCR 551 at 576.

30. For a discussion of coexisting models for governing the education of children of faith: S. Van Praagh, "The Education of Religious Children: Families, Communities and Constitutions" (1999) 47: 3 Buffalo Law Review 1343.
31. See the accompanying papers by, in particular, Yishai Blank and Suzanne Last Stone, for related analysis of the governance of public space.
32. Famille et Aînés Québec, *supra* note 3.
33. K. Dougherty, "Yolande James Says Subsidized Daycares Can't Teach Religion: Have until June 1 to Phase Out Any Religious Teaching or Risk Losing Subsidies" *Montreal Gazette* (17 December 2010).
34. Famille et Aînés Québec, *supra* note 3; I. Peritz, "Quebec Bans Religious Teaching in Publicly Subsidized Daycares" *Globe and Mail* (21 December 2010).
35. Famille et Aînés Québec, *supra* note 3.
36. Ibid.
37. See "Religion Ban in Quebec's Public Daycares Welcomed: Jewish Group Says Government Has Gone Too Far" *CBC* (10 March 2010); and G. Hamilton, "God Tossed from Daycare" *National Post* (18 December 2010).
38. See Fr. R. J. de Souza, "Religion in Retreat" *National Post* (30 December 2010).
39. Indeed, newspaper reports of reactions to the Directive noted that some daycares sought to immediately comply with the new guidelines, worried that they may inadvertently violate them: "At the Friends of Don Bosco daycare centre in Montreal's Rivière-des-Prairies district, this year's Christmas concert omitted the reenactment of the Nativity scene. Instead, the children sang *Twinkle, Twinkle Little Star* and Bing Crosby's *Mele Kalikimaka* Hawaiian Christmas"; I. Peritz, "Quebec Bans Religious Teaching in Publicly Subsidized Daycares" *Globe and Mail* (21 December 2010).
40. Bill: Projet de loi no 94, 2010: Loi établissant les balises encadrant les demandes d'accommodement dans l'Administration gouvernementale et dans certains établissements [*Bill 94*].
41. Van Praagh, "Sharing the Sidewalk" (2010) 8:3 Canadian Diversity 6 and Van Praagh, "Sidewalk Stories: Sites of Encounter and Co-Existence" in S. Azmi, L. Foster & L. Jacobs, eds, *Balancing Competing Rights in a Diverse Society* (Toronto: Irwin Law Books, 2012).
42. Bill 60, *Charter affirming the values of State secularism and religious neutrality and of equality between women and men, and providing a framework for accommodation requests*, 1st Sess, 40th Leg, 2013, Quebec (first reading). [*Charter of Quebec Values*]
43. The constraints and potential of "multiculturalism" as framework with respect to religious norms, are addressed in particular by Michael Karyanni, Victor Muniz-Fraticelli, and Shai Lavi in their contributions to this collection.
44. J. Arnold, "Anti-Veil Bill May Be Unconstitutional, Group Says" *Canadian Jewish News* (28 October 2010), available online: <http://www.cjnews.com/index.php?option=com_content&task=view&id=20135&Itemid=86>.
45. See Commission de consultation sur les pratiques d'accommodement reliées aux différence culturelles, 2007. *Mandat de la commission*, available online: <http://www.accommodements.qc.ca/commission/mandat-en.html>; and *Constitution de la Commission de consultation sur les pratiques d'accommodement reliées aux différence culturelles*, 2007. D. 95–2007, GOQ 2007. IX.1372.
46. For a compelling analysis of normative interactions in the context of governance in Québec, see P. Noreau, "Référents religieux et rapport à la normativité: asymétrie des rapports au droit," in J.-F. Gaudreault-Desbiens, *Le droit, la religion et le raisonnable* (Montréal: Thémis, 2009) 383–423.
47. W. H. Auden, "Law Like Love," in D. Kader and M. Stanford, eds, *Poetry of the Law: From Chaucer to the Present* (Iowa City: University of Iowa Press, 2010) 108.
48. This approach is grounded in critical legal pluralism and, more specifically, draws on insights developed by, inter alia, Sally Engle Merry (see, e.g., "Legal Pluralism" [1988] 22 Law & Society Review 869); R. A. Macdonald (see, e.g., M.-M. Kleinhans and R. A. Macdonald, "What Is a *Critical* Legal Pluralism?" [1997] 12 Canadian Journal of Law & Society 25), and R. Cover (see, e.g., "The Supreme Court, 1982 Term: Foreword: *Nomos and Narrative*," 97 [1983] Harvard Law Review 4).

49. S. Mathieu, *La transmission du judaisme dans les couples mixtes* (Paris: Les Éditions de l'Atelier, 2009).
50. V. Fridman, *Ecriture et identité juive en Argentine dans la transition démocratique* (Paris: Honoré Champion, 2010).
51. For further discussions on this theme, see the chapters by Angela Campbell and Menachem Mautner included in this collection.
52. Silvio Ferrari, in his chapter in this collection, illustrates the varied understandings within the three monotheistic religions for engagement with the secular state. See also the commentary by S. Fish, "Serving Two Masters: Shariah Law and the Secular State" *New York Times* (25 October 2010).
53. As H. Patrick Glenn puts it, "Recognition and acceptance of the diverse legal traditions of the world has implications for the identities which people in the world give themselves... Identity is fuzzier, more multivalent; there are more loyalties claiming your attention": H. P. Glenn, *Legal Traditions of the World*, 3rd edn (New York: Oxford University Press, 2007) at 360. Roderick Macdonald articulates the relevant questions for each one of us, "Who do you think you are?" "How do we know which of our various identities deserve legal recognition? And how do we know when these particular identities should matter?": R. A. Macdonald, *Lessons of Everyday Law* (Montreal: McGill-Queen's, 2002) at 121. See also J. Webber, "Legal Pluralism and Human Agency" (2006) 44 Osgoode Hall Law Journal 167, for a critical discussion of individual agency against a legal pluralist landscape.
54. Rabbi T. Bayfield, "Faith Tests Do Not Fit Judaism" *Times Online* (26 October 2010).

# 7

# Who Is a Jew and the Law

*Between London and Jerusalem*

DAPHNE BARAK-EREZ

## 1. Introduction: Who Is a Jew—Community Membership and the Law

Religious and cultural communities often set criteria regarding membership and affiliation.* These rules are often outside the domain of law, but may get the attention of the legal system when the state is willing to acknowledge community decisions regarding membership in a manner that also has bearing on legal rights.

This chapter assesses the connection between community rules and law in the context of the modern controversies surrounding membership criteria in Jewish communities. Orthodox Jewish tradition has long adhered to the rule of matrilineal lineage as the criterion for inclusion in the Jewish group (and thus one is a Jew only if born to a Jewish mother or converts properly). However, the emergence of other traditions in the modern Jewish world, alongside cultural and national understandings of Judaism, has tended to offer alternatives to this sole criterion.

This controversy has long left its mark on Israeli law where the question of "Who is a Jew" has crucial implications for the application of the Law of Return 1950 ("Law of Return"). This law states that every "Jew" has the right to immigrate to Israel and acquire Israeli citizenship (expressing the historical role of Israel as the homeland of the Jewish people and as a safe haven for every Jew in the world). Surprisingly, the question became a source of controversy in Britain as well following the decision of the Supreme Court on the admissions policy of the Jewish Free School in London.[1] This policy was accused of being discriminatory on the basis of ethnicity as the school declined to accept children who were not born to Jewish mothers, according to the traditional Orthodox criteria.

This chapter compares and contrasts these two case-studies and their respective answers to the question "Who is a Jew?," with a view to further understanding the approach to questions regarding identity raised in legal settings. The definitions applied bear both significant similarities and striking differences simultaneously. In both the British and Israeli contexts, the controversies over who should have the right to determine membership criteria were bitter not only because of their practical consequences, but also due to their symbolic significance. In Britain, the *JFS* decision raised the issue of the autonomy of the Jewish community to shape its borders and rules of inclusion and went far beyond the issue of education for the applicant. Similarly, in Israel, the leading cases did not emerge solely from the need of the parties to receive Israeli citizenship, but rather from the desire to be registered as Jews, and thus receive public recognition as members of the Jewish nation.

## 2. Who Is a Jew in London
### 2.1. British Case Law

As more fully described in the previous chapter, the *JFS* case dealt with the admission policy of a Jewish school in northwest London that did not admit children who were not born to Jewish mothers (either Jewish women by birth or women who converted to Judaism following Orthodox tradition). More specifically, the case concerned the matter of a prospective student, known as M, who was denied admission because his mother's conversion to Judaism failed to meet the comparatively strict standards maintained by Orthodox Judaism. These standards manifest themselves in a long process of study and a requirement to observe many traditional daily practices considered religious duties from the perspective of Orthodox Judaism. While Masorti (Conservative), Reform and Progressive Jews recognized the validity of M's mother's conversion, Orthodox Jews considered it invalid. Since the Jewish traditional doctrine (which Orthodox Judaism strictly follows) adheres to matrilineal lineage (in contrast to merely having Jewish ancestry through the father), M was not considered Jewish by the school.

The majority of the UK Supreme Court (comprising five justices) held that this constituted "direct discrimination" as prohibited by Section 1 of the Race Relations Act 1976,[2] and therefore ruled against the school's decision (whereas two justices thought that the decision constituted "indirect discrimination" and two justices remained in the minority, holding that the school's admissions policy was nondiscriminatory). More concretely, the majority view was that the school had wrongfully distinguished between people based on family origin and accordingly made a distinction based on ethnicity. According to the majority, M was treated differently because of the ancestry of his mother and accordingly fell afoul of the Race Relations Act 1976 (even though the motives for this decision were religious and benign). The justices interpreted the admissions policy, which was based on traditional Jewish rules, as failing to adhere to the prohibition on racial discrimination since it gave weight to ancestry, which has an ethnic component.

The justices were aware of the fact that Judaism is open to conversion and therefore open also to people who are not of ethnic Jewish origin.[3] However, they thought that given the burdensome nature of conversion, which subjects those converted to Judaism to many religious duties in their everyday life (the duties every Orthodox Jew has to follow) the conversion alternative still discriminates against those who were not born Jewish, given that many Jews by birth do not follow these duties in their everyday life.[4] Interestingly, the decision did not address another issue of discrimination that was implied by the facts: the discrimination on the basis of gender against Jewish men who cannot guarantee for their children a "Jewish" status if not married to Jewish women (by birth or by conversion) in comparison to Jewish women.[5]

### 2.2. Criticism: Hidden Cultural Biases

Although the issue of the burden of daily religious practices constitutes a real hurdle in the context of Jewish conversion, the decision of the majority of the Supreme Court, though presented as neutral, was informed by Christian culture. The decision seems to expect that conversion will not necessitate burdensome practical duties. This expectation has been unconsciously inspired by Christian culture. In Christianity, religious affiliation is very much based on the willingness to embrace the faith with less emphasis on daily traditions, especially in comparison to Judaism.[6] By viewing the Jewish requirements as burdensome, the justices in the majority inadvertently relied on their own preconceived notions of justice and fairness regarding religious duties.[7] Taken to the extreme, the Court's decision can be read as implying that the Jewish community should regard as "Jewish" every individual, even with no Jewish ancestry of any form, provided that she is willing to embrace the Jewish faith.[8]

## 3. Who Is a Jew in Jerusalem

### 3.1. Israeli Case Law

The Israeli court decisions regarding the "Who is a Jew?" question were no less controversial or divisive than the British one. The first decision of the Israeli Supreme Court on this question was the *Rufeisen* case,[9] which dealt with the peculiar life story of "Brother Daniel." "Brother Daniel" was born Oswald Rufeisen in 1922 in Poland to a Jewish family. During World War II while being hidden in monasteries, he embraced the Catholic faith and converted to Christianity. In contrast to many other persecuted Jews who decided to return to Judaism when the horrors of the war ended, Rufeisen had become a devout Catholic and even decided to become a Carmelite monk. However he retained a strong attachment to his Jewish ancestry and therefore desired not only to reside in Israel, but to do so by exercising his right as a Jew based on the Law of Return. His fight was symbolic since it was clear that the Government of Israel would let him enter the country and reside in it based on ordinary immigration and citizenship law. At the same time, the Israeli government felt it of great symbolic importance not to recognize Rufeisen as a Jew. Rufeisen brought a petition to the Israeli Supreme Court in its capacity as the High Court of Justice.

The decision of the Court in the *Rufeisen* case was quite intriguing. Formally speaking, Rufeisen could qualify as a Jew, following even the strictest religious standards. He was born to a Jewish mother, and his conversion did not change that, because from the standpoint of the Jewish religion, being Jewish is an immutable trait and an interminable obligation. This case was therefore the mirror, or opposite, of the M decision: while M's case dealt with a Jew who was Jewish culturally yet not religiously (from the Orthodox perspective), Brother Daniel's case dealt with an individual who was a Jew from a religious perspective (even the Orthodox one) yet not Jewish according to common cultural ideas. Eventually, the Israeli Supreme Court dismissed Rufeisen's petition. The majority decision, written by Justice Silberg, who was himself an Orthodox Jew, explained that despite meeting the religious criteria, Rufeisen did not meet the popular understanding of Jewishness. Thus, the court adopted a secular-based criterion for its decision. The minority opinion, written by Justice Cohn, offered another view, based on the subjective conviction of the person.

The next constitutive precedent in this area is the *Shalit* case,[10] which was closer on its facts to the M decision. In this case, the question "Who is a Jew?" concerned the children of a Jewish father and a non-Jewish mother. The mother did not convert to Judaism, but did not practice any other religion. The couple lived in Israel and raised their children as Jews from a social and cultural perspective, and correspondingly identified them as Jews. Since the family resided in Israel there was no question of immigration rights, and the children were granted Israeli citizenship because one of their parents was Israeli (based on ordinary citizenship law). However, since the Israeli registry also mentions the "nationality" of individuals, the Shalit family's request that their children be identified as Jews was denied. The Shalits brought the case to the Israeli Supreme Court, which had to once again face the "Who is a Jew?" question. Like in the *Rufeisen* case, the Court was divided. This time, the petition was accepted based on a minimal majority of five to four. In sharp contrast to the *Rufeisen* case, however, the majority adopted the subjective test, according to which the government has to respect the subjective conviction of the person herself (as long as it is sincere) regarding her identity. Among the dissenting justices, there were essentially two views. Two justices based their decision on the "passive virtue,"[11] that is on the limited role of judicial review in such cases. Accordingly, they refrained from intervening in the decision. The other two justices supported the same result because they thought that Israeli law should follow the old Jewish tradition in this matter, and therefore should adhere to the matrilineal criterion.

The *Shalit* decision did not offer any real closure to the controversy. In addition, it was subject to strong criticism from religious Orthodox political forces, which rejected the subjective test and demanded that Israeli law follow Jewish tradition. As a result, soon after the *Shalit* decision, the Law of Return was amended by the inclusion of a formal definition of the term "Jew."[12] This definition reflects a choice to accept the hegemony of the old religious Orthodox standard, with some adjustments. The term "Jew" is currently defined as "a person who was born of a Jewish mother or has become converted to Judaism and who is not a member of another religion." This definition adopted the religious standard based on the matrilineal test and incorporated the option of following a religious conversion process, but in addition took into account the objection found in the *Rufeisen* case, based on popular understanding of the notion of "non-Jewish Jews." Alongside this Orthodox-inspired narrow definition, and as part of the political compromise, the amendment to the Law of Return included also a new provision that broadened the scope of the law and awarded return rights to people who do not qualify as "Jews" but come from Jewish ancestry. More specifically, according to the amendment, the right of return is awarded to a person who has a Jewish parent or even a Jewish grandparent. Thus, for symbolic purposes, the definition of the legal term "Jew" abides by traditional standards, but for practical purposes the law remained inclusive, and may have even become more inclusive.

## 3.2. Criticism: Different Understandings of Modern Jewish Identity

The main observation regarding the "Who is a Jew" question in Israeli law is the degree to which it reflects anxiety, inner contradictions, and an inability to reach a consensus on these issues in Israeli society. The majority in the *Shalit* case declined to follow the *Rufeisen* precedent, which was shaped, to a large extent, by its unique facts. The Court instead adopted the test that was previously offered by the minority opinion in the *Rufeisen* decision. The legislation on the matter supposedly offered a practical solution, but in fact exacerbated the ongoing controversy. It was based on the halakhic traditional test (of birth to a Jewish mother or conversion), but was supplemented with the secular exception adopted by the *Rufeisen* decision. The willingness of the legislator to give full rights of return even to immediate family relatives of Jews who are not considered Jewish themselves, reflects once again the fact that the formal view of the law does not represent a broad agreement.

It is important to stress that the "Who is a Jew?" debate in Israeli law is not only far from being settled, but is also highly relevant to newer issues in the Israeli public arena. Since the amendment of the Law of Return, the Israeli Supreme Court has started to face new challenges that were not expressly regulated by the text of the law. These new questions address the issue of conversion. The law made it clear that conversion is the decisive act of joining the Jewish group, but it did not specify what forms of conversion would be considered valid for the purposes of the law: the question that was at the heart of the *Jewish Free School* decision. This question has become more pressing since the non-Orthodox movements in Judaism are strong in the Diaspora and thus quite often people who undergo conversion outside Israel and wish to immigrate are not necessarily considered Jewish by Orthodox rabbis. The Israeli Supreme Court decided that it accepts for the purposes of the Law of Return every conversion,[13] but this view is considered controversial by Orthodox rabbis, and more importantly, by the political leaders of the Orthodox public.[14]

Aside from the conversion controversy, the distinction of the amended Law of Return between the relatively narrow definition of the term "Jew" and the practice of also awarding broad citizenship rights to people who do not conform with the strict definition created new questions. It opened the gates of immigration and brought to Israel newcomers who may feel Jewish, but are not treated as such for practical purposes. For example, in Israel, the law of marriage and divorce is based on the religious affiliation of each individual. For Jews, it is the halakha, Jewish religious law. In this context, the law adopted the Orthodox criteria. Accordingly, people who get citizenship and immigration rights according to the Law of Return might not be considered Jewish at a later date for the purpose of family law. The problem is not only theoretical, nor is it relevant to only a small group of newcomers to Israel. The last decades have seen two large waves of immigration to Israel, from the former USSR and from Ethiopia. In the USSR, Jews were often involved in intermarriages and therefore many people of Jewish origin were not necessarily born to Jewish mothers. In Ethiopia, the phenomenon of adopting Christianity has become prevalent in some communities, and hence a whole section of the newcomers consist of relatives of Ethiopian Jews who are not Jewish according to the new definition of the law—not due to their ethnic origin, but rather because they are members of another religion.

## 4. Similarities and Differences between London and Jerusalem

While the British debate on the *Jewish Free School* decision may seem to echo the Israeli case law discussing the question of "Who is a Jew," these comparative case-studies reflect different legal dilemmas.

First and foremost, for the Israeli justices, and in the context of Israeli law in general, the question was which approach best reflected the current stage of development of Jewish civilization and history. In contrast, for the British justices the question was whether the criteria used by the Jewish community (of the school) fit current British (and even more broadly speaking—Western) understandings and ideals of equality. In Israeli law, the interesting and burning question is "Who is a Jew?"[15] In contrast, in British law, the crucial question was "Who is a racist?"[16] The justices accepted the criteria brought to them as given and only assessed them by using external standards of human rights law, as interpreted by them.

Second, the two case-studies differ in their implications on symbolic and practical matters. In Israel, controversies over the "Who is a Jew?" question have been mostly symbolic. Rufeisen could visit Israel and reside in it, but he wanted to do so with the explicit recognition by the Jewish state of his status as a Jew, a symbolic act resisted by the state. Shalit wanted his children to be registered as Jews, although they were entitled to Israeli citizenship anyway. Ultimately, when the Law of Return was amended, following the *Shalit* decision, the amendment adopted a narrow religiously-oriented definition but also included a new provision giving equal rights of return to family members of Jews, who are not considered Jews themselves. Accordingly, the controversy over the definition retained its symbolic nature: the answer to the identity question did not limit the scope of the rights of citizenship under the Law of Return. In contrast, the British decision was also important in terms of its practical results, which were critical for broadening the scope of those eligible to register for the Jewish school.

Third, the two case-studies differ in the degree to which they involve public components. In Israel, the rules debated were at the center of the public sphere and influenced Israel's immigration legislation. In the British case, however, the subject matter for the Court was, at least formally, a decision made by a private school. Accordingly, the Court did not base its decision on those equality standards that apply to public authorities, but rather on legislation that applies to private actors. Formally speaking, the precedent set by the UK Supreme Court applies equally to all religious schools whether they are financially supported by the state or not. Moreover, it is worth noting that, as in other contexts, the division between the public and the private is not that clear. Indeed, the British decision is troubling to the extent that theoretically it is also applicable to private schools that do not aspire to be supported by the state. In other words, the fact that the Jewish Free School was funded by the state could have contributed to the legitimacy of the decision, but it did not form part of its legal basis.[17] Consequently, although one may argue that the existence of public funding justifies a greater level of state intervention with regard to the school's admittance policy, since this was not a justification offered by the court, the decision may equally be applied to an independent school of a minority community not supported by the state. Another perspective on the significance of the decision to public life in Britain, although definitely not part of its legal basis, is its potential to guide judicial review of the practices of other religious communities in Britain. It is probable that the justices addressed the Jewish school, but had other minority groups in their mind as well. In fact, the *Jewish Free School* decision is probably significant for Muslims in Britain no less than it is significant for Jews.

Fourth, the most important distinction between the two case-studies concerns the fact that the first dealt with a Jewish community in the Diaspora, a minority group, whereas the other presented the rules adopted by a majority group in the context of its nation-state. In Israel, the "Who is a Jew?" question was discussed for the purpose of forming the public sphere in a country in which Jews are the hegemonic majority.[18] It was a debate within the majority community between rival understandings of the majority culture. In contrast, the British case dealt with the practices of a religious and cultural minority in Western Europe.[19] In this sense, there is no place for the expectation of similar approaches of judicial review. The Jewish community in Britain adopted criteria that applied only to its own members and therefore had a reasonable expectation that its traditions would be respected, as long as it did not impose them in the public sphere. The decision had an impact on a relatively small and closed group, namely the school community, and opened the door for forced membership to it. By way of contrast, in Israel decisions on the "Who is a Jew?" question have an impact on immigration and citizenship issues, which are part of the public arena.[20]

It is interesting to note that the British decision referenced Israeli case law, but not the classic *Rufeisen* and *Shalit* cases. Rather, it pointed to another decision of the Israeli Supreme Court which intervened in the practice of an Ultra-Orthodox school to maintain separate classes for Jewish girls from Sephardic (mainly Middle Eastern) origin and for Jewish girls from Ashkenazic (European) origin.[21] The Israeli Supreme Court was not deterred from intervening in this segregative policy and considered it to be a case of ethnic discrimination. This decision was cited in concurrence by the UK Supreme Court in the *Jewish Free School* case. However, the comparison is not free from criticism. Sephardic or Ashkenazic identities are solely based on origin and cannot be transformed. This is a very different example from that of Jewish identity, since the latter can be transformed (by going through a conversion process) even according to the most Ultra-Orthodox views.

## 5. Conclusion: Identity Questions and the Limitation

The comparative story unfolded here does not lead to firm conclusions. Its lessons transcend the legal arena. At any rate, it is crucial to distinguish between the existential question for many Jews—what should be the normative view of modern Judaism—and the legal consequences of this question. One may believe that the Jewish group should consider relaxing some of its traditions regarding membership as a matter of cultural and community survival. However, this does not mean, in and of itself, that applying the traditional criteria for affiliation with the Jewish nation should be considered racial discrimination and subject to external legal regulation.

## Notes

* I thank Orna Ben-Naftali for her comments and Ofra Bloch and Naomi Scheinerman for their research assistance. Additional thanks go to the participants in the Faculty Colloquium at Emory Law School, the Legal History and Religion Workshop at the University of Wisconsin, and the Religious Revival in a Post-Multicultural Era conference at McGill Law School for their helpful comments. The chapter was submitted for publication before the author's appointment to the Supreme Court of Israel.
1. *R (on the application of E) (Respondent) v The Governing Body of JFS and the Admissions Appeal Panel of JFS and others (Appellants)* [2009] UKSC 15 [Jewish Free School]. The decision is dealt with in more detail by Shauna Van Praagh, "'Inside Out/Outside In': Coexistence and Cross-Pollination of Religion and State" (in this volume).
2. The *Race Relations Act* 1976 was later replaced by the *Equality Act* 2010, the new general antidiscrimination legislation in England, but its basic features were maintained in the new law.
3. In this sense, the case was a much more complex example in comparison to rules of membership based only on race or ethnicity, as was the case in the famous American case of *Bob Jones University v United States,* 461 US 574 (1983) or in the Canadian case of *Jacobs & Jacobs and Canadian Human Rights Commission v. Mohawk Council of Kahnawake* [1998] CHRD No. 2. TD 3/98 discussed by Van Praagh, *supra* note 1.
4. *Jewish Free School* (Judgment by Lord Phillip), *supra* note 1, at para 42; see also the Judgment by Lord Kerr at para 107.
5. The Jewish rules of group affiliation are the mirror image of the patrilineal test prevalent in many other traditions. Such a patrilineal rule served as the basis for litigation in the case of *Santa Clara Pueblo v Martinez*, 436 US 49 (1978). This case involved a request to

stop the denial of tribal membership to children born to female (not male) tribal members who married outside of the tribe and was presented as a gender discrimination case. The US Supreme Court did not decide the merits of the case and based its decision on the principle of tribal common-law sovereign immunity.
6. The emphasis on faith is very evident in the Gospel according to St. John. See, e.g., John 3:15–18 ("That whosoever believeth in him should not perish, but have eternal life. For God so loved the world, that he gave his only begotten Son, that whosoever believeth in him should not perish, but have everlasting life. For God sent not his Son into the world to condemn the world; but that the world through him might be saved. He that believeth on him is not condemned: but he that believeth not is condemned already, because he hath not believed in the name of the only begotten Son of God").
7. This observation was stated also by Lord Brown, one of the minority justices. See *Jewish Free School, supra* note 1, at para. 258.
8. For additional criticism of the case, see S. Mancini, "To Be or Not To Be Jewish: The UK Supreme Court Answers the Question; Judgment of 16 December 2009, R v The Governing Body of JFS, 2009 UKSC15" (2010) 6 European Constitutional Law Review 481–502.
9. *Rufeisen v Minister of the Interior*, HCJ 72/62, 16 PD 2428 (1962) [Rufeisen].
10. *Shalit v Minister of the Interior*, HCJ 58/68, 23(2) PD 477 (1970) [Shalit].
11. Using the terminology offered by A. M. Bickel. See Bickel, *The Least Dangerous Branch: The Supreme Court at the Bar of Politics*, 2nd edn (New Haven: Yale University Press, 1986) 111–29.
12. The amendment was also applied to issues of registry by the Ministry of Interior, as in *Shalit, supra* note 10, itself.
13. See, e.g., *Rodriguez Toshbeim v Minister of Interior*, HCJ 2597/99, 58(5) PD 412 (2005).
14. For more details on the case law in this area, see G. Sapir, "How Should a Court Deal with a Primary Question that the Legislature Seeks to Avoid? The Israeli Controversy over Who Is a Jew as an Illustration," 39:4 (2006) Vanderbilt Journal of Transnational Law 1233–302.
15. *Rufeisen, supra* note 9 ("The law question at stake is: what is the meaning of the term 'Jew' in the Law of Return 1951, and does it include a Jew that converted his religion and was baptized, but still sees himself and feels like a Jaw, despite his conversion?" at 2432).
16. *Jewish Free School* (Judgment by Lady Hale), *supra* note 1 ("This case is concerned with discrimination on account of 'ethnic origins.' And the main issue is what that means—specifically, do the criteria used by the Jewish Free School to select pupils for the school treat people differently because of their 'ethnic origins'?" at para 54).
17. *Jewish Free School, supra* note 1, at para. 163 ("JFS, formerly the Jewish Free School, is a voluntary aided comprehensive secondary school which is maintained by the local authority, the London Borough of Brent").
18. *Shalit, supra* note 10 ("Although the question at stake is a personal, small and limited one, the dissection concerning it and its ideological elements, requires self-examination and penetrating criticism, with our entity as a people, our meaning as a nation and our Zionist duty in reviving this country" at 493).
19. See *Jewish Free School* (Judgment by Lord Phillip), *supra* note 1 ("In contrast to the law in many countries, where English law forbids direct discrimination it provides no defense of justification. It is not easy to envisage justification for discriminating against a minority racial group. Such discrimination is almost inevitably the result of irrational prejudice or ill-will. But it is possible to envisage circumstances where giving preference to a minority racial group will be justified. Giving preference to cater for the special needs of a minority will not normally involve any prejudice or ill-will towards the majority. Yet a policy which directly favours one racial group will be held to constitute racial discrimination against all who are not members of that group" at para 9).
20. It is important to note that the formal registration as "Jewish" by the Ministry of Interior does not oblige the Israeli Chief Rabbinate in its decisions on registration for marriage and divorce. The Rabbinate has the sole jurisdiction in these matters according to the Rabbinical Courts Law (Marriage and Divorce), 1953.
21. *Noar Kahalach v The Ministry of Education*, HCJ 1067/08 (not published, 9 August 2009); see *Jewish Free School, supra* note 1, at para 159.

# PART FOUR

# WHOSE VOICE? WHICH TRUTH? ONE OR MANY?

# 8

# A Dialogue between a Liberal and an Ultra-Orthodox on the Exclusion of Women from Torah Study

MENACHEM MAUTNER

*What follows is a fictive dialogue between a liberal and an Ultra-Orthodox on the exclusion of women from Torah study.**

*In a typical scholarly text the scholar operates within a certain body of knowledge. The following text is written as a dialogue because that is the appropriate scholarly mode for cases of intercultural encounters in which people located in one culture aim at understanding and evaluating the logic of extant practices in another culture.*

*Being a literary figure, the Ultra-Orthodox party to the dialogue is not your typical member of the Ultra-Orthodox community. He draws on knowledge borrowed from Western academic disciplines such as anthropology and philosophy, as well as on Western literature, in order to make his arguments as accessible and persuasive as possible to his liberal interlocutor, and in the spirit of what John Rawls, in discussing the idea of toleration, calls "reasoning from conjecture": "reason[ing] from what we believe, or conjecture, may be other people's basic doctrines . . . We are not ourselves asserting that ground of toleration but offering it as one they could assert consistent with their comprehensive doctrines."[1]*

*More than a third of the dialogue is devoted to a discussion of the preliminary problems of understanding and normatively evaluating the practices of another culture. These are highly intricate questions that cannot be bypassed in the current age of multiculturalism, yet all too often they have been overlooked.*

*One understanding that emerges from this dialogue is the need to base normative evaluations on a close examination of the facts relevant to the evaluations. Philosophy without thick sociology may prove to be faulty philosophy.*

# 1. Introduction
## 1.1. Problems in Understanding Other Cultures

**Liberal**: Equality is a central value in the political theory of liberalism and the law of the liberal state. One reason why tension arises between the liberal state and non-liberal groups living in it is the discrimination against women in such groups. That is the case with the Ultra-Orthodox group, where women are almost completely excluded from Torah study and consequently also from playing judicial roles and from political leadership. In both law and politics, decisions are made that profoundly affect the lives of women, yet pursuant to their exclusion from Torah study, women are precluded from participation in the processes whereby such decisions are made. Moreover, "Torah study is perceived as the heart of Jewish religious life." A Torah scholar "experiences an encounter with God through the might of God's Torah,"[2] and "makes himself a partner in the cultural and spiritual heritage of Judaism."[3] Why is it, then, that you reserve it only for men and exclude women from it?

**Ultra-Orthodox**: I shall do my best to respond. But I am afraid that you will have difficulty understanding my point of view. Every cross-cultural encounter may give birth to two major problems: the problem of *understanding*, that is, whether people located in one culture are able to understand what goes on in another culture; and the problem of *evaluation*, that is, whether people located in one culture may normatively evaluate practices prevalent in another culture.

**Liberal**: As to understanding, there is a long-standing tradition in Western culture premised on faith in the ability of people living in one culture to grasp the meaning that people of another culture ascribe to their lives. Vico, for example, in a famous passage, expressed astonishment at the fact that human beings invest so much intellectual energy in the study of nature, to the neglect of the study of human society, including "the world of nations."[4] Anthropologists usually work across cultures. The underlying premise of their discipline is that people located in different cultures can "converse" with each other, "translate" each other's meanings, and "understand" them.[5] In the same vein, a series of thinkers have applied Hans-Georg Gadamer's dialogical hermeneutics[6] to cross-cultural encounters,[7] emphasizing the change such encounters may effect in the self-understanding of the parties involved in them.[8]

**Ultra-Orthodox**: And yet, anthropologists, linguists and cultural researchers are well aware of the difficulties involved in attempts to understand foreign cultures and to "translate" the meaning prevalent in one culture into the meaning terms extant in another culture without producing misunderstandings, distortions, and losses,[9] as well as of the difficulties involved in maintaining intercultural communication.[10] Indeed, there have been too many instances in which Western liberals have failed to understand the meaning of cultural practices prevalent in non-liberal groups. It is often the case that liberals attach certain meanings to such practices, while in the groups themselves they bear wholly different meanings. Ironically enough, it is often the case that these latter meanings manifest values that are not only recognized, but even cherished, in the culture of the mainstream liberal society itself, albeit in different social contexts. Here are some examples[11]:

A major campaign has been conducted by Western feminists in recent decades against the practice of female circumcision, common in certain parts of Africa, the Middle East, and Malaysia. The campaign has been premised on the assumption that female circumcision is a way for men to control and suppress female sexuality. However, many writers insist that in many cultural groups this practice embodies meanings having nothing to do with the control of female sexuality by men. Thus, it has been argued that female circumcision is a ritual that signals the transition of a girl from childhood to maturity, and her becoming a member of the social group; that it is a means of demonstrating courage, tenacity, and endurance of pain and suffering on the part of women, particularly in preparation for the pains of labor; that it signals an equalization of women's status to that of men by proving that women can endure severe pain and demonstrate courage; that it signals the initiation of young women into a fraternal bond with older women, while promoting the mutual invigoration of women vis-à-vis men; that it is meant to improve the hygiene and health conditions of women, or their beauty and aesthetics; that it is meant to remove from the female body a remnant of the male sexual organ and thereby complete the transformation of a girl into a woman; that it signifies a commitment to sexual purity, or a shift from sexuality prone to pleasure to sexuality inclined to fertility, or the transition by aging women from involvement in sexual activity to motherly devotion to their family's welfare; that it signals a woman's belonging to a certain religious group, or to a high-status social class within the group.[12]

A second example is veiling, which is often presented by Western feminists as a means for men to control women's bodies and sexuality. Contrarily, Muslim women have argued that girls who veil themselves when they attend school simply wish to acquire the knowledge and professional skills offered by non-Muslim schools, while assuaging their parents' concerns that in doing so they might be corrupted by their classmates' culture. It has also been argued that in the course of Khomeini's revolution in Iran in 1979 middle-class women veiled themselves as a way of identifying with working-class women and symbolizing their opposition to Western cultural imperialism. Likewise, it has been argued that educated Muslim women regard the veil as a symbol of their distinct national and cultural identity, particularly in the context of manifesting opposition to a Western identity. It has also been argued that the veil allows women to be active in arenas controlled by men and thereby expand their autonomy and self-expression.[13]

The third example has to do with Indian women. Western feminists have continuously failed in their attempts to mobilize Indian women on behalf of changing their life conditions. That is because Western feminists have approached Indian women from an individualistic worldview, claiming that certain practices in which Indian women take part in the context of their families constrain their liberty and inhibit their personal self-realization. But in Hindu culture, an individual expresses and realizes his or her humanity not by autonomously determining the contents of his or her life, but by participating in familial and social relations, and by contributing to the economic and spiritual welfare of family and group members. Therefore, Indian women view their contributions to the welfare of others, particularly members of the younger generation in their families, as the most important source of gratification in their lives. It is not only the case, then, that these women do not perceive themselves as victims of injustice; quite to the contrary, they see their contribution as a source of strength, satisfaction, and high social status. Thus, by presenting the Indian family as a site of injury to women, Western feminists have only undermined a central element of meaning in the lives of Indian women.[14]

The fourth example I have in mind has to do with the gap between Western feminists and Third World women. The claim has often been made that middle-class Western feminists fail to understand the problems of Third World women because the lives of the latter are shaped by conditions that are unfamiliar to Western women: slavery, hard physical labor in agriculture, exploitation by multinational corporations, and genocide. Therefore, whereas Western feminists define the condition of Third World women using categories of gender, a true understanding of their condition requires resort to categories of class and race. Likewise, while Western women apply to the condition of Third World women categories that distinguish them as individual persons, Third World women view the sources of their malaise in broader terms: the corrupt political regimes in their countries and the exploitative global political order.[15]

Two famous encounters between Westerners and non-Westerners ended disastrously because the parties held different understandings as to the meaning of the situation in which they were involved. Anthropologist Marshall Sahlins describes the encounter between Captain James Cook and Hawaiian natives in 1779. When Cook and his people landed on the coast of Hawaii, the Hawaiians believed that Cook was an incarnation of the God Lono on his annual return to revive the land's fertility. Cook and his people were therefore given a royal welcome. But for the Hawaiians to enjoy the benefit of their future harvests, according to Hawaiian mythology, their king had to kill the

God Lono. That is exactly what happened a few weeks later: one of the locals took the life of Captain Cook.[16] Historian Barbara Tuchman describes the fall of the Emperor Montezuma and the Aztec state to the Spanish conquistadors headed by Hernan Cortes. When Cortes and his people approached the Aztec capital, Montezuma thought that Cortes was an incarnation of Quetzalcoatl, the founding god of the state who had fallen from glory and departed into the eastern sea and whose return to earth was said to signal the downfall of the empire. Montezuma "convinced himself that the Spaniards were indeed the party of Quetzalcoatl come to register the break-up of his empire and, believing himself doomed, made no effort to avert his fate." This marked the end of the great Aztec empire and the beginning of three centuries of Spanish rule over Mexico.[17]

And in one of the most famous anthropological texts of the second half of the twentieth century, Clifford Geertz said that to understand the piece's plot one "would begin with distinguishing the three unlike frames of interpretation ingredient in the situation, Jewish, Berber, and French, and would then move on to show how (and why) at that time, in that place, their copresence produced a situation in which systematic misunderstanding reduced traditional form to social farce."[18]

In the same vein, I shall argue later that when Susan Moller Okin argues, in her classical article "Feminism and Multiculturalism: Some Tensions,"[19] that Ultra-Orthodox women cannot develop "a sense of equal worth or self-respect," she fails to understand the situation of these women and the conditions in which they live.

**Liberal**: And yet, people from different cultures have been in fruitful contact throughout history, borrowing cultural elements from alien cultures and making them part of their own cultures.[20] Bear in mind also that sometimes the same difficulties arise within the context of a single culture itself (as is manifest in contract law doctrines of mistake and interpretation, which deal with misunderstandings ensuing from interactions in which the parties consciously work to eliminate possible misunderstandings between them).[21]

**Ultra-Orthodox**: I think we can pin down some of the sources of the difficulties.

First, every culture is made of a grid composed of a vast number of categories,[22] as well as of a vast number of practices. It is in cultural categories and practices that cultural meaning lies. But there are no two cultures whose grids of categories overlap, or all of whose practices overlap. "Human societies differ significantly in the ways in which they construct, organize, and control subjective experience."[23] A category or a practice may exist in one culture but be missing from another. "[S]ome cultures have larger inventories of differentiated meanings than others" and thus "more modes of handling meaning."[24]

Therefore, "members of different national communities are not equally likely to draw on the same cultural tools to construct and assess the world that surrounds them."[25] As Ruth Benedict famously has written:

> In culture too we must imagine a great arc on which are ranged the possible interests provided either by the human age-cycle or by the environment or by man's various activities. . . . Its identity as a culture depends upon the selection of some segments of this arc. Every human society everywhere has made such selection in its cultural institutions. Each from the point of view of another ignores fundamentals and exploits irrelevancies. One culture hardly recognizes monetary values; another has made them fundamental in every field of behaviour. . . . One builds an enormous cultural superstructure upon adolescence, one upon death, one upon after-life . . . Aspects of life that seem to us most important have been passed over with small regard by peoples whose cultures, oriented in another direction, have been far from poor.[26]

Second, two cultures may share the same category ("time," "space," "causation," "death," "beauty," "masculinity," "property," etc.) or the same practice, but accord them different meanings. "Shared words do not suffice for shared understandings."[27] And "[t]wo pieces of behavior that look like the same action may have different meanings for those who perform them."[28] Likewise, different cultures may give the same category or practice a different normative meaning. As Wittgenstein writes, "A coronation is the picture of pomp and dignity. . . . But in different surroundings gold is the cheapest of metals, its gleam is thought vulgar. There the fabric of the robe is cheap to produce. A crown is a parody of a respectable hat."[29]

Third, even when cultures recognize the same categories and practices, they may differ in the importance they accord to the meanings embedded in them: "socially available meaning systems privilege the importance and symbolic weight of some distinctions over others."[30] "A field of human behaviour may be ignored in some societies until it barely exists; it may even be in some cases unimagined. Or it may almost monopolize the whole organized behaviour of the society."[31] In a comparative study of schemes of evaluation, it has been found that "cultural repertoires prevailing in the United States make market references more readily available to situations, whereas the French repertoires make principles of civic solidarity more salient and enable a larger number of French people to resort to them across situations, and often precisely in situations in which Americans would resort to market principles. However, this does not mean that market criteria of evaluation are absent from the French repertoires, but only that they are used in a small number of situations by a smaller number of people."[32] Likewise, it has also been found that the category of sexual harassment is more salient to American understandings of the ethics of the workplace than to French.[33]

Fourth, understanding the meaning of cultural categories and practices necessitates an understanding of the contexts of their existence. These contexts may be both spatial ("any principle or value is colored by the others with which it is conjoined")[34] and historical, and they imbue cultural categories and practices with their distinct meaning and standing in a culture. Therefore, taking a category or a practice merely on its own terms may result in distortion and loss of meaning. Yet no two cultures are identical in the spatial and historical contexts of their categories and practices.[35]

Fifth, every culture is composed of some "infrastructural categories."[36] Categories of this type have three dimensions: (1) weight, that is, they play a central role in determining the way people living in a culture perceive themselves, their place in the universe and in society, their relations with others (including the state), the purposes of their lives, and so on; (2) breadth, that is, infrastructural categories influence and inform a wide range of the activities and events that transpire in the lives of those belonging to a culture; and (3) density, that is, these categories are rich in content (borrowed from other categories of the culture). Categories such as "democracy," "liberalism," "religion," "nationalism," or "childhood" are obvious examples. Cultures often differ in the composition of their infrastructural categories.

Because of these differences between cultures, it is often said that cultures are incommensurable.[37] And since meaning-giving processes are premised on a "fusion of horizons" between mind categories and meaning-bearing objects,[38] and since mind categories are always constituted by a culture (we "think through culture," as Richard A. Shweder puts it),[39] it is clear that any simplistic attempt to fuse the categories and practices of one culture with those of another will inevitably result in misunderstandings, distortions, and losses.

## 1.2. The Problems of Cross-Cultural Normativity

**Liberal**: What is the purpose of our dialogue? Why are we conducting this discussion? One purpose is enlightenment, namely an attempt on my part to understand, via your good services, the internal point of view of your culture with regard to the practice of Torah study. But there is a second, normative dimension to this dialogue, which we should not overlook: my interest in your culture is not merely intellectual; I come to this dialogue with certain normative prior judgments about your culture which I wish to test, and which, following this dialogue, I may have to update.[40] The problems you have just identified pertain to the first dimension of our dialogue. Yet, once we acknowledge that our dialogue involves normative judgment as well, it adds new problems to the problem of understanding that we have thus far discussed. These have to do with the problem of normative relativism. Normative relativism holds that "because all standards are culturally constituted, there are no available *trans*cultural standards by which different cultures might be judged on a scale of merit or worth. Moreover, given the fact of cultural variability, there are no universally acceptable *pan*cultural standards by which they might be judged on such a scale.... [S]ince there are no universally acceptable evaluative standards... judgments such as good or bad, right or wrong, normal or abnormal... must be relative to the variable standards of the cultures that produce them."[41] Philosophers sometime refer to this position as "metaethical moral relativism"[42] or as "philosophical relativism."[43]

So, should we adhere to metaethical moral relativism and philosophical relativism? Is it really the case that I can't pass judgment on the practice of an alien cultural group that I find troubling? I don't think so. I think there are two strategies to which we may resort

First, since there is no such thing as "a view from nowhere," I think I am entitled to view your culture from the perspective of my own culture and say that I find what I see unacceptable.[44] Otherwise, much of the value of a Gadamerian dialogue as a means to enlightenment and self-scrutiny is undermined.[45] This seems to be, implicitly, Charles Taylor's position in his pioneering article "Multiculturalism and 'The Politics of Recognition'."[46] On the one hand, Taylor strongly cautions against viewing liberalism as a "[neutral] meeting ground for all cultures." Liberalism is "the political expression of one range of cultures, and quite incompatible with other ranges," he writes. "[L]iberalism can't and shouldn't claim complete cultural neutrality. Liberalism is also a fighting creed."[47] On the other hand, the particularity of liberalism is not a good enough reason for Taylor to abstain from dialogue between Western liberal culture and other cultures. We need to maintain a sense of our own limited part in the whole human story, he writes, and to presume that human cultures that have animated entire societies over some considerable length of time have something important to say to us. And at the end of our encounter with an alien culture, we may find in it things that deserve "our admiration and respect" side by side with things "we have to abhor and reject."[48]

Importantly, in arguing that we may find in an alien culture elements deserving of "our admiration and respect" together with elements that "we have to abhor and reject," Taylor implicitly holds that it would be wrong to take a judgmental stance towards cultures in their entirety ("French culture," "Muslim culture," etc.). Rather, every culture is composed of a vast number of categories and practices, and when we normatively appraise cultures we need to deal with *specific* cultural elements and practices. Indeed, though liberals may have a negative view of the treatment of women by Ultra-Orthodox culture, they may still find that their views on the exploitation of women by the pornography industry overlap with the position of Ultra-Orthodox culture on that topic. Likewise, a liberal may well admire the central place that Ultra-Orthodox culture accords to the task of educating the younger generation, while disagreeing with the contents of that education.

We need to supplement Taylor's stance on cross-cultural dialogue with the virtues that must be displayed and nurtured in conducting a dialogue, according to Gadamer. Conducting a dialogue, maintains Gadamer, "requires that one does not try to argue the other person down but that one really considers the weight of the other's opinion."[49] The purpose of a dialogue "consists not in trying to discover the weakness of what is said, but in bringing out its real strength. It is not the art of arguing (which can make a strong case out of a weak one) but the art of thinking."[50] It is the "art of testing" and "questioning" that challenges "the fixity of opinions."[51] It is characterized by "the mutuality, the respect required, the genuine seeking to listen to and understand what the other is saying, the openness to risk and test our opinions through such an encounter."[52]

Note that both Taylor and Gadamer envision cross-cultural *dialogues*, in the course of which normative evaluations may take place. Wholly different problems arise when cross-cultural evaluations lead to actual *measures* being taken to restrict or uproot a certain cultural practice, most typically when a liberal state takes measures against a certain practice of an illiberal group living in it (denial of funding to the group; denial of legal recognition of a group practice; or criminalization of a practice). When a state takes such measures, three distinct concepts are relevant. The first is *deliberation*, that is, public discourse aimed at clarifying the values that are at stake, with the participation of all parties involved. Deliberation may enrich all parties' understanding of the meaning and justification of relevant practices of theirs, and at times it may even lead to persuasion and change of views.[53] The second concept is *judgment*, in the sense Hannah Arendt uses the term in her discussion of politics (there is a second, nonpolitical, meaning of the term in Arendt's discussion), namely a faculty exercised by actors who share a "common world" in the course of their public deliberation over the political courses of action to be undertaken by them.[54] The third concept is *justification*, that is, providing citizens with reasons to justify state action that adversely affects them. Much like Arendt's concept of judgment, which assumes that all relevant parties belong to the same community, reasons provided as justification of state action should be internal to the culture of the pertinent citizens, for otherwise the action, looked at from the citizens' point of view, would amount to disrespecting them, that is, treating them as a means rather than an end.[55] Thus, both the exercise of judgment and the provision of justification require that the state and its citizens share the same normative system. Thorny questions therefore arise when this is not the case, in other words, when a liberal state must deal with its illiberal citizens.

Thus far I have made one suggestion as to how to break free of the yoke of normative and philosophical relativism: in judging the practices of another culture, although one (inescapably) applies the categories of one's own culture, one should maintain an open mind to the utmost extent. There is, however, a second way of normatively evaluating cultures, which consists of applying the human rights doctrine.

In what is probably the most important development in twentieth-century international law, in the decades following World War II the international community developed a rich doctrine of human rights. Additionally, partly as a result of the influence of the human rights doctrine of international law, the concept of human rights has been widely discussed and applied in the constitutional law jurisprudence of many countries. The human rights doctrine enjoys universality. Not only are its ideals found in many cultures around the world, but it also enjoys widespread acceptance by the international community: many people around the world, living in diverse societies and cultures, endorse the doctrine and would like it to become an important part of the political culture of their country and in their personal lives. "No other ideal seems so clearly accepted as a universal good," writes Oscar Schachter.[56] The doctrine of human rights is therefore available to provide us with standards that may be said to transcend any particular culture for the purpose of evaluating cultural practices.[57]

**Ultra-Orthodox**: But anybody familiar with the human rights doctrine knows that its contents are phrased in highly abstract terms, as general and vague ideals. So anyone who uses it for the evaluation of cultures enjoys substantial leeway in filling it up with concrete elements.

**Liberal**: That is correct. But I cannot think of any other normative system about which it may be said, to borrow from John Rawls,[58] that there is "an overlapping consensus."[59]

## 1.3 A Word on the Parties to this Dialogue

**Ultra-Orthodox**: Before we proceed to clarify the substantive issues of this dialogue, I think we have to address the issue of the identities of the parties to it.

For many years, anthropologists studied the cultures of small, isolated societies. As a result, they developed a perception of culture as a coherent, organic entity that enjoys wide acceptance. In recent decades, anthropologists and other culture researchers have begun to view culture as composed of many elements that often contradict each other. Moreover, culture is now viewed as a highly contested entity: various groups hold competing interpretations of the cultures in which they live and struggle with each other over the status of these interpretations within the culture.[60]

We are two men about to discuss a practice that affects women first and foremost. What does it mean that two men are discussing a practice having to do with women? It means that had two women conducted this dialogue they would most likely have laid emphasis on some other aspects of the problem. But there is nothing unusual about that. Had two different men been parties to this dialogue, their dialogue might well have taken a different direction. But the fact that every culture allows for many perspectives (Gadamer calls them "horizons") in addressing an issue does not mean that there is no single widely (albeit not universally) agreed upon understanding of what the culture means, shared by most members of the cultural group, at the core of the culture. As always, the legal culture is a good metaphor for culture at large: the fact that the law allows for more than one legitimate way of addressing a legal issue does not mean that there is no single widely agreed upon way of doing so, shared by most lawyers, in the law.[61] In that spirit, in what follows I shall do my best to present some of the views widely held in the Ultra-Orthodox group bearing on the topic we are addressing.

## 2. Religion and Tradition

### 2.1. The Religious Argument

**Ultra-Orthodox**: You have asked me why it is that Ultra-Orthodox women are excluded from Torah study. Well, the answer is that Torah study is a religious imperative (*mitzvah*) that under our accepted tradition is incumbent upon men, but not upon women.[62]

In Deuteronomy 11:19 it is said: "[a]nd ye shall teach them your sons." The Talmud, Kiddushin, 29:2, has concluded from these words that the injunction applies to "your sons, not your daughters," that is, a father is duty-bound to teach his son, not his daughter, nor is the daughter herself under a duty to study Torah. And in Mishna, Sotah, 3:4, Rabbi Eliezer said: "[w]hoever teaches his daughter Torah teaches her obscenity [*tiflut*]." Most adjudicators throughout the generations have accepted this position. Noteworthy among them is Maimonides, who writes:

> [O]ur sages have commanded that a man will not teach his daughter Torah, for the minds of most women are not tuned to learning,

and due to the poverty of their minds they would apply the Torah to petty things. Our sages have said: he who teaches his daughter Torah it is as if he teaches her *tiflut*. This applies to the Talmud. But the written Torah [the Bible] he won't teach her in the first place, but if she did study, this does not amount to teaching her *tiflut* [obscenity].⁶³

Maimonides's position has been endorsed by most subsequent adjudicators. However, throughout the generations several approaches have been put forward to restrict the application of Maimonides's ruling.

First, it has been noted that Maimonides himself distinguishes between the study of the Talmud and the study of the Bible: the prohibition on teaching applies to the former, not the latter.

Second, some have interpreted Maimonides's words as applying only to the case of a father teaching his daughter. But when a woman takes the initiative to study on her own, this has been regarded by some as permissible.

Third, some have interpreted Maimonides's words as applying to teaching a young girl, but not to teaching a mature woman who has demonstrated her wisdom and tenacity.

Fourth, some have held that a father is duty-bound to teach his daughter practical *mitzvoth* (such as the rules for observing the Shabbat). According to this approach, then, teaching women is not supposed to be done for its own sake, but rather to be motivated by instrumental, informative considerations. On the more inclusive view, a father teaching his daughter should go beyond the practical-instrumental, with the aim of nurturing piety and virtuous conduct in her. Some have argued that this has become particularly urgent with the disintegration of Jewish communities in the modern era.

Fifth, some have argued that since women of our times receive a secular education at universities, this should be balanced by Torah study. A version of this argument holds that since modern women study at universities, they are accustomed to studying, and their education should therefore include Torah study.

Sixth, some have interpreted the words of Rabbi Eliezer and Maimonides as being merely an educational guideline, but not an imperative unequivocally prohibiting Torah study by women. In practice, "throughout history there were parents who resisted this imperative and took the care of providing their daughters with Torah education, or women who upon maturity resolved to do that.... In every period there were women who studied and acquired knowledge and used it so as to guide their families or their communities as to the appropriate conduct."⁶⁴

**Liberal**: To which out of this gamut of approaches do you subscribe?

**Ultra-Orthodox**: We see the approach expressed by Maimonides as binding upon us. In order for you to fully understand this point, let me say a few words about the place of tradition in our lives.

## 2.2. The Status of Tradition

**Ultra-Orthodox**: I would like to juxtapose the essentials of modern consciousness with the essentials of our culture. I think that this will uncover the roots of the difference between the liberal attitude and ours in the matter with which we are dealing

A major strand in modernity is premised on the denial of any status bestowed by tradition in the life of a person. The self-conscious rejection of traditionalist thinking was "one of the principal badges by which the champions of modernity have, from the beginning of their battle against unenlightened superstition, sought to distinguish themselves from their opponents."[65] "[W]herever modern ideas have gained ground, traditionalist ones have lost it and come under a cloud of moral and intellectual suspicion."[66] This tenet of modernity is usually identified with Kant's celebrated article, "An Answer to the Question: What is Enlightenment?,"[67] in which he praises those individuals who "think for themselves." "'Have courage to use your own understanding!'—that is the motto of enlightenment," Kant famously declares. However, the truth of the matter is that Kant's attitude to tradition is more complex than that,[68] and the real point of departure in modernity's separation from tradition is Descartes's monologist, inward-looking, reason-based philosophy of doubt.

In the spirit of modernity, in *The Subjection of Women*[69] John Stuart Mill contends that the system of inequality between men and women "never was the result of deliberation, or forethought ... of what conducted to the benefit of humanity or the good order of society. It arose simply from the fact that from the very earliest twilight of human society, every woman ... was found in a state of bondage to some man."[70]

There is another strand in modernity, however, which does accord tradition an authority. This is the strand that has to do with nationalism and with romanticism, as well as with communitarianism.[71] The only sphere in which modernity institutionalizes the authority of tradition, however, is the common law: judges are constrained by the precedent-based tradition in which they function. "An argument from precedent asserts that something should be done a certain way now because it was done that way in the past."[72] But beyond that, modernity accords no authority to tradition in any other sphere.

That is not the case with us. For us, tradition has a binding force. It embodies God's imperatives as to the good life, together with the ways these imperatives have been interpreted throughout the generations by halakhic sages. If God's imperatives have been interpreted throughout the generations as prescribing Torah study by men only, that in itself compels us to lead our lives in that way and no other. At times the exclusion of women from Torah study may raise questions for me. I may occasionally say to myself: "There are so many women whose talents for Torah study are manifestly greater than those of many men, but still they don't engage in it. Why is it, then, that we maintain a differentiation between men and women in this context?" Such questions arise from time to time, and not only with me; they have surfaced throughout the generations, and a series of halakhic sages have indeed grappled with them, to the effect that in some instances changes have been proposed in the halakhah. But as someone who observes a religious tradition, I don't regard myself as having the authority to effect changes in this or that element of the tradition that governs my life. Tradition is something you accept and abide by as it is, even if from time to time you have to confront questions about it. The fact that the differentiation between men and women with regard to Torah study is based on nothing less than the authority of Maimonides; the fact that Maimonides himself drew on great authorities that preceded him; and the fact that Maimonides's ruling has been adopted by the greatest halakhic sages throughout the generations to this very day—to me all of that means that I am required to abide by this tradition. If sometime in the future an adjudicator of the caliber of Maimonides rules that equality should prevail between men and women with regard to Torah study and this ruling becomes widely accepted, then our tradition will change, and we shall live in accordance with this new tradition. But so long as that is not the case, we perceive ourselves duty-bound to act in accordance with our tradition as it currently stands.

I shall attempt to explain my position in terms familiar to you. I said before that the common law is the only sphere in modern culture where the authority of tradition has been institutionalized. How many times has a common law judge said to himself or herself, "this precedent looks problematic; it should be overturned," and yet he or she abided by the precedent and did not deviate from it? Why? The answer is that common law judges function within a tradition, and those who function within a tradition undertake to abide by its dictates, even if at times they may find some of them objectionable. And if you read what Karl Llewellyn, leader of the American legal realists in the 1920s and 1930s, has to say about the binding force of precedents, and on how nevertheless it is possible to break away from outdated precedents in the course of time, you will find a great similarity between the world in which common law judges live and the world in which we live.[73]

**Liberal**: But at any given time any tradition, including the legal, allows for various interpretations and gives rise to varying, even conflicting, interpretations. Also, any tradition, including the legal, is constantly developing and changing. You yourself pointed out that some halakhic adjudicators sought to narrow down the ruling of Rabbi Eliezer and Maimonides against women's Torah study, and some adjudicators have even called for it to be overturned.

**Ultra-Orthodox**: This is all true. But the enduring position at the heart of our tradition is that only men study Torah, and so long as that is the case, we see ourselves bound to live that way, without challenging it.

Let me refine my explanation. Remember we talked about cases in which a category exists in one culture but is missing from another? Liberal society does not have a concept of "the right way to live." Liberals believe in a plurality of the good. Not so with us. We do have a concept (category) of the right way to live. This is the way of life that God in his grace granted us and ordered us to follow, to the best of our abilities, in the course of our lives. As Father Arnall tells Stephen Dedalus and his classmates in Joyce's *A Portrait of the Artist as a Young Man*: "[a]nd remember, my dear boys, that we have been sent into this world for one thing and for one thing alone, to do God's holy will ... All else is worthless."[74] We recognize human agency, of course; we don't perceive human beings as robots. We recognize that to be human is to make reason-based, autonomous decisions throughout a lifetime and that human beings are morally responsible for their doings. But whereas liberal thinkers hold that every person has the right to write "the big story" of his or her life as he or she wishes, we believe that there is only one right big story, one right way of life, and that is the way that God has determined for us, and that has been further filled with content by our halakhic sages (the particular halakhic sages we adhere to) throughout the generations. And the way of life God has determined for us, together with the rulings of our halakhic sages throughout the generations, embody the tradition we deem binding upon us.

Rabbi Yosef Dov Soloveitchik well understood this difference between religious tradition and modernity when he wrote, somewhat in the spirit of the words of Father Arnall, that "modern man claims that he is free and that all restrictions on him amount to coercion and harm. In contrast, God's sovereignty requires man to be modest before God and to acknowledge the sovereign that accords him with all his blessings. . . . Life is a godly gift and a right that may be used only for holy purposes."[75]

**Liberal**: I think your argument illuminates the great watershed between our two approaches: the difference in our attitudes toward tradition, or, to be more specific, the opposite place of tradition in our lives. We talked about culture as being composed of categories. "Tradition" is a category recognized in both your culture and mine. But its status in the two cultures is very different. In your culture, it is not only an active category, but an infrastructural category.[76] In my culture, the category is recognized, but by and large inactive. We are dealing here with a major difference between the religious and secular cultures.

**Ultra-Orthodox**: Yes, it seems that in understanding the different role played by tradition in our two cultures, we have reached Wittgenstein's famous "bedrock": "[i]f I have exhausted the justification, I have reached bedrock and my spade is turned. Then I am inclined to say: 'This is simply what I do.'"[77]

**Liberal**: And from my perspective all of this raises many additional, complex, and troubling questions as to the conditions under which your tradition evolves: for example, to what extent those subject to it, such as women, have any meaningful voice in the processes by which it is maintained and changed. Also, for me your approach is unacceptably ahistorical and a-contextual: you are bound by the ruling of a sage who, despite his undeniable greatness, lived in the Muslim world of the twelfth century. And is it merely a coincidence that we do know the name of his father, and the name of his brother, and the name of his son, but we don't know until this very day the name of his wife, nor do we know the name of his daughter (or whether he had one)?

## 2.3. The Hold of Tradition

**Liberal**: I would like to underscore this profound difference between our two cultures by making use of a term that is recognized by both—"human dignity" (the term used in your culture is "God's image")—even though it seems to enjoy greater centrality in our culture than in yours.

The common meaning of the term "human dignity" is connected with Kant: to treat a person as having human dignity is to assume that he or she is able to act autonomously, that is, to make use of reason and determine his or her fate.[78] This interpretation of the term embodies a central tenet of modernity. Mill, in discussing discrimination against women, writes that what is peculiar to the modern world is that "human beings are no longer born to their place in life, and chained down by an inexorable bond to the place they are born to, but are free to employ their faculties . . . to achieve the lot which may appear to them most desirable."[79] "The principle of the modern movement in morals and politics," writes Mill, "is that conduct, and conduct alone, entitles to respect: that not what men are, but what they do, constitutes their claim to deference; that, above all, merit, and not birth, is the only rightful claim to power and authority."[80] In a similar vein, Charles Taylor presents the premodern era as having been governed by the principle of "honor" (the social location of a person rightfully determines his or her fate), and the modern era as being governed by the concept of human dignity.[81] Mill argues that women are the only group in the modern era whose fate continues to be determined at birth.

You may therefore understand why a situation in which the fate of Ultra-Orthodox men and women differs substantially just because of their different sex is troubling from the point of view of secular liberal culture.

**Ultra-Orthodox**: I can understand that. But our culture is different. Reason lies at the core of our concept of humanity, as well. But for us what constitutes human dignity is when someone makes use of his or her reason so as best to comply with God's imperatives as to the right way of life. As I noted earlier, at the current stage in the development of the halakhah, as we perceive it, the right way of life is one in which men study Torah and women don't.

**Liberal**: One of the most far-reaching developments in religious Zionism in Israel in recent decades has been the rise of a vibrant and highly influential religious feminism.[82] The feminist revolution in religious Zionism is manifest first and foremost in the establishment of educational institutions aimed at teaching the Talmud to women. The intention is to provide women with rabbinical knowledge that will enable them to fulfill rabbinical functions, that is, provide rabbinical guidance to other women.[83] I am certain that this development will have an influence on the Ultra-Orthodox group.

**Ultra-Orthodox**: This practice may possibly spread to our group, in one way or another, and developments on the ground will foster a new attitude to the whole issue.[84] But right now we are bound by the ruling of Maimonides and the other halakhic sages. In any event, even if that does happen, it will take time before the next natural development takes place, namely the translation of women's Torah study into women's participation in adjudication and political leadership.[85]

## 3. Humanism and Equality

### 3.1. The Humanistic Argument

**Ultra-Orthodox**: Can you formulate what disturbs you the most about our practice of differentiating between men and women with regard to Torah study?

**Liberal**: I'll try. Human beings have reason and intellectual capabilities. A good human life is one in which a person makes the utmost use of his or her intellectual potential. When certain individuals, for instance women, are prohibited from engaging in a sphere of social activity that exists in a society, they are precluded from fully realizing the intellectual potential that lies within them. Put differently, they are denied reaching the height of their human flourishing.[86]

John Stuart Mill, one of the greatest liberal thinkers, makes a trenchant argument. He writes about "the dull and hopeless life to which [the discrimination of women] so often condemns them, by forbidding them to exercise the[ir] practical abilities."[87] Mill concludes his book by writing about "the positive evil caused to the disqualified half of the human race by their disqualification—first in the loss of the most inspiring and elevating kind of personal enjoyment, and next in the weariness, disappointment, and profound dissatisfaction with life, which are so often the substitute for it."[88] Susan Moller Okin writes about women in the Ultra-Orthodox group in a similar vein: "what of a girl born into this culture who is drawn toward religious study as strongly as [a] boy . . . is repelled by it?" she asks.[89]

**Ultra-Orthodox**: I think I can understand your position. But for me the fact that the halakhah has been interpreted throughout the generations by our greatest sages in a way that establishes a distinction in the present context between men and women means that this distinction is part of the way of life I must follow.

## 3.2. Equality: Human Dignity

**Liberal**: Thus far I have presented the problem with excluding women from Torah study, as well as from adjudication and political leadership, from the perspective of humanism. But the problem also arises from the perspective of the value of equality, which, as I noted earlier, is a central liberal value.

**Ultra-Orthodox**: What is the basis of the liberal value of equality?

**Liberal**: I think it has two major foundations. One is the concept of human dignity.[90] The concept of human dignity is premised on the assumption that all human beings, because of their humanity, regardless of their cultural or identity traits, have equal moral worth, and therefore must be treated equally to some extent.[91] Discrimination, treating persons differently without justification, implies that some persons are regarded as having lesser moral worth than others. From the liberal point of view, therefore, the exclusion of women from Torah study means that women are regarded as having lesser moral worth than men.

The experience of being regarded as having lesser moral worth is particularly injurious to the psyche of an individual in cases of exclusion. The law refers to discrimination as the opposite of equality. But I think that when we talk about the opposite of equality it is helpful to distinguish between "discrimination" and "exclusion." Discrimination is where resources are unequally distributed between groups or individuals, without justification. Exclusion is a subcategory of discrimination. It takes place when a certain individual or group is precluded from acting in a certain social sphere that is open to others, without justification. (Exclusion is not only the opposite of inclusion; in a way, it is also the opposite of solidarity.)[92] I tend to think that the experience of exclusion is more injurious than that of discrimination, because in the case of exclusion a person sees others taking part in a certain activity that he or she finds attractive, yet is barred from participating

Indeed, in *The Double*,[93] Fyodor Dostoyevsky depicts an experience of exclusion—a person who is not allowed into a party—as leading to madness. Jacob Talmon writes that nationalist movements arise when the intelligentsia of a minority national group tries to assimilate into the majority society, but experiences rejection. In such situations, writes Talmon, the minority intelligentsia performs a "u-turn," focuses on cultivating its own people's culture, and works for the attainment of full national sovereignty.[94] Indeed, the history of nationalist movements, such as Zionism or the Québécois nationalist movement, confirms Talmon's suggestion. Exclusion is indeed a powerful force in the lives of both individuals and groups.

### 3.3. Equality: Biases and Stereotypes

**Liberal**: An additional rationale that lies at the basis of the value of equality focuses on the concepts of "bias" and "stereotype."[95] Biases and stereotypes harm individuals because they cause them to be perceived in ways that preclude them from realizing the human potential that lies within them. Biases and stereotypes also cause those to whom they relate to internalize a demeaning self-perception, and this, in turn, breeds in them a diminished self-respect and precludes them from claiming for themselves goods or privileges that are reserved for those exempt from biases and stereotypes (this is the famous "glass ceiling"). These insights stand at the basis of the "politics of identity" conducted in recent decades by a series of groups. What underlies all of this is the value of creating conditions that enable every person to realize his or her human potential to the utmost possible extent in the context of the activities and social relations in the society in which he or she lives. We are back therefore to the humanistic rationale, according to which every individual should be able to make use of his or her reason and capabilities to the utmost extent in the course of his or her lifetime. Biases and stereotypes undermine this humanistic ideal.

From the liberal point of view, then, the problem in the exclusion of women from certain central activities that take place in the Ultra-Orthodox group, including not only Torah study but adjudication and political leadership as well, is that they are barred from fully realizing their human potential.

**Ultra-Orthodox**: But in our group that is not the outcome of any biases or stereotypes against women. It is true that throughout the generations one may find statements by halakhic sages to the effect that women not only differ from men, but are also of inferior (intellectual and moral) capabilities. But these are outdated texts that express understandings prevalent at the time they were written. (Needless to say, one cannot expect a person to think beyond the cultural categories of his or her time.) Moreover, such statements are offset by a long series of pronouncements by halakhic sages praising the capabilities of women and advocating the unmitigated respectful treatment of them. Judaism is a long-lived and enormously rich tradition; one may find in it many conflicting pronouncements made throughout the generations.

Note that Mill in *The Subjection of Women* finds it necessary to argue at length against the claim that the subjection of women to men is "natural" and "universal."[96] He also contests the claim that the intellectual capabilities of women are lesser than those of men.[97] Mill makes the astute comment that "it is not sufficient to maintain that women on the average are less gifted than men on the average, with certain of the higher mental faculties, or that a smaller number of women than of men are fit for occupations and functions of the highest intellectual character. It is necessary to maintain that no women at all are fit for them, and that the most eminent women are inferior in mental faculties to the most mediocre of the men on whom those functions at present devolve."[98] Those functions, he goes on to point out, "are often filled by men far less fit for them than numbers of women, and who would be beaten by women in any fair field of competition."[99] Note that Mill needed to resort to these arguments as late as 1869, on the threshold of the eighth decade of the nineteenth century.

Note that I do not make any of the arguments that were prevalent in Western culture until recently and against which Mill found it necessary to speak out. I do not justify the differentiation we maintain between men and women on the basis of anything having to do with the essences of masculinity and femininity. Rather, my argument is meta-halakhic: it is my existential decision to live my life within the tradition of my religion, and in its current state that tradition dictates a differentiation between men and women with regard to Torah study. Moreover, in what follows I would like to introduce our way of life in a way that shows how very far it goes, in spite of the differentiation we maintain, toward upholding women's human dignity.

**Liberal**: That sounds to me a little bit like legal formalism. Ultra-Orthodox women are being treated in a certain derogatory way. You justify it not by claiming that women are inferior to men in any way, but rather by drawing on the rulings of Maimonides and other great halakhic sages. But these rulings cannot but be based on a derogatory view of women.

## 3.4. "Issachar and Zebulun Agreement"

**Ultra-Orthodox**: I would like to go back to what you said before about discrimination, that it implies that some people have lesser moral worth and are of diminished human dignity. I hope that after you listen to the following argument you will agree with me that it is impossible to maintain that the women of our group are perceived as being of inferior status.

We have talked about the centrality of the value of Torah study in our lives. As we see it, when men study Torah, women study as well, though by proxy, in creating the conditions that enable their husbands to study. This division of labor draws on an ancient notion that exists in Judaism—the "Issachar and Zebulun Agreement." In his blessing to the Children of Israel before his death, Moses said: "Rejoice, Zebulun, in thy going out; and Issachar, in thy tents."[100] This served as the basis for a Midrash which says that after the Children of Israel entered the Land of Canaan, the people of the tribe of Zebulun made a living through maritime commerce and supported the people of the tribe of Issachar, who spent their time studying Torah.[101] Many generations later this model underwent a transformation to serve as the basis for the relations between a wealthy person and a poor Torah scholar: the wealthy person supports the Torah scholar by providing his subsistence. In return, the wealthy person is regarded as a partner to the study, so that the reward for performing the *mitzvah* is shared by both of them.

The model has undergone a further transformation by being applied to the relations between husbands and wives: the husband devotes himself to Torah study, while his wife takes care of the family's subsistence.[102] One therefore cannot claim that our women are perceived as being of inferior status. Rather, we regard them as partners of equal status to men in fulfilling this central value in our lives, Torah study. To hold otherwise is to focus on an external fact, that men study Torah and women don't, and ignore the thicker understanding of the meaning attached to it in our group.

Susan Moller Okin claims that as a result of the differentiation we maintain between the education of boys and girls, "the personality identities cultivated in the girls are much less central to the culture, which raises an immediate question about how they are to develop a sense of equal worth or self-respect."[103] I think Okin is wrong. Ultra-Orthodox women develop a high sense of self-worth and self-respect when they perceive themselves, and are perceived by others, as taking part in Torah study through their husbands.[104]

**Liberal**: But there is something very disturbing here. This division of labor is not dependent on a choice made by this or that couple, or on the fitness or absence thereof of this or that husband's and wife's talents. Rather, the division of labor you maintain is gender based: it is always, without exception, the men who study, and it is always, without exception, the women who support them. Also, the "Issachar and Zebulun Agreement" model cannot in any way justify the exclusion of young, unmarried girls from Torah study.

**Ultra-Orthodox**: That is correct. But maybe what follows will put our practice in a better light from your perspective.

### 3.5. Two Central Values: Torah Study and Raising Children

**Ultra-Orthodox**: I wish to present the differentiation we maintain between men and women with a slight modification. You have argued that according to one common interpretation, the requirement of equality derives from the concept of human dignity: the unequal treatment of persons or groups implies a view of them as having lesser moral worth. But one can't possibly say that the exclusion of our women from Torah study amounts to that. In our group, there are two central values: Torah study and raising children. We uphold these two values by maintaining a division of labor: men are in charge of Torah study, and women are in charge of raising children.

As I have noted, Susan Moller Okin asks whether Ultra-Orthodox women can develop "a sense of equal worth or self-respect."[105] But since we put our women in charge of what is dearest of all to us, how can one hold that we violate our women's sense of worth, self-respect, and human dignity? Discussing the socialization of women, Okin rightly emphasizes the importance of "the realm of domestic or family life" where "persons' senses of themselves and their capacities are first formed *and* in which culture is first strongly transmitted."[106] But if the domestic realm is so important, how can it possibly be said that Ultra-Orthodox women develop a low sense of self-respect, when they are the ones in charge of this realm where a group's culture and heritage are "first strongly transmitted"? Add to that our view of women as participating also in the *mitzvah* of Torah study according to the "Issachar and Zebulun Agreement" model, and it seems to me that any claim that our women suffer from a problem of self-worth, respect, and human dignity is groundless.[107]

**Liberal**: But here, again, as in the case of your "Issachar and Zebulun Agreement" argument, there is something very disturbing: the division of labor between husbands and wives is not dependent on a choice made by this or that couple, or on the fitness or absence thereof of this or that husband's and wife's talents. Rather, the division of labor you maintain is gender based: it is the men who study, and it is the women who are in charge of raising children. Also, this division of labor ignores the possibility that both men and women will study the Torah, and that both men and women will be deeply, and jointly, involved in raising their children.

## 3.6. Separate but Equal

**Liberal**: What you are suggesting is a version of "separate but equal," a doctrine of much disrepute in American law. In *Plessey v. Ferguson*[108] of 1896 the Supreme Court upheld the constitutionality of the doctrine in the context of interracial relations. But in *Brown v. Board of Education*[109] of 1954, "separate but equal" was held to be unconstitutional.

**Ultra-Orthodox**: But note that in the American setting "separate but equal" was part of an entrenched system of racial discrimination that was premised on a perception of blacks as being inferior to whites. That is not the case with us. The differentiation we maintain between men and women is not based on, and does not imply, any perception of women as being inferior to men.

**Liberal**: And yet you have to admit the severe implications of the exclusion of women from Torah study. As I noted at the outset, that exclusion leads to the exclusion of women from adjudication and political leadership. Law and politics are arenas in which decisions of major importance regarding all aspects of the lives of individuals are adopted. This means that the unique perspectives and interests of women systematically and continuously fail to be represented in the legal and political decision-making processes that take place in the institutions of the Ultra-Orthodox group. Also, the exclusion of women from adjudication and politics cannot but symbolically diminish the status of women. All of this adds up to the exclusion of women from other activities of the group: for instance, they don't count toward making up a *minyan*; their testimony is inadmissible in court proceedings[110]; and they are precluded from conducting public rituals.[111]

**Ultra-Orthodox**: That is all true, but note that unlike the American case of "separate but equal," the differentiation we maintain between men and women is not accompanied by any ideology premised on women's inferiority to men. Indeed, as many writers have pointed out, Ultra-Orthodox women do not suffer from low self-esteem. Also, bear in mind that in addition to their participation in Torah study by proxy and to the role they play in child-rearing, the responsibility of Ultra-Orthodox women for the subsistence of their families means that in many instances they attend professional secular studies, thereby gaining not only valuable professional knowledge, but also first-hand knowledge of what goes on in secular society. This gives them lots of self-confidence and self-esteem, as well as winning the respect of their husbands and the community at large.[112] Also, note that women are not completely excluded from Torah study. In many Ultra-Orthodox communities women do study Torah, though in evening classes (conducted by other women). One incidental by-product of these gatherings is that women enjoy the opportunity to exchange experiences and intuitions, and that mutual reinforcement fosters solidarity and bonding among them.[113]

## 4. "Imperial"/Assimilatory Liberalism

**Ultra-Orthodox**: You mentioned Okin, a central feminist-liberal thinker. But note that she comes to far-reaching conclusions with regard to our group. Arguing that "[u]ltra-Orthodox culture is more likely than a more open and liberal culture to harm the individual interests of both its male and its female children,"[114] Okin challenges the Ultra-Orthodox group "to show that the *type* of personality identity one develops in a restrictive and encompassing community such as that of the Ultra-Orthodox is at least as good for persons as, if not superior to, the type they would be likely to develop in a more open and liberal community."[115] She adds that Ultra-Orthodox women "*may* be much better off, from a liberal point of view, if the culture into which they were born were either gradually to become extinct (as its members become integrated into the surrounding culture) or, preferably, to be encouraged and supported to substantially alter itself so as to reinforce the equality, rather than the inequality, of women—at least to the degree to which this is upheld in the majority culture."[116] The reason why Okin comes to this far-reaching conclusion is because she finds the treatment of women in the Ultra-Orthodox group to be problematic. I want to make two comments in that regard.

First, I doubt whether Okin has studied the situation of Ultra-Orthodox women thoroughly enough. Had she done so, she would have realized that even though we maintain a differentiation between men and women with regard to Torah study, still, because of our notion of the "Issachar and Zebulun Agreement" and because we see our women as bearing the primary responsibility for raising the children, we succeed in maintaining our women's human dignity at a very high level.

Second, is it not rather simplistic, far-reaching, even arrogant, to deliver a comprehensive verdict on a rich culture of many centuries' standing, deeming it inferior to liberal culture, and to resolve that it would be better for the women living in it if their culture was assimilated into the mainstream liberal culture? Also, does it make any sense to compare cultures on such a scale? Okin seems to have disregarded what Charles Taylor advised in his classical article "Multiculturalism and 'The Politics of Recognition'," namely that it is wrong to take a judgmental stance toward cultures in their entirety and that when we normatively appraise cultures we need to deal with specific cultural elements and practices.[117]

Stephen Macedo, another prominent liberal thinker, also takes an assimilatory stance toward religious groups. He talks about "a holy war between religious zealots and proponents of science and public reason,"[118] going even so far as to say that the "[a]ssimilation [of fundamentalist groups] is an inescapable and legitimate object of liberal policy."[119] And as if that were not enough, he concludes by declaring: "[W]e will sometimes accommodate dissenting groups, but we must remind fundamentalists and others that they must pay a price for living in a free pluralistic society."[120]

In *The Morality of Freedom*[121] Joseph Raz discusses "communities whose culture does not support autonomy," such as "religious sects." Raz maintains that in insisting on bringing up their children in their own way, these communities are "harming" their children. Therefore, he argues, the question arises whether it would be justified to resort to coercion "to break up" these communities. Raz holds that in cases in which the culture of such a community flourishes and enables its members "to have an adequate and satisfying life," the continued existence of the community "should be tolerated, despite its scant regard for autonomy."[122]

To Raz it is clear that the culture of such communities is "inferior to that of the dominant liberal society in the midst of which they live." This, in turn, raises the question whether the cultures of these communities should be tolerated. Raz responds as follows: "[T]he perfectionist principles espoused in this book suggest that people are justified in taking action to assimilate the minority group, at the cost of letting its culture die or at least be considerably changed by absorption." Eventually, however, he reaches the opposite conclusion: "[W]renching them out of their communities may well make it impossible for them to have any kind of normal rewarding life whatsoever because they have not built up any capacity for autonomy. Toleration is therefore the conclusion one must often reach."[123] Only second-order, prudential considerations, then, restrain Raz from recommending measures for the assimilation of religious groups who don't cherish the liberal value of autonomy.[124] In subsequent writings, however, Raz has added a multicultural perspective to his liberal theorizing and adopted a stance much more respectful of non-liberal groups.[125]

Okin, Macedo, and the early Raz are what Richard Shweder calls "imperial liberals," namely thinkers who hold that liberal conceptions of the good life should be disseminated "in all corners of society and throughout the world"; that "[w]here there are individuals let them transcend their tradition-bound commitments and experience the quality of their lives solely in secular and ecumenical terms"; and that "those liberal principles and conceptions should be upheld using the coercive power of the state and, if possible, exported to foreign lands using the coercive powers of international institutions (such as the World Bank, the IMF, NATO, and the United Nations)."[126] (All three thinkers could as well be referred to as "assimilatory liberals."[127])

Moreover, any call for the assimilation of non-liberal groups into the mainstream liberal society runs counter to the view that all cultures have intrinsic value and should therefore be preserved[128] (even if it may be justified to seek to eliminate some particular practices of theirs).

Also, how can one suggest that it would be better for Ultra-Orthodox women to live in the mainstream liberal society without taking into account the predicaments of women in it, such as discrimination in the workplace, widespread practices (propagated by the advertising and entertainment industries) that reduce women to objects for men's sexual pleasure, cultural pressures to undergo extreme diets and plastic surgeries, pornography and prostitution? And, more generally, how can one ignore the poverty, the inhumane treatment of prisoners, the death penalty, violent sports that jeopardize the health of athletes, and the widespread violence in movies and TV programs, all of which are part of what it is to live in mainstream liberal society?

It seems to me that our dialogue is nearing its conclusion. So let me make two final comments. First, note that we began with cases in which liberal activists have failed to understand the cultures of non-liberal groups, and we are about to conclude by discussing liberal thinkers who have no hesitation advocating the wholesale assimilation of non-liberal groups. Second, we have not yet touched upon the issues of meaning and virtue, which for me are of the utmost importance. In concluding my contribution to this dialogue, let me briefly comment on those topics

Life in our group takes place within a normative framework that has been, and continues to be, determined, generation after generation, by the greatest halakhic sages of the times, people distinguished for their combination of high intellectual capabilities and high personal moral standards (somewhat in the spirit of Plato's vision of the ideal state). Moreover, to live in the Ultra-Orthodox group means to constantly live in the presence of an ideal of the virtuous life and in the light of the example set by persons of virtuous character, as well as to constantly judge one's own character and conduct by those criteria. How can you compare this kind of living to that of a society whose culture does not provide "a comprehensive morality" to regulate "entire lives"[129] and whose values are determined, to a disproportionate extent, by the market and its institutions?

## 5. Conclusion

**Liberal**: No single human being can fulfill all worthwhile human values in the course of his or her lifetime. The same applies to cultural groups. No culture can give adequate expression to all worthy human values. Liberalism gives prominence to the values of liberty and autonomy. It does not directly take issue with the quality of the culture of liberal society. Ultra-Orthodox culture places an overwhelming emphasis on the issues of culture and meaning. It pays a price, however, in terms of the liberty, and to some extent the autonomy, enjoyed by those living in it. And while both cultures endorse the value of equality, they both tolerate inequality: liberal society acquiesces to the inequality between those who have the talents to successfully function in the market and those who lack such talents; the Ultra-Orthodox culture is premised on a hierarchy between the learned and the non-learned, and between men and women.

One cannot deliver a single, simplistic, unequivocal judgment on the status of women in the Ultra-Orthodox group. On the one hand, the exclusion of women from Torah study seems to adversely affect them, both symbolically and in that it brings about their absence from judicial and political institutions in which decisions are made that bear on many important aspects of their lives. Also, the gender-based exclusion of women from Torah study is incompatible with the humanist imperative to enable all human beings to fully flourish by letting their intellectual capabilities manifest themselves in all spheres of activity recognized in the societies in which they live.

On the other hand, the notion of the "Issachar and Zebulun Agreement" and the role women play in raising children serve as highly important sources of meaning, gratification, and self-esteem in the lives of Ultra-Orthodox women. But this raises the intricate question whether the Hegelian-Marxist notion of "false consciousness" is applicable to people living in cultures (all cultures, including the liberal one). Also, Ultra-Orthodox women are not confined to their homes or to their communities. They are active in the surrounding secular society, and that equips them with valuable knowledge that gives them an advantage over their husbands. This in turn adds to their self-confidence and self-esteem.

One understanding that emerges from this dialogue is the need to base normative evaluations on a close examination of the facts. Martha C. Nussbaum put it succinctly when she wrote that "the philosopher, while neither a fieldworker nor a politician, should try to get close to the reality she describes."[130] Though lawyers seem to do a much better job of it than philosophers, this is a valuable reminder to lawyers as well.

# Notes

\* I would like to thank participants of the McGill-Tel Aviv "Religious Revival in Post-Multicultural Age Workshop"; participants of the Faculty Seminar, Faculty of Law, Tel Aviv University; and participants of the Colloquium of the Department of Interpretation and Culture, Bar Ilan University, for their comments. Further gratitude goes to Nissim Mizrachi, Yofi Tirosh, Zvi Triger, Elimelech Westreich, and Shai Wosner for their comments.

1. J. Rawls, *The Law of Peoples* (Cambridge, MA: Harvard University Press, 1999) at 152.
2. C. Navon, "Women's Torah Study" (2008) 28 Tchumin 71 (Hebrew).
3. Y. Leibovitch, "The Status of Women—Halakhah and Meta-Halakhah," in *Belief, History and Values* (Jerusalem: Acadon, 1982) 71 at 72 (Hebrew).
4. "[T]he world of civil society has certainly been made by man ... Whoever reflects on this cannot but marvel that the philosophers should have bent all their energies to the study of the world of nature, which, since God made it, He alone knows; and that they should have neglected the study of the world of nations, or civil world, which, since men had made it, he could come to know." *The New Science of Giambattista Vico*, trans. T. G. Bergin and M. H. Fisch (Ithaca, NY: Cornell University Press, 1984) at section 331.
5. For a review and discussion of "the interpretive approach" and "the subjectivist approach" to this issue, see: S. R. Kirschner, "'Then What Have I To Do with Thee?': On Identity, Fieldwork, and Ethnographic Knowledge" (1987) 2 Cultural Anthropology 211; see also L. Holy, "Introduction: Description, Generalization and Comparison: Two Paradigms," in L. Holy, ed, *Comparative Anthropology* (Oxford and New York: Blackwell, 1987) 1. Mizrachi argues that members of two different networks of meaning are able to activate a set of "bridging techniques" that he calls "modular translation." N. Mizrachi, "On the Mismatch Between Multicultural Education and it Subjects in the Field" (2012) 33:2 British Journal of Sociology of Education 185, 198. Gellner points out the "interesting fact" that "no anthropologist ... has come back from a field trip with the following report: *their* concepts are *so* alien that it is impossible to describe their land tenure, their kinship system, their ritual." E. Gellner, "General Introduction: Relativism and Universals," in B. Lloyd and J. Gay, eds, *Universals of Human Thought: Some African Evidence* (Cambridge: Cambridge University Press, 1981) 1 at 5. Martha Nussbaum writes that "[d]espite the evident differences in the specific cultural shaping of the grounding experiences, we do recognize the experiences of people in other cultures as similar to our own. We do converse with them about matters of deep importance, understand them, allow ourselves to be moved by them." M. C. Nussbaum, "Non-Relative Virtues: An Aristotelian Approach" (1988) 13 Midwest Studies in Philosophy 32, 46.
6. H.-G. Gadamer, *Truth and Method*, 2nd rev edn, trans. D. Marshall and J. Weinsheimer (New York: Continuum, 1993); H.-G. Gadamer, *Philosophical Hermeneutics*, trans. D. E. Linge (Berkeley: University of California Press, 1976).
7. J. Habermas, "A Review of Gadamer's Truth and Method," in F. R. Dallmayr and T. A. McCarthy, eds, *Understanding and Social Inquiry* (Notre Dame, IN: University of Notre Dame Press, 1977) 335, at 342 and 352; C. Taylor, "Understanding the Other: A Gadamerian View on Conceptual Schemes," in J. Malpas, U. Arnswald, and J. Kertscher, eds, *Gadamer's Century* (Cambridge, MA: MIT Press, 2002) at 279, 280, and 296; C. Taylor, "The Politics of Recognition," in A. Gutmann, ed, *Multiculturalism and "The Politics of Recognition"* (Princeton, NJ: Princeton University Press, 1992) 25, at 67, 70 and 73; D. Linge, "Editor's Introduction to Philosophical Hermeneutics," in H.-G. Gadamer, ed, *Philosophical Hermeneutics*, ibid., xi, at xii and xxi; R. Bernstein, *Beyond Objectivism and Relativism: Science, Hermeneutics, and Praxis* (Philadelphia: University of Pennsylvania Press, 1983) 36. For Gadamer, translation, conversation, and understanding are very much the same. See: Gadamer, ibid., at 383–89. See also: C. Geertz, "Thick Description: Toward an Interpretive Theory of Culture," in *The Interpretation of Culture* (New York: Basic Books, 1973) at 3 and 30.
8. Linge, ibid.; Bernstein, ibid.; R. Wagner, *The Invention of Culture*, rev edn (Englewood Cliffs, NJ: Prentice-Hall, 1975) at 9; H. B. Sarles, "Cultural Relativism and Critical Naturalism," in M. Dascal, ed, *Cultural Relativism and Philosophy: North and Latin American Perspectives* (Leiden: E.J. Brill, 1991) 195–214, at 195.
9. G. Lienhardt, "Modes of Thought," in *The Institutions of Primitive Society: A Series of Broadcast Talks* (Glencoe: The Free Press, 1961) 95; A. MacIntyre, "Relativism, Power, Philosophy" (1985) 59 Proceedings and Addresses of the American Philosophical

Association 5, at 9–10; L. Holy, ed, *Comparative Anthropology* (Oxford and New York: Blackwell, 1987); S. B. Schwartz, ed, *Implicit Understandings: Observing, Reporting, and Reflecting on the Encounters between Europeans and Other Peoples in the Early Modern Era* (Cambridge: Cambridge University Press, 1994); T. Asad, "The Concept of Cultural Translation in British Social Anthropology," in J. Clifford and G. E. Marcus, eds, *Writing Culture: The Poetics and Politics of Ethnography* (Berkeley: University of California Press, 1986) 141–64; P. G. Rubel and A. Rosman, eds, *Translating Cultures: Perspectives on Translation and Anthropology* (Oxford and New York: Berg, 2003).

10. M. G. Clyne, *Inter-Cultural Communication at Work: Cultural Values in Discourse* (Cambridge: Cambridge University Press, 1994).
11. In a classic article, "Feminism and Multiculturalism: Some Tensions" (1998) 108 Ethics 661–84, Susan Moller Okin showed that most cases in which the practices of non-liberal groups look problematic to Western liberals involve some violation of the interests of women. So the four following examples deal with Western interventions meant to protect women living in non-liberal cultural groups.
12. B. Shell-Duncan and Y. Hernlund, eds, *Female "Circumcision" in Africa: Culture, Controversy, and Change* (Boulder: Lynne Rienner, 2000); R. A. Shweder, "'What About Female Genital Mutilation?' and Why Understanding Culture Matters in the First Place," in R. A. Shweder, M. Minow, and H. R. Markus, eds, *Engaging Cultural: The Multicultural Challenge in Liberal Democracies* (New York: Russell Sage Foundation, 2002) 216; I. R. Gunning, "Arrogant Perception, World-Travelling and Multicultural Feminism: The Case of Female Genital Surgeries" (1991–1992) 23 Columbia Human Rights Law Review 189; L. A. Obiora, "Female Excision: Cultural Concerns," 8 *International Encyclopedia of the Social & Behavioral Sciences* (2001) 5442–5447; T. Bentzen and A. Talle, *The Norwegian International Effort Against Female Genital Mutilation* (2007) id; M. C. Lam, "Multicultural Feminism: Cultural Concerns," 15 *International Encyclopedia of the Social & Behavioral Sciences* (2001) 10163-10169; O. Hoffe, "Human Rights in Intercultural Discourse: Cultural Concerns," 10 *International Encyclopedia of the Social & Behavioral Sciences* (2001) 7018–7025; S. L. Gilman, "'Barbaric' Rituals?," in J. Cohen, M. Howard, and M. C. Nussbaum, eds, *Is Multiculturalism Bad for Women?* (Princeton, NJ: Princeton University Press, 1999) 53.
13. C. T. Mohanty, "Under Western Eyes: Feminist Scholarship and Colonial Discourse," in C. T. Mohanty, A. Russo, and L. Torres, eds, *Third World Women and Feminism* (Bloomington: Indiana University Press, 1991) 51; N. J. Hirschmann, "Eastern Veiling, Western Freedom?" (1997) 59 Review of Politics 461; Lam, id.; B. Parekh, "A Varied Moral Order," in J. Cohen, M. Howard, and M. C. Nussbaum, eds, *Is Multiculturalism Bad for Women?* (Princeton, NJ: Princeton University Press, 1999) 69.
14. U. Menon, "Neither Victim Nor Rebel: Feminism and the Morality of Gender and Family Life in a Hindu Temple Town," in R. A. Shweder, M. Minow, and H. R. Markus, eds, *Engaging Cultural Differences: The Multicultural Challenge in Liberal Democracies* (New York: Russell Sage, 2002) 288; M. C. Nussbaum, "Public Philosophy and International Feminism" (1998) 108 Ethics 762. Likewise, it has been argued that Western feminists have failed to properly understand the unique history of feminism in China and the unique problems and needs of Chinese women. See: S.-M. Shih, "Toward an Ethics of Transnational Encounters, or 'When' Does a 'Chinese' Woman Become a 'Feminist'?," in M. Waller and S. Marcos, eds, *Dialogue and Difference: Feminisms Challenge Globalization* (New York: Palgrave Macmillan, 2005) 3; Y. Wu, "Making Sense in Chinese 'Feminism'/ Women's Studies," in M. R. Waller and S. Marcos, eds, *Dialogue and Difference: Feminisms Challenge Globalization* (New York: Palgrave Macmillan, 2005) 29.
15. C. T. Mohanty, "Cartographies of Struggle: Third World Women and the Politics of Feminism," in C. T. Mohanty, A. Russo, and L. Torres, eds, *Third World Women and the Politics of Feminism* (Bloomington: Indian University Press, 1991) 1; Wu, *supra* note 14 at 29; Lam, *supra* note 12; Gunning, *supra* note 12; S. E. Merry, "Human Rights Law and the Demonization of Culture (And Anthropology Along the Way)" (2003) 26:1 Political & Legal Review 55–76, at 63–64; L. Volpp, "Talking 'Culture': Gender, Race, Nation, and the Politics of Multiculturalism" (1996) 96 Columbia Law Review 1573–617; L. Volpp,

"Feminism versus Multiculturalism" (2001) 101 Columbia Law Review 1181–218. Pinhas Shifman provides a list of examples of misunderstandings that arise when religious people invoke religious terms in Israel's public discourse. For instance, when a mass accident occurs, religious people often claim that it is God's response to the proliferation of religious sinfulness. Secular people are annoyed by such pronouncements, because they see them as manifestations of a cruel accountancy and flawed causality. But religious people understand such pronouncements very differently, namely as calls for religious soul-searching. P. Shifman, *One Language, Different Tongues* (Jerusalem: Shalom Hartman Institute, 2012) 30–35 (Hebrew). Lawyers often encounter cases of cultural misunderstandings. See: A. D. Renteln, *The Cultural Defense* (Oxford: Oxford University Press, 2004); L. E. White, "Subordination, Rhetorical Survival Skills, and Sunday Shoes: Notes on the Hearing of Mrs. G." (1990) 38 *Buffalo Law Review* 1; R. Shamir, "Suspended in Space: Bedouins Under the Law of Israel" (1996) 30:2 Law & Society Review 231.

16. M. Sahlins, *Islands of History* (Chicago: University of Chicago Press,1985) chapters 1, 4.
17. B. W. Tuchman, *The March of Folly: From Troy to Vietnam* (New York: Ballantine Books, 1984) 11–14.
18. Geertz, *supra* note 7 at 3, 9.
19. Okin, *supra* note 11.
20. A. Martinez, "Cultural Contact: Archaeological Approaches," 5 *International Encyclopedia of the Social & Behavioral Sciences* (2001) 3035-3037; A. Appadurai, "Global Ethnoscapes: Notes and Queries for a Transnational Anthropology," in R. G. Fox, ed, *Recapturing Anthropology: Working in the Present* (Santa Fe: School of American Research Press, 1991); J. Clifford, *Routes: Travel and Translation in the Late Twentieth Century* (Cambridge, MA: Harvard University Press, 1997).
21. See also: J. W. Fernandez, "Cultural Relativism, Anthropology of," 5 *International Encyclopedia of the Social & Behavioral Sciences* (2001) 3110–3113. ("People are usually aware from their domestic everyday experience of the difference of perspective and the relativity in understanding between men and women, the old and the young, the parent and the child, the slow and the quick"; at 3110).
22. R. A. Shweder, "Anthropology's Romantic Rebellion Against the Enlightenment, or There's More to Thinking than Reason and Evidence," in R. A. Shweder and R. A. Levine, eds, *Culture Theory: Essays on Mind, Self, and Emotion* (Cambridge: Cambridge University Press, 1984) 27–66; R. G. D'Andrade, "Cultural Meaning Systems," in R. A. Shweder and R. A. Levine, eds, *Culture Theory: Essays on Mind, Self, and Emotion* (Cambridge: Cambridge University Press, 1984) 88–122; R. Wuthnow, *Meaning and Moral Order: Explorations in Cultural Analysis* (Berkeley: University in California Press, 1987) at 12, 50–52, 69–71 and 86–87; R. Wuthnow et al., *Cultural Analysis* (Boston: Routledge & Kegan, 1984) 77, 82, and 260–61; R. G. D'Andrade, "A Folk Model of the Mind," in D. Holland and N. Quinn, eds, *Cultural Models in Language and Thought* (Cambridge: Cambridge University Press, 1987) 112; R. G. D'Andrade, "Some Propositions about the Relations between Culture and Human Cognition," in J. W. Stigler, R. A. Shweder, and G. Herdt, eds, *Cultural Psychology: Essays on Comparative Human Development* (Cambridge: Cambridge University Press, 1990) 65–129; R. A. Shweder, *Thinking Through Cultures: Expeditions in Cultural Psychology* (Cambridge, MA: Harvard University Press, 1991) 101, 102; S. N. Eisenstadt, "The Order-Maintaining and Order-Transforming Dimensions of Culture," in R. Munch and N. J. Smelser, eds, *Theory of Culture* (Berkeley: University of California Press, 1992) 64, at 68; P. DiMaggio, "Culture and Cognition" (1997) 23 Annual Review of Sociology 263; A. Kuper, *Culture: The Anthropologists' Account* (Cambridge, MA: Harvard University Press, 1999) at 35, 57, 61, and 65.
23. T. Luckman, "Shrinking Transcendence, Explaining Religion?" (1990) 50:2 Sociological Analysis 127, 130.
24. U. Hannerz, *Cultural Complexity: Studies in the Social Organization of Meaning* (New York: Columbia University Press, 1992) at 8.
25. M. Lamont and L. Thevenot, "Introduction: Toward a Renewed Comparative Cultural Sociology," in *Rethinking Comparative Cultural Sociology* (Cambridge: Cambridge University Press, 2000) 1, 9.

26. R. Benedict, *Patterns of Culture* (Boston: Houghton Mifflin, 1934) at 23, 24; Gadamer, *Truth and Method, supra* note 6 at 449, holds that "our experience of the world is bound to language" and that "tradition is . . . expressed in language," at 462; he also writes that every language expresses meaning "in its own way"; at 402.
27. H. Lacey, "Understanding Conflicts between North and South," in M. Dascal, ed, *Cultural Relativism and Philosophy: North and Latin American Perspectives* (Leiden: E.J. Brill, 1991) 243–62, at 243.
28. J. Waldron, "One Law for All? The Logic of Cultural Accommodation" (2002) 59 Washington & Lee Law Review 3, at 4.
29. L. Wittgenstein, *Philosophical Investigations*, trans. G. E. M. Anscombe (New York: Macmillan, 1953) at section 584.
30. Lamont and Thevenot, *supra* note 25 at 9.
31. Benedict, *supra* note 26 at 45.
32. Lamont and Thevenot, *supra* note 25 at 9.
33. L. Thevenot and M. Lamont, "Conclusion: Exploring the French and American Polity," in M. Lamont and L. Thevenot, eds, *Rethinking Comparative Cultural Sociology* (Cambridge: Cambridge University Press, 2000) 307, 316.
34. J. Waldron, "Particular Values and Critical Morality" (1989) 77 California Law Review 561–89, at 583.
35. For example, one cannot understand the spirit of the Israeli workplace, the relations between coworkers, and the relations between employees and employers; nor can one understand the relation between "work" and "leisure" in Israeli culture, without taking into account the spirit of the IDF (Israel Defense Forces) where young Israelis go through a workplace experience—a combination of "work" and "fun"—for the first time in their lives. Likewise, one cannot understand the spirit of the Israeli infantry without understanding its roots in the pre-state paramilitary units that were premised on informal and egalitarian interpersonal relations. And finally, one cannot understand the rulings of Israel's Supreme Court in the past four decades without taking into account its unique location in the war of cultures that erupted in Israel in the late 1970s between secular and religious Jews. See: M. Mautner, *Law and the Culture of Israel* (Oxford: Oxford University Press, 2011).
36. Charles Taylor writes about "hypergoods," i.e., "goods which not only are incomparably more important than others but provide the standpoint from which these must be weighted, judged, decided about." C. Taylor, *Sources of the Self—The Making of Modern Identity* (Cambridge, MA: Harvard University Press, 1989) 63. In a different context, P. Feyerabend calls these "universal principles": they "underlie every element of the cosmos (of the theory), every fact (every concept)," and thus their suspension "means suspending all facts and all concepts." P. Feyerabend, *Against Method*, 3rd edn (London and New York: Verso, 1975) at 205. In still another context, infrastructural categories function similarly to myths (such as those of the book of Genesis) in a culture.
37. J. Overing, "Translation as a Creative Process: The Power of the Name," in L. Holy, ed, *Comparative Anthropology* (Oxford: Blackwell, 1987) 70, 71, 72; M. Dascal, "Introduction," in M. Dascal, ed, *Cultural Relativism and Philosophy: North and Latin American Perspectives* (Leiden: E.J. Brill, 1991) 1–9, at 3.
38. Gadamer, *supra* note 6.
39. Shweder, *Thinking Through Cultures, supra* note 22.
40. Cf. B. Parekh, "Minority Practices and Principles of Toleration" (1996) 30 International Migration Review 251.
41. M. E. Spiro, "Cultural Relativism and the Future of Anthropology" (1986) 1 Cultural Anthropology 259, at 260–61. See also: A. Barnard, *History and Theory in Anthropology* (Cambridge: Cambridge University Press, 2000) at chapter 7; G. Harman, "Moral Relativism Defended" (1975) 84 The Philosophical Review 3 (moral judgments are in a logical sense made in relation to implicit agreements on morality; this is not to deny, however, that some moralities are "objectively" better than others or that there are objective standards for assessing moralities). On normative relativism and its history, see: Fernandez, *supra* note 21. A famous statement of the normative relativist position may be

found in the 1947 Statement of the American Anthropological Association (AAA) submitted to the United Nations Commission on Human Rights: "[N]o technique of qualitatively evaluating cultures has been discovered.... Standards and values are relative to the culture from which they derive ... Ideas of right and wrong, good and evil, are found in all societies, though they differ in their expression among different peoples. What is held to be a human right in one society may be regarded as anti-social by another people, or by the same people in a different period of their history." "Statement on Human Rights" (1947) 49 American Anthropologist 539–43, at 540. The significant involvement of anthropologists, as well as the AAA, in the human rights movement since the 1990s, signals a reversal of this relativistic stance. See: M. Mautner, "From 'Honor' to 'Dignity': How Should a Liberal State Treat Non-Liberal Cultural Groups?" (2008) 9 Theoretical Enquiries in Law 609–42, at 629–30. Another well-known relativist position is found in Michael Walzer's discussion of justice: "Justice is relative to social meaning... We cannot say what is due to this person or that one until we know how these people relate to one another through the things they make and distribute.... A given society is just if its substantive life is lived in a certain way—that is, in a way faithful to the shared understandings of the members . . . Every substantive account of distributive justice is a local account." M. Walzer, *Spheres of Justice* (New York: Basic Books, 1983) 312–14. John Rawls's transition from *A Theory of Justice* (Cambridge, MA: Harvard University Press, 1971) to *Political Liberalism* (New York: Columbia University Press, 2005) signals a shift from universalistic theorizing to theorizing that fits the particular conditions of certain societies only, namely liberal democratic ones.

42. "The truth or falsity of moral judgments, or their justification, is not absolute or universal, but is relative to traditions, convictions, or practices of a group," C. Gowans, "Moral Relativism," in *The Stanford Encyclopedia of Philosophy (Spring 2014 Edition)*, Edward N. Zalta (ed.), URL = <http://plato.stanford.edu/archives/spr2014/entries/moral-relativism/>.

43. "At the point of cultural intersections, there must be a breakdown of critical or comparative discourse because there are no pertinent trans-cultural yardsticks of evaluation." M. Krausz, "Crossing Cultures: Two Universalisms and Two Relativisms," in M. Dascal, ed, *Cultural Relativism and Philosophy: North and Latin American Perspectives* (Leiden: E.J. Brill, 1991) 233–42, at 239.

44. A. Dundes Renteln, "Relativism and the Search for Human Rights" (1988) 90 American Anthropologist 56, at 63–64; G. Obeyesekere, "Methodological and Philosophical Relativism" (1966) 1:3 MAN (n.s.) 368–74 (arguing that cultural comparison is possible).

45. See text to *supra* notes 6–8.

46. Taylor, "Politics of Recognition," *supra* note 7.

47. Ibid., at 62.

48. Ibid., at 72–73. See also: Renteln, *supra* note 44 ("where the act is in accordance with the society's internal standards, but violates the critic's own standard (an external one), criticism of an ethnocentric sort is possible"; at 64)

49. Gadamer, *Truth and Method, supra* note 6 at 367.

50. Ibid.

51. Ibid. See also at 303, 361–62, 363, 383.

52. Bernstein, *supra* note 7 at 162.

53. A. Gutmann and D. F. Thompson, *Democracy and Disagreement* (Cambridge, MA: Harvard University Press, 1996); J. Bohman, *Public Deliberation: Pluralism, Complexity and Democracy* (Cambridge, MA: MIT Press, 1996); J. S. Dryzek, *Deliberative Democracy and Beyond* (Oxford: Oxford University Press, 2000); J. M. Valadez, *Deliberative Democracy, Political Legitimacy, and Self-Determination in Multicultural Societies* (Boulder: Westview Press, 2001); A. Gutmann and D. F. Thompson, *Why Deliberative Democracy?* (Princeton, NJ: Princeton University Press, 2004).

54. H. Arendt, "The Crisis in Culture," in *Between Past and Future* (New York: Penguin Books, 2006) 197–226; R. Beiner, "Hannah Arendt on Judging," in H. Arendt and R. Beiner, eds, *Lectures on Kant's Political Philosophy* (Chicago: University of Chicago Press, 1982) 89; M. Passerin d'Entrèves, *The Political Philosophy of Hannah Arendt* (London and New

York: Routledge, 1994) at chapter 3; J. Nedelsky, "Communities of Judgment and Human Rights" (2000) 1 Theoretical Inquiries in Law 1–38; L. Bilsky, *Transformative Justice: Israeli Identity on Trial* (Ann Arbor: University of Michigan Press, 2004) at chapter 5.

55. Much ambiguity seems to surround John Rawls's concept of "public reason," i.e., whether it applies to democratic deliberation or to democratic justification. I think that the latter is the better understanding of the concept. See: M. Mautner, "Religion in Politics: Rawls and Habermas on Deliberation and Justification," in H. Dagan, S. Lifshitz, and Y. Z. Stern, eds, *The Role of Religion in Human Rights Discourse* (Jerusalem: Israel Democracy Institute, expected 2014).
56. O. Schachter, "Human Dignity as a Normative Concept" (1983) 77 American Journal of International Law 848, at 849.
57. Renteln, *supra* note 44 at 64.
58. Rawls, *Political Liberalism*, *supra* note 41 at 133–72.
59. For use of the term "overlapping consensus" with regard to the human rights doctrine see: C. McCrudden, "Human Dignity and Judicial Interpretation of Human Rights" (2008) 19 European Journal of International Law 655; C. Taylor, "A World Consensus on Human Rights" (Summer 1996) *Dissent* 15; Mautner, *supra* note 41 at 632–33. For the same approach see: A. Gutmann, "The Challenge of Multiculturalism in Political Ethics" (1993) 22 Philosophy & Public Affairs 171; Renteln, *supra* note 44; MacIntyre, *supra* note 9; Nedelsky, *supra* note 54. On the relation between the relativist position and human rights doctrine see: J. Waldron, "How to Argue for a Universal Claim" (1995) 30 Columbia Human Rights Law Review 305.
60. R. Brightman, "Forget Culture: Replacement, Transcendence, Relexification" (1995) 10 Cultural Anthropology 509; P. DiMaggio, *supra* note 22; W. H. Sewell Jr., "The Concept(s) of Culture," in V. E. Bonnell and L. Hunt, eds, *Beyond the Cultural Turn: New Directions in the Study of Society and Culture* (Berkeley: University of California Press, 1999) 35.
61. M. Mautner, "Three Approaches to Law and Culture" (2011) 96 Cornell Law Review 101.
62. The following is based on: Navon, *supra* note 2; Rabbi Sg'r, "Between Personal Perfection and Social Labeling: 'Talmud Torah' for Women According to the Rambam," in Z. Maor, ed, *The Two Great Lightings: Women's Equality in the Family from a New Jewish Point of View* (2007) 35 (in Hebrew); Rabbi Sg'r, "'Seeing the Voices': 'Yeshivesh' Scholarlinessand the 'Female Voice' in Torah Studying," in Z. Maor, id, at 63 (Hebrew); A. Weinroth, *Feminism and Judaism* (Tel Aviv: Yedioth Ahronoth Publishers, 2001) (Hebrew); E. Fisher, "Normative Considerations in the Rulings on Women's Torah Study," in M. Shilo, ed, *To Be a Jewish Woman* (Jerusalem: Urim, 2001) 94 (Hebrew); "Women," in *Oztar Israel Encyclopedia*, vol. 7 (1924) 117 (Hebrew); "Women," in Encyclopedia Judaica, vol. 21, 2nd edn (Farmington Hills, MI: Gale, 2007)2007), at 156; Z. Zohar, "The Attitude of Rabbi Yosef Masas Towards Women's Torah Study" (2000) 82 Pe'amim 150 (Hebrew).
63. Maimonides, Mishne Torah, Torah Study Rules, Chapter 1, 13.
64. M. Raz, "She Opened Her Mouth in Wisdom and Piety on her Tongue, On Scholary Women Through History," in *The Jewish People Today: Belonging and Commitment* http://www.macam.ac.il/
65. A. T. Kronman, "Precedent and Tradition" (1990) 99 Yale Law Journal 1029–1068, at 1044.
66. Ibid.
67. I. Kant, *An Answer to the Question: What is Enlightenment?*, Berlinische Monatsschrift, iv (1784) 193.
68. Kant draws a distinction between the "private" and "public" use of reason, and elaborates on the role of this distinction in the context of the church: a pastor may disseminate and perpetuate the church's dogma among his congregation because that is his function performing a role in a religious organization. But as a public scholar, that same person should face no constraints whatsoever in expressing his thoughts and speaking his mind about the church's dogmas.

69. J. S. Mill, in S. M. Okin, ed, *The Subjection of Women* (Indianapolis, IN: Hackett Publishing, 1988).
70. Ibid., at 5.
71. For communitarians, a community's way of life "forms the basis for a public ranking of conceptions of the good, and the weight given to an individual's preferences depends on how much she conforms or contributes to this common good. A communitarian state ... encourages people to adopt conceptions of the good that conform to the community's way of life, while discouraging conceptions of the good that conflict with it." W. Kymlicka, "Community," in R. E. Gooding and P. Pettit, eds, *A Companion to Contemporary Political Philosophy* (Oxford: Blackwell, 1993) 366, at 370.
72. Kronman, *supra* note 65 at 1032. Indeed, Karl N. Llewellyn titled his last book *The Common Law Tradition* (Boston and Toronto: Little Brown, 1960).
73. See, e.g., K. N. Llewellyn, *The Bramble Bush* (Oxford: Oxford University Press, 2008) ("Often the prior cases push so strongly toward one line-up that [the judge] will not even see the chance ... to line them up differently. Then, unless the result raises the hair (*his* hair, not yours!), and forces a different outcome to speak at the muzzle of a gun, the judge will never get as far as inquiring into justice. He will decide 'by law' and let it go at that"; at 77).
74. J. Joyce, *A Portrait of the Artist as a Young Man* (1930) 113.
75. Rabbi Y. Dov Soloveitchik, "God's Three Names in the Bible," in Avraham Beit Din, ed, *Chapters in Rabbi Y. D. Halevi Soloveitchik's Thought* (1984) 11, 17 (Hebrew).
76. See Feyerabend, *supra* note 36.
77. Wittgenstein, *supra* note 29, section 217.
78. McCrudden, *supra* note 59 at 659–60, 686; D. G. Reaume, "Discrimination and Dignity" (2003) 63 Louisiana Law Review 645, 689.
79. Mill, *supra* note 70 at 17.
80. Ibid., at 88–89.
81. Taylor, "The Politics of Recognition," *supra* note 7.
82. The rise of religious feminism has been discernible since the 1970s in Christianity, Judaism, and Islam. See: M. Shmueli, "The Power to Define Tradition: Feminist Challenges to Religion and the Israeli Supreme Court" (PhD dissertation, University of Toronto, 2005).
83. There are many other manifestations of this emergent religious feminism: rabbis' rulings and conduct (e.g., sexual harassment) are being scrutinized from a feminist perspective; new theologies devised that integrate traditional Jewish elements with feminist insights; and new interpretations of traditional texts offered by reading feminist insights into them, emphasizing the autonomy and personal self-realization of women. Since the early 1990s, women have been serving as rabbinical advocates in rabbinical courts and as members of municipal bodies in charge of providing religious services. Synagogues are being designed in ways that diminish the separation between men and women and that do not convey the inferiority of women (e.g., seating women in parallel to men, as opposed to seating them in the rear of synagogues); and women have begun actively participating in religious rituals previously reserved for men. See Mautner, *supra* note 35 at 205–6.
84. It is interesting to note that even though Ultra-Orthodox speakers often criticize the positions and practices of the religious-Zionist group, the feminist practices of religious Zionism have not been criticized.
85. The Ultra-Orthodox group deviates from certain of Maimonides's rulings with regard to women. Thus, Maimonides held that women should spend most of their time at home and be allowed out only once a month. The Ultra-Orthodox group certainly does not abide by this ruling. Mishne Torah 13, 14.
86. E. Frankel Paul, F. D. Miller, Jr., and J. Paul, eds, *Human Flourishing* (Cambridge: Cambridge University Press, 1999).
87. Mill, *supra* note 70 at 107–8. Interestingly enough, Mill's remarks on "the dull and hopeless life" of those forbidden "to exercise the[ir] practical abilities" very much apply to the fate of many Ultra-Orthodox *men* who, because of the centrality of the value of Torah study in their group, spend their lives in *yeshivot* even though they lack the talent, skill,

and curiosity required to devote one's life to learning, and therefore spend many hours a day chatting, gossiping, etc.
88. Mill, ibid., at 108.
89. Okin, *supra* note 11 at 673. See also: A. Margalit, *The Decent Society* (Cambridge, MA: Harvard University Press, 1996) ("working is the unique essence of humans, and the more a person actualizes his essence, the more human he is.... It is certainly wrong for a decent society to hinder anyone from attaining a meaningful occupation"; at 253).
90. McCrudden, *supra* note 59 at 689–90, 690–91; Reaume, *supra* note 78 at 663 and 667.
91. Reaume, ibid., at 674–75.
92. R. Rorty, "Solidarity," in *Contingency, Irony, and Solidarity* (Cambridge: Cambridge University Press, 1989) 189.
93. F. Dostoyevsky, *The Double: A Poem of St. Petersburg*, trans. G. Bird (London: Harvill, 1957).
94. J. L. Talmon, "National Revival," in D. Ohana, ed, *The Riddle of the Present and the Cunning of History* (Jerusalem: The Bialik Institute, 2000) 68, at 69 (Hebrew). See also: H. Arendt, "We Refugees," in J. Kohn and R. H. Feldman, eds, *The Jewish Writings* (New York: Schocken Books, 2007) 264.
95. R. Post, "Prejudicial Appearances: The Logic of American Antidiscrimination Law" (2000) 88 California Law Review 1–41; Reaume, *supra* note 78 at 667, 673, and 679–86.
96. Mill, *supra* note 70 at 12 and 13.
97. Ibid., at chapter 3.
98. Ibid., at 54.
99. Ibid., at 55.
100. Deuteronomy 33:18.
101. Midrash Tanchuma, Pinhas, 5.
102. This division of labor is a new phenomenon in the history of the Ultra-Orthodox group in Israel. Until the 1950s, only a minority of Ultra-Orthodox men devoted their lives to Torah study. But then the group transformed itself into a "learners' society," to use a term coined by M. Friedman, i.e., a group in which a large number of men devote their lives to Torah study. Interestingly enough, Ultra-Orthodox women played a major role in this great transformation. In the years following World War I, Ultra-Orthodox women established an educational system for women in Eastern Europe. In the 1950s, Israeli Ultra-Orthodox women who had studied in that system took it upon themselves to work (at the time, mainly as teachers) and provide their families' subsistence and thereby allow their husbands to devote their lives to Torah study. The transformation was also made possible by the Israeli welfare state, whose allowances substantially contribute to the subsistence of Ultra-Orthodox families whose men devote their lives to Torah study. Also, the Israeli state took it upon itself to substantially finance the Ultra-Orthodox educational system (for both male and female students). M. Friedman, *The Ultra-Orthodox Woman* (Jerusalem: The Jerusalem Institute for Israel Studies, 1988) (Hebrew). See also: M. Friedman, *The Ultra-Orthodox Society: Origins, Trends and Processes* (Jerusalem: The Jerusalem Institute for Israel Studies, 1991) chapter 4 (Hebrew); T. El-Or, *Educated and Ignorant: On Ultra-Orthodox Women and Their World* (Boulder, CO: Lynne Rienner, 1992) chapter 2 (Hebrew).
103. Okin, *supra* note 11 at 673. The fact that women are regarded as of lower status than men in a society has immediate material consequences for the life conditions of women: poor women give up food to feed their husbands and children, fail to make use of medical treatment, etc.
104. Friedman, *Ultra-Orthodox Woman*, *supra* note 102; T. El-Or, "The Length of the Slits and the Spread of Luxury: Reconstructing the Subordination of Ultra-Orthodox Jewish Women Through the Patriarchy of Men Scholars" (1993) 29:9/10 Sex Roles 585–98, at 585 and 594 ("The scholars' families are socially rewarded for their poverty, and women are given a prominent role in furthering the community's goals and ideals. Rejecting the idea of prosperity and presenting the surrounding world as a vanity fair helps denounce the values of that world."); ibid., at 596 ("Marriage takes them beyond individual gains and into the collective effort to maintain the society of men scholars.... Thus, marriage is not presented

as an ideal, but as an important relationship that offers these modern women relevant and authentic meaning for their situation. . . . Being the modest wife of a scholar becomes a highly desired state among contemporary ultra-Orthodox women."); B. Morris, "Agents or Victims of Religious Ideology? Approaches to Locating Hasidic Women in Feminist Studies," in J. S. Belcove-Shalin, ed, *New World Hasidism: Ethnographic Studies of Hasidic Jews in America* (Albany: State University of New York Press, 1995) 161 (discussing the considerable activism demonstrated by Hasidic women in the 1950s); ibid., ("the 'victim' portrait of Hasidic women must be reconsidered in light of new evidence on Hasidic activism. Often it is the Hasidic woman who actively promotes her own role and who serves as an advocate for the Hasidic ideology of separate spheres"; at 62).

105. Okin, *supra* note 11 at 673.
106. Ibid., at 664. (Emphasis in the original text). See also: J. T. Levy, *The Multiculturalism of Fear* (Oxford: Oxford University Press, 2000) ("In modern multicultural, multiethnic, and multireligious societies, there is constant pressure on minority cultures. It is difficult to maintain and transmit a culture when surrounded by alien influences. . . . [In such circumstances] the home becomes the primary location for culture to be transmitted and carried on. This makes mothers especially central to the nationalism or cultural traditions of minority groups, and raises the pressure on them to maintain the purity of the old ways"; at 53).
107. See also: Nussbaum, *supra* note 14 ("For many Western women, an especially deep part of the search for the meaning of life is played by romantic love, whether of a woman or of a man; this tie, and the search for this tie, to some extent pull against women's solidarity with other women in groups. Everywhere I went in India, by contrast, women related to the group as to their primary community and source of emotional sustenance; the Western woman's focus on romance and (in many cases) on men is regarded as somewhat strange, and not necessarily conducive to women's functioning"; at 790–91). Reuven Rubin (1893–1974) was one of Israel's greatest painters. His wife Esther devoted her life to promoting and managing his career. In her memoirs she writes: "I have often been asked whether I don't have a sense of loss for not devoting my life to the promotion of a career of my own . . . My choice to be Rubin's assistant and partner was conscientious; it was made out of recognition of my self-worth. A full partnership existed between the two of us and we both invested the best of our talents and virtues in it." E. Rubin, *Bouquet of Memories* (Steimatzky, 1999) 153–54 (Hebrew).
108. *Plessey v Ferguson*, 163 US 537 (1896).
109. *Brown v Board of Education*, 347 US 483 (1954).
110. Bavli, Shvuot, 30, 1; Baba Kamah, 88, 1; Shulchan Aruch, Choshen Mishpat, 35, 14.
111. Bavli, Megilah, 23, 1.
112. El-Or, *supra* note 104; Morris, *supra* note 104 at 172–73; T. El-Or, "Paradoxical and Social Boundaries," in E. Fuchs, ed, *Israeli Women's Studies: A Reader* (New Brunswick, NJ: Rutgers University Press, 2005) 133; B. Greenberg, "Ultra-Orthodox Women Confront Feminism," (June 1996) 63 Moment 36. On the face of it, there is an interesting development here: Ultra-Orthodox women joining secular women to take advantage of the opportunities offered by the modern job market. In many instances, however, because they lack higher education and high professional skills, Ultra-Orthodox women perform low-level jobs in the secular job market.
113. El-Or, *supra* note 104.
114. Okin, *supra* note 11 at 672.
115. Ibid. Emphasis in the original text.
116. Ibid., at 680. Emphasis in the original text. For a similar approach, see: S. M. Okin, "Is Multiculturalism Bad for Women?," in J. Cohen, M. Howard, and M. C. Nussbaum, eds, *Is Multiculturalism Bad for Women?* (Princeton, NJ: Princeton University Press, 1999) 7, at 9 and 22–23.
117. See text following *supra* note 48.
118. S. Macedo, "Liberal Civic Education and Religious Fundamentalism: The Case of God v. John Rawls" (1995) 105 Ethics 468, at 470.
119. Ibid.

120. Ibid., at 496.
121. J. Raz, *The Morality of Freedom* (New York: Oxford University Press, 1986).
122. Ibid., at 423.
123. Ibid., at 424.
124. Note that Raz concludes his discussion with the following proviso: "These remarks are of course abstract and speculative. They are meant to indicate the direction in which the conclusions of this book lead, rather than to deal with the issue in depth." Ibid., at 424
125. J. Raz, "Multiculturalism: A Liberal Perspective," in *Ethics in the Public Domain: Essays in the Morality of Law and Politics* (Oxford: Clarendon Press, 1994) 155; J. Raz, "How Perfect Should One Be? And Whose Culture Is It?," in J. Cohen, M. Howard, and M. C. Nussbaum, eds, *Is Multiculturalism Bad for Women?* (Princeton, NJ: Princeton University Press, 1999) 95.
126. Shweder, *supra* note 12 at 235–36. Paul Kahn writes about "that particular form of academic imperialist: the liberal theorist." Paul Kahn, *Putting Liberalism in its Place* (Princeton, NJ: Princeton University Press, 2005) 13.
127. There are liberal thinkers who may be termed "diversity liberals." They hold that the central liberal value is not autonomy, but diversity: it is the function of the liberal state to serve as a framework for the peaceful coexistence of people with diverse conceptions of the good life. These thinkers therefore call for "restraint" on the part of the state in its relations with non-liberal groups. For sources, see: Mautner, *supra* note 41 at 611.
128. R. Dworkin, *Life's Dominion: An Argument About Abortion, Euthanasia, and Individual Freedom* (New York: Knopf, 1993) at chapter 3; Kronman, *supra* note 65; S. C. Rockefeller, "Comment," in A. Gutmann, ed, *Multiculturalism and "The Politics of Recognition"* (Princeton, NJ: Princeton University Press, 1992) 87; A. W. Musschenga, "Intrinsic Value as a Reason for the Preservation of Minority Cultures" (1998) 1 Ethical Theory & Moral Practice 201; B. Oomen and S. Tempelman, "The Power of Definition," in Y. Donders et al., eds, *Law and Cultural Diversity* (Utrecht: SIM, 1999) 7, at 16–18.
129. A. Gutmann, "Communitarian Critics of Liberalism," in S. Avineri and A. de-Shalit, eds, *Communitarianism and Individualism* (Oxford: Oxford University Press, 1992) 120, at 126.
130. Nussbaum, *supra* note 14, at 765. On the connection between philosophy and empirical knowledge, see also: R. Beiner, *What's the Matter with Liberalism?* (Berkeley: University of California Press, 1992) at 20–21, 32; J. Bohman, *supra* note 54, at 3-4.

# 9

# Religious Claims as Public Reason?

*Polygamy as a Case Study*

ANGELA CAMPBELL

## 1. Introduction

This chapter explores the value of framing claims about controversial practices in terms of "religion."[*] It will ask whether the expression of public arguments in terms of faith enhances or stunts effective discussion and understanding across cultures, perspectives, beliefs, and traditions. These questions are assessed through the use of a case study of polygamy in a Canadian community where this practice is openly taken up by residents, and whose leaders have claimed publicly that the group's practice of polygamy is grounded in religious convictions. This community, known as "Bountiful," British Columbia, is comprised of about 1000 followers of the Fundamentalist Church of Jesus Christ of Latter Day Saints ("FLDS"). They adhere to plural marriage as a central tenet of their faith, believing that a man's taking of plural wives not only leads to a good terrestrial life, but also facilitates entry into the "Celestial Kingdom."

Media representation of Bountiful has not been flattering. The press has portrayed this community as a space in which lecherous older men prey upon young women, taking them as their teenage brides without the consent of anyone except, possibly, their parents and the community "bishop" or leader. This image is also fueled by the isolation of many FLDS communities like Bountiful, typically situated in rural locations removed from cosmopolitan life, as well as by women's conventional appearance in the FLDS Church, which requires ankle-length pioneer dresses and untrimmed braided hair.

Bountiful's residents practice polygamy openly even though it is criminalized in Canada. Until recently, this situation was of no practical consequence. However, in 2009, the attorney general of British Columbia ordered, for the first time, the arrest and prosecution of two male community leaders. This was a notable move, given that prior to this, there had been just one successful prosecution (in 1899) for polygamy since the Canadian Parliament established this offence in 1890.[1] While the two men subject to these 2009 criminal charges were on conditional release, public discussion focused on whether their claims contesting the charges as an unconstitutional violation of religious freedom would succeed.[2] Conversations concentrated on the appropriate breadth of protection, or "accommodation," to give religious and cultural practices that apparently run counter to core "Canadian values" like gender equality, dignity, and even a "Christian" perception of marriage.[3]

The debate over whether Canada's legal treatment of polygamy squares with protection for religious freedom continues to simmer, even though the charges against the two Bountiful men were quashed pursuant to a September 2009 judgment, which ruled that the acting attorney general had exceeded his jurisdiction by bringing these arrests.[4] Nevertheless, issues at the core of the halted criminal case were adjudicated in a reference case heard by the British Columbia Supreme Court (the "Polygamy Reference"). The Court was asked to determine whether Canada's prohibition of polygamy in section 293 of its Criminal Code (CC) infringes on rights protected by the *Canadian Charter of Rights and Freedoms* and if so, whether any infringement could be reasonably justified in a "free and democratic society."[5] Beyond this initial constitutional question, the Court was also asked to identify the "necessary elements" of section 293 CC and in this connection was directed to consider whether the offence of polygamy requires the Crown to establish factors such as exploitation, involvement of a minor, abuse of authority, or a context of dependence.[6]

Arguments led by *Amicus* counsel—appointed to respond to claims advanced in the Polygamy Reference by the attorneys general of British Columbia and of Canada—stressed that the ban on polygamy in section 293 CC interferes with religious freedom.[7] This is not surprising. While section 293 CC was argued to contravene a number of constitutionally protected rights (e.g., equality, liberty, freedom of association), polygamy has been publicly discussed and evaluated almost exclusively as a religious practice.[8] Moreover, of the rights potentially compromised by section 293 CC, religious freedom may have been the most straightforward for the *Amicus* to establish as infringed by the polygamy ban.[9] Social and legal appreciations of polygamy thus pressed arguments to be framed with reference to faith-based claims, forcing the litigation and the parties concerned—notably FLDS community members—into a "religious corner."

In a decision rendered in late 2011,[10] the British Columbia Supreme Court held that the polygamy ban within section 293 CC should be upheld. In his reasons for judgment, Bauman CJSC found the provision to infringe on none of the fundamental liberties protected by the Canadian constitution, with two exceptions. First, Bauman CJSC deemed that the application of section 293 CC to minors was overbroad and violated the principles of liberty in a manner that failed to accord with the principles of fundamental justice, as protected by section 7 of the Canadian *Charter*. Thus, section 293 CC was read down to exclude application to persons under the age of 18.

The second exception to the general finding that s. 293 did not encroach upon constitutional rights pertained, unsurprisingly, to religious freedom. Bauman CJSC held that for at least some practitioners of polygamy, the practice had religious meaning and therefore, its legal prohibition interfered with the right to freedom of religion guaranteed by section 2(a) of the *Charter*. The judgment proceeded, however, to find that this limitation on religious freedom was justified given the harm the Court deemed inherent to polygamy, which threatened women, children, society, and "the institution of monogamous marriage."[11]

This essay does not seek to offer a critique or normative evaluation of the Polygamy Reference. Rather, it comments on religion's centrality within conversations concerning polygamy's moral and legal propriety. Having conducted doctrinal and empirical research on polygamy, specifically on polygamy in Bountiful, over the last four years, the religious roots of this practice for residents of this community are clear to me. Plural marriage is a central tenet within FLDS, or fundamentalist Mormon, theology.[12] Indeed, it was over this very practice that fundamentalists broke away from the mainstream Mormon Church, when the latter issued edicts calling for the cessation of plural marriage in 1890.[13]

While my research and fieldwork have affirmed the sincerity of claims grounding Bountiful's plural marriage in FLDS theology, I think it is erroneous to focus exclusively on religion in current discussions about this difficult and controversial practice. In my own research, I have visited Bountiful twice, once for five days and a second time for seven days, with a view to meeting and interviewing women to learn about how they understand formal state-made rules regarding polygamy and how these intersect with community norms about this form of marriage. In this connection, I have formally interviewed 22 women, all adults, and have spoken to a variety of other women who wished to share their thoughts with me only off the record. During these discussions, it became apparent that for many women in Bountiful, polygamy is taken up not only because it is perceived as religiously mandated, but it is also looked upon favorably for economic, social, and even political reasons. Participants in my research spoke in clear terms about the way in which having "sister wives" helps to increase financial security in a household, facilitates the pursuit of personal goals like undertaking postsecondary education, provides companionship, and strengthens women's decision-making power in the domestic sphere.

In this chapter, I want to explore the particular value of framing claims about polygamy in terms of religion, while also examining the risk this poses for neglecting other crucial dimensions. This chapter is thus divided in two parts. The first draws on John Rawls's notion of "public reason." It examines whether religiously rooted claims are conducive to dialogue and understanding across different social and cultural groups as these claims pertain to controversial beliefs and attitudes. In the second part, I discuss why religious claims, although potentially valuable to public debate and discussion, are "incomplete." For Rawls, a political conception that lacks completeness will not be an "adequate framework of thought in the light of which the discussion of fundamental political questions can be carried out."[14] I will argue that religious claims do not satisfy this requirement of completeness, as they fail to account for the multifaceted rationales that exist, even within devout communities, for ostensibly "religious" practices. They also will not necessarily be comprehensible to all citizens to whom these claims are made. Religious claims on their own thus do not provide an adequate structure for assessing politically and socially controversial practices.

In discussing these two key points in this chapter, I use the case study of polygamy in Bountiful to illustrate my argument. My use of a case study also aims, indirectly, at elucidating the analytical helpfulness and inherent limitations of canonical liberal political theorists such as Rawls. It takes up a process of "normative reflection"[15] upon first principles. David Thacher argues that case studies can provide such reflection by "bringing into view situations we had not previously envisioned."[16] Thus, through this chapter I hope both to nuance conventional perceptions of polygamy through the lens of liberal political theory, while also pointing to fault lines in theory where it shows itself unable to account for the heterogeneity and blurriness of "political" and "public" expression within real communities.

## 2. Religion's Political Relevance

In this first section, I will examine the value of framing claims about controversial practices in religious terms. I look specifically at claims made in "public" settings. However, before engaging in this analysis, a brief comment on what is meant by "public" is required. As discussed in Section 2, I am alert to the inherent problems with this terminology and of any blunt bifurcation between "private" and "public" zones. Nevertheless, I use the term "public" here as referring to its conceptual significance in the political-theory debates upon which I rely in this section. My own appreciation of this term, and the way that I use it here, is that of a space or a conversation that can be legitimately observed or accessed by anyone, even though it is the case that a number of factors might obstruct this access for certain members of society.

Such "public" discussions about polygamy in Canada—for example, those that have unfolded in the media,[17] legislatures,[18] or online blogs and commentary[19]—have cast this as a practice grounded almost exclusively in religion. In the Canadian Polygamy Reference, two competing representations of the prohibition of polygamy under Canadian criminal law were presented: a first cast the ban as leading inexorably to religious persecution; the other contends that any limitation of rights is justified and necessary to protect against harms, especially those posed to women and children.[20]

The discussion in this part examines the relevance and the limitations of religiously rooted claims in public debate over morally controversial practices like polygamy. It will draw on John Rawls's prescription, for political debates in a liberal state, for "public reason": the requirement that political positions should be deliberated upon publicly by means of reasons that citizens from diverse religious and cultural backgrounds can understand and accept.[21] It will examine whether Rawls's notion of public reason is helpful for evaluating the political relevance of religion, and in exploring whether claims about religion in Canada's polygamy debate are politically reasonable, practically accurate, intellectually satisfying, and morally credible. To this end, two particular questions are addressed in this part. A first considers whether advancing claims in religious terms meets Rawls's requirement of public reason; a second asks whether religious claims effectively facilitate rational public conversation in a plural society.

## 2.1. Religious Claims as Public Reason

When residents of a religious community adopt a controversial practice, is it enough for them to engage in discussions and seek out accommodation and acceptance of this practice in terms framed only in the language of religion? Is this enough to foster rational public conversation? Specifically, what is at stake in the pluralistic liberal state's demand that religious citizens adopt "secular reasons" when making demands for rights or protections from the state? What may be "lost in translation" in the process of converting religious reasons to secular ones, and is this loss justified by the need for a common ground for public exchange on controversial practices, like polygamy, which appear anchored to religious belief?

For Rawls, political reasons need to be logically correct, open to rational appraisal, and evidentially supportable.[22] This emerges from *Political Liberalism* where Rawls spells out how citizens have a duty to adopt a certain *form* of public discourse.[23] Specifically, there is an onus to give reasons for attitudes and behavior that others can understand and with which they can engage What is not entirely clear from Rawls, however, is whether the requirement of public reason implies that public claims grounded in *religion* (e.g., "I think or behave this way because it is what my god commands, or because I would otherwise be committing a sin.") be *translated* into civil or *"secular"* terms. Rawls himself seems to question whether a firm division can be drawn between what is on the one hand "religious," and, on the other, "secular" or "public."[24] Nevertheless, his work suggests that faith-based claims alone will not be conducive to rational political discussions and that some work is needed to transform them into terms more susceptible to understanding outside of the religious group that advances the claim.

In thinking about this requirement of translation of religious claims into "public" or "secular" claims, three concerns are quickly apparent. A first pertains to the possibility that some religious claims may simply be untranslatable into secular terms. One might ask whether there is a way for a person to grasp the experience and meaning of a religious doctrine to which she does not adhere. James Boyd White takes this position, noting the "deep disjunction" between religious experience and public language, and insists that different ways of discussing ideological concepts or views (as he terms them, "modes of discourse") *can* share a public space, but only if there is no insistence that parties "make complete sense in terms of the other."[25] White ultimately concedes that religion and rationality cannot be so simply divided, and he accepts that religion will seep into public spaces but that law should accept it will never fully or accurately appreciate religious reasons.[26]

White's observations reflect his concern about plurality and difference, and his caution is well taken. Having said this, White's view seems unduly bleak to me and unrealistic in a pluralistic state, where practical necessity demands dialogue between and within secular and religious groups. Conversations about religion should expect some measure of understanding to transfer from the religious realm into public debate. In the polygamy example, abandoning the hope that law might account, at least in part, for how a polygamist sees her marriage and family structure as connected to her god suggests that there are some practices just too "different" for us to comprehend. This risks alienating and marginalizing minority religious groups.

A second concern is whether the requirement of translating a religious claim into more accessible "public reasons" compromises the dignity of a devout individual. Habermas alludes to this in his writings on Rawls and public reason. Habermas seems to question, or at least be ambivalent about, the need for "generally accessible reasons" in regard to religious beliefs and practices. He does not see secularism as commanding citizens "personally to supplement their public statements of religious convictions by equivalents in a generally accessible language."[27] He further asks whether the requirement of providing "secular" reasons, or at least a balance between religious and civic convictions, would be overly onerous for devout people. We can foresee in particular that where a person's sense of belief "nurtures his or her entire life," a requirement to move from religious to political/civic reasoning when in the public sphere may be untenable. From this perspective, excluding religiously based discussion in the public sphere risks curtailing discussion and losing opportunities for meaningful dialogue.[28] As discussed in Section 2 below, this point is particularly germane in the community of Bountiful where faith permeates diverse (and for many, all) aspects of daily life, not just decisions about polygamy and marriage. Further, requiring reasons articulated in secular terms for religiously motivated views and behavior can adversely affect the religious believer's sense of dignity and respect by precluding their full recognition as believers in the eyes of the state and by requiring them to simplify or contort the reasons underlying their beliefs so that these can be intelligible outside their respective faith communities.

Allowing religious practices and views to be explained in their own (faith-based) terms may, then, be acceptable for Habermas. He sees this as possible and acceptable provided that "secular citizens . . . open their minds to the possible truth content" of claims made by "citizens of faith" such that even when such claims are not necessarily framed in religious terms, there remains openness to the possibility of religious reasons emerging and being accepted as "generally accessible arguments."[29] Preserving the dignity of a religious citizen, then, is not only about removing the requirement of translation. Rather, even if the citizen is not compelled to "self-censor," Habermas accepts that *some* translation might be required to make her views accessible and compelling, and this entails engagement and collaboration in public settings. Yet his model is a collaborative one. It imagines that substantive religious and "secular" voices may be heard together in the same discussions, with an openness to the possibility that even reasons articulated in secular terms by devout people will be connected to ideas or rationales rooted in faith that can be generally understood and accessible "in the broader political process."[30] This potentiality of shared understanding seems crucial to Habermas, particularly for practices that seem ostensibly oppressive. He indicates that tolerance of such practices requires "compelling reasons," and these must be reasons "that all sides can equally accept."[31] Habermas may overstate the potential for shared understanding and broadly accessible political dialogue, however. As discussed more fully below,[32] his position overlooks the obstacles that many citizens, both secular and religious, will face in participating in political conversations. Because the idea of a shared, accessible political dialogue is so central for Habermas, his neglect of forces that may repel or distance certain actors from the public spaces where such debate occurs creates a noticeable gap in his analysis.

A third concern is whether a requirement of "reasonable" over "religious" language/claims will lead to disingenuous argument in public debate.[33] Wolterstorff is particularly critical of the restraint on religious reason that liberalism appears to promote; he is skeptical of Rawls's requirement that religious citizens engage in public discourse using only secular reasons.[34] He further suggests that respect for religious diversity should allow more space for religious claims so that the respondent to the claim can respect the person fully, namely with respect to her identity as a person of a particular faith.[35] This point is clearly connected to the foregoing concern related to the dignity of devout citizens who may be required to recast claims about practices and beliefs motivated by their faith.

Yet Wolterstorff's critique may be too severe, since sincerity does not seem dispensable to public reason. For example, Dombrowski indicates that public reason may just demand that religious believers *include* nonreligious reasons to be assessed on their own merit, even if they are nonetheless generated by religious reasons.[36] That said, Audi's response to Wolterstorff does suggest that liberalism's exclusion of religious reasons in the public domain risks inciting "leveraging" in a way that conceals one's true perspective and thus forecloses possibilities for knowing or understanding that perspective.[37]

Thus, while for Rawls, religiously framed claims may not clearly count as "public reason," others who have engaged with this concept in political theory warn that requiring religious practices to be explained outside the parameters of faith may be ill advised. Specifically, this requirement might pose an impossible burden to satisfy upon devout citizens since some practices and beliefs might be simply unsusceptible to explanation outside of religion. Requiring a "translation," then, will only result in misunderstanding about the practice or belief. Moreover, this process might impair the dignity of devout citizens and create a risk that "public" (or "secular") claims about religious traditions will be misleading or inaccurate. These risks suggest that there may be some value in allowing religious reasons to "count" as public reason as conceptualized by Rawls. Yet before reaching this conclusion, it is necessary to assess first whether religious claims can facilitate and enrich conversations in a plural society such as Canada.

## 2.2. The Potential of Religious Claims to Facilitate and Enrich Conversations in a Plural Society

While the potential of religious claims to generate public discussion that is accessible across different social constituencies has been questioned, theoretical analyses of such claims indicate that they bear at least two important potential virtues, each reflecting a unique ability to facilitate rich conversations and engagement in a plural society. First, religion is generally a concept amenable to respect and understanding by different communities. In this way it is an expedient basis for dialogue among individuals of diverse backgrounds and views. Second, listening to religious claims should prompt some degree of "reflexivity" among citizens in these different communities, and this in turn should lend itself to greater openness and understanding across these groups. I will discuss each of these features below.

### 2.2.1. Expediency

In many ways, religion can be seen as a practical concept for grounding public debate. Specifically, it is a generally understandable concept, which acts as a type of cognitive shortcut to respecting another's reasons without necessarily engaging in substantive evaluation of them. Put differently, most people can appreciate what religion itself is, even though the teachings of particular religions many not be known, accessible, or acceptable to all. On some level, then, religious claims should help us understand each other and the source of our convictions, even when we do not agree on the correctness or acceptability of those convictions.

Thus, in the context of polygamy, an opponent of this practice may firmly reject the practitioner's religious views. Nevertheless, the fact that the latter articulates reasons for her behavior, choices, or perspective as being linked to religion facilitates some understanding and offers, at a minimum, a starting point for discussion. This being so, even though the practice may alienate outsiders, its religious motivation garners some measure of automatic respect. This point finds some support from Habermas who notes that the claim of religious freedom allows for an argument accessible to all even though deep ideological conflicts persist.[38] The invocation of religion should also prompt "sensitive" dialogue that calls for explanations of both a controversial practice and any attempt to limit it.[39] This notion of sensitive listening is critical to promoting understanding and discussion, even about the most controversial practices asserted as religious. An extreme example is female genital cutting. Sensitive listening to reasons for this practice would rarely—if ever—result in its quick acceptance. Rather, sensitive dialogue requires the listener to resist any visceral horror or outrage she might feel about the practice and prompts her to engage in a conversation about this custom and its origins. Such a conversation would have inherent value, given the social and political outreach and debate that it compels. This remains true even when the conversation does not spark tolerance for "problematic" religious and cultural practices.

On the other hand, it may be argued that rather than serving as a point of departure for conversations about morally controversial topics, religion is actually an effective device for cutting such discussions short. Rorty alludes to this in his work that refers to religion as a "conversation-stopper."[40] Originally Rorty asserted that religion should be left out of public debate and that even if it could influence or motivate a person's position, public arguments should drop or omit references to religion. Instead, he urged that democracy compels reasons that may be endorsed by people of radically different worldviews. From this, we can infer that initially, Rorty perceived faith-based claims to repel, rather than facilitate conversation, which is of course inimical to achieving mutual exchange and understanding.

However, Rorty later—in his own words—"backpedals" from this position in an essay inspired by Wolterstorff in which he maintains that a person should be able to bring her own valued texts—whether or not religious—into public settings. Nevertheless, Rorty continues to protest claims that invoke religious texts that are "sadistic" (pointing to the example of biblical arguments against same-sex relationships). For Rorty, religion can be relevant when used as basis for informing and articulating rules; but citing passages to scripture alone is insufficient to count as serious political discussion.[41] Thus in his revised position, he casts religion as a conversation-stopper only when it is invoked without further discussion or reason.[42] This seems compelling, although it may be limited where the reason that is subsequently relied on to discuss one's position is also framed in terms of faith. It also presumes a broad consensus on what constitutes sufficient "further discussion" to justify a claim or practice: for many religious believers, their faith's imperatives alone constitute the whole of justification.[43]

Connected to Rorty's original point characterizing religion as a "conversation-stopper" is the concern over whether listening seriously to religious claims necessarily leads to, or at least fosters, the accommodation of "problematic" religious practices, especially those aligned with fundamentalist doctrine. The matter can be framed as such: to what extent does engagement with religion, on religious terms, risk abdication to cultural or religious relativism? Some guidance on this is offered by Dombrowski, who favors a "sensitive" hearing of people of faith outside the mainstream, but does not see this as leading to acquiescing to their demands where these are "unreasonable." He notes that restrictions on fundamentalist practices should be "based on the concept of justice itself rather than on fear."[44] This point is notably relevant to fundamentalist Mormon belief, which promotes polygamy as a central practice. It again begs the question, though, of the basis upon which a faith practice's "reasonableness" may be assessed.

Thinking about these principles with reference to polygamy in Canada, we can imagine the following question. Has a FLDS believer in Bountiful who states that she has become a plural wife because this is consistent with the teachings of her religious founder, Joseph Smith, and those set out in the

Doctrine & Covenants, offered a rationale that can facilitate an elucidating conversation about whether plural marriage should be tolerated in Canada? Given that such a wide bredth of protection is offered to religious freedom claims in Canada,[45] it seems likely that this type of argument will be respected by the state, or least give rise to some degree of pause and reflection before the state interferes with the believer's choice and behavior in relation to polygamy. The FLDS follower's argument is inherently uncontroversial and inoffensive, and can set the groundwork for discussions that lead to richer understandings about what polygamy means to FLDS communities. The claim of the FLDS follower can do this work without necessarily being "translated" or "converted" to secular terminology; that is, she does not have to conceive of reasons to explain to a non-FLDS listener why she has become a plural wife. Instead, her claim alone should be enough to count as public reason that initiates dialogue and understanding across different social and cultural groups about an unorthodox or unusual form of marriage.

The above scenario seems, on the surface, to be an acceptable outcome to a volatile political issue. However, whether this claim about polygamy and religion is, by itself, a "compelling" justification for particular attitudes or choices is less clear. Faith may not be enough to respond satisfactorily to the range of challenges and objections to the practice of polygamy. This will be discussed more fully below, in Section 3.2 of this chapter, which considers the "incompleteness" of religion as a focal point for public conversation. Further, as discussed in Section 3.2, even though they are perhaps expedient or pragmatic, religious explanations fail to capture the spectrum of rationales given for polygamy beyond faith and God, even by religious adherents to this practice.

Before engaging with these points, though, a second potential value of claims grounded in religion merits consideration. This value arises from the need for collaboration to reach mutual understanding between "religious" and "non-religious" citizens, which should prompt these parties' self-reflection on the moral or religious doctrines underlying their respective public claims. As explored below, this seems to be a potential virtue of allowing religious claims to "count" as public reason.

### 2.2.2. Reflexivity

To what extent does engagement in public discourse about religion require citizens from different communities to think reflexively about their own assumptions and benchmarks?[46] What value does this reflexive exercise have for public dialogue and understanding? As Habermas notes, "whether the liberal response to religious pluralism can be accepted by the citizens themselves as the single right answer depends not least on whether secular and religious citizens, each from their own respective angle, are prepared to embark on an interpretation of the relationship of faith and knowledge *that first enables them to behave in a self-reflexive manner toward each other* in the political public sphere."[47] Therefore, by requiring collaborative engagement among citizens, political conversations about religion may be intrinsically useful in fostering a stance of self-reflection on the part of citizens, which turn supports pluralism, democracy, and mutual understanding.

Engagement with politics is thus pitched as a possible method for religious citizens to reflect upon and develop deeper understandings of their own faith or moral views ("comprehensive doctrines" per Rawls) and to connect these to secular law and notions of morality.[48] Here, too, Habermas suggests that the exercise involves looking at one's own moral or religious[49] precepts and thinking about where and how it fits with public politics. Yet this point also cuts the other way; that is, the "non-religious" citizen should be pushed, through engagement with religious people, to be reflective and self-questioning about the foundations of her perceptions and conduct.

These ideas resonate with a strand of feminist literature that calls for introspection as a measure for revisiting presumptions about "difference" or "exoticism" among women, especially women who form part of a cultural minority. This line of reasoning maintains that understanding practices and beliefs that initially seem far removed from one's own standpoint meaningfully begins with a critical assessment of the values, experiences, and perceptions tolerated (or perhaps even promoted) within one's own cultural framework. As Matsuda notes, "[w]e are not the same. But we are not so different that we are bereft of the chance of knowing anything at all about one another and thereby about ourselves."[50]

In the polygamy debate, the nonreligious person who encounters religious claims to support plural marriage may be prompted to reflect critically on her own views and values, which might not be so drastically removed from the polygamist's claim that her desire for plural marriage should not be subject to state interference (that is, provided there is meaningful consent and no incest). In particular, listening to religiously rooted claims about polygamy can prompt an introspective process that disturbs one's assumptions about conduct and beliefs viewed as acceptable within one's own cultural context. Termed by Cossman as a process of "turning the gaze back on itself,"[51] the observer may identify parallels and intersections between the multiple experiences of different people and reconsider the "otherness" of the practices and persons forming the subject of her inquiry.[52] All of this should be conducive to openness in the face of controversial practices rooted in religious doctrines, albeit a careful openness that does not necessarily lead to full acceptance of these practices. Such openness is crucial to textured dialogue that can yield meaningful social understandings about these practices and their meaning to those who take them up.

## 3. Religion's "Incompleteness"

As outlined in the foregoing section, concerns about the justice of demanding that religious citizens adopt secular reasons in conversations beyond their respective communities may infuse religiously rooted claims with a measure of political salience. Nevertheless, as alluded to earlier, relying solely or even predominantly on religious reasons to explain practices or beliefs that generate social debate may frustrate the ability to understand these phenomena fully and to speak about them meaningfully. In this part, I discuss three primary shortcomings of an exclusive reliance on religious claims and consider these through the particular lens of polygamy in Bountiful, Canada. My observations, drawn from my fieldwork, of what religious explanations for polygamy in Bountiful overlook suggest that religious claims are, for the purposes of public reason, "incomplete." Such claims are also potentially pernicious in their tendency to oversimplify the beliefs and perspectives held within socially and politically marginalized communities.

### 3.1. Religion as One among Several Forces Explaining "Sacred" Practices

To begin, speaking only in terms of religion ignores the diversity of factors and forces that may drive decisions to take up particular practices. For example, a Catholic who baptizes her child will likely believe that this ritual is one that will cleanse the child and make her free from original sin. At the same time, this act can have a host of other meanings and relevancies for the parent. The baptism may be viewed as a moment of introducing the child to her Christian community. While this factor may be characterized as having a religious dimension, it also has a measure of social and cultural significance. The baptism might also offer an occasion to introduce the child, shortly after birth, to her extended family, which gathers to celebrate this event. Perhaps more mundanely, the baptism may be undertaken by the parent without extensive thought or reflection; it might be simply done as rote matter of course: something that she just does because she herself was baptized and there is no real reason to object to doing this for her own child. Finally, on a more cynical level, we might imagine a situation where a parent baptizes her child even though she does not see herself as particularly devout, but because she wants her child to have the option to be Catholic later in life, and this requires a baptism, or because her spouse, her parents, or her extended family pressure her to baptize the child, and she feels pressure to meet these expectations.

In each of these scenarios religion is present, but the degree to which it is determinative of action varies. It shifts between the shadow and foreground, depending on the particular frame of mind of the protagonist in the different situations. The point remains, however, that faith alone does not explain the baptismal act, even though it bears some measure of relevance in the justification. Other forces and factors may accompany religion in explaining this act, such as social expectations generated by family and community connections or the desire for membership (either for the self or for the child) in a particular group.

While baptism is a single event and a common ritual not usually subject to controversial debate in Canada, polygamy is both more controversial and affects many dimensions of a person's existence for much of her life and for the generations that follow her. The points emerging from the hypothetical example of baptism thus may find even clearer expression in women's decisions about polygamy in Bountiful. From my research in this community, I have found a variety of determinants underlying the belief in and practice of polygamy. Research participants' accounts are diverse and indicate that there is no single "sacred experience" that can yield one primary religious "reason" for polygamy.

Thus, in my research, I have encountered women who have attributed their decision to live polygamously to *religious teachings*. Several women made statements to the effect that polygamy is part of their religion and what they believe God expects from them. So, given the dictates of their faith, several participants have suggested that the criminalization of polygamy does not affect the practice of plural marriage. One woman, for example, indicated: "I grew up knowing that polygamy was in my life, and it's part of my religion so I mean, there was nothing that was going to stop me from doing what God wanted me to do" (Participant #2). Another explained that accessing "the highest Kingdom of Heaven" requires one to marry polygamously (Participant #4).

At the same time, for some women, marrying according to FLDS teachings was linked not specifically to theological requirements, but rather, to *community expectations* that people from Bountiful marry individuals who share the same beliefs. Thus, rather than being connected to religion itself, this motivation for marriage seemed more closely connected to the aspiration of adhering to community norms with a view to retaining membership in the group. As one participant suggested, this is perceived as important for the ongoing survival of the community into future generations and as a prerequisite to a harmonious spousal relationship: "[m]arrying within the faith is important to many of us, because to have a strong and happy marriage, you need to have the same values as your partner. Also, passing on your beliefs to your children has got to be easier if both parents share them" (Participant #1).

Women in Bountiful have also spoken about the primary benefit or motivation of their polygamous lifestyle in terms seemingly unrelated to faith. Some women thus alluded to the *economic viability* that having multiple income-earners in a domestic setting allows. For plural marriage families, women typically seemed to be the key administrators of household finances. They explained that they share and manage the responsibility of keeping track of and paying bills. Often husbands took part in women's meetings where accounting matters were handled, but this was not always the case. These arrangements frequently seemed to be premised on the value of helping and supporting family members who did not earn an income.[53] While no woman ever told me, "I became a plural wife because it's economically preferable to monogamous marriage," the multiplicity of incomes was cast as beneficial for women, especially where some opted not to be income-earners, choosing instead to pursue postsecondary education or to work within the home.

In a related vein, a number of participants stressed that living polygamously is valuable to them because having sister wives offers individual women the *flexibility to pursue independent goals* and projects related to education and employment. Because women in Bountiful tend to marry before pursuing postsecondary studies, they will typically be mothers by the time they enroll in college. These women thus considered it invaluable to have a sister wife to care for their children, and to keep up with domestic work, while they took their courses and studied. Other women who worked outside of the home felt a similar appreciation for this social network. This sentiment is captured in participants' statements such as the following:

> When I first started college I was a little bit . . . I was kind of drawn back. But then I got thinking, "I am who I am, and I can't change myself to please everyone in the world," and so I just started to be myself. And actually more people accepted me for who I was. Like one lady said, "Who has your baby?" when my little boy was younger, and I said, "Oh, my sister wife." I just said that. And she said, "I envy you, I envy you. I struggle every morning to find a babysitter. You have these wonderful support systems and I envy you in that way." (Participant #2)

> I go to school and I've got a babysitter, right there at home. He [my son] doesn't have to go anywhere. They're already home. They're in their own environment. And they are already cared for by their own

family. You know and, myself, I can stay home and baby-sit for someone else who has to go to work. (Participant #1)

I go to work and support her and she tends my kids. And we really and truly and honestly are partners.... Honestly there's not any [sic] two ladies that live as a couple as we do. (Participant #5)

The interdependence that many sister wives experience in Bountiful seems to serve as a basis for the *companionship and solidarity* that several women counted among the benefits of being a plural wife. While acknowledging that sister wives' relationships might be adversely affected by feelings of jealousy or competition at times, most women referred to their sister wives as their "best friends" or "companions." Sister wives typically spent more time together than individual plural wives did with their husband. I met women who lived and took holidays together, often without their husband. I also met two sister wives who were not in a legal relationship with their polygamist husband, who felt that their connection with each other was so intense that they opted to marry formally under British Columbia law, which permits same-sex marital unions.[54] The strength of the bond between some sister wives emerges in comments like the following:

My sister wives are like my very best friends... I do more things with my sister wives than I do with my husband. I'm with my sister wives 24/7... Sometimes I feel like I'm more married to my co-wives than I am to him! (Participant #2)

It's kind of like in a monogamous relationship where you and your husband are really close. Well, a lot of us get actually that closeness with each other that you would have with your husband... We know everything about the other person. Feel what they feel, we think what they think. (Participant #7)Q: What about the biggest thing you would lose [if you lived monogamously]?A: My sister wives, their children. I really do love them. (Participant #8)

Women also described how the solidarity forged among sister wives might became useful in moments of disagreement or conflict with a shared husband:

When we want something [it's] pretty hard for him to stand up to two of us so, if we could [sic] afford it, we can make it happen. And if it's something you know we want to do to the house. We say, honey, we're doin' this, right, okay. And so, it happens. (Participant #3)

> I feel sorry for the guys. They're very outnumbered [chuckle] even if they're with two wives. (Participant #1)

Finally, some women reasoned that polygamy might be taken up purely because it leads to *personal fulfilment and happiness*. Participants noted that some community members will marry monogamously where they believe that plural marriage would not be satisfying. Although polygamy was considered by some participants as required for entry into the Celestial Kingdom of God in the FLDS faith, some women indicated that "openness" to polygamy can be sufficient to be devout, even if in practice, one marries monogamously. Thus, some participants spoke of the necessity of being happy in marriage and choosing polygamy only if this will lead to personal fulfillment. The comments that follow are illustrative:

> I, growing up, I never felt like I wanted to be a plural wife but, and I thought about this quite a bit because you could say it was because of how I was raised or whatever but I have friends my same age who, we basically grew up together in the same environment. And I have several friends who said that they wanted to be in a polygamous relationship and that was different for me, I didn't want to ... I guess you could say it's an individual thing because you know, we grew up the same and had the same influences and they chose to be polygamous and I chose to be a monogamous wife. I most certainly did think of being in a plural marriage as a possibility, but I had set my heart for someone and he didn't have a wife so that meant I would not be a polygamist. Upon my marriage I never assumed that I would never be a polygamist. The matter is an individual choice for people. (Participant #10)

> [I]t's [marriage's] such an individual experience for each woman ... she chooses to have the experience that she wants. That's what I tell my children all the time. In every situation, no matter who you're living with, no matter what the situation is, you have to have two choices: you can choose to be happy and you can choose to be miserable, and it all depends on your attitude and how you plan to deal with it. (Participant #9)

This collection of excerpts from research interviews provides some indication of the diversity of factors that may explain why some women, in at least one polygamous community, may become plural wives. These points may not be representative of the experiences of all women in Bountiful, and they cannot speak to the way polygamy is lived in other communities either in Canada or internationally. Nevertheless, they remain helpful for illuminating the potential dimensions that might be lost or overlooked by relying exclusively on faith-based claims and debates in seeking to appreciate the meaning of controversial beliefs and practices adopted within minority groups.

## 3.2. What Religious Claims Overlook

A second key shortcoming of relying on religious explanations and dialogue to appreciate controversial practices and belief arises from the fact that it is not, in many cases, a "complete"[55] political conception. This is illustrated concretely by the testimonies of some women in Bountiful canvassed above. Yet the example of Bountiful is evocative of a general problem, for the purposes of public reason, of exclusively religious explanations for a practice. These explanations are "incomplete" in that they do not yield reasonable answers to "fundamental questions" associated with such practices or controversies.[56] Specifically, rooting the discussion solely in terms of faith goes very little distance in addressing concerns related to gender equality, dignity, democracy, liberty, and security of the person. Where these principles are perceived as thwarted by a practice or perspective, more is needed, in terms of both process and substance, than a simple claim from a religious leader that the conduct or belief is in line with what a group's faith mandates. Meaningful public discussion and legitimacy instead require the devout claimants to respond persuasively to the "secular" concerns associated with the practice or attitude that has generated social disquiet.

The "incompleteness" of religious claims about controversial practices emerges clearly in the case study of polygamy in Bountiful. As indicated above, religious leaders have founded their objection to Canada's ban on this practice primarily by casting the latter as a breach of their freedom of religion.[57] This type of claim does not do much, however, to quell the strongest social anxieties that exist about plural marriage in Canada. These anxieties are associated primarily with the inherent gender inequality that appears to exist within polygamy.[58] They are further fueled by stories about young women being forced to marry polygamist men who are much older than them and who might even be relatives.[59] Concerns have also arisen from narratives of women who fled unhappy polygamous settings, recounting experiences of being trapped in situations of domestic abuse and violence.[60] There is a further worry about women and girls being trafficked internationally (specifically, between Canada and the United States) to become brides.[61] Finally, objections to polygamy are not premised on concerns just for women; many opponents raise questions about the "lost boys" of polygamous groups, that is, adolescent boys and young men reportedly pushed out of their communities to eliminate competition for young brides.[62]

Each of these represents a serious concern, and where such claims are substantiated, a simple reference to God, scripture, or sacred ritual will not respond to concerns about the equality and security of the persons involved in the practice; nor does it go any distance toward establishing the legitimacy and propriety of polygamy in Canada.[63] Rather, a more textured, accessible, and morally convincing explanation for the practice is needed to overcome these concerns and to offer reassurance about the outcomes of those made seemingly vulnerable by polygamy. As such, this situation is one where religious reasons on their own are markedly incomplete and cannot alone count as "public reason" in Rawls's terms.

At the moment, claims about polygamy evade, rather than engage, one another. There is a considerable gap between arguments couched in freedom of religion and those positing that women, children, and young boys are harmed by this form of marriage. What seems necessary at this point is a common framework for thinking about this practice or some shared conceptual terrain, where proponents and opponents each engage in debate using language and ideas that bear some meaning and purchase to the other. This may call for some "translation," as considered above, of religious concepts to the secular, and vice versa, while remaining cognizant of the artificiality of a rigid divide between what is "of faith" and what is "secular."[64] Perhaps more importantly, however, finding a common ground for discussants requires participants to recognize and respond to competing concerns. Thus, the polygamist or libertarian who sees polygamy's criminalization as unconstitutional must acknowledge and discuss persuasively the concerns listed above that portray polygamy as potentially threatening. Similarly, a proponent of prohibiting polygamy must respond robustly to religious-freedom claims, recognizing the right to religious freedom as a constitutionally entrenched principle in most liberal democracies and asking whether and when the state can justifiably limit this right, especially through the threat of criminal sanction. This individual would also do well to acknowledge the *religious* roots of many *political* concepts and the reality that "public reasons" will always be determined by the identity and context of the person articulating them, regardless of whether she considers herself "religious" or not.[65]

This type of enriched conversation is entirely possible in Canada's polygamy debate. Those who advocate decriminalization could marshal evidence in addition to religious-freedom arguments that wrestle more intensely with concerns about polygamy's harms. For example, discussions by women explaining how and why they choose this form of marriage,[66] how they recognize and address the challenges of polygamy while seeing these as less important than polygamy's benefits, and how they feel and exhibit considerable autonomy in their communities would be helpful to this discussion. Facts about how often monogamy is taken up, with a view to "evening out" gender demographics, in a plural marriage community would be helpful to respond to concerns about "lost boys" ostracized from places like Bountiful. Polygamist community members' perceptions about age of marriage requirements and the fact that certain plural wives have lobbied for a higher age of consent to sexual contact law are also relevant.[67] The same is true with respect to addressing whether anyone in Bountiful or other polygamist communities is free to leave and to divorce or end a spousal relationship that leaves her unhappy.[68]

This information is necessary to support or complement religiously grounded claims that challenge fundamental liberal values and rights. It is required to fill in gaps left by religious-freedom arguments that, in the polygamy context, do not respond to deep social and political concerns related to gender equality and personal security. Instead, relying on religion alone can engender two outcomes, neither of which is helpful or promising for intercultural understanding. Specially, religious claims alone, when found to be unconvincing, will be overlooked or not seriously addressed. Conversely, they might be considered so convincing that the secular state allows a practice to occur only because it is faith based. In the former situation, little information or understanding is transmitted about the controversial practice to those who do not adhere to it, and the result may be that a practice warranting respect is shunned or prohibited. In the latter, the analysis may be eclipsed by religious or cultural relativism, at the peril of those who may be harmed by the practice under scrutiny.

Thus, allowing or calling upon devout citizens to supplement claims based on faith in regard to socially controversial, or morally ambiguous, practices with explanations that respond to the "secular" concerns of the liberal state is necessary. This is needed, in particular, to engage critically and meaningfully with objections that may have been (or may ultimately be) raised in regard to the practice, with a view to developing a broader and fuller social understanding in its regard. As the case study of polygamy in Bountiful shows, this requires a full reckoning, by those who oppose the practice, with religious-freedom claims. It also necessitates a willingness, on the part of the religious practitioner, to engage with the rights-based claims of a "secular" opponent.

### 3.3. Relevance of "Private" Reasons and Power

While the foregoing discussion takes issue with the sole reliance on religious claims as public reason, the language of "public reason" itself also poses inherent limitations for shared understanding and interaction among communities. Namely, both religious discourse and public reason generally fail to account for the idea of *private* power and debate, as well as the diversity of reasons that might be advanced for a practice that, publicly, is cast only as grounded in religion. Discussions as to whether religious claims may count as "public reason" presume that public and private domains can be neatly extricated from one another and that claims demanding political, and potentially also legal, attention and scrutiny are only those advanced in the "public" realm.[69] This notion misses the mark on a number of fronts. First, it seems to take for granted that every citizen has access to "public fora" and that the latter are spaces where individuals' ideological and religious values will not and should not be invoked as justifications. This is connected with Habermas's argument that devout people should be permitted to speak out in religious terms since they will still see themselves as members of the "civitas terrena, which empowers them to be the authors of laws to which as its addressees they are subject."[70]

Yet this position seems at odds with the experiences of many citizens vis-à-vis the state. Specifically, many citizens, regardless of whether they speak in "religious" or "non-religious" terms, will feel disconnected from secular public and political spaces, or Habermas's "civitas terrena." The disjuncture is acutely manifest in the context of polygamy in Bountiful, especially if the "laws" that Habermas is referring to are formal, state-originating laws.[71] Whether members of minority religious communities assume a uniform sense of belonging in secular/public spaces (or the "civitas terrena") is debatable. Thus, liberal theorists' efforts to carve out a space for respecting religious claims in public domains might inadvertently entrench the myth of a monolithic community voice and blanket the actual diversity present within communities.

Research participants I interviewed in Bountiful shared a discernible sense of stigma and exclusion on account of law's rejection of polygamy in Canada.[72] They do not seem to feel particularly engaged in public debate about this topic. Rather, they expressed views that their realities were ignored by political actors outside of their community. In the words of one woman: "[There are] all these people that want to help women escape from Bountiful; what about those of us who want to stay here? Why don't you help us stay here?" (Participant #1).

This substantiates Baehr's point about political discourse/decisions as occurring "behind the backs of the persons party to them" such that distributional outcomes repeat themselves.[73] Of course, in Bountiful, this could be linked also to issues of gender, class, and education, not just participants' identities as religious women. Thus, as guilty as "secular" political actors might be of leaving women out of public debates on polygamy, the patriarchs of this community might be just as culpable, as they have assumed front-line positions and spoken exclusively and generally for Bountiful about polygamy in this discussion.

Beyond this, however, it is worth thinking about the relevance of *private* reasons, power, and relationships, especially if public spaces and reasons are not uniformly accessible. Thus, of what theoretical and practical relevance are the *private* explanations of a practice, shared within a community on terms accessible to its residents? Furthermore, can internal community conversations bear a level of authenticity and recognition outside this terrain for those of us who do not "belong" to the community? In responding to these lines of inquiry, it is crucial to remain critical of the distinction drawn between the public/political and the private/religious. As noted, this is an artificial divide,[74] and some feminist scholars have taken issue with drawing sharp lines between these two spheres, stressing the view that "the personal *is* political" and noting the nefarious consequences for women of ignoring gendered experience in contemporary political theory.[75] Specifically, this body of feminist literature has focused on how family and intimate relationships can be sites of political power and exploitation[76] and how calling things "private" shields them—in a potentially dangerous way—from scrutiny and contestation.[77] Feminists further maintain that labeling spaces that women have traditionally inhabited as "private," and distinguishing these zones from "public" spheres, has disempowered women and curtailed their abilities to advance moral and political claims.[78]

At the same time, it remains important not to overlook the ways in which women have developed agency even despite the effects of the constructed public–private divide. Recasting notions of "privacy" and "publicity" can illuminate the innovative and effective ways that women have gained political mobility within and beyond their family and community settings.[79] For example, feminist literature on "consciousness-raising" (that is, the process of building on collective discussions and common gendered experiences to challenge existing hierarchies), depict these activities as publicly meaningful even though their origins and momentum developed in spaces traditionally viewed as private.[80]

The feminist revision of public and private categories is a useful lens for understanding the distribution of authority in Bountiful, where women have taken part in activities like contacting and speaking with the media; hosting public summits on polygamy; lobbying for elevating the age of consent to sexual contact; speaking out within their congregation's meetings and among themselves about polygamy and other distinctive practices within their community (e.g., reproduction, women's dress and aesthetic appearance). Are these activities properly cast as "private" or "public"? Although not necessarily open or observable to everyone outside of the community, calling these events "private" seems to belittle the mobilizing power that they have for individuals who otherwise bear minimal political voice and visibility.

While helpful for illuminating these points, feminist scholarship does not help to fill in some of the critical gaps left by modern political theorists' ideas on religion and public claims. Specifically, feminists have not asked three crucial questions, namely:

1. What is the value of examining *internal* debates and reasons developed within ostensibly private settings (e.g., families, communities) for understanding, at the level of formal law and politics, controversial practices that appear connected to a religious belief? More particularly, in the Bountiful setting, do residents see intra-community discussions and debates as private or public?

In some cases, these internal conversations may indeed be viewed as public. For example, within Bountiful some disagreement, especially among women, has emerged about how women should dress. Some women continue to wear traditional FLDS attire, while others have taken to wearing modern clothes, such as jeans and t-shirts. Those who dress in more "mainstream" attire have drawn some criticism and disapproval from conservative community members. While this division in the community about appearance is not widely known and unlikely to be of much interest outside of Bountiful, it is a "political" question in the community insofar as it concerns issues of power and authority. Women thus referred to the notion of "winning over" or "convincing" younger girls to choose to adopt the more conservative dress style. All of this bolsters Benhabib's point that only the parties themselves can and should decide what is public and what is private as an argument—there is no objective determinant of this distinction.[81]

2. Why might internal, or intra-community, reasons never reach the domain of "mainstream" public politics?

On the question of how intra-community debates should be classified, it is worth noting Pellizzoni's argument that reasons can be framed with regard to any subject and any language, but what matters most to an argument's legitimacy is "the inclusion of everyone's viewpoint."[82] This emphasis on procedure is intriguing, suggesting that paying attention to form over substance may be the route to the most just and inclusive public debates. But again, recurrent presumptions and questions arise here regarding: (a) access to spaces for sharing viewpoints and (b) what counts as sharing a viewpoint in a "public" context. As illuminated by using Bountiful as a case study, explicitly secular and "political" spaces are not universally viewed as open or accommodating by religious citizens. Moreover, decisions and ideas articulated by religious citizens within their respective group may be considered to have "public" meaning and relevance in these settings.

3. What should we make of reasons developed in these internal/informal/private settings (e.g., families, communities) when they are *not linked to religion* but instead to factors such as social expectations, economic necessity,

or personal preference, even though the issue or practice in question is touted as anchored to faith? To what extent do these "other" reasons push conversations in different and more robust ways than simple claims about religion which, on their own, may be a possible "conversation-stopper"?

In this connection, the example of polygamy in Bountiful illuminates the varied factors that may motivate seemingly "religious" practices. Finding opportunities and methods for unearthing these factors and integrating them within public discussions could yield a deeper and more nuanced understanding of practices under scrutiny. In particular, this process may diffuse gridlocked and heated discussions grounded in ideas of religious freedom and accommodation, and highlight the insight that religion might not be the only, or even the most important, reason for conduct and choices that generate social controversy. This being the case, accepting religion within the ambit of "public reason" for a particular practice requires a concomitant effort to learn about "private," intra-family or intra-community, reasons for that practice, which may be unrelated to faith.

## 4. Conclusion

Within a pluralistic, liberal state, social and political controversies over practices and beliefs rooted in diverse religious traditions are inevitable and even salutary. These controversies are less likely to precipitate discord, however, if they can be discussed in a reasoned way, on terms that foster shared understandings across differences. Initiating and sustaining such reasoned discussion, however, is difficult. It requires the articulation of reasons and arguments that can be understood and accepted by multiple constituencies in civil society. This requirement, which reiterates John Rawls's conception of public reason, compels the development of a framework for broadly accessible public dialogue.

This chapter has examined whether and how religious claims can fulfill the objectives of public reason as conceived by Rawls and as developed by other liberal political theorists. It does so through the lens of a case study on polygamy in Canada. Ultimately, this work assesses the efficacy of religious claims for facilitating inclusive public dialogue aimed at reaching a broad social understanding of plural marriage in Canadian society.

As discussed in Section 1, religious claims on their own may not count as public reason as imagined by Rawls. Rather, some work may be needed to translate these claims into secular language and concepts that are more readily accessible to lay citizens. Yet, making translation a prerequisite for religion to count as public reason raises important concerns. Specifically, such translation might be impossible; it might adversely affect the dignity of the religious person who makes the claim; and it may result in disingenuous secular explanations regarding practices that are in fact grounded in faith. As such, it is worth thinking about religious arguments being intrinsically acceptable as public reason. Moreover, as developed above, theoretical analyses of faith-based claims indicate that they bear at least two potential virtues, each of which may foster rich debate in a plural society. First, religion can be seen as *expedient*, in that it is a concept that automatically generates a basic measure of understanding and respect in a liberal state. Second, religion may also prompt *self-reflection* among those who engage in public debate, which should be conducive to greater openness and understanding toward diverse religious beliefs and practices.

While recognizing the political salience that religious claims may bear, as explained in Section 2, religion is also an incomplete framework for reasoned public debate. That is, relying on these claims alone gives rise to significant risks in public debates about controversial practices ostensibly rooted in faith. The polygamy case study illuminates three such risks. First, an exclusive focus on religion ignores the plurality of factors that might in fact underlie practices and beliefs. Second, discussions grounded in religion alone may bury valid concerns worthy of political attention. Thus, in the polygamy context, a fixation with religion leaves aside pressing anxieties about gender equality and personal security that this practice engenders. Third, thinking about religion with reference to the notion of public reason leads one to overlook the dimensions of "private" power and discussions that might be essential to understanding a controversial practice or idea. In this chapter, I have drawn on my conversations with women in Bountiful to demonstrate how liberal theory's efforts to find a space for religious arguments in public reason have two competing effects. Specifically, these efforts at once reveal the potential of religious claims to strengthen dialogue across communities, while inadvertently constricting the avenues through which communities on the margins, like Bountiful, are understood and heard.

Given all of this, religion has a clear place in public debates on plural marriage. It also retains weight within juridical argument and analysis, as witnessed through the Polygamy Reference. This being said, taken in isolation, claims tethered to religion will not suffice to develop reasoned debate and judgments in regard to polygamy and juridical approaches to it. Rather, a textured and broadly understood discussion about this practice, and its tolerability under Canadian law, requires that religious claims be accompanied by arguments and reasons better characterized as economic, social, or personal, as articulated in both public and private domains.

# Notes

* This paper was prepared with support from the Social Sciences and Humanities Research Council of Canada and the McGill Ratpan fund. Thanks go to Joanna Baron for extremely able research assistance and insightful commentary and to participants in the McGill–Tel Aviv University Workshops on Religious Revival in a Post-Multicultural Age for rich suggestions and feedback.
1. *The Queen v Bear's Shin Bone* (1899), 3 CCC 329 (SCNWT (S Alta Jud Dist)).
2. The *Canadian Charter of Human Rights and Freedoms and Freedoms*' section 2(a) protects "freedom of conscience and religion" as a "fundamental freedom": *Canadian Charter of Rights and Freedoms*, Part I of the *Constitution Act, 1982*, being Schedule B to the *Canada Act 1982* (UK) 1982, c 11 [*Charter*]. Public discussion about legal action in relation to polygamy in Bountiful has noted prosecutorial concerns about the strength of religious-freedom arguments that defense counsel would raise. See R. C. C. Peck, "Report of the Special Prosecutor for Allegations of Misconduct Associated with Bountiful, BC: Summary of Conclusions," available online (*Vancouver Sun*): <http://www.canada.com/vancouversun/news/extras/bountiful.pdf>; J. Hainsworth, "Canada: Leaders of Polygamist Group Arrested" *Huffington Post* (7 January 2009), available online: <http://www.huffingtonpost.com/2009/01/07/canada-leaders-of-polygam_n_156,082.html>.
3. See, e.g., A. Mayeda, "Tories Prepared to Stand Ground on Polygamy: Documents" *National Post* (24 March 2009), available online: <http://www.nationalpost.com/news/story.html?id=1,423,616>; L. Ferretti, "La polygamie pour tous ou pour personne," *Le Devoir* (4 March 2009) A9.
4. *Blackmore v British Columbia (Attorney General)*, 2009 BCSC 1299.
5. This language derives from the constitutional justificatory provision in the *Charter*, *supra* note 2. Section 1 of the *Charter* provides: "[t]he *Canadian Charter of Rights and Freedoms* guarantees the rights and freedoms set out in it subject only to such reasonable limits prescribed by law as can be demonstrably justified in a free and democratic society."
6. *Reference re: Criminal Code*, section 293, 2010 BCSC 1351 at para 9.
7. "Anti-Polygamy Law a 'Relic': Lawyer" *The Canadian Press* (12 April 2011), available online: <http://www.cbc.ca/news/canada/british-columbia/story/2011/04/11/bc-polygamy-hearing-dickson.html>.
8. See, e.g., M. Bailey et al., "Expanding Recognition of Foreign Polygamous Marriages: Implications for Canada," Queen's University Legal Studies Research Paper No. 07–12, available online (SSRN): <http://papers.ssrn.com/sol3/papers.cfm?abstract_id=1,023,896##> at 20–21 who discuss the issue of whether *Criminal Code* section 293(1) violates any right guaranteed by the Canadian *Charter* with sole reference to religious freedom protected by section 2(a) of the *Charter*. For an analysis of public and political narratives concerning polygamy, specifically in relation to issues of gender equality, see A. Campbell, "Bountiful's Plural Marriages" (2010) 6:4 International Journal of Law in Context 343–61. The centrality of the religious freedom argument in the Polygamy Reference was even anticipated by one woman whom I interviewed in Bountiful before pleadings began: "I gather just from reading the media reports that the, the person representing ... is going to make an argument based on freedom of religion, you know" (Participant #1).
9. Since the Supreme Court of Canada's 2004 decision in *Syndicat Northcrest v Amselem*, [2004] 2 SCR 551, section 2(a) of the *Charter* has been given a relatively broad application, requiring only an individual's "sincere belief" in a practice as being religiously mandated to qualify for constitutional protection: see *Amselem*, ibid., at para 51. The broad reading of section 2(a) is particularly striking when contrasted with the higher thresholds established by this Court to find a breach of section 7's "principles of fundamental justice." See, e.g., *R v Malmo-Levine* 2003 SCC 7, where the majority stated that a law would have to be "arbitrary and irrational" to find a violation of section 7. This threshold must be met to establish the violation of one's rights to life, liberty, and security of the person, which are protected under section 7. The standard for establishing a breach of

religious freedom under section 2(a) is also wide in comparison to that created for section 15(1)'s promise of "equality before and under the law": see *R v Kapp* 2008 SCC 41, where the Supreme Court majority distanced itself from an earlier decision, which held that a violation of section 15(1) required a violation of human dignity in addition to a finding of differential treatment and perpetuation of prejudice, yet still maintained that human dignity was an "essential value underlying the s. 15 equality guarantee" at para 21.

10. *Reference re: Section 293 of the Criminal Code of Canada*, 2011 BCSC 1588..
11. Ibid. at para 5.
12. The necessity of marriage for achieving celestial existence is made explicit in the Doctrine and Covenants, which forms part of the canon of the Mormon Church and contains early revelations to the Church's founders, where it is written: "In the celestial glory there are three heavens or degrees; And in order to obtain the highest, a man must enter into this order of the priesthood [meaning the new and everlasting covenant of marriage] [i.e., the covenant of polygamous marriage]; And if he does not, he cannot obtain it." See The Doctrine and Covenants of the Church of Jesus Christ of Latter-day Saints at 131:1–3.
13. R. L. Bushman, *Mormonism: A Very Short Introduction* (New York: Oxford University Press, 2008) at 98–99.
14. J. Rawls, "The Idea of Public Reason Revisited" (1997) 64 University of Chicago Law Review 765–807 at 777 [Rawls, "Public Reason Revisited"].
15. D. Thacher, "The Normative Case Study" (2006) 11:6 American Journal of Sociology 1631–676, at 1632.
16. Ibid., at 1632.
17. See, e.g., C. Lewis, "Bountiful B.C. Case Likely to Stir Up Religious Freedoms Debate" *National Post* (6 January 2009), available online: <http://www.nationalpost.com/news/story.html?id=1,152,461>, R. Matas and W. Trueck, "Polygamy Charges in Bountiful," *Globe and Mail* (7 January 2009), available online: <http://www.theglobeandmail.com/news/national/article963758.ece>; N. Hall, "Winston Blackmore Sues B.C. Government for Polygamy Prosecution" *Vancouver Sun* (14 January 2010), available online: <http://www.vancouversun.com/news/Winston+Blackmore+sues+government+polygamy+prosecution/2441672/story.html>.
18. See, e.g., British Columbia, Legislative Assembly 2008, *Official Report of Debates of the Legislative Assembly (Hansard)*, No 9 at 12, 183 (B. Bennett). For an example of the early twentieth-century discourse about polygamy in the Parliament of Canada, see, e.g., Debates of the Senate, Fourth Session, Sixth Parliament (25 February 1890) at 142 (Hon. Mr. Kaulbach).
19. See W. Blackmore's blog, Share the Light, online: <http://sharethelight.ca/b2/>, comment chain at <http://www2.macleans.ca/2009/01/08/blogging-from-bountiful-winston-blackmore-in-his-own-words/>, <http://www.huffingtonpost.com/2009/01/07/canada-leaders-of-polygam_n_156,082.html>.
20. Arguments are summarized in the closing submissions of the three principal parties to the reference. See Closing Submissions of the Attorney General of British Columbia; Closing Submissions of the Attorney General of Canada; and Closing Submissions of the Amicus Curiae in *Reference re: Criminal Code*, section 293 (on file with the author).
21. Rawls, "Public Reason Revisited," *supra* note 14 at 799.
22. Ibid., at 784–85.
23. J. Rawls, *Political Liberalism* (New York: Columbia University Press, 2005) at 241 and 243 [Rawls, *Political Liberalism*].
24. Rawls, "Public Reason Revisited," *supra* note 14 at 779–80.
25. J. B. White, "Talking about Religion in the Language of the Law," in J. B. White, ed, *From Expectation to Experience: Essays on Law and Legal Education* (Ann Arbor: University of Michigan Press, 1999) at 149.
26. Ibid., at 128–30.
27. J. Habermas, "Religion in the Public Sphere" (2006) 14:1 European Journal of Philosophy 1–25, at 5.
28. D. Dombrowski, *Rawls and Religion* (Albany: State University of New York Press, 2001) at 111–12.

29. Habermas, *supra* note 27, at 11.
30. Ibid., at 11.
31. Ibid., at 4.
32. See "3.3 Relevance of 'Private' Reasons and Power" below.
33. Dombrowski, *supra* note 28, at 41. See also R. Audi and P. Wolterstorff, *Religion in the Public Square* (Lanham, MD: Rowman & Littlefield, 1997) at 135–37.
34. Audi and Wolterstorff, ibid., at 77 and 95–96.
35. Ibid., at 110–11.
36. Dombrowski, *supra* note 28. On sincerity see also Rawls, *Political Liberalism*, *supra* note 23, at 240.
37. Audi and Wolterstorff, *supra* note 33, at 135–36.
38. Habermas, *supra* note 27, at 4.
39. Recall Dombrowski, *supra* note 28, on "sensitive" listening.
40. R. Rorty, "Religion in the Public Square: A Reconsideration" (2003) 31:1 Journal of Religious Ethic 141–49 at 148.
41. Ibid., at 147.
42. Ibid., at 148–49 thus writes, "[s]o, instead of saying that religion was a conversation-stopper, I should have simply said that citizens of a democracy should try to put off invoking conversation-stoppers as long as possible. We should do our best to keep the conversation going without citing unarguable first principles, either philosophical or religious."
43. See A. Abizadeh, "'Because Baha'u'llah Said So': Dealing With a Non-starter in Moral Reasoning" (1995) 5:1 Baha'i Studies Review at 83, where the "bankruptness" of these types of arguments and beliefs from a Baha'i perspective is considered.
44. Dombrowski, *supra* note 28, at 111.
45. See discussion on *Amselem*, *supra* note 9.
46. Within this collection, chapters by Mautner and Van Praagh offer further contemplation as to the way in which intercultural engagement prompts such self-reflection.
47. Habermas, *supra* note 27, at 20, emphasis added.
48. Ibid., at 14.
49. Note Habermas's point that religious claims can be subject to justification/reflexivity: "They have lost their "purported immunity to the impositions of modern reflexivity," ibid., at 9.
50. See especially M. J. Matsuda, "Pragmatism Modified and the False Consciousness Problem" (1989–90) 63 Southern California Law Review 1763–782 at 1777. See also A. Bunting, "Theorizing Women's Cultural Diversity in Feminist International Human Rights Strategies" (1993) 20 Journal of Law and Society 6; B. Cossman, "Turning the Gaze Back on Itself: Comparative Law, Feminist Legal Studies, and the Postcolonial Project" (1997) Utah Law Review 525; M. Malik, "'The Branch on Which We Sit': Multiculturalism, Minority Women and Family Law," in A. Diduck and K. O'Donovan, eds, *Feminist Perspectives on Family Law* (New York: Routledge, 2006) 211; I. R. Gunning, "Arrogant Perception, World-Travelling and Multicultural Feminism: The Case of Female Genital Surgeries" (1991–92) 23 Columbia Human Rights Law Review 189–248.
51. Cossman, *supra* note 50.
52. This approach is suggested also by Malik, *supra* note 50 who considers the value of connecting practices cast as "different" to "a similar or analogous home practice." at 228–29.
53. Not all polygamous households operate this way in Bountiful; some research participants stressed their economic *independence* over the value of pooling financial resources. Other polygamous families do not share a household; each wife might have her own separate living arrangement. These circumstances will depend on the desires of the particular family members and their means. Nevertheless, the point remains that for some women in Bountiful, plural marriage enables a sharing of incomes and resources that benefits some families.
54. For a discussion of this relationship and how it has been perceived in Bountiful see Campbell, *supra* note 8.
55. Rawls, "Public Reason Revisited," *supra* note 14, at 777.
56. Rawls, *Political Liberalism*, *supra* note 23, at 227.

57. See Blackmore's blog, *supra* note 19. Note, however, that counsel for the Fundamentalist Church of Jesus Christ of Latter Day Saints and Bountiful community leader James Oler, who made submissions in the Polygamy Reference as an interested party, argued that section 293 CC is unconstitutional because it violates not only religious freedom, but also liberty and freedom of association as protected by the *Canadian Charter*. See Closing Submissions of The Fundamentalist Church of Jesus Christ of Latter Day Saints and James Oler in *Reference re Criminal Code*, section 293 (on file with the author).
58. With few exceptions, polygamous societies involve men with plural wives and not the reverse. Thus, because men and women do not have equal entitlements in marriage, polygamy has been cast as a "fundamentally unequal relationship." N. Javed, "GTA's Secret World of Polygamy; A Toronto Mother Describes Her Ordeal, Imam Admits He Has 'Blessed' Over 30 Unions," *Toronto Star* (24 May 2008), available online: <http://www.thestar.com/News/GTA/article/429490>, citing Professor Nicholas Bala.
59. See, e.g., the coverage of Bountiful leader Winston Blackmore's 2009 arrest, which spoke to alleged marriage to "9 child brides." D. Bramham, "Some Bountiful Brides only 15, Affidavit States; Nine of Accused Fundamentalist's 25 Wives Under 18, Document Says," *Ottawa Citizen* (1 July 2009) C10.
60. See D. Palmer and D. Perrin, *Keep Sweet: Children of Polygamy* (Lister, BC: Dave's Press, 1994); and C. Jessop, *Escape* (New York: Broadway Books, 2007).
61. The notion of bride trafficking has been discussed in both the legislative and media spheres. See, e.g., British Columbia, Legislative Assembly 2008, *Official Report of Debates of the Legislative Assembly (Hansard)*, No 9 at 12,183 (B. Bennett); and CanWest MediaWorks Publications (2007) "B.C. Government has a Duty to Protect Bountiful's Children while Challenging Polygamy," *Vancouver Sun* (3 August 2007) A8.
62. B. M. Billie, "The Lost Boys of Polygamy: Is Emancipation the Answer" (2008–9) 12 Journal of Gender Race & Justice 127; A. Tresniowski, "Castaways: In Utah and Arizona Hundreds of Teenage Boys are Being Torn from Their Families and Expelled from an Extreme Mormon Sect. Is It Because They Compete for Teen Girls that the Sect's Grown Men Want to Marry?" *People Weekly* (25 July 2005) (CPI.Q.).
63. The point is also recognized by *Amicus* counsel in the Polygamy Reference, who argued that section 293 CC, which prohibits polygamy in Canada, results in violations of religious freedom for those who take up polygamy as a faith-based practice. According to the *Amicus*, practices such as sexual exploitation and abuse as well as child maltreatment and trafficking "could not for one moment be protected under banner of freedom of religion." Closing Submissions of the Amicus Curiae in *Reference re Criminal Code*, section 293, at para 236 (on file with the author). See also ibid., at para 9.
64. Within this collection, chapters by Ferrari, Last Stone, and Lavi persuasively contest strict demarcations between religion and secularism, reflecting particularly on the cultural and religious roots of secular traditions.
65. See White, *supra* note 25, at 146–47; L. Pellizzoni, "The Myth of the Best Argument: Power, Deliberation and Reason" (2001) 52:1 British Journal of Sociology 59–86, at 74.
66. On the notion of women's ability to "choose" polygamy, see, e.g., M. D'Amour, "Sect Wives Defend Lives: Women Say Polygamy Choice Is Theirs," *The Calgary Sun* (29 July 2004) A4.
67. See "B.C. Polygamists Want Age of Consent Raised," *CTV News* (19 February 2005), available online: <http://www.ctv.ca/servlet/ArticleNews/story/CTVNews/11087601 02803_29/?hub=CTVNewsAt11>.
68. Some of these points emerge from the narratives recounted by women who have participated in my qualitative research in Bountiful. See A. Campbell, "Bountiful Voices" (2009) 47 Osgoode Hall Law Journal 183–234 and A. Campbell, "Bountiful's Plural Marriages" (2010) 6:4 International Journal of Law in Context 341–61.
69. Rawls especially divides the political from the personal/familial. See Rawls, *Political Liberalism, supra* note 23, at 137.
70. Habermas's optimism about public debate is equally optimistic in the following passage: "The democratic procedure has the power to generate legitimacy precisely because it both includes all participants and has a deliberative character; for the

justified presumption of rational outcomes in the long run can solely be based on this." Habermas, *supra* note 27, at 12.
71. See N. Fraser, "Rethinking the Public Sphere: A Contribution to the Critique of Actually Existing Democracy," in C. Calhoun, ed, *Habermas and the Public Sphere* (Cambridge, MA: MIT Press, 2002) 109–42 at 115 on Habermas, suggesting that he "idealizes the liberal public sphere" and "fails to examine other, non-liberal, non-bourgeois, competing public spheres" at 115.
72. A related critique suggests that it not just the idea of common debate that is too hopeful, but rather the notion that citizens with varying fundamental views and values will reach a form of *agreement* at the political level despite deep ideological differences, as unrealistic. See Dombrowski, *supra* note 28, at 113 on Rawls and Charles Larmore: "to try to force one religion or club of friends at the political level is to engage in fantasy regarding an imagined agreement among free and equal citizens regarding one comprehensive religious or political doctrine," and Audi, *supra* note 33, at 137, who states that it is "hopeless" to expect a pluralistic society to operate as a single community.
73. A. R. Baehr, "Toward a New Feminist Liberalism: Okin, Rawls and Habermas" (1996) 11:1 *Hypatia* 49–66, at 59.
74. See S. Benhabib, "Models of Public Space: Hannah Arendt, the Liberal Tradition, and Jürgen Habermas," in C. Calhoun, ed, *Habermas and the Public Sphere* (Cambridge, MA: MIT Press, 2002) 73–98 at 90, who sees a "fundamental ambiguity governing the term 'privacy.'"
75. Ibid., at 92.
76. See, e.g., S. M. Okin, "Political Liberalism, Justice, Gender" (1994) 105 Ethics 23–43, at 27; Benhabib, ibid., at 92–93.
77. Fraser, *supra* note 71, at 131.
78. Benhabib, *supra* note 74, at 89; M. P. Ryan, "Gender and Public Access: Women's Politics in Nineteenth-Century America," in C. Calhoun, ed, *Habermas and the Public Sphere* (Cambridge, MA: MIT Press, 2002) 259–88, at 259, citing Michelle Zimbalist Rosaldo.
79. Fraser, *supra* note 71, at 115–16.
80. Bunting, *supra* note 50, at 12; K. T. Bartlett, "Feminist Legal Methods" (1990) 103 Harvard Law Review 829–88, at 863–65; and Matsuda, *supra* note 50.
81. Benhabib, *supra* note 74; Pellizzoni, *supra* note 65, at 74.
82. Pellizzoni, ibid., at 74–75. Recall Benhabib, ibid., at 89, who speaks of the conversation being "radically open."

# PART FIVE

# MULTICULTURALISM, RELIGION, AND THE GEOGRAPHY OF POWER

# 10

# The Acute Multicultural Entrapment of the Palestinian-Arab Religious Minorities in Israel and the Feeble Measures Required to Relieve It

MICHAEL M. KARAYANNI

## 1. Introduction

Liberal multiculturalism has become a major normative theory for justifying the accordance of minority-group rights.[1] This justification stems from an authentic concern for the well-being and autonomy of minority-group members who, though entrenched in their community culture, are at the same time also vulnerable to the pull of the hegemonic majority.[2] Accommodation of minority groups serves to enhance their members' sense of belonging and autonomy. Indeed, the assertion focuses on individual autonomy—lending a strong liberal cast to the quest of accommodating minority groups—since the accommodation's target beneficiaries are the individual members who form the group, rather than the group per se.[3]

As this theory of group rights crystallized, however, a major problem arose: how should liberal multiculturalism relate to religious minority groups that adhere to practices viewed as illiberal, for which they seek accommodation—in the form of jurisdictional autonomy over their members in matters of family law, recognition of their dress codes, absolution from criminal liability when they perform certain religiously motivated activities, or other judicial leniencies?[4] I shall refer to this problem as "multicultural entrapment." In this respect, the seminal essay by Susan Moller Okin, *Is Multiculturalism Bad for Women?*[5] was an eye-opener, albeit a controversial one,[6] showing how internal group practices can be especially problematic for women.

Children, too, are vulnerable to illiberal group practices. For example, the United States Supreme Court decision in *Wisconsin v. Yoder*,[7] concerning Amish parents who asked to be absolved of criminal liability for removing their children from school at the age of 14 instead of at the legally mandated age of 16, justified their actions on the basis of their and their community's protected freedom of conscience. Ultimately, the Court absolved the parents from criminal liability based on their individual freedom of conscience, given the norms and practices of their group.[8] Important as it may be for a community to sustain its existence by indoctrinating its children, this same interest, if accommodated, will make these children less capable of becoming active and productive citizens of the general society with the ability to understand and appreciate the complexity and advantages of modern life.[9]

Much thought has been devoted to considering the propriety of accommodating minority religious groups, especially if such groups adhere to patriarchal norms and practices.[10] Some scholars have proposed that such religious groups should not be accommodated at all, for how could individuals who reject liberalism as a guiding principal in their internal conduct be accommodated in the name of liberalism?[11] On a more fundamental level, the claim is that the classical liberal right of freedom of association is in itself sufficient to accommodate all groups who want to come together and promote their joint ideals, interests, and aspirations. Therefore, no active support or accommodation need be afforded by the state to any of the existing groups, minorities or otherwise. Yet those who take seriously the claim that one's individual capacity to evaluate reality and decide how to act in a normative manner is inherently embedded in one's group identity (cultural, ethnic, religious, racial) cannot be indifferent to the weakening of this identity, even when the particular group is illiberal in its internal practices. Therefore, something more than a guarantee of the basic freedom of association is needed. Proponents of multiculturalism as a normative political-legal structure designed to accommodate minority groups are ready to endow special rights on such illiberal groups, along with certain guarantees that such an accommodation will not undermine the rights of minority individuals. One scholar has proposed that the accommodation of minority groups take the form of "external protection," that is, protection of the minority group from the hegemonic majority.[12] Accordingly, it is legitimate for the state to recognize the official status of a minority language and minority holidays, and to ensure that the minority has representatives in governmental bodies. However, if the accommodation grants the minority the power to apply its internal norms to its members, these prerogatives should be "internally restricted." Such is the case when a minority is granted jurisdictional powers over its members in matters of personal status. This approach has been criticized, given the fact that it is not always clear if the accommodation is of the "internal restriction" type or the "external protection" type, and even if it is the latter, it will indirectly give rise to the imposition of internal restrictions.

Other theorists are ready to accommodate illiberal religious groups with an extensive jurisdictional authority over their members as long as such members have the option to "exit" and thus relieve themselves from the imposition of illiberal practices.[13] At the core of this approach is the claim that groups will be unable to exist as such without their internal restrictions, at least some of such restrictions. However, such groups must be accommodated with the condition that if certain members are uncomfortable with the internal norms and practices, they can "opt out" and leave the group. However, the mechanism of exit has also been questioned.[14] In cases where group membership is ascribed by birth, rather than by choice, exit can be very difficult in practice.[15] Moreover, the choice to remove oneself from such an affiliation can lead to harsh consequences, requiring a complete break with the community that one was raised in and that features certain characteristics one might still cherish.[16] Age is also a factor. How can children as young as twelve years old decide that they want to leave their group? More nuanced propositions argue that the best way to handle illiberal intra-group practices is by promoting reforms from within that can be realized by such mechanisms as "deliberative democracy."[17] According to this approach, mechanisms can be instituted within illiberal groups that would facilitate deliberation of internal group norms, which would then be agreed upon by group institutions before they become enforceable. Such internal deliberation will eventually cause internal norms and practices to become more accommodating to vulnerable group members.

The discussion of multicultural entrapment, intensive and rich as it is, is nonetheless lacking in one major aspect. It takes place within the confines of a western liberal democracy where accommodation, especially of religious minorities, has been minimal at best. While in such a context one can detect how influential the hegemonic culture can be on a minority religion, still the existing socio-legal order is sufficiently powerful to promote and protect the well-being of individual minority-group members. Consequently, it is almost a given that such a socio-legal order offers a sphere to which a minority-group member can "exit" and that public institutions are attuned, at least formally, to the needs and concerns of individual members just as much as the minority group is. This is often not the situation with regard to religious minorities in nation-states, especially vulnerable minority members such as women and children. In many nation-states there are a number of factors that operate simultaneously in justifying why minority groups, particularly religious groups, should continue to exist as such. More importantly, in many nation-states, the mechanisms suggested for the elimination or the easing of multicultural entrapment become inapplicable. First, in the nation-state context, there is often no perceived benefit in assimilating the minority religions; on the contrary—in an effort to preserve the character of the nation-state, the religious minorities are maintained as such. Since the accommodation of minority religions is commonly conceived as a form of compensation for the biased identity of the state as a whole, both the majority and the minority religions perceive the jurisdictional authority granted to minority religions over matters of family law as a form of multicultural accommodation and compensation. Additionally, in nation-states there is no inclusive civic identity that all citizens connect with equally. Consequently, minority group members who wish to exit their religious group are not only burdened by the usual constraints of leaving an entire way of life, but in addition have nowhere to exit to. The absence of an all-inclusive civic identity also diminishes the capacity of the various branches of government, naturally identified with the nation-state's ideals and aspirations, to intervene on behalf of members of religious minorities against their religious community's jurisdiction. Such intervention will be regarded as meddling by "outsiders," thereby denying state institutions the leverage of legitimacy and public cause they ordinarily enjoy in western democracies when intervening in minority affairs. As a result of this situation, an acute condition of multicultural entrapment is created, which in turn gives rise to one of the most challenging questions in the theory and practice of multiculturalism: how can such entrapment be remedied or contained, if at all?

It is this acute form of multicultural entrapment that I wish to describe as well as to suggest mechanisms for its alleviation. As a case study, I intend to take the jurisdictional authority accorded to the Palestinian-Arab religious communities in Israel in matters of family law.

## 2. Internal Restrictions in Context

Israel is a highly diverse society. Nationally, there exists a Jewish majority that at the end of 2012 numbered 5,999,600, forming about 75.1 percent of a total population of 7,984,500.[18] About 20.6 percent of the population is Palestinian-Arab (1,647,200).[19] The remaining portion (337,800) are unidentified as Jews or Arabs but are mostly immigrants who have acquired Israeli citizenship under a special provision in the Law of Return, 1950[20] (being the relative of a Jew) or have acquired permanent residence in Israel under special circumstances.[21] Another group is that of foreign workers, estimated at 202,000, who do not appear in the official census.[22]

In terms of religion, too, Israeli society comprises many groups. The Jewish majority is divided into secular, traditional, and religious groups, with the latter including a well-established Ultra-Orthodox community.[23] Within the Jewish traditional and religious communities other divisions exist, such as between Ashkenazi and Sephardi Jews, and between Orthodox, Conservative, and Reform Judaism.[24] However, as far as Israeli law is concerned, none of these Jewish communities forms a separate religious community. In respect of the Palestinian-Arab community there are three main divisions: Muslims, numbering about 1,200,000 (16 percent of the total population); Druze, numbering about 120,000 (1.6 percent); and Christians, numbering about 150,000 (2 percent).[25] The Palestinian-Arab Christian community is divided into ten recognized religious communities: (1) the Eastern (Orthodox) community; (2) the Latin (Catholic) community; (3) the Gregorian Armenian community; (4) the Armenian (Catholic) community; (5) the Syrian (Catholic) community; (6) the Chaldean (Uniate) community; (7) the Greek (Catholic) Melkite community; (8) the Maronite community; (9) the Syrian (Orthodox) community; and (10) the Evangelical Episcopal Church in Israel.[26] In addition to these there is the Baha'i Community—a religious group recognized since 1971.[27]

These divisions have legal implications. Under the long-standing Ottoman *millet* system these religious communities were empowered to establish their own religious courts and apply their religious norms to their members in a number of personal status matters.[28] The religious courts of the recognized religious communities were and still are accorded exclusive jurisdiction over the matters of marriage and divorce of their local members. In other matters of personal status, like those pertaining to alimony, child custody, and inheritance, the religious courts have the judicial capacity to deal with such issues and apply their religious norms only if all the concerned parties consent to their jurisdiction. Without such consent, the parties must resort to the regular civil courts (the Court for Family Affairs), which on certain issues, like alimony, will still apply the relevant religious law of the parties instead of the usual civil territorial norm. So in essence the religious identity of local Palestinian-Arab citizens of Israel serves in a number of spheres to connect the individual to a particular legal system. It can determine the governing law (*lex causae*) for a certain relationships, exactly as the law of the place where the tort was committed or that where the contract was concluded can determine the governing law in each of these disciplines.[29]

- The jurisdictional capacity granted to the Palestinian-Arab religious communities I take to be a major multicultural accommodation, and I seek to uncover and challenge some of the assumptions that lie behind this view.[30]

Since the accommodation is in the form of a judicial and prescriptive capacity granted to religious communities over their members, the accommodation causes the creation of a number of "internal restrictions" that severely undermine the rights of women and children in particular—so at least when judged from a liberal point of view.[31] Here is a list of examples from the norms prescribed by Palestinian-Arab religious communities in matters that can come under their jurisdiction: Polygamy is sanctioned (though not mandated) by Islamic law (sharia), enabling a man to marry up to four wives;[32]

- Upon remarriage a widowed Muslim woman can lose custody over her minor children to relatives of her deceased husband;[33]
- Divorce (*tallaq*) is possible under sharia and Druze family law if the husband decides to unilaterally dissolve the marriage (unless provided otherwise in the marriage contract);[34]
- Marriage of minors (girls as young as 12 years old) is sanctioned by Greek Orthodox family law as well as sharia;[35]
- Divorce, even if consensual, is unavailable under certain Christian family laws, and if available is much more considerate of the husband than of the wife.[36]

It is noteworthy that Palestinian-Arab religious communities differ in this respect from the jurisdiction accorded to rabbinical courts in Israel in matters of marriage and divorce. Although this is also a source of internal restrictions that can undermine the rights of women,[37] as in the case of wives refused divorce by their husbands, the *agunah*[38]—literally anchored—woman, these superficial similarities mask a radical difference in intent, norms, and practice.[39]

As I have shown elsewhere, there is an essential difference between the justifications for the religious accommodations of the Palestinian-Arab community and those behind the religious accommodations of the Jewish majority.[40] I will try to explain the difference.

The accommodations granted to the Palestinian-Arab religious communities are taken to be a form of minority (group) accommodation that is multicultural and liberal in nature.[41] The authority granted to the Palestinian-Arab religious communities to adjudicate the matters of personal status of their members is presumably given because of Israel's proclaimed democratic norms that seek to respect religious diversity among its non-Jewish communities. As Izhak Englard has noted, in respect of the Palestinian-Arab minority the conflict between religion and state has become entangled in the "age-old Israel-Arab conflict over Palestine,"[42] and this politicization has in turn contributed to the "[shift] in concern from individual freedom of religion to collective autonomy."[43] Thus, in terms of normative justification, the religious accommodations for the Palestinian-Arab minority in Israel are no more than a continuation of the long-standing Ottoman *millet* system by which minority religions were granted prescriptive and judicial jurisdiction over their members. Moreover, the perceived democratic justification for the jurisdiction accorded to the Palestinian-Arab religious communities relegates these religious affairs to Israel's "private" sphere. The jurisdiction is the private matter of the religious minority rather than of the state. These attributes are inherently different from those characterizing the jurisdiction accorded to Jewish religious institutions and Jewish religious norms. Given the Jewish nature of the State of Israel, the jurisdiction accorded to Jewish religious institutions and norms is perceived as yet another public feature, albeit controversial at times, of the State of Israel as a Jewish state.[44] This is obviously the result of the intertwining of religion and state within Judaism itself.[45] But still, it is Israel's definition as a Jewish state, and not its definition as a democratic state, that justifies the religious accommodations granted to Jewish religious institutions and norms. Consequently, after the establishment of the State of Israel as a Jewish state it can no longer be said that the Jewish community in Israel is just another *millet* or ethno-religious group.[46] Rather, the matter of Jewish religious jurisdiction has been "nationalized" in the sense that it has become part of Israel's "public" sphere. Consequently, the policies directing the Israeli establishment's actions when coming to recognize Jewish religious institutions and norms refer to and contain the need to preserve Jewish identity and Jewish unity, even when such recognition was anathema to the liberal ideals of considerable portions among the Jewish community.[47]

One significant implication of this basic distinction is the ease with which the Israeli establishment is willing to recognize non-Jewish religious communities and grant them official status. The Druze community was recognized in 1957,[48] the Evangelical Episcopal Church in 1970,[49] and the Baha'i Community in 1971.[50] Recognition was given to Christian communities comprising not more than a few thousand members.[51] On the other hand, though Reform and Conservative Judaism are major streams among Jews worldwide and have a considerable following in Israel as well, their quest for recognition by the Israeli establishment has always been an uphill battle, and a largely unsuccessful one.[52] Whereas for Jewish communities recognition has always been determined by the public demands and dictates of Jewish identity and unity in the State of Israel—strictly maintained by hegemonic Orthodox Judaism—the recognition of non-Jewish religious communities is determined by the state's commitment to religious pluralism.

This distinction between the normative justification behind the jurisdictional capacity of the rabbinical courts on the one hand and the justification used for Palestinian-Arab religious communities on the other hand has a direct bearing on the configuration of the multicultural entrapment in the Israeli context. While the Jews in Israel are entrapped within the jurisdiction of the rabbinical courts, this entrapment cannot be regarded as either liberal or multicultural. As we have seen, this jurisdictional authority is not derived from a will to accommodate a politically under-powered minority group, who without the accommodation might lose its collective identity. On the contrary, as much as the jurisdiction of the rabbinical courts is justified in terms of accommodating Jewish religious communities in Israel, it has been acknowledged that these groups have traditionally been granted excessive political power and also happen, at least in terms of the Ultra-Orthodox community, to be expanding rather than assimilating. The case is different in respect of the Palestinian-Arab religious communities. Perceptions of liberal multiculturalism have traditionally been behind granting them their jurisdictional capacity over marriage, divorce, and other family law matters. Thus, by definition, only Palestinian-Arabs in Israel can be regarded as being in multicultural entrapment.

## 3. The Acute Multicultural Predicament of Palestinian-Arabs in Israel

There are several major forces that work to strengthen the existing jurisdiction of the Palestinian-Arab religious communities in Israel, making the entrapment of vulnerable individual Palestinian-Arabs particularly acute.

Before outlining the different factors a note is in order. Jeff Spinner-Halev was the first to suggest that the Muslim community in Israel is differently situated than the Jewish community in terms of its internal restrictions.[53] The reason he gives is that the Muslim community in Israel is an oppressed group, whereas the Jewish majority is not.[54] The oppressive nature of the state also makes it less credible and less able to intervene in the internal restrictions of the minority group. I agree with Spinner-Halev that the differences exist but believe less in oppression as being the main factor. If a factor at all, it is a corollary of much deeper currents in the character of Israel as a nation-state. If Spinner-Halev is correct in his assessment of oppression as being the major factor then it would have been logical to find that internal restrictions in other non-Jewish religious communities who are less oppressed, say Druze and Christians, will be situated differently from those of the Muslim and Jewish communities. But this is not the case. Though these groups are oppressed less than Muslims in Israel they still experience the same acute state of the multicultural predicament. As will become clear from the ensuing discussion, the major factor has to do with the different forces exerted by the social, political and constitutional characteristics of Israel as a nation state.

## 3.1. Israel as a Non-assimilative State

It is acknowledged that when it comes to relations among Jews and Arabs in Israel, as well as among the different religious communities, that Israel is a non-assimilative state.[55] Israel does not have a general melting-pot policy, and the state provides little incentive to assimilate the non-Jewish religious minorities. Indeed, social scientists have contended that part of maintaining the Jewish identity of Israelis is by demarcating the differences between Jews and non-Jews.[56] In this respect the existing jurisdictional capacity of the different *millets* preserves endogamy, in line with this general policy.[57] In Israel, therefore, the hegemonic group wants not to weaken the religious identity of the minority religious groups but rather to strengthen it so that the identity of the majority can be better maintained, and thus to bolster the national identity of the State of Israel as a Jewish state. One example of Israeli identity politics at work in maintaining the religious divides and the regulation of family law that I have examined is that of Israel's adoption law. A strict norm mandates religious matching between the adopters and the adopted child, whatever group they belong to, thus dictating the limits of adoption across religious lines. I was able to show that religious Jewish norms at work in national policy-making bodies crafted the adoption law as part of public Jewish interests, embedded in the sphere of interreligious relations in Israel—a norm that seeks to advance the separateness among the religious communities rather than their unity.[58]

By now, it should be clear how the multicultural entrapment of the Palestinian-Arab minority in Israel differs in its acuteness from that of other religious minority members in western democracies. As opposed to these other minorities, the Palestinian-Arab religious communities are actively encouraged to maintain their religious identity, if not explicitly then by a range of implicit policies that work to deny the establishment of any other identity that seeks to replace the religious one. Yet in western democracies the process seems to be exactly the opposite—to create an environment that works to weaken the religious identity of minorities by formal as well as implicit means.

## 3.2. The Absence of a Common Israeli Identity

A corollary to what has been stated so far is the absence of a civic identity that could contest the religious identity of Israelis—at least as far as the Israeli establishment is concerned.[59] There has never been an established policy or active pursuit of creating a single, unified Israeli identity for all those who possess Israeli citizenship. Indeed, petitions on behalf of Jewish organizations to change the labeling in Israeli identity cards from ethno-religious affiliation—for example "Jewish"—to "Israeli" have recently been dismissed by the Israeli

Supreme Court.[60] Citizenship in Israel is based on membership in an ethnic group,[61] and being an Israeli is synonymous with being a Jew.[62]

Studies on the meaning and content of Israeli citizenship support to a great extent the idea that Palestinian-Arab community members in Israel do not share a sense of being part of a certain collective with shared ideals and aspirations[63] and are depicted as "invisible,"[64] the "odd man out,"[65] and "citizens without citizenship."[66] Gad Barzilai, today the dean of the University of Haifa Faculty of Law and both a political scientist and a legal scholar, succinctly concluded that the Palestinian-Arab minority in Israel is the "most remote, excluded community from the state's meta-narratives."[67]

Given the excessively weak civic linkage between the state and its Palestinian-Arab citizens, little leverage exists for legitimizing state intervention in the religious affairs of the Palestinian-Arab religious communities, especially when this intervention is called for in order to protect members against internal restrictions of their religious communities. State institutions will be perceived as "outsiders" meddling in the affairs of "others."[68] Again, Israel's national identity as a Jewish state exerts immense power in demarcating the groups' "ours" and "theirs," with the state having more leverage in the religious matters of the first and less in those of the latter.[69]

### 3.3. The Power of Historical Inertia

Historically, a strong connection was established between the recognition accorded to a Jewish (and later an Arab) state as a nation-state and the need to grant autonomy to the religious minorities that will come to exist under it, especially in matters of family law.[70] The essence of this linkage is in perceiving the recognition in a religious minority's autonomy as a partial consolation prize, as it were, for according of a nation-state status to the state as a whole. Therefore, if autonomy is not granted to religious minorities over family law matters, then the nation-state will have less legitimacy. The seeds of this linkage can be seen in the Balfour Declaration of November 2, 1917. Immediately after the statement in which the British Government is said to "view with favour the establishment in Palestine of a national home for the Jewish people ... ," the document states that it is "clearly understood that nothing shall be done which may prejudice the civil and religious rights of existing non-Jewish communities. ... " The British Mandate over Palestine, conferred by the League of Nations on July 24, 1922, is even more explicit in this matter.[71] After conceding in the preamble that the Mandate over Palestine is responsible for "putting into effect" the Balfour Declaration, Article 9 of the Mandate states: "Respect for the personal status of various peoples and communities and for their religious interests shall be fully guaranteed." The article then goes out of its way to say that such respect should extend to "the control and administration of Waqfs"—that is, religious endowments conferred in accordance with Islamic sharia. In Chapter 2, Article 4 of the UN General Assembly Resolution 181 of November 29, 1947, commonly known as the "partition plan," it was provided that in each of the proposed Arab and Jewish nation-states "[t]he family law and personal status of the various minorities and their religious interests, including endowments, shall be respected."[72] So when Israel was established in 1948, part of its quest then and for a long time thereafter in gaining international legitimacy was to actively maintain the jurisdictional authority of the various Palestinian-Arab religious communities. In this sense the maintenance of Israel's character as a Jewish nation-state was, and to a great extent still is, an additional force for according recognition to the jurisdictional capacity of Palestinian-Arab religious communities over their family law matters.[73]

### 3.4. Control by Fragmentation

Another force that worked, at least traditionally, to lock Palestinian-Arab members within their religious communities is Israel's policies for controlling minorities. Ian Lustick in his influential book *Arabs in the Jewish State*, published in 1980,[74] starts off the analysis by noting how in spite of Israel's deep divisions, especially among Arabs and Jews, Israel has not witnessed ethnic disturbances as other countries did. The cause for this, Lustick goes on to argue, is the quiescence of the Israeli Arabs, achieved through different means of control.[75] One important instrument of control is segmentation and fragmentation.[76] In this respect the religious divisions among the Palestinian-Arab community, as ordered by the traditional *millet* system, proved to be a resource that could be exploited by the Israeli establishment in order to further this control policy.[77] Indeed, Israel did not invent the *millet* system; but given its existence and Israel's policy of control, it served it better if it was enforced rather than weakened.[78] Yet enforcing the *millet* system meant actively maintaining the jurisdiction of the Palestinian-Arab religious communities, which in turn works to reinforce internal restrictions, making yet more vulnerable minorities within the communities.

### 3.5. Limitations on Exit

The existence of a viable exit route from the minority group has been instrumental in legitimizing the grant of autonomy or other accommodations to minority groups. This is especially the case when the minority seeks to apply internal restrictions on its members, as religious groups commonly do. Exit possibilities mean that individual members who are uncomfortable with internal restrictions can chose to leave the group and by doing so relieve themselves from such internal limitations. The existence of exit options is also a force that can transform the group from within. Given that groups generally aim to maintain their constituency, they will respond to group members leaving because of internal restrictions and work to reform their internal practices. In short, exit possibilities promote the interests of individuals from within and makes their voices heard. In this sense exit options do for the internal handlings of the group what opting-out mechanisms do for class actions. In order to legitimize the initiation of a civil claim on behalf of a large group of individuals who are similarly situated because of a similar substantial claim against a defendant, the process provides for those who are not interested in the initiation of the claim on their behalf to opt out and thus relieve themselves from the adverse effect of an unfavorable judgment. Additionally, the option that class members have to opt out also serves as an incentive for the class representative (effectively the lawyers in charge of litigation) to do the best job possible in order that class members should not choose to leave—for the size of the class effects the size of judgment and the size of judgment affects the returns of the representative. Opting out, in turn, benefits the class in that it helps control the agency problem associated with class actions.

But exit in the context of religious and cultural groups has been severely criticized.[79] Essentially, the claim is that religious and cultural groups for individuals are not what class actions are for claimants. Individuals, even if uncomfortable with certain internal restrictions, do not just leave their group. To do so is like leaving a whole life behind and not just what might be conceived as detrimental practices by the group representative. Additionally, for some individuals, children for example, exit from their religious groups is not an option at all. Be the case as it may, exit assumes that there is an alternative regime of norms that one can connect to after exit. In many western countries such a sphere conceivably exists. An Amish woman in America bothered by its group's practices and norms may chose to leave the group and will probably find a society and a sphere of norms that she can connect to and be part of. But for many Palestinian-Arab individuals in Israel there is no such sphere to which they can exit. Israel lacks a civil regime of marriage and divorce that Palestinian-Arab individuals can opt out to, given that Israel has no civil territorial law that regulates marriage and divorce for those who belong to one of the recognized religious communities.[80] A Palestinian-Arab member of a religious group who would seek to live a purely secular life but yet would like to maintain her national identity, culture, and language will find no social context in Israel that can supply her needs. As in our identity cards, we can be Jewish, Arab, Druze—or have nothing indicated.

## 3.6. Minority Politics

Another important force that works to strengthen jurisdictional authority has to do with the fact that both the secular and the traditional political forces representing the Palestinian-Arabs would like to maintain the jurisdictional authority as it is. The secular parties, such as the communist Democratic Front for Peace and Equality (*Hadash—Al-Jabhah*) party or the National Democratic Assembly (*Balad—Al-Tajamou*) have a national agenda for the Palestinian-Arab minority, but it is not a secular one that calls, for example, for the abolishing of religious authority or even for the creation of a territorial civil regime to which Palestinian-Arabs can opt out. The parties seem to feel that such calls would probably create internal rifts that will weaken the minority's national struggle. Given that patriarchy is still a major social characteristic of the Palestinian-Arab minority, it is clear also why the traditional religious-political leadership seeks to reinforce rather than weaken the existing jurisdictional authority of Palestinian-Arab communities. The religious norms of family law seek to preserve the patriarchal structure of the family and thus are perfectly aligned with the social agenda of such factions. These forces overlap with the other factors indicated above, adding yet another force that preserves the jurisdiction of the Palestinian-Arab religious communities.

The factors I have specified have combined to exert a force that strengthens the jurisdictional authority of the various Palestinian-Arab religious communities. As this jurisdictional authority gathers strength, multicultural entrapment becomes more and more acute in nature, for the strengthening of communal jurisdiction means further locking in and circumvention of individual rights and choices.

# 4. Jurisdictional Interventions

The foregoing should not be taken to mean that no effort has been made to intervene in the jurisdictional authority of the Palestinian-Arab religious communities. Over the years a number of measures were taken to safeguard individual well-being against the encroaching effect of group religious norms.[81] The Knesset has taken the following steps:

- Criminalizing polygamy,[82] unilateral divorce,[83] and the solemnization of marriage of minors (under the age of 18);[84]
- Guaranteeing equal rights for women;[85]
- Recognizing common law marriages, thereby offering individuals who are unable to marry according to their relevant religious norms the possibility of instituting a form of partnership;

- Restricting the exclusive jurisdiction of Muslim shari'a courts and Christian courts to matters of marriage and divorce alone.

The Israeli Supreme Court has also rendered a number of important decisions to protect individual Palestinian-Arabs from their religious jurisdiction. One noticeable decision in this respect is *Sultan v. Sultan*.[86] The question here was whether a Muslim wife who was unilaterally divorced by her Muslim husband can bring a civil claim for damages, even though the divorce is valid under sharia. The court recognized the claim, basing its decision on an explicit provision in the Israel Penal Law, 1977 (section 181) that criminalizes the act of unilateral divorce, irrespective of the fact that the relevant law regarding the personal status of the parties recognizes it as a valid act. A major component of the court's reasoning was the objective behind the criminalization of unilateral divorce: to achieve equal treatment of women on an individual basis as well.[87]

Another important decision is that of *Bader (Mari'ee) v. Mari'ee*.[88] In this decision the Court reversed the line of a previous holding under which the Druze religious courts were considered to have exclusive jurisdiction in matrimonial property claims when raised as an incidental matter to a divorce proceeding. Under the new holding, for such an incidental jurisdiction to exist there needs to be an explicit provision in the law, which the current law lacks.

Probably the most eloquent decision in this line of precedents is *Plonit v. Ploni*.[89] Here, a Muslim mother and her daughter were successful in challenging the exclusive jurisdiction of the sharia court over a declaration of paternity between Muslims in Israel. The crux of the Court's reasoning here was to protect the daughter's basic right to know who her real father is—something that would not have been possible, so the Court assumed, if this paternity action were to remain under the jurisdiction of the sharia court. Under Islamic law there is a very strong presumption that a married person can only be the parent of the children of his or her legally (sharia) recognized spouse—*Al walad lil firash*: the child belongs to the marriage bed.[90]

Recently, another important decision was handed down by the Court in *Plonit v. High Shari'a Court of Appeals*.[91] The High Shari'a Court of Appeals held that a woman cannot serve as an arbitrator in a specially designed arbitration process in a divorce action that was pending before it. The Court overturned the decision because it stands against the principle of equality as it was prescribed by the Women's Equal Rights Law, 1951.

These developments beg the question of whether the multicultural predicament is really as acute as I have claimed it to be, at least today as opposed to the past. Both the Knesset and the Israeli Supreme Court have seemingly made an impressive effort to safeguard individuals, including Palestinian-Arab citizens, against illiberal norms in their respective religious communities.

To answer this, let me first note that by framing the multicultural predicament of the Palestinian-Arab in Israel in respect of the religious jurisdiction over their family law matters as acute does not mean that they receive no protection from the liberal norms as prescribed by these measures.

But when it comes to actual enforcement of some of the restrictions enumerated above, law enforcement authorities are dilatory in prosecuting such cases.[92] Studies were conducted, for example, on the effectiveness of the restrictions on the age of marriage among the Palestinian-Arab Muslim community. The conclusion these studies reached was that enforcement by the authorities was minimal and courts were lenient in their sentencing,[93] if and when indictments were filed.[94] Indicative in this respect is the Age of Marriage Law, promulgated in 1950. In a survey taken some ten years after the enactment of this law, it was shown that 42.7 percent of all Muslims were married before the age of 17. The number could have been higher, since there may have been marriages that were not registered, and others that were registered were originally underage marriages that were confirmed retroactively.[95] Additionally, in the case of an underage marriage, it was Islamic law that governed whether the marriage was valid or not, according to which a female girl becomes eligible for marriage when she reaches sexual maturity, "determined in almost all cases on the basis of the onset of menstruation," which can be as early as the age of 12.[96] The decrease of underage marriages was attributed to changing social norms rather than to criminal prohibition. Similar conclusions were reached in the case of polygamy,[97] which is still widely practiced among the Bedouin community in southern Israel.[98] Also here the intervention by the Knesset did not directly deal with the validity of polygamous marriage, criminal prosecution was minimal, sentences were lenient, and the decrease was more due to the changing social values than due to criminal liability.[99]

At times the problem of not putting equitable norms and policies into effect is not so much the passivity of law enforcement authorities but that of courts that allow the control of patriarchal norms within the Palestinian-Arab community. One of the long-standing hallmarks of the patriarchal nature of the Palestinian-Arab community is women's renunciation of their inheritance rights in favor of the male heirs in the family.[100] Thus, even if female and male heirs in the family are entitled to equal shares of an inheritance, the women often give up their share. Though women probably do so as a result of social pressure and their inferior status in this patriarchal society, courts have not been forthcoming in helping such women to secure their rights as heirs.[101]

Probably the boldest move in favor of Palestinian-Arab women's individual rights was the amendment to the Family Court Law in 2001 whereby the exclusive jurisdiction of the sharia and Christian religious courts was confined to matters of marriage and divorce. This in turn afforded Palestinian-Arab Muslim and Christian women the option of filing their alimony claims before the Court for Family Affairs rather than solely before their respective religious courts, as was the case until this amendment. It is generally believed that granting such an option improves the status of women, given the general tendency of civil courts to be more equitable and more supportive and understanding than religious courts of women's claims.[102] Even if this assumption is true,[103] it should be borne in mind that the same option was granted to Jewish women already in 1953, with the enactment of Rabbinical Jurisdiction (Marriage and Divorce) Law.[104] Whatever the reasons for this 47-year delay in the equalization of the religious courts, clearly the major normative obstacle is that for Palestinian-Arab religious groups, the group comes first and the individual second.

## 5. Feeble Measures

I propose that the acute state of multicultural entrapment can be more effectively dealt with by more nuanced and specific measures than criminal sanctions. In the following I will suggest three such basic measures.

### 5.1. Cut and Paste Policies

One idea is to review liberal family law reforms that have already taken place in other Middle Eastern countries where the same religious communities are accorded similar jurisdictional authority over matters of family relations and to learn from them what could be implemented in respect of the relevant Palestinian-Arab religious community in Israel. This type of selective adoption of similarly situated family law reforms can never thrive in a paternalistic, prescriptive form or as an imposition of "foreign" values, but only as an organic development of existing community norms. In fact, one such case has already taken place with respect to the Israeli Druze community. The Druze community gained full official recognition as an independent religious community in 1957.[105] Some four years later, the religious leadership of the community adopted the Druze family law in effect in Lebanon.[106] The Israeli establishment, represented by the Ministry of Religions, saw no need to intervene in the substantive norms pertaining to the Druze community, perceiving such a matter as "an internal matter of the community."[107] Yet it should be noted that this code of family law was known as a most advanced code of norms, prescribing that the husband should treat his wife as an equal partner, completely restricting polygamy, making the husband's adultery a cause for divorce, and entitling the wife to monetary compensation if unjustly divorced.[108] I suggest that similar importations can be made with reference to other Palestinian-Arab religious communities. For example, today Egypt grants Muslim women the option to initiate a divorce proceeding if she is willing to give up some of her matrimonial property rights. While this is not an ideal solution, it is an improvement over the existing situation in Israeli Muslim communities, in which a woman may not initiate divorce proceedings at all.

Another method of importation that can be utilized and is organic to the Israeli legal system rather than the Palestinian-Arab religious community itself is to draw on liberalizing precedents of a secular nature that have taken place in the jurisdictional authority of the Jewish rabbinical courts, and apply them to the Palestinian-Arab religious communities. The jurisdiction of the Jewish rabbinical courts in Israel and the imposition of a religious norm in matters of family law are resented by many Israeli Jews, who perceive them to be a form of religious coercion and thus illiberal. Yet given the primacy of Jewish identity in the Israeli nation-state, the jurisdiction of the rabbinical courts has taken on a public nature.[109] As part of the nation-state apparatus, jurisdiction over family law matters is a means of preserving the Jewish identity of the state. This constellation of the rabbinical court's jurisdiction as illiberal and public is an exact mirror image of the courts of the Palestinian-Arab religious communities, commonly taken as multicultural/liberal and private in nature. One implication of this distinction is that the Israeli Supreme Court is more willing to intervene in the jurisdictional authority of the rabbinical courts in the name of liberal norms than it is when dealing with the jurisdiction of the Palestinian-Arab religious courts. For, once again, if the accommodation of the Palestinian-Arab religious communities at the group level is itself liberal in nature, the Court's liberal quest will be less forceful in introducing a liberal norm that seeks to protect individual members from a jurisdictional authority that is conceived as coercive and illiberal in nature. Nonetheless, once an intervention in the jurisdiction of the rabbinical courts takes place, which is relatively more common, then the outcome can be applied more easily to the jurisdiction of the Palestinian-Arab religious courts as well. Indeed, the impetus for such application came in 2001, when a law was enacted equating the exclusive jurisdiction of sharia and Christian courts to that of the rabbinical courts—until then, the exclusive jurisdiction of these two courts was wider than that of the rabbinical courts. Currently, the justification for intervening in the affairs of a minority is based on pressure to level the jurisdictional authority of the various religious communities that operate in the same legal system; however, intervention can be used more pointedly to advance more liberal norms that would protect individual members of religious minorities.

## 5.2. Accountability

A second measure is to strengthen the accountability of religious community officials in charge of the agencies with judicial authority over their members. It is only reasonable that officials with administrative powers be subject to some kind of administrative control, whether in their appointment or judicial performances. Such administrative control can also be subject to input by the relevant religious constituency, such as electing these judiciary officials directly or electing a general body that will oversee their activities. The primary advantage of such measures is that they can be used as platforms for activists and politicians representing the minorities to promote reforms through the support of officials who will seek to adopt such reforms. It is widely acknowledged that groups whose internal norms are contested should play, whenever possible, the central role in any reform movement.[110] Promoting accountability of officials can serve as a powerful promoter of internal reform movements.

The lack of any accountability of officials serving in religious courts is particularly noticeable in the ten recognized Christian communities. The judges of these courts are appointed at the sole discretion of each of the communities, with no intervention or oversight by any public body. Israeli law is not concerned with the qualifications of such judges, who may lack any formal credentials or qualifications for serving the relevant Christian community. Moreover, since such judges are financially dependent on the religious community rather than on the state (which is the case of sharia and Druze courts' *qadis*) there never can be full confidence that such officials are sufficiently neutral to render just judgment or sufficiently independent to reform religious law from within. There is a strong case to be made for requiring that judges serving in Christian courts should be granted official status and undergo the same procedure of appointments as the judges of the other religious courts do, without jeopardizing the jurisdictional authority of the Christian communities. One important move in this direction has already been made. A new judicial body that deals with complaints against judges was created in 2002.[111] The definition of the "judges" that are under the supervisory authority of the ombudsman office includes judges in the Christian courts, even though, unlike all other judges, they are not appointed to office by any statutory body.[112] I suspect that this move was taken given the realization that such judges fulfill an important judicial function that demands some kind of supervision. This may ensure that judges in the Christian courts will undergo a public appointment procedure that will probe into their personal and professional qualifications.

## 5.3. Transparency

Although the religious law of the Palestinian-Arab religious communities has official standing, and thus courts are considered to have judicial notice of it, there exists no official publication or collection where one can turn to and find the contents of such law. This makes it extremely difficult not only to learn about the contents of the law but also to attain any proper analysis of its contents, attributes, and characteristics generally. Things are different in respect of the Jewish communities, where much effort has been made in collecting the body of laws that govern the Jewish family. Furthermore, given that judgments rendered by the religious courts are also of a public nature, at least in those parts of the judgment where the court identifies the applicable law, analyzes, and applies it, there is a strong case to be made in mandating the publication of these judgments. If these judgments will be made public it is anticipated that courts will be much more cautious in determining the appropriate law and applying it, and more importantly it will make it possible to oversee and criticize the judicial process undertaken by the court.

## 5.4. Concurrent Jurisdiction as Competing Jurisdiction

The fourth measure is to capitalize on an already existing mechanism that seeks to promote competition between the religious courts and the civil courts when it comes to adjudicating family law disputes. The idea is to create the widest possible concurrent jurisdictional capacity between the civil and religious courts over family law matters. The option of initiating litigation before a civil court, when it becomes available, will serve as an incentive for the religious courts to reform their norms and procedures in order to maintain their relevance for their entire constituency, women included. The envisioned concurrent jurisdictional authority of civil courts in matters of family law need not lead to the abolishment of the religious norm as the governing norm. The concurrent jurisdictional capacity can be limited only to the sphere of adjudicative jurisdiction while maintaining that the jurisdiction to prescribe the governing norm will remain in the hands of the religious community. Even then, the prospects of seeking justice in another court will serve as a partial exit that can empower the voice of community members, including that of women, from within. As indicated above, the religious community wants to maintain its hold over its members and therefore should want to attend to their demands so as to better serve their interests. There is always the danger that the religious community would want to make up for losing exclusive power over its members by radicalizing its religious norms, which would continue to govern the substantive issues. However, there exists an important precedent that shows that concurrent jurisdiction authority does not radicalize the religious norm, but does even the opposite. From 2001, as mentioned, Muslim and Christian women have the power to initiate an alimony claim before a civil court instead of being obliged to file it before their respective religious court, which until then had exclusive jurisdiction in such a matter. Yet the substantive norm that governs an alimony claim between spouses continues to be that of the religious law of the parties, even when the claim is initiated in the civil court. But there is no indication that the religious norm became more radical in nature as a result of the reform. Indeed, activists and lawyers working in the realm of family law indicate that since the 2001 amendment these religious courts have raised the amounts of alimony, and by doing so were competing with the civil courts and paying more attention to the interests of women. This shows that such measures can be taken in other matters that are still under the exclusive jurisdiction of the Palestinian-Arab religious communities, such as marriage and divorce. Relative to the other measures, this would no doubt be considered the boldest. It would seek to abolish the exclusive jurisdiction of the religious courts over matters of marriage and divorce, a sphere thus far considered a taboo. The Palestinian-Arab community may have a certain advantage over the Jewish community in this respect. If Palestinian-Arabs are able to concede the fact that their primary identity is their national identity rather than their religious one—which cannot be as easily done in respect of the Jewish majority in Israel—then the demarcating of identities through the existing exclusive jurisdiction over matters of marriage and divorce among Muslims, Christians, and Druze will be less called for. As a matter of fact, a serious attempt was taken in this direction of introducing civil marriage in Lebanon, and signs that it might eventually succeed there already exist.[113] What seems to be the driving force behind this initiative is a shared national Lebanese citizenship instead of the traditional confessional one.[114] A similar initiative can be adopted among the Palestinian-Arabs in Israel. Already, their shared national identity serves as a unifying force.[115] Moreover, the suggested mechanism here does not do away with the religious law altogether in matters of marriage and divorce. It only makes it optional to turn to the civil court rather than the religious court in marriage and divorce actions—knowing in advance that the applicable law in both is the religious law of the parties.

## 6. Conclusion

The social, political, and constitutional context in which jurisdiction is accorded to different religious communities could have a profound impact on how such a jurisdiction is to be characterized. As we have seen, even if the

Jewish community's rabbinical courts are accorded the same jurisdictional capacity as that of the Islamic, Christian, and Druze religious courts, this still does not mean that the normative justification for these jurisdictional capacities is the same for all. Israel's identity as a Jewish nation-state (i.e. Jewishness as both religious and national), the social reality within the Jewish community that has a fairly large secular population, and the political reality of a major political rift between Jewish religious and nonreligious politics have all contributed to making the existing jurisdictional competency of the rabbinical court a necessity and illiberal in character at the same time. The jurisdiction of the rabbinical courts is not of a multicultural nature to start with, so speaking of multicultural entrapment in respect of Jews in Israel is genuinely flawed. Things are different in terms of the Palestinian-Arab religious communities in Israel. The jurisdictional competency of their courts was indeed conceived as multicultural and liberal in nature, notwithstanding the fact that serious question might rise in this respect if such a jurisdictional capacity is closely scrutinized. Thus, the discussion of the multicultural predicament is relevant only to the Palestinian-Arab religious communities. Given the different factors that work to lock Palestinian-Arab individuals in their respective religious communities, it is safe to say that the predicament of secular Palestinian-Arabs in Israel is much worse than that of secular Jews. Yet as I have also tried to show, this does not mean that there is nothing to be done. I have proposed a number of mechanisms that have a real chance of becoming law, and if so can reform the practices and norms of the Palestinian-Arab religious communities from within. Given the relatively feeble nature of the mechanisms, these reforms might not happen overnight. However, their prospects of bringing effective reforms in the long run are much more real than those of criminal sanctions and external intervention.

# Notes

1. W. Kymlicka, *Multicultural Citizenship: A Liberal Theory of Minority Rights* (Oxford: Oxford University Press, 1995); J. Raz, "Multiculturalism: A Liberal Perspective" (1994) 41 Dissent 67.
2. W. Kymlicka, *Liberalism, Community, and Culture* (Oxford: Oxford University Press, 1989).
3. J. Raz, "Multiculturalism" (1998) 11 Ratio Juris 193; P. Kelly, ed, *Multiculturalism Reconsidered* (Malden, MA; Cambridge, UK: Polity Press in association with Blackwell Publishers, 2002).
4. L. Green, "Internal Minorities and their Rights," in W. Kymlicka, ed, *The Rights of Minority Cultures* (Oxford: Oxford University Press, 1995) 257; A. Shachar, *Multicultural Jurisdictions: Cultural Differences and Women's Rights* (Cambridge: Cambridge University Press, 2001); A. Eisenberg and J. Spinner-Halev, eds, *Minorities within Minorities: Equality, Rights and Diversity* (Cambridge: Cambridge University Press, 2005).

5. S. M. Okin, "Is Multiculturalism Bad for Women?," in J. Cohen et al., eds, *Is Multiculturalism Bad For Women?* (Princeton, NJ: Princeton University Press, 1999) 7.
6. L. Volpp, "Feminism Versus Multiculturalism" (2001) 101 Columbia Law Review 1181.
7. 406 US 205 (1972).
8. On the controlling effect of *Yoder* in light of later United State Supreme Court holdings, see M. A. Hamilton, *"Employment Division v. Smith* at the Supreme Court: The Justices, the Litigants, and the Doctrinal Discourse" (2011) 32 Cardozo Law Review 1671.
9. R. J. Arneson and I. Shapiro, "Democratic Authority and Religious Freedom: A Critique of *Wisconsin v. Yoder*," in I. Shapiro and R. Hardin, eds, *Political Order* (New York: New York University Press, 1993) 365.
10. W. Kymlicka and R. Cohen-Almagor, "Democracy and Multiculturalism," in R. Cohen-Almagor, ed, *Challenges to Democracy: Essays in Honour and Memory of Isaiah Berlin* (Aldershot, UK and Brookfield, VT: Ashgate, 2000) 89.
11. B. Barry, *Culture and Equality: An Egalitarian Critique of Multiculturalism* (Cambridge, MA: Harvard University Press, 2001).
12. Kymlicka, *supra* note 1 at 35–44.
13. C. Kukathas, *The Liberal Archipelago* (Oxford: Oxford University Press, 2003); C. Kukathas, "Are There Any Cultural Rights?" (1992) 20 Political Theory 105.
14. O. Reitman, "On Exit," in A. Eisenberg and J. Spinner-Halev, eds, *Minorities within Minorities: Equality, Rights and Diversity* (Cambridge: Cambridge University Press, 2005) 189.
15. L. Green, "Rights of Exit" (1998) 4 Legal Theory 165.
16. Shachar, *supra* note 4 at 41–42; W. Kymlicka, "The Rights of Minority Cultures: Reply to Kukathas" (1992) 20 Political Theory 140.
17. M. Deveaux, *Gender and Justice in Multicultural Liberal States* (Oxford: Oxford University Press, 2006) at 89–126.
18. Central Bureau of Statistics, Statistical Abstract of Israel 2013, available online: <http://www1.cbs.gov.il/reader/shnatonenew_site.htm>, at Table 2.1 [CBS Statistical Abstract].
19. Ibid.
20. The relevant provision is that of a 1970 amendment: *Law of Return (Amendment no. 2)* 5730–1970, 14 LSI 28 (1969/70), article 4A(a): "The rights of a Jew under this Law and the rights of an *oleh* under the Nationality Law, as well as the rights of an *oleh* under any other enactment, are also vested in a child and a grandchild of a Jew, the spouse of a Jew, the spouse of a child of a Jew and the spouse of a grandchild of a Jew, except for a person who has been a Jew and has voluntarily changed his religion." The amendment adds in article 4B: "For the purposes of this Law, 'Jew' means a person who is born of a Jewish mother or has become converted to Judaism and who is not a member of another religion." See generally, M. Shava, "Comments on the Law of Return (Amendment No. 2), 5730–1970 (Who is a Jew?)" (1977) 3 Tel-Aviv University Studies in Law 295.
21. CBS Statistical Abstract, *supra* note 18 at 30.
22. Ibid.
23. See S. Levy et al., *A Portrait of Israeli Jewry: Beliefs, Observations, and Values among Israeli Jews 2000* (Jerusalem: The Israeli Democracy Institute, 2002) at 5–6.
24. See E. Tabory, "The Israel Reform and Conservative Movements and the Market for Liberal Judaism," in U. Rebhun and C. I. Waxman, eds, *Jews in Israel: Contemporary Social and Cultural Patterns* (Hanover and London: University Press of New England and Brandeis University Press, 2004) 285; B. E. Genut, "Competing Visions of the Jewish State: Promoting and Protecting Freedom of Religion in Israel" (1996) 19:5 Fordham International Law Journal 2120–179, at 2210 and 2151; I. Englard, "Law and Religion in Israel" (1987) 35 American Journal of Comparative Law 185, at 191.
25. CBS Statistical Abstract, *supra* note 18 at Table 2.2.
26. See R. Gottschalk, "Personal Status and Religious Law in Israel" (1951) 4 International Law Quarterly 454, at 455. The Evangelical Episcopal Church was recognized in 1970; see *Order of Recognition of a Religious Community (Evangelical Episcopal Church in Israel)*, 1970, KT 2557, at 1564.

27. *Order of Recognition of a Religious Community (The Baha'i Faith)*, 5731-1971, KT 2673, at 628.
28. See M. Galanter and J. Krishnan, "Personal Law and Human Rights in India and Israel" (2000) 34 Israel Law Review 101; A. Rubinstein, "Law and Religion in Israel" (1967) 2 Israel Law Review 380, at 384–88 [Rubinstein, "Law and Religion in Israel"]; A. Rubinstein, "State and Religion in Israel" (1967) 2 Journal of Contemporary History 107, at 111–12. See also A. Maoz, "Religious Human Rights in the State of Israel," in J. D. van der Vyver and J. Witte, Jr., eds, *Religious Human Rights in Global Perspectives: Legal Perspectives* (The Hague: Kluwer, 1996) 349–90, at 355; A. Maoz, "Enforcement of Religious Courts' Judgments under Israeli Law" (1991) 33 Journal of Church and State 473.
29. Indeed, throughout history there has been a close interaction between conflict-of-law rules and personal law regimes. See E. Vitta, *The Conflict of Laws in Matters of Personal Status in Palestine* (Tel Aviv: Bursi, 1947).
30. Some have called such a jurisdictional capacity "strong multiculturalism." See A. Shachar, "Group Identity and Women's Rights in Family Law: The Perils of Multicultural Accommodation" (1998) 6 Journal of Political Philosophy 285. For a general survey of the different types of group accommodations see J. T. Levy, "Classifying Cultural Rights," in I. Shapiro and W. Kymlicka, eds, *Nomos XXXIX: Ethnicity and Group Rights* (New York: New York University Press, 1997).
31. See R. Hirschl and A. Shachar, "Constitutional Transformation, Gender Equality, and Religious/National Conflict in Israel: Tentative Progress through the Obstacle Course," in B. Baines and R. Rubio-Marin, eds, *The Gender of Constitutional Jurisprudence* (Cambridge: Cambridge University Press, 2005) 205, at 221–22.
32. J. L. Esposito, *Women in Muslim Family Law* (Syracuse: Syracuse University Press, 1982) 20.
33. Cf. HCJ 8906/04 Plonit v. Ploni (July 20, 2005), Nevo Legal Database (by subscription).
34. See Sultan v. Sultan, CA 245/81, [1984] IsrSC 38(3) 169; HCJ 2829/03 *Plonit v. Druze Appellate Court in Acre* HCJ 2829/03, [2006] IsrSC 60(4) 159. ).
35. The Byzantine Family Law, Article 30(2); R. H. Eisenman, *Islamic Law in Palestine and Israel: A History of the Survival of Tanzimat and Shari'a in the British Mandate and the Jewish State* (Leiden: E.J. Brill, 1978).
36. M. Karayanni, "Rikoshetim Yehudi'im ve-Deimokrati'im" ["Jewish and Democratic Ricochets"] (2006) 9 Mishpat u-Mimshal 461, at 493.
37. As a matter of fact, in the scholarly literature dealing with multiculturalism the manner in which Jewish law undermines the rights of women is indicated as yet another example of the multicultural predicament. See Shachar, *supra* note 30 at 291–92.
38. S. M. Weiss and N. C. Gross-Horowitz, *Marriage and Divorce in the Jewish State* (Lebanon, NH: Brandeis University Press, 2013).
39. See R. Biale, *Women and Jewish Law: An Exploration of Women's Issues in Halakhic Sources* (New York: Schocken Books, 1984) at 102–13. Under Jewish law the husband must hand the divorce papers (*get*) to the wife and the wife needs to accept the divorce for the divorce to take place. Under Jewish law the husband and wife have an equal say on whether the divorce should happen or not. Yet the norms become bluntly unequal when one of them decides not to proceed with the divorce. If the wife refuses to accept the *get* the husband can seek a permission to marry another woman, and if he fathers children from any other woman these children will be considered legitimate. If, however, the husband is unwilling to grant his wife the *get*, even though she is willing to accept it, she will not receive permission to marry another man, and if she has children while in this limbo they will be considered illegitimate (*mamzer*), which carries various restrictions in law, which are enforced by the rabbinical courts. Women in this situation, refused divorce by their husbands, have no recourse and are thus become anchored in the marriage.
40. See M. M. Karayanni, "The Separate Nature of the Religious Accommodations for the Palestinian-Arab Minority in Israel" (2006) 5 Northwestern University Journal of International Human Rights 41 [Karayanni, "The Separate Nature"]; M. M. Karayanni, "Living in a Group of One's Own: Normative Implications Related to the Private Nature of the Religious Accommodations for the Palestinian-Arab Minority in Israel" (2007) 6

UCLA Journal of Islamic & Near Eastern Law 1 [Karayanni, "Living in a Group of One's Own"].
41. See I. Saban, "Minority Rights in Deeply Divided Societies: A Framework for Analysis and the Case of the Arab-Palestinian Minority in Israel" (2004) 36 New York University Journal of International Law & Politic 885, at 900, 942–48, 954–60 (characterizing the religious accommodations granted to the Palestinian-Arab minority in Israel as a "group-differentiated right" and as a "modest form of self-government"); D. Kretzmer, *The Legal Status of the Arabs in Israel* (Boulder: Westview Press, 1990) at 163–68 (discussing the religious organization of the Palestinian-Arab religious communities under the heading of "group rights"); see also I. Zamir, "Shivyon Zekhuyuot Klappey ha-Aravim be-Yisra'el" ["Equality of Rights for the Arabs in Israel"] (2005) 9 Mishpat u-Mimshal 11, at 26 and 30 (Hebrew) (regarding the jurisdiction of Palestinian-Arab religious communities to adjudicate matters of marriage and divorce as a group right); A. Rubinstein and B. Medina, *Ha-Mishpat ha-Hukati shel Medinat Yisra'el* [*The Constitutional Law of the State of Israel*], 6th edn (Jerusalem: Schocken, 2005) at 429–35 (in Hebrew) (referring to the religious organization of the Palestinian-Arab religious communities as a limited form of self-government).
42. England, *supra* note 24 at 189.
43. Ibid.
44. Z. Wahrhaftig, "Medinat Yisra'el ke-Medina Yehudit" ["The State of Israel as a Jewish State"], in M. Rotenberg, ed, *Ha-Dat ve-ha-Medina* [*Religion and the State*] (Tel-Aviv: The National Religious Party Public Relations Dept., 1964) 72 (Hebrew).
45. See A. Maoz, "State and Religion in Israel," in M. Mor, ed, *International Perspectives on Church and State* (New York: Fordham University Press, 1994) 239, at 243 ("[d]ivest Jewish culture and heritage from religious elements and one is left rather empty handed."). Therefore, scholars in Israel who seek to legitimize the Jewish character of the State of Israel go out of their way to stress how wrong it is to impose Jewish religious norms on members who do not opt for a religious lifestyle. See A. Yakobson and A. Rubinstein, *Yisra'el u-Mishpahat ha-Amim: Medinat Le'om Yehudit ve-Zekhuyot ha-Adam* [*Israel and the Family of Nations: Jewish Nation-State and Human Rights*] (London: Routledge, 2003) at 150–65 (Hebrew); A. Kasher, *Ruah Ish: Arba'ah She'arim* [*Spirit of a Man: Four Gates*] (Tel-Aviv: Am Oved, 2000) at 19 (Hebrew).
46. Rubinstein, "Law and Religion in Israel," *supra* note 28 at 408 (noting that while under Ottoman rule and the British Mandate the religious accommodations granted to the Jewish community were motivated by the value of autonomy and the interest of not intervening in the internal affairs of the Jewish community, the reason today is the "reverse: the interest is that of preserving the unity of the Jewish People").
47. M. Cohn, "Women, Religious Law and Religious Courts in Israel—The Jewish Case" (2004) 27 Retfærd: Nordic Journal of Law and Justice 57, at 58 (characterizing the problem of institutionalizing the religion of the Jewish community as an infringement on the rights of a liberal majority instead of the right of a religious majority to express their beliefs); M. Edelman, *Courts, Politics, and Culture in Israel* (Charlottesville: University Press of Virginia, 1994) at 60–61 (noting the troublesome fact that rabbinical courts in Israel decide matters of personal status on the basis of halakhic norms to which the majority of the Jewish community does not subscribe).
48. See A. Layish and S. H. Fallah, "Ha-Irgun ha-Adati shel ha-Druzim" [Communal Organization of the Druze], in *Ha-Aravim be-Yisra'el: Retsifut ve-Tmura* [The Arabs in Israel: Continuity and Change] (Jerusalem: Magnes Press, 1981) 123, at 124 (Hebrew).
49. *Supra* note 26.
50. *Supra* note 27.
51. See U. McGahern, *Palestinian Christians in Israel: State Attitudes towards Non-Muslim in a Jewish State* (Abingdon, Oxon; New York: Routledge, 2011) 43.
52. See generally, England, *supra* note 24; O. Seliktar, "Separating the Synagogue from the State: American Jews and the Struggle for Religious Pluralism in Israel" (2002) 18 Israel Studies Forum 57.

53. J. Spinner-Halev, "Feminism, Multiculturalism, Oppression and the State" (2001) 112 Ethics 84.
54. Ibid. at 86, 92–98.
55. S. Smooha, "The Model of Ethnic Democracy: Israel as a Jewish and Democratic State" (2002) 8 Nations and Nationalism 475, at 485; M. A. Tessler, "The Middle East: The Jews in Tunisia and Morocco and Arabs in Israel," in R. G. Wirsing, ed, *Protection of Ethnic Minorities* (New York: Pergamon Press, 1981) 245, at 246.
56. Smooha, *supra* note 55 at 483.
57. Ibid. at 488.
58. M. Karayanni, "In the Best Interests of the Group, Religious Matching Under Israeli Adoption Law" (2010) 3 Berkeley Journal of Middle Eastern and Islamic Law 1.
59. G. Shafir and Y. Peled, *Being Israeli: The Dynamics of Multiple Citizenship* (New York: Cambridge University Press, 2002) at 110. See also A. Ghanem, "State and Minority in Israel: The Case of Ethnic State and the Predicament of Its Minority" (1998) 21 Ethnic & Racial Studies 428, at 432–34; A. H. Sa'di, "Israel as Ethnic Democracy: What Are the Implications for the Palestinian Minority?" (2000) 22 Arab Studies Quarterly 25, at 25; R. Cohen-Almagor, "Cultural Pluralism and the Israeli Nation-Building Ideology" (1995), 27 International Journal of Middle East Studies 461, at 462; S. Smooha and D. Peretz, "The Arabs in Israel" (1982) 26 Journal of Conflict Resolution 451; B. Kimmerling, "Sociology, Ideology, and Nation-Building: The Palestinians and Their Meaning in Israeli Sociology" (1992) 57 American Sociological Review 446, at 450 ("Arabs in Israel remained... outside of the collectivity's boundaries as non-members of 'Israel.'"); M. Walzer, *On Toleration* (New Haven, CT: Yale University Press, 1997) at 41 (noting how the Palestinian Arab minority in Israel, though citizens of the state, nevertheless "do not find their history or culture mirrored in its public life").
60. See CA 8573/08 Ornan v. Ministry of Interior (Oct. 2, 2013), Nevo Legal Database (by subscription).
61. K. M. Firro, *The Druzes in the Jewish State: A Brief History* (Leiden: Brill, 1999) at 157.
62. See I. Peleg and D. Waxman, *Israel's Palestinians, The Conflict Within* (Cambridge: Cambridge University Press, 2011) at 30.
63. Y. Peled, "Ethnic Democracy and the Legal Construction of Citizenship: Arab Citizens of the Jewish State" (1992) 86 American Political Science Review 432.
64. Smooha and Peretz, *supra* note 59 at 451.
65. J. S. Migdal and B. Kimmerling, "The Odd Man Out: Arabs in Israel," in J. S. Migdal, ed, *Through the Lens of Israel: Explorations in State and Society* (Albany: State University of New York Press, 2001) 173.
66. N. Sultany, *Citizens without Citizenship* (Haifa: Mada, Arab Center for Applied Social Research, 2003).
67. G. Barzilai, *Communities and Law: Politics and Culture of Legal Identities* (Ann Arbor: University of Michigan Press, 2003) at 7.
68. Edelman, *supra* note 47 at 87.
69. Spinner-Halev, *supra* note 53 at 84–85.
70. See M. M. Karayanni, "Two Concepts of Group Rights for the Palestinian-Arab minority under Israel's Constitutional Definition as a 'Jewish and Democratic' State" (2012) 10 International Journal of Constitutional Law 304, at 329–30.
71. League of Nations, Mandate for Palestine (1922), Art. 2, available at <http://avalon.law.yale.edu/20th_century/palmanda.asp>.
72. *Partition Plan with Economic Union*, annexed to Resolution Adopted on the Report of the Ad Hoc Committee on the Palestinian Question: Future Government of Palestine, G.A. Res. 181(II), U.N. Doc. A/RES/181(II) (Nov. 29, 1947), chap. 2, art. 4.
73. England, supra note 24 at 189 (noting how the existence of the Israeli-Arab conflict was a major force "why the traditional system of legally recognized religious communities exercising jurisdiction over their members has been rigorously maintained in contemporary Israel...").
74. I. Lustick, *Arabs in the Jewish State: Israel's Control of a National Minority* (Austin: University of Texas Press, 1980).

75. Ibid. at 25–26.
76. Ibid. at 82–83.
77. Ibid. at 133.
78. See Tessler, *supra* note 55 at 264–65.
79. Reitman, *supra* note 14.
80. Karayanni, "The Separate Nature," *supra* note 40 at 65–66.
81. For a general survey of the improvements civil norms have brought to Muslim women in Israel, see A. Layish, *Women and Islamic Law in a Non-Muslim State: A Study Based on Decisions of the Shari'a Court in Israel* (New York: Wiley; Jerusalem: Israel Universities Press, 1975).
82. Penal Law, 5737-1977, art. 176, LSI Special Volume: Penal Law (1977).
83. Penal Law, art. 181.
84. Marriage Age Law, 5710-1950, 4 LSI 158 (1949–50).
85. Women's Equal Rights Law, 5711-1951, 5 LSI 171 (1950/51).
86. *Sultan v Sultan* CA 245/81, [1984] IsrSC 38(3) PD 169.
87. Ibid. at 176.
88. *Bader (Mari'ee) v Mari'ee* HCJ 9611/00, [2004] 58(4) IsrSC 256.
89. CA 3077/90 Plonit v. Ploni, 49(2) PD 578 [1995].
90. H. I. Sa'adu, "Proof of Paternity under Islamic Law" (2005) 2 University of Ilorin Law Journal 41, available at <www.unilorin.edu.ng/publications/proof.rtf>.
91. HCJ 3856/11 (June 27, 2013), Nevo Legal Database (by subscription).
92. See F. Raday, "Kol ha-Isha ba-Demokratiya ha-Yisra'elit" ["The Woman's Voice in the Israeli Democracy"], in R. Cohen-Almagor, ed, *Sugiyot Yessod ba-Demokratiya ha-Yisra'elit [Basic Issues in Israeli Democracy]* (Tel-Aviv: Po'alim Library, 1999) 143, at 158.
93. Peled, A. R. "Shari'a under Challenge: The Political History of Islamic Legal Institutions in Israel" (2009) 63 Middle East Journal 241, at 259.
94. See Eisenman, *supra* note 35 at 171–77.
95. A. Treitel, "Conflicting Traditions: Muslim Shari'a Courts and Marriage Age Regulation in Israel" (1995) 26 Columbia Human Rights Law Review 403.
96. Eisenman, *supra* note 35 at 175–76. In the case of underage marriage, the Age of Marriage Law, 1950 made an innovative prescription by providing that a state official, the Welfare Officer, can together with the girl's parents or guardians ask for the dissolution of the marriage. However, the Welfare Officer has seldom intervened in this respect. Ibid. at 173.
97. Ibid. at 178–86.
98. See Rubin Peled, *supra* note 93 at 251 (stating how in practice the Bedouin community found many ways to circumvent the restriction on underage marriage and polygamous marriages)
99. A. Lapidot-Firilla and R. Elhadad, *Forbidden yet Practiced: Polygamy and the Cyclical Making of Israeli Policy* (Jerusalem: Hebrew University of Jerusalem, 2006); Rubin Peled, *supra* note 93 at 259.
100. See H. Sandberg and A. Hofri, "Arab Israeli Women's Renunciation of their Inheritance Shares: A Challenge for Israel's Courts" (2012) 8 International Journal of Law in Context 253.
101. Ibid. For an anthropological analysis of the phenomenon in the Palestinian-Arab society in general, see A. Moors, *Women, Property and Islam: Palestinian Experiences, 1920–1990* (New York: Cambridge University Press, 1995) at 48–76.
102. Ecclesiastical Courts in Israel: A Gender-Responsive Analysis, <http://www.jadaliyya.com/pages/index/12559/ecclesiastical-courts-in-israel_a-gender-responsiv>.
103. Though some doubts were raised earlier as to whether this amendment will indeed improve the status Muslim and Christian women. See M. Shawa, "Hatsa'at Hok Beit ha-Mishpat le-Inyanei Mishpaha (Tikkun Mis. 4) (Hashva'at Samkhuyot Shipput), 5758-1998—Ha-Omnam Brakha la-Nashim ha-Muslimiyot ve-ha-Notsriyot?" ["The Proposed Family Court Act (Amendment No. 4) (Comparing Jurisdiction), 1998—Is It Truly a Blessing for Muslim and Christian Women?"] (1999) 44 Ha-Praklit 358 (Hebrew).

104. Rabbinical Courts Jurisdiction (Marriage and Divorce) Law, 5713-1953, 7 LSI 139 (1952–53), art. 4 (Israel). See also M. Chigier, "The Rabbinical Courts in the State of Israel" (1967) 2 Israel Law Review 147, at 165–166.
105. See N. Dana and S. Fallah, "Ma'mad ha-Druzim ve-Irgunam ha-Edati" ["The Status of the Druze and their Community Organization"], in *Ha-Druzim* [*The Druze*] (Ramat-Gan: Bar-Ilan University Press, 1998) 159, at 166.
106. Ibid. at 169.
107. Ibid. at 168–169.
108. See Layish and Fallah, *supra* note 48 at 134–135.
109. Karayanni, "Living in a Group of One's Own," *supra* note 40 at 4.
110. Deveaux, *supra* note 17 at 27.
111. Ombudsman for Complaints Against Judges Law, 5762-2002, S.H. No. 1864, p. 590.
112. Karayanni, "Living in a Group of One's Own," *supra* note 40 at 39.
113. "Lebanese Government Approves First Ever Civil Marriage," *The Commentator*, April 26, 2013, http://www.thecommentator.com/articles/tag/civil_marriage/13316; "Civil Marriage is Legal in Lebanon: Experts", *The Daily Star*, January 10, 2014. http://http://www.dailystar.com.lb/News/Lebanon-News/2014/Jan-10/243642-civil-marriage-is-legal-in-lebanon-experts.ashx#axzz33s24OPMo.
114. See Z. Naboulsi, "Civil marriage is more than just the will of two people to get legally wed. In Lebanon it is the feeling of citizenship," <http://www.yourmiddleeast.com/opinion/ziad-naboulsi-civil-marriage-in-lebanon-more-than-just-married_12,614>.
115. M. A. Tessler, "The Identity of Religious Minorities in Non-Secular States: Jews in Tunisia and Morocco and Arabs in Israel" (1978) 20 Comparative Studies in Society and History 359, at 370.

# 11

# Localizing Religion in a Jewish State

YISHAI BLANK

## 1. Introduction

Throughout the world, legal systems are required to accommodate religious diversity and manage heightened tensions that arise from radically conflicting religious beliefs and practices. In some countries, there is a battle of whether some religious attire should be prohibited in public spaces (the Muslim veil, for example); in other places, it is debated whether certain religious symbols should be banned from public spaces (or at least from spaces which are governmental as in the case of the USA); while in other countries the fight is over architectural symbols of religion (the Swiss initiative to ban Muslim minarets is a case in point). These conflicts between religious and secular groups, as well as among different religious groups, often take place in smaller polities, in the form of a battle over the shape and content of local public spaces, controlled and regulated by local governments. In Israel such conflicts include, for example, the closure of stores and of roads during religious holidays and days of rest,[1] the display of religiously offensive objects (such as pork meat or leavened dough on Passover) in streets and showcases,[2] holding religiously contentious parading in streets (in the case of gay parades, for example),[3] the allocation of municipal budgets and lands for religious activities,[4] the presentation of religious symbols in town halls and city parks,[5] and more. The immediacy of these issues, the fact that the traditional powers—business licensing, traffic and road control, spending and more—of local authorities touch upon many of them, and the inability of the central government to obtain a nationwide consensus over religious matters have caused the *localization* of religious liberty in Israel.

The localization of religion in Israel has two meanings: first, it refers to the legal mechanisms by which local governments are empowered to manage religious liberty; second, it means that many local governments in Israel are internally fairly homogeneous in the religious beliefs and practices of their population. With few important exceptions, the study of the legal relationship between religions and the state has tended to focus on the role that central state organs have played in this regard, ignoring the complexities of the interplay between different levels of government.[6] This chapter shifts this focus by exploring the role local governments have been playing in structuring and regulating religious-secular tensions in Israel.

Lacking meaningful constitutional constraints against the establishment of religion,[7] Israel has a history of legislative impositions of religious norms[8] and of governmental efforts to give religious considerations priority over others. Local governments in particular have been trying to use their authorizations in order to advance religious interests and express religious norms. Although some of these attempts were curbed by the Israeli Supreme Court, in many cases localities were either explicitly or implicitly authorized to take religious considerations into account. Localities were able to use their powers in order to establish religion within their jurisdictions also due to the relative religious homogeneity within localities in Israel. This homogeneity enabled localities to reach an internal consensus where the national legislator failed. As compared with the religious diversity of the entire population of Israel and of the Knesset—comprised of Ultra-Orthodox Jews, modern Orthodox Jews, secular Jews, Muslims, Christians, Druze, and more—localities are indeed homogeneous. This chapter also documents the various mechanisms by which this religious homogeneity is achieved and perpetuated.

The Israeli case of the localization of religion indeed presents us with a most vivid example of the famous Madisonian "risk of faction." Lacking sufficient constitutional constraints, localities might express—and enact into law—the most radical and violent views of religious factions, often targeting weak and vulnerable minorities. As Susan Moller Okin and other scholars noted, granting cultural communities—especially religious ones—control over their jurisdictions puts minorities-within-minorities at a greater risk of domination and abuse.[9] Thus, instead of Madison's "positive pluralism" we might in fact face what he termed the "violence of faction."[10] Indeed, Madison was concerned with the risk that the federation would deteriorate into a multitude of radical religious factions combating each other with ever increased zeal. In his view, a structure of weak federal institutions and too strong states (and localities) could bring about the deprivation of individual rights within states and localities, and the radicalization of the entire federation.[11] Madison's cure—"extending the sphere"—would potentially de-radicalize the local zeal and result in the moderation of extreme politics in light of the large number of people with opposing views throughout the federation that would balance each other and the restraining effect of federal elites.[12]

But the localization of religion in Israel might have also been beneficial to the protection of religious (or secular) minorities. Localities that are active in shaping and developing the discourse and doctrine of religious liberty can be highly effective institutional safeguards—rather than mere judicially enforced barriers such as a disestablishment principle—against the monopolization of one religion over the entire state.[13] The fact that localities have been able to exercise their powers in a way that benefitted their preferred religion is imperative given the monopoly that Orthodox Judaism enjoys in the central government. Other religions, as well as other Jewish denominations, are discriminated against and suffer from chronic weakness and underrepresentation in the government, hence the only avenue left for them are local governments. Obtaining power at the local level allows such marginal and minority religions to use the coercive power of local governments to advance the interests of their members. An additional advantage of the localization of religion is that it facilitates and enables religious minorities to "dissent by deciding."[14] Permanent minorities at the national level, argues Heather Gerken, are sometimes able to form local majorities (or powerful local coalitions), and if these jurisdictions are given decision-making powers, they can express their views not only by "talking" but by "deciding." Religious minorities, too, are thus able to form a local majority and express their radically different views by acting upon them at the local level. This ability makes for an extremely powerful dissent, exposing the hegemony of the majority religion and its oppression of other religions.

In order to benefit from the advantages of the localization of religion without, however, deteriorating into an all-out war of factions, and without jeopardizing the individual liberty of persons who wish to live side by side despite their belonging to different religious communities, I offer in this chapter several broad-brush principles. While maintaining, and even further empowering localities to deal with, religious liberty, more stringent constitutional protections need to be given to individuals who happen to live in a locality where the majority belongs to a different creed. Furthermore, I argue, state-mandated segregation on the basis of religion must entirely cease. Ultra-Orthodox Jews are no longer a small minority in need of protection from cultural annihilation. This forced segregation only serves to perpetuate the economic weakness of religious communities and the separation between Jews and Arabs. Lastly, the various local powers described above need to be applied in a manner that will induce integration and interfaith dialogue rather than in a segregation-inducing fashion.

## 2. Religious Freedom in Israel

In this section I present in very broad terms the basics principles of religious freedom in Israel. I make no attempt to cover the topic in depth since this chapter highlights a rather narrow and hidden aspect of religious freedom in Israel—the unique role local governments play in its development and application. While some scholars might argue that there is no real religious freedom in Israel since there is integration—rather than separation—between religion and state, the reality is far more complex. The fact that Judaism, as well as other religions, are indeed established in various state laws and governmental policies is crucial for understanding the doctrine of religious freedom in Israel, but is far from exhausting it. I now describe six fundamental principles that lie at the heart of Israel's unique doctrine of religious freedom.

First, Israel is constitutionally defined as a "Jewish and democratic state" in two of its Basic Laws (Human Dignity and Freedom of Occupation) as well as in other pieces of legislation.[15] Courts and scholars are divided over whether the term "Jewish" should be read as referring to Judaism as a religion, to Jewish nationality, or to Jewish morality.[16] The constitutional reference to the "Jewishness" of the state is therefore at the heart of endless legal debates pertaining to the ability of the state to enforce Jewish prohibitions or to express Jewish religious values. And while the majority of views is that this constitutional provision does not mandate the state to become a theocracy, but rather to "integrate" or "harmonize" the two poles—Judaism and democracy—this expression leaves ample room for competing interpretations, including religious-friendly ones.

Second, although there is no explicit mention of freedom of religion in either of Israel's Basic Laws, the Supreme Court read it into the term "dignity," which is protected by Basic Law: Human Dignity and Liberty.[17] The exact content and meaning of this constitutional freedom of religion is, however, unclear. Most agree that it has a negative and a positive aspect: the negative one being freedom *of* religion—a version of the free-exercise clause, which prohibits the state from interfering with individuals' right to worship and express their faith; the positive aspect being freedom *from* religion—a version, albeit a diluted one, of the disestablishment clause, prohibiting the state from coercing people to worship or act religiously.

Third, until the enactment of two Basic Laws—which hold normative superiority over ordinary legislation—the Knesset was able to enact any law that it wished to since there were no constitutional rights on the basis of which courts could review and strike down laws.[18] The Knesset thus continuously enacted laws that reflected a perception of religion–state relationship that was radically different than two of the most prominent models of relationships between religion and state in the West: the American notion of "disestablishment" (a "wall" between church and state) and the French principle of state secularism (the concept of "laïcité").[19] The most (in)famous example of the Israeli "integration" between religion and state is the lack of civil laws of marriage and divorce.[20] As a continuation of the Ottoman *millet* system and the British Mandate of Palestine, Israel only recognizes marriage and divorce that are performed by religious state officials—rabbis, priests, or *qadis*—according to the religious laws of the various "recognized" religious communities.[21] While religious liberty is maintained in the narrow sense that individuals are not forced to marry or divorce against their faith, it is severely jeopardized since there is no nonreligious option for marriage or divorce within Israel.[22] The only way to opt out of a religious ceremony is to either settle for common law marriage or to marry outside of Israel and ask the state to recognize this marriage (which the Supreme Court ruled the state must do).[23]

There are numerous other examples of the enmeshing of religion and state in Israel. The state regularly appoints clergy and funds state religious activities according to explicit legislation that orders the transfer of money to religious schools and religious services. Jewish, Christian, and Muslim schools are almost fully funded by the state. The operation of the rabbinical and of the non-Jewish denomination religious courts is the responsibility of the state and fully funded by it. The Ministry of Religious Affairs is responsible for the operation of a huge system of religious courts and services. Indeed, Israel is anything but a secular state. There are only very few laws, however, which explicitly endorse religious prohibitions or commandments. There are no laws forcing a certain dress code, imposing modesty, or prohibiting sexual behaviors such as infidelity, homosexuality, and so on. What prevented the Knesset from enacting such laws even before 1992 were not legal constraints, but rather political ones: for decades the secularist political parties enjoyed a solid majority in the parliament, preventing the religious parties from enacting laws which would explicitly endorse religious prohibitions. Attempts to entirely prohibit the selling of pork meat, for instance, have failed due to the opposition of secularist forces.[24] This is one of the major reasons that have indeed caused the localization of religion: unable to reach nationwide consensus due to religious diversity and strong secular opposition, religiously inspired groups opted for the local arena.

The fourth principle of religious freedom in Israel is that while parliament has been rather free to establish religion (save for the lack of political will to do so), the Supreme Court has developed a jurisprudence which severely curtailed—but did not entirely eliminate—the ability of the administrative branch, including local governments, to do so. In a series of rulings dating back to the 1950s, the Court has held that unless specifically authorized by the Knesset, state authorities cannot take into account "religious considerations" as "dominant factors" when using their powers.[25] The Court, however, did not prohibit any religiously motivated use of governmental power. If these religious considerations were not "predominant" but only "additional," ruled the Court in *Lazarovitz v Food Controller*, governments—including local ones—could be influenced by them in their decision making.[26] In fact, a governmental decision would have been "deficient" had the administrative agency ignored the relevant religious considerations.[27] Only when religious considerations became dominant, overshadowing the relevant professional considerations, would the Court invalidate the action. This basic principle prevented government officials from further enmeshing state and religion unless specific "enabling" legislation was enacted.[28]

The fifth principle is that a distinction is made between "religious motivations" and "religious sentiments" or "feelings" (*rigshot dat*). Indeed, it was often the case that state agents took religious considerations into account not because they themselves shared the religious belief, but since they thought they were obligated to accommodate the religious communities. Thus, for instance, certain roads were blocked by traffic authorities during the Sabbath since religious communities rioted, demanding their closure. The need to balance the religious "sentiments" of religious people with various other considerations became one of the dominant paths through which religious considerations were let into Israeli law. While the government was prevented from being "motivated" by religion, it was allowed—even mandated—to take into account the religious "sentiments" of an affected community. It was therefore legal for a locality to use its ordinary traffic- and road-control powers to close down streets and roads during the Sabbath in order to prevent "the direct infringement" on the lives of the religious community living nearby.[29]

The sixth principle was set in *Axel v Netanyah*, where the Court has ruled that religion is a "nationwide problem," resting solely in the hands of the central government and outside of the jurisdiction of cities. Any attempt made by localities to use their powers in order to reflect religious beliefs or considerations was considered *ultra vires* and null.[30] Thus, the city of Netanyah was prohibited from banning the selling of pork by using its business-licensing powers since religion "is a general, nationwide problem" whose solution must rest on the shoulders of the national legislators.[31] As we shall now see, this did not prevent localities from becoming highly active in regulating religion. Indeed, localities played an important role in the evolution of the doctrine of religious liberty, since cities were at the forefront of secular–religious tensions, and they often took into account various "religious" considerations when closing down roads on the Sabbath, refusing to grant business licenses, allocating resources, and more. In the following section I examine this local involvement in depth.

## 3. The Localization of Religion

As I already indicated, when I argue that religion was localized I do not suggest that the central state gave up on its role as a regulator and legislator of religious matters; on the contrary, what marks the process of the localization of religion in Israel was that local governments became heavily involved in mediating religious tensions and in regulating religion in the public sphere alongside—and not instead of—the constant involvement of the state in these affairs. Furthermore, the authorization of localities to regulate religious matters and to express religious norms in their public spheres was often a result of concrete decisions of various central state organs, primarily the executive branch and the Knesset. Such acts were contested, fought over, and regularly challenged in courts, which had to determine the exact role of local governments in expressing religious beliefs and norms.

I argue that the significant involvement of local governments in the regulation of religious freedom and in expressing religious norms and beliefs was a result of a set of legal principles and of residential patterns of religious communities (themselves a result of legal rules, as I shall explain later). The set of legal principles comprised the regular powers that localities possess—business licensing, road closures and traffic control, planning and zoning, control of speech (parades, marches, municipally owned poster stands), spending and land allocation—and special enablement laws, individually legislated in order to allow localities to take religious consideration into account in various circumstances. What made the application of these powers by cities so unique and interesting, however, was that the religious identity of local communities was much more homogeneous than the religious identity of the nationwide population. When one studies the religious composition of localities in Israel, one can rather easily classify them as "Ultra-Orthodox Jewish," or "national Zionist Orthodox," or "Muslim," or "Druze," or "Christian," or "secular Jewish," and so on. Indeed, theological dividing lines have somehow turned in Israel into municipal lines. While history and individual preferences explain some of this surprising overlap between local jurisdiction and religious population composition, there are some legal mechanisms that have contributed to it, too. These rules, which I document in this chapter, are still incentivizing and even forcing people to live within their religious communities.

Thus, it was the combination of legal powers given to localities and of various government actions and court decisions that influenced the residential patterns of religious communities in Israel and that eventually resulted in the localization of religion. I begin by describing the powers vested in local governments, which had given them such a crucial role in the doctrine of religious freedom in Israel.

## 3.1. The Legal Principles that Enable Localities to Express Religious Norms and Regulate Religious Liberty

Whether expansively or narrowly authorized, local governments are uniquely positioned vis-à-vis tensions that arise from daily, mundane interactions between individuals and groups over the character of the shared spaces in which they live, study, work, and rest. Indeed, the powers of local governments in many jurisdictions throughout the world often include the same cadre of authorities, enabling localities to promote "the peace and security" of a local jurisdiction: zoning, land use, business licensing, road and traffic control, sanitation, water, housing, safety, spending, and more. Israel is divided into roughly 255 localities (and hundreds of additional sub-localities that are organized as local committees [*va'ad mekomi*] within larger regional councils), ranging in population from over half a million residents to less than two thousand. Each of these localities possesses a large variety of legal powers and duties,[32] ranging from the duty to provide education, sewage, and water, to controlling local planning and zoning, to managing local business licensing, to providing welfare services, to levying local taxes.[33]

As I already indicated, these traditional powers are applied in many issues that touch upon religious freedom, and their application rests on the locality's attitude towards it. Whether to grant a special exception from a zoning law to a synagogue or a religious kindergarten, for example, depends on the local authority's position regarding the desirability of synagogues.[34] And when a coffee shop asks for a business license, the town might prohibit it from playing "western music" if it views such music as sacrilegious, or it might easily allow it, if it holds a different view on the matter.[35] Cities did not just merely abuse their legal powers, however, when they were influenced by religious considerations. They were acting according to the legal guidelines laid down by the Supreme Court.

### 3.1.1. Cities Using their Powers While Taking into Account Religious Considerations: Between a "Nationwide Problem" and a "Local Matter"

As a general rule, as I already noted, the Supreme Court has ruled that the state must abstain from giving dominance to religious considerations unless explicitly authorized by the legislator to do so.[36] The same rule applied also to cities as administrative agents. The issue of cities taking into account religious considerations was raised most dominantly in the context of the selling of pork. Given the importance of the religious prohibition on eating pork in Judaism (and Islam), localities throughout Israel have tried to limit its sale within their jurisdiction. Lacking any specific authorization to do so, they tried to regulate the sale by using their regular business-licensing powers. In *Axel v Netanyah* the Court voided the city's prohibition on the selling of pork within its jurisdiction, ruling that it was not specifically authorized to do so by the legislature.[37]

But the Court went further. Instead of merely repeating the formal rule according to which religious affairs required explicit authorization by the Knesset, President Olshen based his decision on the fact that religious matters such as the prohibition on selling pork were not a "local" matter. In fact, Olshen ruled, religion is "a general, nationwide problem that is not specific to a particular place, and its solution is within the exclusive purview of the national legislator."[38] Although the Court repeated this reasoning in other cases, it did not explain why pork selling is a "nationwide problem" that required the attention of the Knesset.[39] Perhaps the Court hinted to the fact that the entire nation was interested in the outcomes of the judicial battle over pork shops and that every Israeli citizen had a strong opinion regarding pork selling. But are these considerations enough to centralize the issue and take it out of the hands of localities? Normally, other reasons are mentioned in order to legitimate central control over an issue: the existence of externalities and spillovers, the need to coordinate between several locations, and the need to protect minorities from abusive local majorities. While the first two reasons seem irrelevant to the consumption of pork (it involves no tangible externalities on other localities, and there is no need to coordinate it nationally), it is possible that the Court wanted to protect secular minorities from local religious majorities.[40]

*Axel* thus establishes a *structural* principle according to which religious liberty and the regulation of religious matters should not belong to localities, but rather be seen as a nationwide problem, requiring central solutions. I argue, however, that this principle was severely undercut by a competing principle that the Supreme Court developed.

This competing principle was that even though religion was a "nationwide problem" that required explicit authorization by the legislature, the authorized governmental agency was in fact at liberty—and sometimes even under the duty—to take into account religious considerations, whenever those were relevant for the efficient and professional use of power. In *The League for the Prevention of Religious Coercion v The City Council of Jerusalem*, the Court was faced with a challenge to the decisions of the city of Jerusalem and of the regional traffic controller to close several street sections in Jerusalem during the Sabbath.[41] The petitioners argued that the city and the traffic controller were prohibited from taking religious considerations into account when using their professional authority to close down streets. The Court rejected this claim, ruling that there is nothing wrong in considering the interests of the religious residents who live near the roads and balancing them against other considerations such as the volume of traffic, alternative roads, and other factors.[42] Although there is no doubt that the city and the controller "took into account interests which are religious by nature," they were allowed to do so, opined the Court, as long as those considerations pertain to a "significant" part of the population.[43]

In *Baruch v The Tel-Aviv District Traffic Controller*, also dealing with the closure of numerous roads and streets during the Sabbath, the Court affirmed a decision made by the professional traffic authorities since there was nothing wrong in taking into account religious sentiments and the need to protect the religious interests of individuals.[44] In fact, citing *Lazarovitz* the Court reasoned that it is possible that had the authority failed to consider religious needs and interests, its decision would have been invalidated.[45] And in *Horev*, although the Court struck down the decision of the traffic controller and the city of Jerusalem to close down a major road during the Sabbath, it did so because they failed to balance the competing interests properly, not because they were prohibited from taking any religious considerations into account. Indeed, the Court ruled that it is acceptable to consider the religious needs of the population, so long as this consideration did not overcome all other considerations.[46]

The tension between these two principles stands at the basis of the jurisprudence regarding the role of localities in the regulation of religious liberty in Israel. On the one hand, localities are prohibited from regulating religious practices since they are seen as a nationwide problem requiring the explicit mandate of the legislature; on the other hand, since many of these issues pertain to religious local populations for whose safety and interests the locality is responsible, local governments are necessarily empowered to take religious considerations into account. Thus, the Supreme Court oscillates between prohibiting localities from weighing religious considerations and allowing them to do so.

Such judicial oscillation is evident also in the area of sex-oriented businesses and other religiously objectionable establishments. The Druze village of Ussafiyah decided to issue a business license to a coffee shop under the condition that it could not play "western music." Despite clear evidence that the decision was based on religious prohibitions—no alcohol was allowed either at the coffee shop—the Court ruled in *Halon v Ussafiyah* that it was legal for the locality to do so, since "we see no justification to deny the elected body's right to maintain the unique characteristics of their village ... according to the spirit and the culture of the vast majority of its residents."[47] Although the Court casts these religious prohibitions in cultural terms, it is rather obvious that the prohibitions are indeed religious in their origin and in their nature. The "majority" to which the Court refers is not a "cultural" group, but a religious one—the Druze. Put differently, I think it is hard to be convinced by the Court's attempt to legitimate the application of religious norms by merely calling such norms "cultural"; it seems more plausible that the Court is willing to accept the adoption of such norms by governmental agencies when dealing with small religious communities.

And indeed, in another case, the Court was much less willing to accept the legitimacy of such religious/cultural considerations. In *SZM Ltd v The Mayor of Jerusalem*, the Court invalidated the decision of the mayor of Jerusalem, operating as the local licensing board, to deny a sex shop a business license.[48] Distinguishing the case from *Halon*, the Court reasoned that while the village of Ussafiyah is rural and the majority of its residents share the same "culture and traditions," Jerusalem is a "mixed and diverse" city that has no "unified life style."[49] Hence, it seems that the Court is indeed willing to give more deference to local governments that represent religious minorities than it is to localities that represent religious majorities. The Court, however, did not only distinguish the two cases; it also qualified and modified the general principle, limiting the city's ability to take into account religious and moral considerations. Such considerations were permissible only where there was a "serious harm to the religious sentiments of a majority of the people" living near the controversial establishment.[50]

### 3.1.2. Special Enablement Laws

The tension between the competing principles I articulated above have spurred different responses among localities, with some taking more active roles in establishing religion and accommodating religious sentiments and other cities either being inactive in this regard or even expressing their secularity and hostility toward religion. But another result of these evolving principles was that the Knesset enacted numerous special laws that explicitly enable localities to shape the public space within their jurisdiction in a religious fashion. Thus, over the course of the years, the Israeli parliament enacted special permissions for localities to limit or even prohibit the sale of pork in their jurisdiction[51] and to take into account "religious considerations" when they grant business licenses and determine establishments' ability to operate on religious holidays and days of rest.[52]

The decision to authorize localities to regulate the selling of pork and the closure (complete or partial) of shops on the Sabbath was a result of intense political fights between secularists, nationalists, moderates, and religious politicians.[53] Until 1992, Parliament was unlimited in its legislative capacity.

Nonetheless, there were political constraints that prevented the adoption of laws establishing religion: religious parties were a minority in the Knesset and were unable to pass a nationwide prohibition on pork selling or on various activities during religious days of rest. Thus, these enabling laws were a compromise between religious and secularist members of Knesset.[54] At the national level, this compromise seems to have worked: the Knesset has not attempted to legislate a nationwide prohibition on the selling of pork or on operating businesses on the Sabbath in almost over two decades, since the 1990s.

The battle shifted from the Knesset elsewhere. Following these special authorizations, many localities throughout Israel enacted bylaws that severely limited the selling of pork within their jurisdiction[55] and that put serious restrictions on the operation of various businesses during the Sabbath. Other localities, however, actually allowed more and more businesses to open during the Sabbath and were filled with butcher shops that sell pork. Indeed, one of the most obvious effects of these special enablement laws was a growing divergence among cities regarding religious prohibitions. While some became more religious, others simply did not use—or used minimally—these laws and expressed their overt secularism. In other cities, however, wars of religion broke out, with residents trying to impact the locality into adopting their view.[56] These battles were particularly noticeable where the demographic composition of the population was less homogeneous.

Especially in the case of pork, "pig wars" have broken out throughout the country since the 1990s, making this issue salient and alive at the local level (and thus also at the central level). The reasons for this were legal, political, and social: first, religious parties increasingly wanted to use their political power to exert more influence over the shaping of public spaces in Israel (trying to pass laws that would prohibit the selling of pork throughout the state, rather than only in localities with a large religious majority). Indeed, the religious revival and the desire to re-inscribe religion into the public sphere did not leapfrog over Israel.[57] This religious revival was strengthened by the high birthrate of the Ultra-Orthodox Jews, which caused this previously almost-insignificant minority to become a visible and substantial minority: in less than two decades (from 1990 until 2008), the percentage of Ultra-Orthodox Jews rose from only 3 percent to 9 percent of the Jewish population of Israel.[58] While this fact enabled Ultra-Orthodox Jews to exert more political power and influence in the national and local levels, it also created a backlash that was mobilized by "secularist" political parties that fed on the intensification of the conflict.[59]

Second, massive waves of immigration from the former Soviet Union changed the demography of Israeli society in an unprecedented manner. Within less than a decade, about a million immigrants arrived in Israel. These immigrants were highly secularized and shared very few religious customs with the "traditionalist" Jews (often of Mizrahi decent) or with Orthodox Jews. Their distaste for religious prohibitions—pork laws, religious marriages, and so on—became a political agenda, which the parties that represented them pursued. Moreover, some of the newcomers were housed in towns that were densely populated with Ultra-Orthodox Jews or traditionalists. This has caused the friction between two opposing views on public space to share a local space and a local jurisdiction.

Third, the enactment of Basic Law: Freedom of Occupation and Basic Law: Human Dignity and Liberty brought about not only judicial review of the Knesset; it also shifted the balance between various basic principles and values of the Israeli legal system, elevating some of them to a protected constitutional status. Thus, it became easier to challenge in courts local decisions that infringed basic liberties. And when cities balanced "religious sentiments" with other rights and interests (such as freedom of contract and commerce of pork sellers), it was argued that they had to modify this balance, following the enactment of the Basic Laws.

Fourth, a shift in the jurisprudence of the Israeli Supreme Court in favor of decentralization and delegation of powers to local governments has taken place since the 1990s. This shift has made the courts more susceptible to ideas according to which local governments could serve as locations for political action, democratic legitimacy, and norm setting no less—sometimes even more—than the central government.[60]

As a result of these new legal battles and the changing circumstances in Israel, the Supreme Court refined, perhaps entirely reformed, its jurisprudence regarding the local exercise of special enablement laws. In the case of *Solodkin v City of Beit Shemesh*,[61] secular residents and a Member of Knesset from a party identified with immigrants from Russia petitioned the Court, challenging the legality of bylaws that limited, or entirely prohibited, the selling of pork in three localities. The Supreme Court ruled that there are two competing interests, which must be balanced by the local government when it regulates pork selling: on one hand, it needs to take into account the freedom of occupation of pork sellers and the right of pork eaters to consume whatever they wish to eat; on the other hand, local governments need to protect the religious beliefs and conscience of those who oppose the consumption of pork.

What is unique about this balance, the Court added crucially, is that the legislature vested it in the hands of the local authority, which means that a special balancing needs to be carried out: one that would take into account the unique demographic composition and geographic dispersion of the local populace throughout the local jurisdiction. The maps that the municipality draws—where pork may or may not be sold—should reflect this demographic balance. The Court ruled that if there exists only a "tiny minority" of "pork eaters" or "pork haters," the locality can prohibit it altogether, since that minority can either purchase pork in a nearby village or choose to exit the locality and live in a another locality, where they would form a majority. The same goes to the internal division of the locality: if homogeneous neighborhoods can be found within the local jurisdiction, the local government can prohibit (or permit) the sale of pork within these neighborhoods.[62]

The *Solodkin* decision thus further localized religion. It pronounced a very clear principle according to which the balancing between freedom from religion, freedom of occupation, and religious sentiments is a "local matter," which is to be based on local facts, such as demography and geography. Yet, it also localized religion in the sense that it fragmented each locality into smaller "locales," mandating a more nuanced regulation, based on the character of each neighborhood within it. What is particularly striking about the test that the Court adopted is that it is based on social-science-positive data regarding the demography and geography of the place, not on its history, context, and character or on real normative evaluation of the competing interests, values, and rights. In this regard, although it might be said to leave only a little discretion in the hands of the local governments, there is still room left to maneuver since the locality gets to decide on it, even if theoretically they could be checked by courts in retrospect.

Hence, the *Solodkin* decision incentivized religious and secular local groups to obtain a clear majority in the entire locality, or at least in the neighborhood where they lived. It has put premium on homogeneous, "pure" spaces and posited, perhaps unwittingly, an ideal of "geographic separatism," as Rosen-Zvi claims.[63] Following *Solodkin*, it was argued before courts that municipalities that wish to open synagogues and other religious public facilities should do so only in religious neighborhoods.[64] Although the Supreme Court rejected this claim, the message sent by the Court in *Solodkin* was that if people want to have a residential environment that would fit their religious (or secularist) preferences, they should advance homogeneity in their locality and preferably also in their neighborhood.

### 3.1.3. Taxing and Spending

Another extremely important area in which local governments constantly reflect and express their religious beliefs and sentiments is taxing and spending. Both spending and taxing lie well within the traditional powers of local governments in Israel and throughout the world. In their application of these powers, too, cities use religious considerations and try to benefit their favored religions, provoking a fierce debate in courts, in the executive branch, and in the parliament. In *Yekutieli v The Minister of Interior*, local tax exemptions and deductions to residents of Jerusalem were challenged.[65] The basis for these exemptions were regulations promulgated by the Minister of Interior—a member of the Ultra-Orthodox Shas party—in which he enabled localities to exempt two groups of persons from local property taxes. The first group included persons who dedicate their entire time to the study of the Jewish religious texts; the second group included families with four or more children. The Jerusalem local council/municipality decided to use its power to give these exemptions. Both exemptions benefitted Ultra-Orthodox Jews, as families with that number of children almost exclusively belong to the Ultra-Orthodox community. While the legal challenge was raised against the Minister of Interior as well as against the Jerusalem local council/municipality, it was clear that the main problem was not with the way the city applied the regulations—they were very straightforward and clearly empowered the city to give such exemptions—but against the regulations themselves.

The Supreme Court invalidated the regulations, ruling that they violated the principle of equality, which every governmental entity had to respect. Exempting Ultra-Orthodox Jews from paying local taxes imposes a heavy burden on the rest of the local population. If the state wants to give Ultra-Orthodox Jews or Jewish religious scholars tax benefits and exemptions, it should do so in primary legislation of the Knesset and not in executive regulations. This legislation, too, might be subject to judicial review, but what the legislature—which enjoys greater judicial deference—might be allowed to do is clearly impermissible for the executive branch. The Court explained in length why local government should not be allowed to decide for themselves on local tax breaks: since they are smaller and therefore depend on solidarity, they cannot afford to alienate groups by discriminating against them, and they have a tighter budget and therefore cannot afford any breaks at all.

Indeed, the issue of local tax exemptions and deductions has long been centralized and taken out of the hands of localities—whether the exemption is religiously motivated or not. The reasons for that are numerous, undoubtedly involving the fear that some localities will abuse these powers and simply go bankrupt, believing that the government will bail them out. But the fear of local majorities using their power to exempt themselves and milk minorities is also significant. Yet despite the formal prohibition on localities to grant tax exemptions and deductions, localities try to use their taxation powers to benefit various religious communities. For example, they can expansively interpret the tax break given to synagogues, churches, and mosques (by the Knesset), or they can interpret it narrowly.[66] Since the current exemption is given only to "synagogues" (and other places of religious worship), some localities impose local taxes on buildings that only partly serve as synagogues. Other localities, on the other hand, read the exemption very generously, thus giving tax breaks to wedding parlors and other establishments that dedicate a small room for a synagogue and claim the exemption on its basis.[67] Cities can also act informally: measure and assess religious property with greater leniency, refrain from collecting the taxes, and so on.

As compared, however, with the relative centralization of local taxing and the ensuing difficulty of cities to infuse taxing with religious motivations and preferences, cities are more easily able to use their spending power—and to allocate their property—in a manner that expresses their religious sentiments. As a legal matter, it is not only legitimate but also desirable that localities spend their money on projects that they deem appropriate. Indeed, except for municipal services, which they are required to provide by law, local governments are expected to form a budget that is based on the unique local preferences and needs of their residents. And if those residents happen to be religious and wish to spend money on religious enterprises, it is legal for the local government to do so. However, once a locality decides to spend money on a religious enterprise, it must not discriminate between the different religions. This legal principle enables localities to express their religiosity by giving money to synagogues, churches, and other religious enterprises. And despite the requirement to allocate money and other municipal resources "equally and transparently," this is a source for much contention and legal battles.

Already in the early 1960s, the Supreme Court ruled that while a locality was allowed to let religious activities take place within its property, it could not discriminate between different Jewish denominations and had to give them equal access. In *Peretz v Kfar Shemaryahu* the Court invalidated the decision of a small and affluent Jewish suburb to refuse a group of Reform Jews (a modern, non-Orthodox Jewish denomination) to hold prayers in the suburb-owned synagogue.[68] A city was under the duty to treat all its residents with equality, regardless of their religious denomination. Freedom of religion meant, the Court ruled, that each religious group was entitled to the same treatment by the locality; it meant that no one religion could be preferred over the other one.[69] The fact that the religious sentiments of Orthodox Jews might be hurt by a Reform prayer—since they find it offensive and sacrilegious—is insufficient to disallow Reform Jews from holding prayer, as they have religious sentiments, too, that are obviously hurt when prevented from using the suburb's property.[70]

Thus, alongside their support for religious activities that they favor, localities have made an attempt to *refrain* from budgeting activities that were offensive to their religion, even though they could not explicitly admit that (as they were prohibited from doing that due to their duty to allocate budgets and lands equally). In the case of the *Jerusalem Open House*, such discriminatory local practices came under the scrutiny of the Supreme Court. The Jerusalem Open House, a local LGBT organization, has been leading a long and protracted legal campaign, challenging the refusal of the city of Jerusalem to fund its activities.[71] Over the past two decades Jerusalem had undergone a tremendous demographic transformation of "ultra-orthodoxization:" the percentage of Ultra-Orthodox Jews in the city increased dramatically, a result of migration and natural growth of this community and of an exodus of secular and moderately religious Jews.[72] Ultra-Orthodox parties form a rather solid coalition in city hall and from 2003 until 2008 the mayor of Jerusalem was an Ultra-Orthodox Jew (Mayor Lopolyanski). Although Jerusalem denied that it was motivated by religious sentiments, the Open House's requests for municipal support were consistently refused. The city argued that all the budgetary allocations that the Open House applied for were either irrelevant considering the activities of the organization or that the organization simply did not meet the standard for which the locality was aiming. A District Court judge accepted the city's claims, ruling that the city had "equal and transparent" guidelines that did not discriminate against gays and lesbians; they simply did not fit the specific activities that the Open House wished the city to fund.[73]

The Supreme Court overruled the District Court's ruling and ordered the city to revise its policy and allocate equal funds to the Open House. In a groundbreaking decision, Justice Amit adopted the American "strict scrutiny" test, finding that gays and lesbians are a "discrete and insular minority" deserving special protection. Historically oppressed, discriminated against, politically underrepresented, and geographically dispersed, gays and lesbians are worthy of unique protection.[74] The reason Justice Amit needed to adopt the special review test was that it was very difficult to find any *intentional* discrimination against the Open House. Indeed, the broad fiscal powers of cities enable them to reflect religious sentiments by tailoring the criteria for spending in a manner that will exclude activities that are abhorrent to its religious creed. Thus, Jerusalem could refuse the funding requests of the petitioner by carefully crafting the "objective criteria."

Although the Supreme Court ruled that the Open House was discriminated against and that it should receive funds from the municipality, the case actually manifests the ease with which local governments can overcome the prohibition to refuse funding based on religious animus. Despite the fact that overt discriminatory criteria-crafting would be deemed unlawful, in many such cases, discriminatory intent or impact would be very hard to prove and thus localities will be able to manifest their religious sentiments.

The combination of their regular local powers, special enablement laws, and fiscal powers (taxing and spending) make localities prime sites for the consideration of religious sentiments and for the regulation of religious liberty in

Israel. Cities prohibit or allow selling pork meat, limit or permit the opening of stores on the Sabbath and other religious holidays, ban or sanction sex stores, close down or open up roads during the Sabbath, and spend money on and give tax breaks to synagogues or LGBT centers. Given their democratic structure, they are responsive to demands made by their residents. It is therefore imperative to understand the demographic composition of localities in Israel, and analyze how the law constrains and shapes them.

### 3.2. Formal Segregation and the Forced Creation of Pure Religious Communities

It is impossible to appreciate the impact of the localization of religion in Israel without giving due attention to the relative religious homogeneity of localities in Israel. This homogeneity enabled localities to reach a consensus where the national legislature failed. Compared to the religious diversity of the entire population of Israel and of the Knesset, localities are extremely homogeneous. Only very few localities have representative portions of Ultra-Orthodox Jews, modern Orthodox Jews, secular Jews, Muslims, Christians, Druze, and so on. This homogeneity is a result of historical contingencies as well as of a uniquely Israeli legal structure, which forces and induces religious residential segregation. As many scholars have shown, this was a result of the historical background, market forces, but also of clear governmental policies.[75]

While some of the separating lines were blurred over the years,[76] the segregation between secular Jews and religious Jews has not weakened. If anything, it has strengthened. Several new purely Ultra-Orthodox Jewish towns have appeared since the 1990s, and numerous Ultra-Orthodox neighborhoods have appeared in mixed towns.[77] In addition, religious-Zionist Jews, who used to live in fairly integrated environments, have developed new residential patterns, which are more segregated than before. In part a result of the expanding settlement project in the occupied territories and in part a result of internal pressures to create religious environs, a growing number of religious-Zionist Jews form and live in majority-religious localities or in majority-religious neighborhoods.

I now turn to describe them. Much was written about the residential separation between Jews and Arabs,[78] but very little attention was given to the fact that the state also induced the segregation *among* Jews, based on their faith and denominational affiliation.

#### 3.2.1. History and Market Forces that Support Segregation

Historically, already in the nineteenth century, Ultra-Orthodox Jews lived in separate neighborhoods, which were later on recognized by the British

Mandate authorities as independent localities. Christian Arabs and Muslim Arabs also often lived in separate villages and towns. The market prices of houses in Arab villages and neighborhoods (Christian as well as Muslim) and in Ultra-Orthodox Jewish areas were significantly lower than that of houses in central Jewish secular communities. There were also vast discrepancies among the different social groups in funds available for purchasing an apartment; the income levels of Arabs and Ultra-Orthodox Jews were significantly lower than those of secular Jews.[79] The social capital of the former groups was similarly low. Accordingly, Arab or Ultra-Orthodox homeowners who sought to sell their houses and purchase ones in a secular Jewish town would be forced either to compromise on the size of the new house (if they succeeded in finding a smaller one and lived in crowded quarters) or else live in a poor neighborhood in which the schools and other municipal services were inferior.[80]

Thus, Ultra-Orthodox Jews, Christians, and Muslims were economically "steered" to reside in communities where they could afford to buy or rent. Often, these localities were similar to those in which they were born, since they reflected their purchasing power. This is not to deny that individual preferences influenced these choices, but merely to suggest that economy, too, played a role in the perpetuation of religious segregation in Israel.

### 3.2.2. Formal Exclusionary/Segregationist Mechanisms

While undoubtedly individual preferences to live with one's peers and within one's economic means play a significant role in determining one's residential decision, the State of Israel adopted various mechanisms that incentivized and even forced people to live within their communities. First, Ultra-Orthodox Jews were formally excluded from many rural secular settlements; second, secular Jews were excluded from Ultra-Orthodox towns.

The exclusion of Ultra-Orthodox Jews from secular—and even modern Orthodox—settlements was a byproduct of the unique legal structure of rural settlements with state-sanctioned screening boards. Concerned with the concentration of the majority of the population in the center of Israel, and worried about the scarce "Jewish presence" in its northern and southern parts, the state began establishing dozens of new settlements in the rural periphery of the country.[81] Since the state owns about 92 percent of the land in Israel, it could easily implement this policy by allocating lands in these remote areas to groups of individuals who organized themselves as collective associations. These associations would regularly appoint "acceptance committees" (screening boards) that interviewed candidates and decided who could become a member of the association and purchase land in the settlement. The contracts that the residents signed with the collective association and the Jewish Agency (the official owner of some of these state lands) regularly included restrictive covenants requiring the consent of the screening board for any future land transaction. But most crucial was the condition that most associations included in their minutes and founding documents, which was that the candidate served in the Israeli military.

While this condition was mostly aimed at excluding Arabs from these settlements, it incidentally excluded Ultra-Orthodox Jews who, by and large, very seldom serve in the army. The military service requirement was voided by the Court as unconstitutional in the famous *Kaadan* case for violating the principle of equality.[82] However, such screening boards are still alive and well. These boards use various mechanisms, including psychological evaluations and other tests aimed at examining the candidate's "fit" for the settlement in order to exclude various individuals. Indeed, only in 2011 the Knesset passed a law formalizing the right of small settlements (that is, with less than 400 families) to screen their residents based on their "fit for community life" and "fit for the social fabric" of the settlement.[83] Various studies show that such screening processes serve to exclude individuals belonging to minority communities.[84] In some cases, even religious communities living in such settlements—religious-Zionist communities whose members do serve in the military—have used their screening boards to exclude Ultra-Orthodox Jews.[85]

Perhaps more surprising than the exclusion of Ultra-Orthodox Jews from various rural settlements is the relatively new policy according to which secular Jews cannot buy property in new Ultra-Orthodox cities. In the face of increased housing shortage among the growing Ultra-Orthodox community, the Israeli government began, during the 1990s, constructing new towns to meet the demand. Both within Israel proper and in the West Bank, the state allocated lands to erect new Ultra-Orthodox towns. The state adopted a clear policy of allowing only Ultra-Orthodox Jews to purchase apartments in these towns. The screening, it should be noted, was not done by using acceptance committees but rather by the contractors, who won the governmental tenders and who built the various real estate projects.

When this governmental policy was challenged by secular Jews, the Supreme Court ruled in *Am Hofshi v The Ministry of Building and Housing* that as long as secular Jews could purchase an apartment with the same governmental benefits, it was legal for the state to adopt and implement a "separate but equal policy," under the condition that it was aimed at enabling the religious community "to sustain its [unique] ways of life."[86] The Court stressed that recognizing the right of the religious community to sustain its lifestyle "represents a well accepted contemporary notion among jurists, philosophers, social scientists and educators according to which the individual is entitled—among his many other rights—to fulfill his belonging to a community and its unique culture, as part of his right for personal autonomy."[87]

This ruling proved to be of crucial importance, as it opened the gate for the establishment of more and more settlements for Ultra-Orthodox Jews only.[88] In other cities, new Ultra-Orthodox neighborhoods are being constructed. Although the Ultra-Orthodox segregation is often presented as self-segregation—there is indeed no doubt that many Ultra-Orthodox Jews seek such radical segregation—the fact that it is mandated by the government makes it hard to assess whether it is voluntary or not. It seems plausible that at least some Ultra-Orthodox Jews would have chosen to have secular neighbors; and it is possible that some secular Jews would have liked to live near Ultra-Orthodox Jews. Indeed, according to a recent survey, only 61 percent of Ultra-Orthodox Jews prefer to live in purely Ultra-Orthodox settlements; the rest—a significant minority counting for 39 percent of the community—would actually rather live in integrated localities. Among the general population, there is even greater willingness to live in integrated areas, with less than the majority (48 percent) preferring not to live near Ultra-Orthodox Jews.[89]

## 4. Evaluating the Localization of Religion

The localization of religion in Israel is one of the founding elements of Israel's unique mode of state religiosity: it allowed the state to be theorized and understood as religious by some and as secular by others; it enabled the expression of religious sentiments and norms by public bodies, funded and established by the state; it produced the mitigation of some of the "religion wars" at the national level, while encouraging and inducing them at the local level; and although it was built upon an already existing residential segregation between persons of different creeds, it also exacerbated it. In this part I evaluate the desirability of this specific Israeli legal structure.

### 4.1. The Advantages of Localizing Religion in Israel

#### 4.1.1. Localization as Protection against One Religion's Hegemony

The greatest promise of the dispersal of authority to express and reflect religious sentiments and beliefs to local governments is that it would counter and destabilize the monopoly that one dominant religion might have if all political power is held by central authorities. Richard Schragger noted that "political decentralization ensures that the national councils do not have a monopoly on the power to regulate religion" in America.[90] The role of localities in the discourse and doctrine of religious liberty was of crucial importance as it provided incentive for the creation of religious groups, "a necessary precondition for the robust competition among sects that prevents any one sect from gaining political dominance in the whole."[91] Indeed, what Madison feared most—the violence of the religious faction—is, claims Schragger, the antidote against the dangers of *one* religious group becoming all too dominant. Decentralization is an institutional safeguard—rather than a mere judicially enforced barrier—against the monopolization of one religion over the entire national territory.

That local governments in Israel have been routinely involved in regulating matters pertaining to religious liberty—much like localities in the United States—has been crucial to the check both on government's ability to establish one religion and on religious power to spread through the entire federation. Even if the localization of religion that I describe in this chapter has not truly dismantled the hegemony of Jewish orthodoxy, it still managed to create "pockets" of resistance to this hegemony. Theorized this way, we can begin to see that localities are in fact the only places where non-hegemonic religions are able to flourish and become powerful in Israel, and thus possibly challenge the hegemony that Orthodox Judaism currently enjoys. Taking some of the power in religious matters away from the central government and vesting it in a multitude of local governments, each applying it somewhat differently, allocating budgets and jobs to non-Orthodox strands of Judaism, might have actually weakened, at least to a certain degree, the monopolistic power of Ultra-Orthodox Judaism. In this view, the greatest threat to religious liberty comes, of course, from the central government and the Knesset establishing religion, since it will always be one dominant religion: Orthodox Judaism. Decentralization is the antidote since it incentivizes people to form religious sects that would fight against such dominance.

### 4.1.2. Localization as Enabling Religious Dissent by Deciding

Given the monopoly that Orthodox (even Ultra-Orthodox) Judaism enjoys in the government and in parliament, there is very little hope that Reform Judaism, other Jewish denominations, and other religions will ever be able to express their beliefs and norms publically or to assume power positions. Other religions, as well as other Jewish denominations, are discriminated against and suffer from chronic weakness and underrepresentation in the central government. However, in cities where religious minorities constitute a locally significant constituency—or even a local majority—that can exert meaningful political clout they are further empowered and might be thought of as exercising, to a certain extent, self-rule. This point lies at the heart of a compelling argument made by Heather Gerken.[92] Permanent minorities—those that could never become a majority of the votes at the federal level—who radically differ from the majority, she claims, are often thought to be able to do nothing more than voice their dissent or compromise their radical views. They can "speak truth *to* power" but they can never be powerful.

The American structure of government, argues Gerken, enables such minorities to "dissent by deciding," thus act radically and "speak truth *with* power."[93] Permanent minorities can do so since they are enabled to form local majorities, which the law grants with decision-making powers. The strength of dissenting by deciding lies not solely with the immediate benefits and consequences of a particular action, say prohibiting pork meat within one local jurisdiction or allowing women to be elected for a religious council in another. Such a powerful local "disobedience" enables religious minorities to give their dissenting viewpoint salience on the national plane. The nationwide ripple effects caused by different religious governmental actions—closing of roads on the Sabbath, but also refusing to enforce religious laws in a case of a secularist locality—are felt at the national level as other communities with similar views follow suit.

### 4.1.3. Localization as De-privatization

The localization of religion enables religious minorities to express their values not only in the private sphere but also publicly, albeit at close quarters. Indeed, one of the troubles with religious freedom is that in secular societies it is often limited to the private sphere, while the public sphere is shaped by the secular majority. And this sphere, although experienced by secular individuals as "neutral" is in fact experienced as profane by (some) believers. Streets, parks, and other public spaces are filled with expressions that are abomination for (some) religious people. Therefore, in order to create a public sphere that will be experienced as holy by Ultra-Orthodox Jews, by observant Muslims, or by members of other religious denominations, their localities need to be able to express their religious values in public, too.

The broad powers vested in the hands of localities in Israel indeed enable them to create such "holy communities." Control over what shops and establishments operate within their jurisdiction, over the opening of businesses during religious holidays and days of rest, over the closure of roads during the Sabbath, and over the presentation of Hammetz (leavened dough that is prohibited from being eaten and presented during Passover) in public during Passover—all these afford religious communities an opportunity to escape the privacy of their homes and engage in public religious lives. This is particularly true for "nomic" communities, to use Robert Cover's term, whose mutual cultural world is not limited to a single and compartmentalized field of action, but rather stretches into a wide range of human activities and guides the group members in the most profound ways.[94] For such communities, only self-regulated and segregated spaces can serve as an approximation to their radically alternative utopia. The intense segregation that I have described also contributes to the de-privatization of religion as it provides a safeguard against "surprises" in the public sphere. For instance, having only Ultra-Orthodox Jews around means that modest dress codes are kept also in the streets.

### 4.1.4. Localization as Pluralism

Since localities can use their powers to express their endorsement as well as rejection of religious values and beliefs, the range of religious and secular attitudes is broad, reflecting the real plurality that exists among Israelis. According to David Barron, towns and cities should be understood as "important political institutions that are directly responsible for shaping the contours of 'ordinary civic life in a free society'."[95] Enabling cities to deal with religious matters is part of such pluralistic and democratic vision of society. Instead of viewing localities as mere instruments for the protection of individuals against governmental (or private) encroachment upon their negative liberties, we can see them as fostering "public freedom," based on a positive rather than a negative conception of liberty.[96]

Harnessing local governments' powers to positively advance the goals, ideas, and desires of religious communities and not merely to protect individual believers from discrimination goes beyond negative liberty, affording them with the capability to advance their shared worldview and enriching the society with profound diversity. In Israel, especially, such pluralism can indeed be fostered through localizing religion, since religion often overlaps with other identity traits such as nationality and ethnicity. The majority of Muslims and Christians being Arab, and other denominations also signifying ethnicities, localities' use of their religious authorities can become an instrument for racial and ethnic pluralism. These minorities, put differently, make use of their religious powers to express not merely "religion" but also their cultures. It is therefore no coincidence that in the case of *Halon*, the Supreme Court refers to the prohibition on western music that the Druze village imposed on a coffee shop, not as a religious prohibition but as an expression of "*the spirit and the culture* of the vast majority of its residents."[97] Their empowerment to express religion and the overlap between culture and religion thus enables such minority communities to be able to self-construct and self-regulate, at least to a degree, their shared spaces.

But there is a danger in the reconfiguration of religion into culture, as it moves it from the realm of actions to the realm of identity: religion is beginning to be understood as an ethnicity or race, rather than as a set of codes, beliefs, norms, or practices. Religious norms, practices, and motivations are reinscribed as expressions of "culture," and religious freedom is reconceived as cultural autonomy. Religion thus becomes immutable and impossible to change or transform, as this conceptual maneuver reifies individual choices and congeals fluid practices. Ironically, secularism is also reconceived as a culture. As the percentage of secular Jews is dropping and as their political power is in decline, there are more and more voices that try to conceptualize liberal secularism as a culture, perhaps one that is on the verge of being extinct in Israel. In the last round of battles between secular and Ultra-Orthodox Jews, such claims were made in an attempt to grant secular Jews the desired status of a minority that is entitled to "separate" allocation of land or of an environment free of religious symbols altogether.[98] Although until now such challenges have been rejected by the courts, it is too early to tell what lies in the future for such attempts.

### 4.1.5. Localization as Pacification

In Israel, where radical disagreements exist between competing communities such as Ultra-Orthodox Jews and seculars and between Jews and Muslims, decentralizing religion enables sidestepping those tensions, at least partly. Much like in federal regimes, where the decentralization of various decisions enables vastly different cultures and communities to enjoy some degree of cooperation while maintaining their different cultures, the localization of religion in Israel allows people of very different religious creeds to share the same national territory. Indeed, where it is impossible—or terribly painful—to reach a national agreement, it is sometimes better to let territorial subdivisions such as local governments decide for themselves. According to this argument, localizing religion in Israel mitigates some of the potential tensions between religious communities, thus weakening the violence that might occur had religion stayed entirely centralized.

## 4.2. The Shortcomings of Localizing Religion in Israel

### 4.2.1. Localization as Radicalization and Fragmentation

Religion, Madison warned, was a particularly "virulent form of faction."[99] As such, it had the potential to do much more than merely curb centralized political power or dismantle religious monopolies; it was one of the greatest risks to the American federation, which needed to be met with crystal-clear central norms (constitutional protections of individual rights) and powerful central institutions. Religion was able to move people in the wildest directions, and it could bring about the most destructive ideas.[100] Thus the healthy interreligious competition that we imagined earlier on can deteriorate into a multitude of radical religious factions combating each other with ever-increased zeal. Madison's cure of "extending the sphere"—enlarging the political units in a way that each becomes more moderate with more people whose ideologies and preferences "balance out" each other's—is supposed to de-radicalize the local zeal and result in the moderation of extreme politics in light of the large number of people with opposing views throughout the federation that will balance each other and the restraining effect of federal elites.[101]

Sadly, there is evidence that the Israeli combination of empowering localities to regulate religion and allowing—if not forcing—religious-based residential segregation is spiraling Israel into increased religious and political radicalization. Religious radicalization of the Ultra-Orthodox Jewish communities has been recently documented. There are reports that segregation between men and women began seeping from the public and religious spheres into the privacy of their homes.[102] As late as in 2011 the Supreme Court was confronted with another case resulting from the growing religious extremity of the Ultra-Orthodox community. In *Ragan v Ministry of Transportation*, a group of Orthodox Jewish feminists challenged the practice of public transportation providers to force gender segregation in buses that passed through Ultra-Orthodox neighborhoods and localities: men were let in through the front door and allowed to sit at the front of the bus, while women had to enter through the rear door and sit at the back.[103] The Court invalidated the practice, ruling that it violated the principle of equality and the antidiscrimination law, inasmuch as it was forced upon the passengers. However, if passengers were willingly entering these "Kosher buses" (as they became known) through different doors and voluntarily sitting in different parts of the bus, there was nothing wrong in bus companies accommodating this desire.[104]

A thorough discussion of this extremely controversial decision and its problematic assumptions regarding voluntary behavior in such circumstances exceeds the limits of this chapter.[105] What is important to note, however, is that such a radical—and new—practice could not have developed unless a fairly strict spatial segregation existed between Ultra-Orthodox Jews and the rest of society. Indeed, only because these communities live in such insular localities and neighborhoods can bus companies cater to this desire. In more integrated residential environments, secular and moderate-Orthodox Jews would have revolted or simply disobeyed the practice. Lacking meaningful internal opposition, the spatial insularity of the community enables the most radical elements within it to push forward their extreme policies.

As Madison predicted, unchecked by strong central powers, extremism can spread like fire. Once given the legitimacy of the law, the logic of segregation infiltrates deeper, into other domains of life and into other social groups. Residential segregation is now observed in Israel not only between Ultra-Orthodox Jews and secular Jews. Modern Orthodox Jews are starting to demand segregated environments,[106] and so are secular Jews.[107] Baffled by these developments, courts are oscillating between condemning such segregationist tendencies and accepting them as legitimate, desirable, or simply unavoidable.[108] The logic of segregation is particularly noxious where social solidarity collapses and where the traditional majority seems to lose its majority status. According to recent data, secular Jews are losing their clear majority status, and religious Jews are becoming an extremely large minority. Indeed, it is no longer clear that a majority, demographically speaking, truly exists. In such an environment, every group begins to demand its own homogeneous spaces, from which it could exclude all the rest. Once such a dynamic of accelerated fragmentation begins, it becomes very hard to retract from it. And as time goes by, and segregation becomes the rule, people are less and less able to imagine that secular individuals and religious ones ever lived together or that they could ever share a space again.

### 4.2.2. Localization and the Oppression of Minorities

The radicalization just described does not end, however, in theological extremism and growing disparity between the different parts of the country. One of the greatest dangers stemming from such radicalization is that it puts minorities who reside within religious communities at risk of greater abuse and infringement of their rights. The danger lurking to "minorities within minorities" has been theorized already by Madison, who was worried that radical religious factions would infringe on people's property rights by coming up with "[a] rage for paper money, for an abolition of debts, for an equal division of property, or for any other improper or wicked project."[109] But not only property owners are at risk under a structure of religious decentralization. Women, gays and lesbians, and other minorities are also jeopardized by too powerful religious localities. As we have seen above, some of the most radical religious plans indeed involve the subordination of women and of gays and lesbians.[110] Giving religious communities control and autonomy over their jurisdictions exposes minorities within minorities to risks of domination and abuse by the powerful within their community.[111]

### 4.2.3. Localization as Racial Steering and Discrimination

Spatial segregation of religious communities can be turned into a mechanism of "racial steering," which could be used in order to discriminate against racial or ethnic minorities. In the case of Israel, this risk is particularly high, since, as I already noted, religious distinctions overlap national ones. Instead of diverse and empowered communities, we might end up with minorities who are discriminated against on the basis of their places of residence. Exclusion on the basis of religion can thus serve as a guise for exclusion on the basis of race, ethnicity, or nationality. For example, instead of explicitly excluding Arabs—a practice prohibited by law since the ruling in *Kaadan*—companies adopt a policy of selling apartments only to "Zionist-religious" buyers, thus ensuring that no Arab will be allowed to buy in the project. Surprisingly, this practice was affirmed by the District Court of Tel Aviv, in a highly contentious decision.[112]

Furthermore, in some cases, religion has been used to justify ethnic discrimination, such as the discrimination of Mizrahi Jews (Jews of Oriental descent) in the schooling system.[113] Religious leaders claimed that the Mizrahi or "Sephardic" girls were spiritually/religiously "inferior," thus justifying the separation between Mizrahi and Ashkenazi (Jews of European decent) girls in a religious school in an Ultra-Orthodox locality. The Supreme Court invalidated this repugnant practice (sending some of the parents to jail for failing to send their daughters to the integrated school), yet it was a telling example of the ways in which religion can serve as pretext for racial and ethnic discrimination.

## 5. Conclusion: Where To Go from Here? Some Preliminary Suggestions

The various negative outcomes of mandated and induced segregation that I just mentioned should not be understood, however, as reasons to entirely oppose the localization of religion. Localizing religion has advantages that could be kept by attempting to counter the harmful effects of the radical segregation and the separatist ideology that is currently underwriting it. In this chapter I will not specify the legal rules that should replace the existing ones, yet I would like to broadly sketch several principles that might overturn some of the detrimental effects that the specific form of the localization of religion in Israel has had.

The first is that the starting point should indeed remain that, at least currently, local governments should be authorized to express the religious norms of their residents in a significant manner. As I demonstrated, there are advantages that cannot be underestimated: the localization of religion provides a *structural protection*, unmatched by any other judicially enforced rule, against the dominance and hegemony of one religion.

Second, the state should be able to compel residential segregation only in rare and extreme cases. Not every religious community need obtain the status of a minority worthy of a segregated locality of its own. If at all, only extremely small and extremely radical religious communities—nomic communities—that explicitly reject modern lifestyle (such as Satmar Haredi Jews, for instance) should enjoy such status.

Third, it is necessary to address the spatial and social context of the group that seeks segregation. It is different when a group wishes to establish a new city and when it wishes to construct a neighborhood or a project in an already existing area. For example, when a group of national Orthodox Jews wish to settle in Jaffa (a predominately Arab neighborhood of Tel-Aviv), granting them the license to exclude nonreligious persons is highly problematic given the possible motivation and the clear results of such exclusion.

Fourth, it is important to relax the connection between crude demography and clear legal outcomes. When one considers the nature of a neighborhood in order to decide whether, for example, pork could be sold in it or not, it is not enough to count how many secular and religious Jews live there. The history of the area, the symbolic meaning of the battle, the exact articulation of the positions in the specific context, and the importance of enabling minorities to settle in the neighborhood—all are crucial factors in determining the legal rule that needs to be applied. Combined, these very broad principles are aimed at creating more heterogeneous localities and neighborhoods, which might begin the undoing of the radical segregation between different religious communities in Israel. The vision of "pure communities" that was advanced through the localization of religion needs to be replaced with a more integration-oriented vision.

## Notes

1. *Horev v Minister of Transportation*, HCJ 5016/96, 1997 PD 51(4) 1 [*Horev*] (holding that the closure of a major road in Jerusalem during the Sabbath was "unreasonable" since it gave too much weight to religious consideration). In the American context see *McGowan v Maryland* 366 US 420 (1961) (ruling that state Sunday closing laws did not violate the due process or equal protection clauses).
2. *Solodkin v City of Beit Shemesh*, HCJ 953/01, 2004 PD 58(5) 595 [*Solodkin*] (ruling that a local authority can limit the selling of pork meat to certain areas in order to balance between "religious feelings" and freedom of occupation).

3. *Marzel v Police Chief of the District of Jerusalem*, HCJ 5277/07 (holding that the municipality's refusal to let the gay parade march is unreasonable).
4. See *Jerusalem Open House v The City of Jerusalem*, AdminA 343/09 (unpublished, 2010) [Jerusalem Open House, AdminA 343/09]; *Peretz v The Chairman, the Council Members and the Residents of Kfar Shemaryahu*, HCJ 262/62 1962 PD 16 2101 [Peretz].
5. See, e.g., *County of Allegheny v ACLU* 492 US 573 (1989) (ruling that the display of a crèche on government property violated the establishment clause, but that a menorah on display was not unconstitutional).
6. See, for example, R. C. Schragger, "The Role of the Local in the Doctrine and Discourse of Religious Liberty" (2004) 117 Harvard Law Review 1810; D. Barak-Erez, *Outlawed Pigs: Law, Religion, and Culture in Israel* (Madison: University of Wisconsin Press, 2007); I. Rosen-Zvi, "Pigs in Space: Geographic Separatism in Multicultural Societies," in M. Freeman, ed, *8 Law and Sociology: Current Legal Issues 2005* (Oxford: Oxford University Press, 2006) 225 [Rosen-Zvi, "Pigs in Space"].
7. There are, however, limitations on government religious activities. Israeli courts have acknowledged and protected the freedom *from* religion—the limitation on the government's ability to impose religious prohibitions and rules—already in the 1950s. Since Israel had no constitutional limitations on legislative power until 1992—when two Basic Laws were passed—there was a crucial difference between legislative and executive power to establish religion and infringe on individual freedom from religion. While parliament was able to legislate religious laws and to infringe on basic liberties as it saw fit, the government was limited by judicially invented and enforced "fundamental rights," which only the legislature could infringe.
8. Prime examples for such religious pieces of legislation are *Rabbinical Courts Jurisdiction (Marriage and Divorce) Law*, 1953 and the *Law of Return*, 1950. The first is of special importance as it sets up a religious system of marriage and divorce, prohibiting any marriage that is not religious in Israel and assigning individuals to their "official" religion, thus forcing them to marry within that religion.
9. S.M. Okin, "Is Multiculturalism Bad for Women?," in J. Cohen et al. (eds), *Is Multiculturalism Bad For Women?* (Princeton: Princeton University Press, 1999) 7.
10. J. Madison, "The Federalist No. 10," an essay published 22 November 1787.
11. Ibid.; see also discussion at Part 3.2.1.
12. Ibid. The idea to "extend the sphere" means that the larger the political units are, the less susceptible they will be to the risk of faction. Larger political units would include more individuals, thus leading to a more moderate constituency.
13. Schragger, *supra* note 6.
14. H. K. Gerken, "Dissenting by Deciding" (2005) 57 Stanford Law Review 1745, at 1764–65.
15. Basic Law: Human Dignity and Liberty, 1992, SH 1391, 150; Basic Law: Freedom of Occupation, 1994, SH 1454, 90.
16. See A. Ravitzky and Y. Z. Stern, eds, *The Jewishness of Israel* (Jerusalem: The Israel Democracy Institute, 2007).
17. See, for example, *Horev v Minister of Transportation*, HCJ 5016/96, 1997 PD 51(4) 1, 34.
18. Until the enactment of *Basic Law: Human Dignity and Liberty* in 1992 there was almost no limitation on the power of the Israeli parliament to legislate religion. The only barrier between religious laws becoming state law was the political situation in which religious parties were a minority, unable to obtain a majority. Since 1992, however, the Israeli parliament has been constrained by various constitutionally protected individual rights (including the right to a free exercise of religion, which the Court read into it), yet there is no general prohibition on establishing religion.
19. The French principle of *laïcité* establishes a strict prohibitions on any form of state establishment of religion. Obviously, the principle as well as its application have been criticized by many.
20. See G. Stopler, "The Free Exercise of Discrimination: Religious Liberty, Civic Community and Women's Equality" (2004) 10 William & Mary Journal of Women and the Law 459, at 485–92.

21. Ibid. See also *Rabbinical Courts Jurisdiction (Marriage and Divorce) Law*, 1953. The recognized religious communities are Judaism, Islam, and several Christian denominations.
22. Some scholars also pointed to the fact that this system established de facto anti-miscegenation since members of different religious denominations cannot marry each other in Israel.
23. Due to the serious infringement that the religious-only marriage system imposed on the liberty of individuals, the Supreme Court ordered the state, already in the 1960s, to recognize and register marriages that were performed outside of Israel. See *Funk Slezinger v Minister of Interior*, HCJ 143/62, 1962 PD 17 225. Indeed, the recognition of extra-territorial marriage has been so expansive that in 2006 the Israeli Supreme Court ordered the state to recognize same-sex marriage that were performed outside of Israel (Canada in this case). See *Ben-Ari v The Registrar of Population in the Ministry of Interior*, HCJ 3045/05.
24. Barak-Erez, *supra* note 6 at 43–57.
25. *Lazarovitz v Food Controller*, HCJ 98/54, 1956 PD 10 40 (ruling that the exercise of power by government authorities cannot be guided chiefly by religious motivations, but can be influenced by it) [*Lazarovitz*]. See also *Isramax Ltd. v The State of Israel*, CrimA 217/58, 1962 PD 22 343.
26. *Lazarovitz*, *supra* note 25.
27. Ibid., 55; *Baruch v The Tel-Aviv District Traffic Controller*, HCJ 531/77, 1978 PD 32(2) 160, 163 [*Baruch*].
28. Indeed, since the 1950s, the Knesset enacted a few "special enablement laws" granting localities with specific powers to limit or even prohibit the sale of pork meat in their jurisdiction, and to take into account "religious considerations" when granting various establishments business licenses and determining their ability to operate during religious holidays. See *Local Authorities Act (Special Enablement)*, 1956 s 249(21), *The Municipalities Act* (religious holidays and days of rest), 1964; *Prohibition of Opening of Amusement Places (Special Enablement)*, 1997 (regarding Tish'a Be'av—the day of fasting and atonement marking the destruction of the Jewish Temple).
29. *Baruch supra* note 27; *The League for the Prevention of Religious Coercion v The Council of Jerusalem*, HCJ 174/62, 1966 PD 16 2665 [The League for the Prevention of Religious Coercion].
30. *Axel v Mayor, Councilors and Residents of Netanyah*, HCJ 122/54, 1954 PD 8 1524 [*Axel*].
31. Ibid., at 1528 (translation of the Hebrew in Barak-Erez, *supra* note 6), 48–49.
32. This mode of authorization was coined "bundling of jurisdictions" by Richard Ford. See R. T. Ford, "Law's Territory (A History of Jurisdiction)" (1999) 97 Michigan Law Review 843, at 844–45.
33. See *Compulsory Education Law*, 5719–1959, LSI (1959) (Isr.) (education); *The Water Law*, 1959 (sewage and water); *The Planning and Building Law*, 1965 (planning and zoning); *Business Licensing Law*, 1968 (business licensing); *The Welfare Law*, 1958 (welfare services); *The Municipalities Act* (levying taxes). Most of these powers are determined in laws that date back to Mandatory Palestine (and in some cases even to the Ottoman period) and that were amended through the years quite significantly. Local powers can be changed in regular legislation with a regular majority of the Knesset; localities can be established or abolished; and local jurisdictions can be redrawn by a simple act of the Minister of Interior.
34. Such zoning exceptions were the issue in the case of a religious kindergarten in Ramat Aviv Gimel, a secular neighborhood in the north of Tel Aviv, which became a "target" for Ultra-Orthodox Jews. For an equivalent case in the United States see *Bethlehem Christian Fellowship Inc v Planning & Zoning Comm'n*, 807 A.2d 1089 (Conn. App. Ct. 2002).
35. See *Halon v The Mayor of Local Council Ussafiyah*, HCJ 166/71, 1971 PD 25(2) 591 [*Halon*].
36. See *supra* notes 25-28 and accompanying text.
37. *Axel*, *supra* note 30.
38. Ibid. (translation of the Hebrew in Barak-Erez, *supra* note 6 at 48–49).

39. *Freidi v Municipality of Tel Aviv*, HCJ 72/55, 1955 PD 10 734.
40. This reading seems implausible in this concrete case, since the towns where such restrictions were enacted were in fact secular in their demographic composition, yet supportive of these restrictions due to the relative consensus—even among secular Jews—over the symbolic importance of the prohibition against selling and buying pork meat. However, the people who wanted to consume pork meat were indeed a small minority, deserving the Court's protection.
41. *The League for the Prevention of Religious Coercion, supra* note 29.
42. Ibid., at 2668.
43. Ibid.
44. *Baruch, supra* note 27 at 164–65.
45. Ibid., at 163.
46. *Horev, supra* note 1.
47. *Halon, supra* note 35.
48. *SZM Ltd v The Mayor of Jerusalem*, HCJ 230/73, 1974 PD 28(2) 113.
49. Ibid., at 117.
50. Ibid., at 119 and 121. In another, later, case, the Court upheld a decision by a locality to restrict the location of a sex store for similar reasons. See *Yanovitz v Chair of the Council of Ramat Ha-Sharon*, HCJ 809/86, 1987 PD 41(4) 309.
51. Local Authorities Act (Special Enablement), 1956.
52. S 249(21), *The Municipalities Act* (religious holidays and days of rest); *Prohibition of Opening of Amusement Places (Special Enablement)*, 1997 (Tish'a Be'av, a day of fasting and atonement marking the destruction of the Jewish Temple).
53. The reason for this is a combination of political reality and the legal structure. The religious parties in the Knesset believe that they cannot obtain the required majority in order to enact such nationwide prohibition. It is particularly true since such law would most probably require the amendment of a Basic Law, a measure that mandates a special majority of the Knesset. In the case of the importation of non-kosher meat such amendment to the Basic Law: Freedom of Occupation was obtained, but it was a difficult process that only demonstrated the difficulty to enact such nationwide religious legislation.
54. Barak-Erez, *supra* note 6 at 43–57.
55. Ibid., at 59–79; Rosen-Zvi, "Pigs in Space," *supra* note 6, at 226–27.
56. A prime example was the battle that took place in Petah Tiqwa (in 1983–84) and in Jerusalem (in 1986–87) concerning the opening of cinemas during the Sabbath. See *The State of Israel v Kaplan*, CrimC (Jerusalem) 3471/87, PM 5748(2) 26 (1988). See also E. Schweid, "The Sabbath in Israel," in Uri Dromi, ed, *Brethern Dwelling Together: Orthodoxy and Non-Orthodoxy in Israel—Positions, Propositions, and Accords* (Jerusalem: The Israel Democracy Institute, 2005), 220–25.
57. See M. Mautner, *Law and the Culture of Israel* (Oxford: Oxford University Press, 2011).
58. See U. Rebhun and G. Malach, *Demographic Trends in Israel* (Jerusalem: The Metzila Center, 2009) 27.
59. The rise of "Shinui," the political party that set out to combat the increased influence of religious parties, is commonly understood to be a manifestation of such backlash. See Mautner, *supra* note 57, especially chapter 5.
60. Israeli local government law oscillates between two competing conceptions of what localities are and what they should be: the first and the most dominant one is the bureaucratic conception. According to it, localities are mere subdivisions of the state, an administrative convenience, with little or no discretion over the functions they perform, almost entirely subordinated by the central state apparatus. The second conception, the democratic self-rule one, conceives localities as mini-governments that represent the will of the local populace, as voluntary associations of the communities residing within them, thus exerting significant discretion over a wide range of matters they deal with. Each of these conceptions has its own advantages and shortcomings, and each has its roots in the history and in legal doctrine. Even though the bureaucratic conception is far more intuitively accepted by jurists, political theorists, and the general public, the democratic self-rule idea has a wide support not only as a normative ideal, but also as describing historical

and present processes as well as legal rules. See Y. Blank, "Local Frontiers: Local Government Law and Its Impact on Space and Society in Israel" (SJD dissertation, Harvard Law School, Cambridge, MA, 2002); I. Rosen-Zvi, *Taking Space Seriously: Law, Space and Society in Contemporary Israel* (Aldershot: Ashgate, 2004) [Rosen-Zvi, *Taking Space Seriously*].The balance between the bureaucratic and the democratic conceptions has been slowly shifting over the past 25 years, not only at the ideological level but also as a matter of legal reforms, governmental policies, and Court decisions. This shift has a contradictory character. On one hand, local governments were given more planning powers, more fiscal discretion, and their general authorities were expansively construed in some important court rulings; on the other hand, and especially since 2004, following the financial crisis that many localities experienced, the fiscal supervision over local governments tightened, and it became easier for the Minister of Interior to interfere with the internal affairs of "failed" localities (including to put them under receivership, etc.). Despite this contradictory nature of the change, it is safe to say that the democratic-localist conception has been strengthened since the 1990s, and that the bureaucratic-centralist one, while still being very dominant, is no longer the hegemonic perception of Israeli local government theory. See, e.g., *Greenberg v Local Council of Katzrin*, HCJ 2838/95, 1997 PD 53(1) 1.
61. *Solodkin, supra* note 2.
62. Ibid. For a detailed discussion of the decision see Rosen-Zvi, "Pigs in Space," *supra* note 6 at 226–28.
63. Rosen-Zvi, ibid., at 228–31.
64. See *Solodoch v Municipality of Rehoboth*, HCJ 10907/04 (unpublished, 2010).
65. *Yekutieli v The Minister of Interior*, HCJ 6741/99, 2001 PD 55(3) 673.
66. Over the past year there has been an attempt to amend the tax exemption given to synagogues, churches, and mosques so that it will also include places "whose main use is for prayers." This way, localities will have to give this break even to buildings that only partly serve as synagogues. See The Knesset Finance Committee, "Protocol of Session of the Knesset Finance Committee Concerning the Proposed Amendment to the Municipality Taxes and the Government Taxes Ordinance (Exemptions) (Synagogues), 2009 of Member of Knesset Nissim Zeev (p/662)," 2 March 2010; available online: <http://oknesset.org/committee/meeting/52/> (Hebrew).
67. Ibid.
68. *Peretz, supra* note 4.
69. Ibid., at 2106.
70. Ibid., at 2107.
71. The list of petitions to the District Court and to the Supreme Court is lengthy. The most important decision by the Supreme Court was delivered a few months ago. See *Jerusalem Open House*, AdminA 343/09, *supra* note 4.
72. S. Hasson and A. Gonen, *The Cultural Tension within Jerusalem's Jewish Population* (Jerusalem: The Floersheimer Institute for Policy Studies, 1997); S. Hasson, *The Cultural Struggle over Jerusalem: Accommodations, Scenarios and Lessons* (Jerusalem: The Floersheimer Institute for Policy Studies, 1996).
73. *Jerusalem Open House v The City of Jerusalem*, AdminC (Jerusalem) 8187/08 (unpublished, 2008). This decision itself reversed a previous District Court decision in which Justice Yehudit Tzur requested that the municipality reconsider its policy. See *Jerusalem Open House v The City of Jerusalem*, AdminC (Jerusalem) 219/06 (unpublished, 2006).
74. *Jerusalem Open House*, AdminA 343/09, *supra* note 4 at paras 53 and 56–57.
75. Y. Blank, "Brown in Jerusalem: A Comparative Look on Race and Ethnicity in Public Schools" (2006) 38 The Urban Lawyer367, at 384–89; see also Rosen-Zvi, *Taking Space Seriously, supra* note 60.
76. I refer mostly to the segregation between Mizrahi Jews (Jews of Oriental descent) and Ashkenazi Jews (Jews of European and American descent), which was extremely prevalent until the late 1980s. While a significant spatial segregation of impoverished Mizrahi Jews in development towns and poor neighborhoods in large cities still exists, the radical isolation of Mizrahis has been mitigated due to governmental policies and a gradual

upward mobility of second- and third-generation Mizrahis. Another segregation that still exists, but which has begun changing recently, is that between Palestinian-Arabs and Jews. Though the vast majority of Arabs still live in localities that are purely Arab, and although most Jews live in all-Jewish localities, a new phenomenon started unsettling this clear divide. If until the late 1990s, there existed only very few "mixed towns"—in which Jews and Arabs lived together (albeit in different neighborhoods)—during the past decade a few more mixed towns began appearing, as a result of new residential patterns. Arabs started moving into previously all-Jewish towns, thus changing the demographic nature of these towns, and weakening the radical segregation which previously existed.

77. Such new localities include El'ad, Beitar Illit, and Modi'im Illit. See N. Gurovich and E. Cohen-Kastro, "Ultra-Orthodox Jews: Geographic Distribution and Demographic, Social and Economic Characteristics of the Ultra-Orthodox Jewish Population in Israel, 1996–2001," July 2004; available online: <http://www.cbs.gov.il/www/publications/int_ulor.pdf> (Hebrew).

78. The separation between Jews (secular and religious alike) and Arabs (Muslim and Christian alike) was obtained mostly through the allotting of lands exclusively to Jews. See Blank, *supra* note 75, at 386–89.

79. Ibid., at 384–89.

80. Ibid.

81. See O. Yiftachel and A. (Sandy) Kedar, "Landed Power: The Making of the Israeli Land Regime" (2000) 16 Theory and Criticism 67.

82. *Kaadan v Israel Land Authority*, 6698/95, 2000 PD 54(1) 258. See also A. (Sandy) Kedar, "'A First Step in a Difficult and Sensitive Road'—Preliminary Observations on Qaadan v. Katzir" (2000) 16 Israel Studies Bulletin 3.

83. *Amendment to the Collective Associations Ordinance Act* (no 8), 2011, section 1 and 2. The Association for the Civil Rights in Israel filed a petition in the name of numerous individuals challenging the constitutionality of this amendment. See *Sabach v The Knesset*, HCJ 2311/11 (filed 23 March 2011); the petition is available online: <http://www.acri.org.il/he/wp-content/uploads/2011/03/hit2311.pdf> (Hebrew).

84. N. Ziv and C. Tirosh, "The Legal Battle against the Screening of Candidates to Communal Settlements: A Trap in a Pierced and Muddy Web," in A. Lehavi, ed, *Gated Communities* (Tel Aviv: Nevo Press, 2010) 311 (in Hebrew).

85. This happened when an Ultra-Orthodox family tried to be admitted to the religious-Zionist settlement of Bar Yochai. The screening board disqualified the family on the grounds that it didn't "fit" its way of life. See N. Ziv, "An Appeal on the Rejection Decision in the Settlement of Bar Yochai" (letter to Israel's Land Authority sent by the family's lawyer, 11 April 2011) (on file with author).

86. *Am Hofshi v The Ministry of Building and Housing*, HCJ 4906/98, 2000 PD 54(2) 503, 508 [*Am Hofshi*]. One of the sources of inspiration for the *Am Hofshi* decision was another case in which state-coerced segregation was challenged. In the *Avitan* case, the Court affirmed the decision of Israel's Land Authority to establish towns only for Bedouins. The Court ruled that it was a legitimate state interest to settle the nomadic Bedouins and that excluding Jews as well as other non-Bedouins was imperative for this policy's success. The Court also mentions the unique history and culture of the Bedouins as legitimating the state segregation. *Avitan v Israel Land Authority*, HCJ 528/88, 1989 PD 43(4) 297. In *Am Hofshi* the Court ignores the uniqueness of the Bedouin community, extending the license to segregate between communities to any minority group with "unique ways of life."

87. *Am Hofshi* 508–509. It is important to note that the Court in fact voided the Ministry's decision as it found that the policy was separate and unequal. The Court ordered the ministry to establish an equally beneficial project for secular Jews.

88. Such new towns include El'ad, Beitar Ilit, Modi'in Ilit, Kiryat Sefer, and Immanuel. Two additional Ultra-Orthodox cities—Kasif and Harish—are currently planned by the government.

89. The survey was conducted by the Geocartography Institute. See A. Dagani, "61 percent of the Ultra Orthodox Prefer to Live in Separate Settlements," 15 February 2011; available

online: <http://www.relevanti.com/פרוף-אבי-דגני/גלובס/עמוד-הבית/m7329_61--נפרדים מהחרדים->
<מעדיפים-לגור-בישובים> (Hebrew).
90. Schragger, *supra* note 6 at 1815–816.
91. Ibid.
92. Gerken, *supra* note 14.
93. Ibid., at 1750.
94. R. M. Cover, "The Supreme Court, 1982 Term: Foreword: Nomos and Narrative" (1983) 97 Harvard Law Review 4; see also A. S. Greene, "Kiryas Joel and Two Mistakes about Equality" (1996) 96 Columbia Law Review 1.
95. D. J. Barron, "The Promise of Cooley's City: Traces of Local Constitutionalism" (1999) 147 University of Pennsylvania Law Review 487, at 490.
96. Gerald Frug defines public freedom as "the ability to participate actively in the basic societal decisions that affect one's life." G. E. Frug, "The City as a Legal Concept" (1980) 93 Harvard Law Review 1057, at 1068. (Frug attributes the concept of "public freedom" to philosopher Hannah Arendt).
97. *Halon, supra* note 35 at 594 (my emphasis).
98. In the city of Beit Shemesh, which is experiencing waves of Ultra-Orthodox migration into it, secular residents demanded that Israel's Land Authority allocate lands to a secular neighborhood, like it regularly does for Ultra-Orthodox neighborhoods. The District Court of Jerusalem refused to intervene with the Authority's refusal, reasoning that the logic of the *Am Hofshi* decision did not apply to secular Jews who were a majority group with no unique lifestyle worthy of protection. See *Edri v The Minister of Building and Housing*, AdminC (Jerusalem) 1888/09 (unpublished, 2009) [*Edri*, AdminC 1888/09]. The Supreme Court affirmed on procedural grounds. See *Edri v The Minister of Building and Housing*, AdminA 68/10 (unpublished, 2011) [*Edri*, AdminA 68/10].
99. Schragger, *supra* note 6 at 1815.
100. Madison, *supra* note 10, argues: "The influence of factious leaders may kindle a flame within their particular States, but will be unable to spread a general conflagration through the other States. A religious sect may degenerate into a political faction in a part of the Confederacy; but the variety of sects dispersed over the entire face of it must secure the national councils against any danger from that source. A rage for paper money, for an abolition of debts, for an equal division of property, or for any other improper or wicked project, will be less apt to pervade the whole body of the Union than a particular member of it; in the same proportion as such a malady is more likely to taint a particular county or district, than an entire State." at pinpoint.
101. Ibid.
102. According to the report, in various Ultra-Orthodox communities families began separating between men and women even in small family gatherings, squeezing women in separate tables in the kitchen. Until very recently, such custom has never been observed and has very little religious basis. See T. Rotem, "Separate Tables" *Haaretz* (1 July 2011); available online: <http://www.haaretz.com/weekend/week-s-end/separate-tables-1.370695>.
103. *Ragan v Ministry of Transportation*, HCJ 746/07 (unpublished, 2011) [*Ragan*]. See Y. Ettinger, "High Court: Gender Segregation Legal on Israeli Buses—But Only with Passenger Consent" *Haaretz* (6 January 2011); available online: <http://www.haaretz.com/news/national/high-court-gender-segregation-legal-on-israeli-buses-but-only-with-passenger-consent-1.335567>. For a supportive position of the practice see A. Harel, "Benign Segregation: A Case Study of the Practice of Gender Separation in Buses in the Ultra-Orthodox Community" (2004) 20 South African Journal on Human Right 64.
104. The Court in *Ragan* therefore required that the buses put signs that made it clear that entering and getting off the bus through different doors was not mandatory and that so were the sitting arrangements. These signs, ruled the Court, will make it clear that it was illegal to force anyone to respect these practices. Many commentators have criticized this ruling, calling it naïve at best.
105. Many have criticized this decision, calling it a dangerous compromise and caving in to the most radical sections of the Ultra-Orthodox communities.

106. There are many projects throughout Israel that are currently marketed to national-religious families and individuals only. While some rely on market and social dynamics, in other cases the exclusion is overt and explicit. See, e.g., the website of "Be'emuna," who prides itself for marketing its apartments only to the national-religious sector, available online: <http://www.bemuna.co.il/show.asp?id=5861> (Hebrew).
107. See *Edri*, AdminC 1888/09, *supra* note 98; *Edri*, AdminA 68/10, *supra* note 98. See discussion above at Part 3.1.4.
108. Ibid.
109. Madison, *supra* note 10.
110. See the discussion above of the *Open House* case.
111. S. M. Okin, *supra* note 9.
112. Tel Aviv's District Court recently held that a private development company was allowed to refuse to sell apartments to anyone who was not "Zionist-religious." The court ruled that there was "nothing wrong in a group of people organizing in order to live next to each other to be able to lead their life according to their ways of life." See *Saba'a v Israel Land Administration*, AdminC 2002/09 (unpublished, 2010). An appeal to the Supreme Court was rejected since the project was already being constructed and the Court ruled that it was a "done deal." However, the Court made remarks which could be understood as expressing dissatisfaction with the District Court's ruling as well as with the practice. See *Saba'a v Israel Land Administration*, AdminA 1789/10 (unpublished, 2011).
113. *Amutat No'ar Ka-Halacha v Ministry of Education*, HCJ 1067/08 (unpublished, 6 August 2009).

# BIBLIOGRAPHY

*Books and articles in books*

Achour, Y. B. "Nature, raison et révélation dans la philosophie du droit des auteurs sunnites," in E. E. Dais et al. (eds), *Consequences of Modernity in Contemporary Legal Theory* (Berlin: Duncker & Humblot, 1998).

Agamben, G. *Homo Sacer: Sovereign Power and Bare Life* (Stanford: Stanford University Press, 1998).

Al-Ghazali. *Tahafut al-falasifah* [*Incoherence of the philosophers*] (Lahore: Pakistan Philosophical Congress, 1963).

Al-Haj, M. *Education, Empowerment, and Control: The Case of the Arabs in Israel* (Albany: State University of New York, 1995).

Anderson, E. *Value in Ethics and Economics* (Cambridge, MA: Harvard University Press, 1993).

Anidjar, G. *Semites: Race, Religion, Literature* (Stanford: Stanford University Press, 2007).

Anidjar, G. *The Jew, the Arab: A History of the Enemy* (Stanford: Stanford University Press, 2003).

Arendt, H. "The Crisis in Culture," in *Between Past and Future* (New York: Penguin Books, 2006), 194.

Arendt, H. *On Revolution* (New York: Viking Press, 1965).

Arendt, H. "The Decline of the Nation-State and the End of the Rights of Man," in *The Origins of Totalitarianism*, 3rd edn (London: George Allen & Unwin, 1966).

Arendt, H. "We Refugees," in J. Kohn and R. H. Feldman (eds), *The Jewish Writings* (New York: Schocken Books, 2007) 264.

Arneson, R.J. and I. Shapiro, "Democratic Authority and Religious Freedom: A Critique of *Wisconsin v. Yoder*," in I. Shapiro and R. Hardin, eds, *Political Order* (New York: New York University Press, 1993) 365.

Asad, T. *Formations of the Secular: Christianity, Islam, Modernity* (Stanford: Stanford University Press, 2003).

Asad, T. "The Concept of Cultural Translation in British Social Anthropology," in J. Clifford and G. E. Marcus (eds), *Writing Culture: The Poetics and Politics of Ethnography* (Berkeley: University of California Press, 1986) 141–64.

Auden, W. H. "Law Like Love," in D. Kader and M. Stanford (eds), *Poetry of the Law: From Chaucer to the Present* (Iowa City: University of Iowa Press, 2010) 108.

Audi, R. and P. Wolterstorff. *Religion in the Public Square* (Lanham, MD: Rowman & Littlefield, 1997).

Avineri, S. "The Paradox of Religion and the Universality of Human Rights", in A. Sajo, *Human Rights with Modesty: the Problem of Universality* (Dordrecht: Springer, 2004) 317.

Avishai, O. "'Doing Religion' in a Secular World: Women in Conservative Religions and the Question of Agency" 22:4 *Gender & Society* (2008) 409.

Banting, K. & W. Kymlicka, "Introduction: Multiculturalism and the Welfare State: Setting the Context," in K. Banting & W. Kymlicka, eds, *Multiculturalism and the Welfare State*, (Oxford: Oxford University Press, 2006) 1.

Barak-Erez, D. *Outlawed Pigs: Law, Religion, and Culture in Israel* (Madison: University of Wisconsin Press, 2007).

Barnard, A. *History and Theory in Anthropology* (Cambridge: Cambridge University Press, 2000).

Barry, B. *Culture and Equality: An Egalitarian Critique of Multiculturalism* (Cambridge, MA: Harvard University Press, 2001).

Barzilai, G. *Communities and Law: Politics and Culture of Legal Identities* (Ann Arbor: University of Michigan Press, 2003).

Bauman, Z. "What Chance of Ethics in the Globalized World of Consumers?," in *Does Ethics Have a Chance in a World of Consumers?* (Cambridge, MA: Harvard University Press, 2008) 31.

Beiner, R. "Hannah Arendt on Judging," in H. Arendt and R. Beiner (eds), *Lectures on Kant's Political Philosophy* (Chicago: University of Chicago Press, 1982) 89.

Beiner, R. *What's the Matter with Liberalism?* (Berkeley: University of California Press, 1992).

Benedict, R. *Patterns of Culture* (Boston: Houghton Mifflin, 1934).

Benhabib, S. "Models of Public Space: Hannah Arendt, the Liberal Tradition, and Jürgen Habermas," in C. Calhoun (ed), *Habermas and the Public Sphere* (Cambridge, MA: MIT Press, 2002) 73–98.

Ben-Haim, L. "Harediut, National Religiousness and Secularization in Higher Education: A Multi-Modern Perspective," in U. Cohen et al. (eds), *Israel and Modernity* (Eilat: Ben Gurion University of the Negev, 2006) 395 (Hebrew).

Ben-Menahem, H. *Judicial Deviation From Talmudic Law: Governed by Men, Not by Rules* (New York: Hardwood Academic Publishers, 1991).

Ben-Rafael, E. & Y. Peres, *Is Israel One? Religion, Nationalism, and Multiculturalism Confounded* (Leiden: Brill, 2005).

Berger, P. "Afterword," in J. D. Hunter and O. Guinness, eds, *Articles of Faith, Articles of Peace* (Washington, DC: Brookings Institution Press, 1990) 114.

Berman, H. *Law and Revolution: The Formation of the Western Legal Tradition* (Cambridge, MA: Harvard University Press, 1983).

Bernstein, R. *Beyond Objectivism and Relativism: Science, Hermeneutics, and Praxis* (Philadelphia: University of Pennsylvania Press, 1983).

Betts, R. B. *Christians in the Arab East: A Political Study* (Atlanta: John Knox Press, 1978).

Biale, R. *Women and Jewish Law: An Exploration of Women's Issues in Halakhic Sources* (New York: Schocken Books, 1984).

Bickel, A. M. *The Least Dangerous Branch: The Supreme Court at the Bar of Politics*, 2nd edn (New Haven, CT: Yale University Press, 1986).

Bilsky, L. *Transformative Justice: Israeli Identity on Trial* (Ann Arbor: University of Michigan Press, 2004).

Blank, Y. "Local Frontiers: Local Government Law and Its Impact on Space and Society in Israel" (SJD dissertation, Harvard Law School, Cambridge, MA, 2002).

Blidstein, G. "On Lay Legislation in Halakha: The King as Instance," in S. Last Stone (ed), *Rabbinic and Lay Communal Authority* (New York: Yeshiva University Press, 2006) 1–18.

Böckenförde, E.-W. "Der säkularisierte Staat. Sein Charakter, seine Rechtfertigung und seine Probleme im 21. Jahrhundert," in *Der säkularisierte Staat* (Munich: Carl Friedrich von Siemens-Stiftung, 2007).

Böckenförde, E.-W. "Die Entstehung des Staates als Vorgang der Säkularisation," in *Der säkularisierte Staat* (Munich: Carl Friedrich von Siemens-Stiftung, 2007).

Bohman, J. *Public Deliberation: Pluralism, Complexity and Democracy* (Cambridge, MA: MIT Press, 1996).
Bolz, N. *Das konsumistische Manifest* (Munich: Fink, 2002).
Bouchard, G. *L'Interculturalisme* (Montréal: Boréal, 2012).
Bourdieu, P. *Firing Back: Against the Tyranny of the Market 2*, translated by Loic Wacquant (New York: New Press, 2003).
Bowen, J. R. *Can Islam Be French? Pluralism and Pragmatism in a Secularist State* (Princeton, NJ: Princeton University Press, 2009).
Boyd White, J."How Should We Talk About Religion?," in J. Boyd White ed, *How Should Talk About Religion? Perspectives, Context, Particularities* (Notre-Dame: University of Notre-Dame, 2006) 1.
Brague, R. *The Law of God* (Chicago: University of Chicago Press, 2007).
Brownlie, I. and G. S. Goodwin-Gill (eds). *Basic Documents on Human Rights*, 6th edn (Oxford: Oxford University Press, 2010).
Brugger, W. and M. Karayanni (eds). *Religion in the Public Sphere: A Comparative Analysis of German, Israeli, American and International Law* (Heidelberg: Springer, 2007).
Bubner, R. "Zur Dialektik der Toleranz," in R. Forst (ed), *Toleranz im Konflikt. Geschichte, Gehalt und Gegenwart eines umstrittenen Begriffs* (Frankfurt/M.: Campus, 2003).
Burke, E. *Reflections on the Revolution in France* (Stanford: Stanford University Press, 2001).
Bushman, R. L. *Mormonism: A Very Short Introduction* (New York: Oxford University Press, 2008).
Calhoun, C. et al., eds, *Rethinking Secularism* (Oxford: Oxford University Press, 2011).
Carter, S. L. *God's Name in Vain: The Wrongs and Rights of Religion in Politics* (New York: Basic Books, 2000).
Casanova, J. *Europas Angst vor der Religion* (Berlin: Berlin University Press, 2009).
Casanova, J. *Public Religions in the Modern World* (Chicago: University of Chicago Press, 1994).
Casanova, J. et al. in H. Joas. and K. Wiegandt (eds), *Säkularisierung und die Weltreligionen* (Frankfurt/M.: Fischer, 2007).
Caspar, R. *Traité de théologie musulmane* (Roma: Pontificio Istituto di Studi Arabi e d'Islamistica, 1996).
*Catechism of the Catholic Church* (Città del Vaticano: Libreria Editrice Vaticana, 1993).
Chelini-Pont, B., N. Ferchiche and by C. K. Papastathis in J. Martínez-Torrón and W. Cole Durham, Jr., eds, *Religion and the Secular State/La religion et l'État laïque: Interim National Reports/Rapports Nationaux Intermédiaires, issued for the occasion of the XVIIIth International Congress of Comparative Law, Washington, D.C.—July 2010* (Provo, UT: International Center for Law and Religious Studies, Brigham Young University, 2010).
Clifford, J. *Routes: Travel and Translation in the Late Twentieth Century* (Cambridge, MA: Harvard University Press, 1997).
Clyne, M. G. *Inter-Cultural Communication at Work: Cultural Values in Discourse* (Cambridge: Cambridge University Press, 1994).
Cohen, L. *Let Us Compare Mythologies* (Montreal: Contact Press, 1956).
Cohen, A. and B. Susser. *Israel and the Politics of Jewish Identity: The Secular-Religious Impasse* (Baltimore: The John Hopkins University Press, 2000).
Cover, R. "Nomos and Narrative," in M. Minor, M. Ryan, and A. Sarat, eds, *Narrative, Violence, and the Law: The Essays of Robert Cover* (Ann Arbor: University of Michigan Press, 1993).
Dalla Torre, G. *Infedeli, in Enciclopedia del diritto*, vol. 21 (Milano: Giuffrè, 1971).
D'Andrade, R. G. "A Folk Model of the Mind," in D. Holland and N. Quinn (eds), *Cultural Models in Language and Thought* (Cambridge: Cambridge University Press, 1987) 112.
D'Andrade, R. G. "Cultural Meaning Systems," in R. A. Shweder and R. A. Levine (eds), *Culture Theory: Essays on Mind, Self, and Emotion* (Cambridge: Cambridge University Press, 1984) 88–122.

D'Andrade, R. G. "Some Propositions about the Relations between Culture and Human Cognition," in J. W. Stigler, R. A. Shweder, and G. Herdt (eds), *Cultural Psychology: Essays on Comparative Human Development* (Cambridge: Cambridge University Press, 1990) 65–129.

Dana, N. and S. Fallah, "Ma'mad ha-Druzim ve-Irgunam ha-Edati" ["The Status of the Druze and their Community Organization"], in *Ha-Druzim [The Druze]* (Ramat-Gan: Bar-Ilan University Press, 1998) 159.

Dane, P. "Constitutional Law and Religion," in D. Patterson (ed), *Blackwell Companion to Philosophy of Law and Legal Theory* (Oxford: Wiley-Blackwell, 1999) 113–25.

Dascal, M. "Introduction," in M. Dascal (ed), *Cultural Relativism and Philosophy: North and Latin American Perspectives* (Leiden: E. J. Brill, 1991) 1–9.

David, J. E. "Maïmonide, la nature et le droit: un vieux problem revisité," in Louis-Léon Christians et al., dir, *Droit naturel: relancer l'histoire?* (Bruxelles: Bruylant, 2008) 233.

Depoortere, F. *Christ in Postmodern Philosophy: Gianni Vattimo, René Girard and Slavoj Žižek* (London and New York: T & T Clark International, 2008).

Deveaux, M. *Gender and Justice in Multicultural Liberal States* (Oxford: Oxford University Press, 2006).

Dombrowski, D. *Rawls and Religion* (Albany: State University of New York Press, 2001).

Dostoyevsky, F. *The Double: A Poem of St. Petersburg*, translated by G. Bird (London: Harvill, 1957).

Druart, T.-A. "Al-Fârâbi (870-950): une éthique universelle fondée sur les intelligibles premiers," in Louis-Léon Christians et al., dir, *Droit naturel relancer l'histoire?* (Bruxelles: Bruylant, 2008).

Dryzek, J. S. *Deliberative Democracy and Beyond* (Oxford: Oxford University Press, 2000).

Dumas, A. "Intérêt et usure," in *Dictionnaire de droit canonique*, vol. 5 (Paris: Letouzey & Anè, 1953).

Dworkin, R. *Life's Dominion: An Argument about Abortion, Euthanasia, and Individual Freedom* (New York: Knopf, 1993).

Edelman, M. *Courts, Politics, and Culture in Israel* (Charlottesville: University Press of Virginia, 1994).

Eisenman, R. H. *Islamic Law in Palestine and Israel: A History of the Survival of Tanzimat and Shari'a in the British Mandate and the Jewish State* (Leiden: E.J. Brill, 1978).

Eisenstadt, S. N. "The Order-Maintaining and Order-Transforming Dimensions of Culture," in R. Munch and N. J. Smelser (eds), *Theory of Culture* (Berkeley: University of California Press, 1992) 64.

Eisenberg, A. and J. Spinner-Halev (eds). *Minorities within Minorities: Equality, Rights and Diversity* (Cambridge: Cambridge University Press, 2005).

El-Or, T. *Educated and Ignorant: On Ultra-Orthodox Women and Their World* (Boulder, CO: Lynne Rienner, 1992).

El-Or, T. "Paradoxical and Social Boundaries," in E. Fuchs (ed), *Israeli Women's Studies: A Reader* (New Brunswick, NJ: Rutgers University Press, 2005) 133.

Emon, A. E. *Islamic Natural Law Theories* (Oxford: Oxford University Press, 2010).

Englard, I. "The Conflict between State and Religion in Israel: Its Ideological Background," in M. Mor (ed), *International Perspectives on Church and State* (New York: Fordham University Press: 1993) 219.

Esposito, J. L. *Women in Muslim Family Law* (Syracuse: Syracuse University Press, 1982) 20.

Ezzati, A. *Islam and Natural Law* (London: Icas Press, 2002).

Feldman, N. *Divided by God: America's Church-State Problem—And What We Should Do About It* (New York: Farrar, 2005).

Fernandez, J. W. "Cultural Relativism, Anthropology of," in *International Encyclopedia of the Social & Behavioral Sciences* vol. 5 (Oxford: Pergamom Press, 2001) 3110–3113.

Ferrari, S. "Canon Law as a Religious Legal System," in A. Huxley (ed), *Religion, Law and Tradition: Comparative Studies in Religious Law* (London: RoutledgeCurzon, 2002) 49–60.

Ferrari, S. "Religion et constitution," in M. Troper and D. Chagnollaud (eds), *Traité international de droit constitutionnel*, vol.3: *Suprématie de la Constitution* (Paris: Dalloz, 2013), 437.
Feyerabend, P. *Against Method*, 3rd edn (London and New York: Verso, 1975).
Firro, K. M. *The Druzes in the Jewish State: A Brief History* (Leiden: Brill, 1999).
Fonrobert, C.E. "Gender Politics in the Rabbinic Neighborhood: Tractate Eruvin," in *Introduction to the Feminist Talmud Commentary—Seder Moed* (Tubingen: Mohr Siebeck, 2007) 43.
Frankel Paul, E. F. D. Miller, Jr., and J. Paul, eds, *Human Flourishing* (Cambridge: Cambridge University Press, 1999).
Fraser, N. "Rethinking the Public Sphere: A Contribution to the Critique of Actually Existing Democracy," in C. Calhoun (ed), *Habermas and the Public Sphere* (Cambridge, MA: MIT Press, 2002) 109–42.
Fridman, V. *Ecriture et identité juive en Argentine dans la transition démocratique* (Paris: Honoré Champion, 2010).
M. Friedman, *The Ultra-Orthodox Society: Origins, Trends and Processes* (Jerusalem: The Jerusalem Institute for Israel Studies, 1991) chapter 4 (Hebrew).
Friedman, M. *The Ultra-Orthodox Woman* (Jerusalem: The Jerusalem Institute for Israel Studies, 1988) (Hebrew).
Furet, F. and F. Mélonio (eds). *The Old Regime and the Revolution*, translated by A. Kahan (Chicago: University of Chicago Press, 1998).
Gadamer, H.-G. *Philosophical Hermeneutics*, translated by D. E. Linge (Berkeley and Los Angeles: University of California Press, 1976).
Gadamer, H.-G. *Truth and Method*, translated by D. Marshall and J. Weinsheimer, 2nd rev edn (New York: Continuum, 1993).
Garnett, R. "Religious Liberty, Church Autonomy, and the Structure of Freedom," in J. Witte, Jr. and F. S. Alexander (eds), *Christianity and Human Rights: An Introduction* (Cambridge: Cambridge University Press, 2010) 267–82.
Garnett, R. "Two There Are: Understanding the Separation of Church and State," in M. Hogan and L. Frederking (eds), *The American Experiment in Religious Freedom* (Portland: Garaventa Center, 2008) 319–30.
Gauchet, M. *The Disenchantment of the World*, translated by Oscar Burge (Princeton, NJ: Princeton University Press, 1999).
Geertz, C. "Thick Description: Toward an Interpretive Theory of Culture," in *The Interpretation of Culture* (New York: Basic Books, 1973).
Gelasius I, Pope. "Letter to the Emperor Anastasius," in K. F. Morrison et al. (eds), *University of Chicago Readings in Western Civilization: The Church in the Roman Empire*, vol. 3 (Chicago: University of Chicago Press, 1986).
Gellner, E. "General Introduction: Relativism and Universals," in B. Lloyd and J. Gay (eds), *Universals of Human Thought: Some African Evidence* (Cambridge: Cambridge University Press, 1981).
Gilman, S. L. "'Barbaric' Rituals?," in J. Cohen, M. Howard, and M. C. Nussbaum (eds), *Is Multiculturalism Bad for Women?* (Princeton, NJ: Princeton University Press, 1999) 53.
Glendon, M. A. *Rights Talk: The Impoverishment of Political Discourse* (New York: Free Press, 1993/1991).
Glenn, H. P. *Legal Traditions of the World: Sustainable Diversity in Law* (Oxford: Oxford University Press, 2010).
Goadby, F. M. *International and Inter-Religious Private Law in Palestine* (Jerusalem: Hamadpis Press, 1926).
Gowans, C. "Moral Relativism," in *The Stanford Encyclopedia of Philosophy (Spring 2014 Edition)*, Edward N. Zalta (ed.), URL = <http://plato.stanford.edu/archives/spr2014/entries/moral-relativism/>.
Green, L. "Internal Minorities and their Rights," in W. Kymlicka (ed), *The Rights of Minority Cultures* (Oxford: Oxford University Press, 1995) 256–74.

Griffel, F. "The Harmony of Natural Law and Shari'a in Islamist Theology," in A. Amanat and F. Griffel (eds), *Shari'a: Islamic Law in the Contemporary Context* (Stanford: Stanford University Press, 2007) 38–61.
Gutmann, A. "Communitarian Critics of Liberalism," in S. Avineri and A. de-Shalit (eds), *Communitarianism and Individualism* (Oxford: Oxford University Press, 1992) 120.
Gutmann, A. and D. F. Thompson. *Democracy and Disagreement* (Cambridge, MA: Harvard University Press, 1996).
Gutmann, A. and D. F. Thompson. *Why Deliberative Democracy?* (Princeton, NJ: Princeton University Press, 2004).
Haakonssen, K. "Republicanism," in R. E. Goodin and P. Pettit (eds), *A Companion to Contemporary Political Philosophy* (Oxford: Blackwell, 1993) 568.
Habermas, J. "A Review of Gadamer's Truth and Method," in F. R. Dallmayr and T. A. McCarthy (eds), *Understanding and Social Inquiry* (Notre Dame, IN: University of Notre Dame Press, 1977) 335.
Halbertal, M. "Co-existing with the Enemy: Pagans and Jews in the Mishnah," in G. N. Stanton and G. G. Stroumsa (eds), *Tolerance and Intolerance in Early Judaism and Christianity* (Cambridge: Cambridge University Press, 1998) 159–73.
Hall, T. L. *Separating Church and State: Roger Williams and Religious Liberty* (Urbana: University of Illinois Press, 1998).
Hallaq, W. B. *A History of Islamic Legal Theories* (Cambridge: Cambridge University Press, 1997).
Hannerz, U. *Cultural Complexity: Studies in the Social Organization of Meaning* (New York: Columbia University Press, 1992).
Hart, H. L. A. *The Concept of Law*, 2nd edn (Oxford: Oxford University Press, 1994).
Harvey, D. *A Brief History of Neoliberalism* (Oxford: Oxford University Press, 2005).
Hashemi, K. *Religious Legal Tradition, International Human Rights Law and Muslim States* (Leiden and Boston: Nijhoff, 2008).
Hasson, S. and A. *The Cultural Struggle over Jerusalem: Accommodations, Scenarios and Lessons* (Jerusalem: The Floersheimer Institute for Policy Studies, 1996).
Hasson, S. and A. Gonen. *The Cultural Tension within Jerusalem's Jewish Population* (Jerusalem: The Floersheimer Institute for Policy Studies, 1997).
Heelas, P. "Introduction: On Differentiation and Dedifferentiation," in P. Heelas (ed), *Religion, Modernity and Postmodernity* (Oxford: Blackwell, 1998) 1–18.
Henaff, M. and T. B. Strong. "Introduction: The Conditions of Public Space: Vision, Speech and Theatricality," in M. Henaff and T. B. Strong (eds), *Public Space and Democracy* (Minneapolis: University of Minnesota Press, 2001) 1–33.
Heredia, L. "From Prayer to Protest: The Immigrant Rights Movement and the Catholic Church," in K. Voss and I. Bloemraad (eds), *Rallying for Immigrant Rights* (Berkeley: University of California Press, 2011) 101–22.
Hirschl, R. and A. Shachar. "Constitutional Transformation, Gender Equality, and Religious/National Conflict in Israel: Tentative Progress through the Obstacle Course," in B. Baines and R. Rubio-Marin (eds), *The Gender of Constitutional Jurisprudence* (Cambridge: Cambridge University Press, 2005) 205.
Hobbes, H., in E. Curley (ed). *Leviathan: With Selected Variants from the Latin Edition of 1668* (Indianapolis: Hackett, 1994).
Holy, L. "Introduction: Description, Generalization and Comparison: Two Paradigms," in L. Holy (ed), *Comparative Anthropology* (Oxford and New York: Blackwell, 1987).
Hoodfar, H. "More Than Clothing: Veiling as an Adaptive Strategy" in S. Alvi, H. Hoodfar and S. McDonough, eds, *The Muslim Veil in North America: Issues and Debates* (Toronto: Women's Press, 2003).
Hostovsky Brandes, T. "The Hand in Hand Bilingual Education Model: Vision and Challenges" in A. Sagi & O. Nachtomy, eds, *The Multicultural Challenge in Israel* (Boston: Academic Studies Press, 2009).

Hunt, L. *Inventing Human Rights: A History* (New York: W.W. Norton, 2007).
Huster, S. *Die ethische Neutralität des Staates* (Tübingen: Mohr Siebeck, 2002).
Isak, A. *Das Selbstverständnis der Kirchen und Religionsgemeinschaften und seine Bedeutung für die Auslegung des staatlichen Rechts* (Berlin: Duncker & Humblot, 1994).
Jellinek, G. "Die Erklärung der Menschen- und Bürgerrechte," in R. Schnur (ed), *Zur Erklärung der Menschen- und Bürgerrechte* (Darmstadt: Wissenschaftliche Buchgesellschaft, 1964) 1.
Jessop, C. *Escape* (New York: Broadway Books, 2007).
Joppke, C. "The Retreat of Multiculturalism in the Liberal State: Theory and Policy" 55:2 *British Journal of Sociology* (2004) 237.
Joyce, J. *A Portrait of the Artist as a Young Man* (1916, 1930)
Kahn, P. *Putting Liberalism in its Place* (Princeton, NJ: Princeton University Press, 2005).
Kallen, H. *Cultural Pluralism and the American Idea* (Philadelphia: University of Pennsylvania Press, 1956).
Kant, I. *An Answer to the Question: What is Enlightenment?*, Berlinische Monatsschrift, iv (1784).
Kasher, A. *Ruah Ish: Arba'ah She'arim* [*Spirit of a Man: Four Gates*] (Tel-Aviv: Am Oved, 2000) (Hebrew).
Kelly, P. ed, *Multiculturalism Reconsidered* (Malden, MA; Cambridge, UK: Polity Press in association with Blackwell Publishers, 2002).
Khadduri, M. "Nature and Sources of Islamic Law," in I. Edge (ed), *Islamic Law and Legal Theory* (Aldershot: Dartmouth, 1996).
Khadduri, M. *The Islamic Conception of Justice* (Baltimore: Johns Hopkins University Press, 1984).
Klassen, D. J. *Le Droit naturel dans le pensée de Thomas d'Aquin*, in Louis-Léon Christians et al., (dir), *Droit naturel: relancer l'histoire?* (Bruxelles: Bruylant, 2008) 257–92.
Konvitz, M. (ed). *Judaism and Human Rights* (London: Rutgers, 2001).
Korioth, S. "Jeder nach seiner Facon," in *Kritische Justiz, Beiheft 1* (Baden-Baden, Nomos 2009),
Korioth, S. "Loyalität im Staatskirchenrecht?," in W. Erbguth et al. (eds), *Gedächtnisschrift Jeand'Heur* (Berlin: Duncker & Humblot, 1999).
Krausz, M. "Crossing Cultures: Two Universalisms and Two Relativisms," in M. Dascal (ed), *Cultural Relativism and Philosophy: North and Latin American Perspectives* (Leiden: E.J. Brill, 1991) 233–42.
Kretzmer, D. *The Legal Status of the Arabs in Israel* (Boulder: Westview Press, 1990).
Kuper, A. *Culture: The Anthropologists' Account* (Cambridge, MA: Harvard University Press, 1999).
Kukathas, C. *The Liberal Archipelago* (Oxford: Oxford University Press, 2003).
Kymlicka, W. "Community," in R. E. Gooding and P. Pettit (eds), *A Companion to Contemporary Political Philosophy* (Oxford: Blackwell, 1993) 366.
Kymlicka, W. and R. Cohen-Almagor, "Democracy and Multiculturalism," in R. Cohen-Almagor, ed, *Challenges to Democracy: Essays in Honour and Memory of Isaiah Berlin* (Aldershot, UK and Brookfield, VT: Ashgate, 2000) 89.
Kymlicka, W. "Disentangling the Debate" in *Uneasy Partners: Multiculturalism and Rights in Canada* (Waterloo: Wilfrid Laurier University Press, 2007) 137–56.
Kymlicka, W. *Liberalism, Community, and Culture* (Oxford: Oxford University Press, 1989).
Kymlicka, W. *Multicultural Citizenship: A Liberal Theory of Minority Rights* (Oxford: Oxford University Press, 1995).
Kymlicka, W. "The Current State of Multiculturalism in Canada and Research Themes on Canadian Multiculturalism 2008–2010" Citizenship and Immigration Canada (Minister of Public Works and Government Services Canada, 2010).
Lacey, H. "Understanding Conflicts between North and South," in M. Dascal (ed), *Cultural Relativism and Philosophy: North and Latin American Perspectives* (Leiden: E.J. Brill, 1991) 243–62.

Ladeur, K.-H. and I. Augsberg. *Toleranz—Religion—Recht. Die Herausforderung des „neutralen" Staates durch neue Formen von Religiosität in der postmodernen Gesellschaft* (Tübingen: Mohr Siebeck, 2007).
Lam, M. C. "Multicultural Feminism: Cultural Concerns," in *International Encyclopedia of the Social & Behavioral Sciences* vol. 15 (Oxford: Pergamom Press, 2001) 10163.
Lamont, M. and L. Thevenot. "Introduction: Toward a Renewed Comparative Cultural Sociology," in *Rethinking Comparative Cultural Sociology* (Cambridge: Cambridge University Press, 2000).
Lapidoth, R. and M. Corinaldi. "Freedom of Religion in Israel," in A. M. Rabello (ed), *Israeli Reports to the XIV International Congress of Comparative Law* (Jerusalem: Harry and Michael Sacher Institute for Legislative Research and Comparative Law, 1994).
Larmore, C. "Public Reason," in S. Freeman (ed), *The Cambridge Companion to Rawls* (Cambridge: Cambridge University Press, 2003).
Larrière, C. "Grotius: droit naturel et sociabilité," in Louis-Léon Christians et al., dir, *Droit naturel: relancer l'histoire?* (Bruxelles: Bruylant, 2008), 293–330.
Layish, A. *Women and Islamic Law in a Non-Muslim State: A Study Based on Decisions of the Shari'a Courts in Israel* (New York: Wiley, 2006).
Layish, A. and S. H. Fallah, "Ha-Irgun ha-Adati shel ha-Druzim" [Communal Organization of the Druze], in *Ha-Aravim be-Yisra'el: Retsifut ve-Tmura* [The Arabs in Israel: Continuity and Change] (Jerusalem: Magnes Press, 1981) 123 (Hebrew).
Legaré, C. and A. Bougaief. *L'Empire du sacre Québécois* (Québec: Presses de l'Université du Québec, 1984).
Leibovitch, Y. "The Status of Women—Halakhah and Meta-Halakhah," in *Belief, History and Values* (Jerusalem: Acadon, 1982) 71.
Lerner, H. "Constitutional Incrementalism and Material Entrenchment" in Avi Sagi & Ohad Nachtomy, eds, *Multicultural Challenge in Israel* (Boston: Academic Studies Press, 2009).
Lévinas, E. *Entre Nous: Thinking-of-the-Other*, trans. M. Smith and B. Harshav (New York: Columbia University Press, 1998)
Levy, S. et al. *A Portrait of Israeli Jewry: Beliefs, Observations, and Values among Israeli Jews 2000* (Jerusalem: The Israeli Democracy Institute, 2002).
Levy, J. T. "Classifying Cultural Rights," in I. Shapiro and W. Kymlicka (eds), *Nomos XXXIX: Ethnicity and Group Rights* (New York: New York University Press, 1997).
Levy, J. T. *The Multiculturalism of Fear* (Oxford: Oxford University Press, 2000).
Lichtenstein, A. "Does Jewish Tradition Recognize an Ethic Independent of Halakha?," in M. Fox (ed), *Modern Jewish Ethics: Theory and Practice* (Columbus: Ohio State University Press, 1975).
Lienhardt, G. "Modes of Thought," in *The Institutions of Primitive Society: A Series of Broadcast Talks* (Glencoe: The Free Press, 1961) 95.
Lilla, M. *The Stillborn God: Religion, Politics and the Modern West* (New York: Knopf, 2007).
Lindbeck, G. A. *The Nature of Doctrine: Religion and Theology in a Postliberal Age* (Philadelphia: Westminster Press, 1984).
Linge, D. "Editor's Introduction to Philosophical Hermeneutics," in H.-G. Gadamer (ed), *Philosophical Hermeneutics*, translated by D. E. Linge (Berkeley and Los Angeles: University of California Press, 1976).
Lippert, R. K. *Sanctuary, Sovereignty, Sacrifice* (Vancouver: UBC Press, 2005).
Llewellyn, K. N. *The Bramble Bush* (Oxford: Oxford University Press, 2008).
Llewellyn, K. N. *The Common Law Tradition* (Boston and Toronto: Little Brown, 1960).
Luhmann, N. *Die Religion der Gesellschaft* (Frankfurt/M.: Suhrkamp, 2000).
Luhmann, N. *Funktion der Religion* (Frankfurt/M.: Suhrkamp, 1977).
Luhmann, N. "Funktionale Methode und juristische Entscheidung," in *Ausdifferenzierung des Rechts* (Frankfurt/M.: Suhrkamp, 1981).
Luhmann, N. "Funktionale Methode und Systemtheorie," in *Soziologische Aufklärung, Bd. 1*, 4th edn (Opladen: Westdeutscher Verlag, 1970).

Luhmann, N. *Grundrechte als Institution. Ein Beitrag zur politischen Soziologie*, 2nd edn (Berlin: Duncker & Humblot, 1975).
Luhmann, N. *Soziale Systeme. Grundriß einer allgemeinen Theorie*, 4th edn (Frankfurt/M.: Suhrkamp, 1994).
Lustick, I. *Arabs in the Jewish State: Israel's Control of a National Minority* (Austin and London: University of Texas Press, 1980).
Macdonald, R. A. *Lessons of Everyday Law* (Montreal: McGill-Queen's, 2002).
MacIntyre, A. *After Virtue: A Study in Moral Theory* (Notre Dame, IN: University of Notre Dame Press, 1981).
Maclure, J. and C. Taylor. *Laïcité et liberté de conscience* (Montréal: Boréal, 2010).
Maclure, J. "Multiculturalism and Political Morality" in D. Ivison, ed, *The Ashgate Research Companion to Multiculturalism* [Farnham: Ashgate, 2010] 39.
Mahmood, S. *Politics of Piety: The Islamic Revival and the Feminist Subject* (Princeton: Princeton University Press, 2005).
Makdisi, G. "Ethics in Islamic Traditionalist Doctrine," in *Religion, Law and Learning in Classical Islam* (Hampshire: Variorum, 1991) 336.
Malik, M. "'The Branch on Which We Sit': Multiculturalism, Minority Women and Family Law," in A. Diduck and K. O'Donovan (eds), *Feminist Perspectives on Family Law* (New York: Routledge, 2006) 211.
Maoz, A. "Constitutional Law," in I. Zamir, S. Colombo, and I. Zamir (eds), *The Law of Israel: General Survey* (Jerusalem: Hebrew University of Jerusalem, 1995).
Maoz, A. "Religious Human Rights in the State of Israel," in J. D. van der Vyver and J. Witte, Jr. (eds), *Religious Human Rights in Global Perspectives: Legal Perspectives* (The Hague: Kluwer, 1996) 349–90.
Maoz, A. "State and Religion in Israel," in M. Mor (ed), *International Perspectives on Church and State* (New York: Fordham University Press, 1994) 239.
Margalit, A. *The Decent Society* (Cambridge, MA: Harvard University Press, 1996).
Maroto, P. *Institutiones iuris canonici ad normam novi codicis* (Rome: Commentarioum pro Religiosis, 1921).
Marshall, T. H. *Citizenship and Social Class, and other Essays* (Cambridge: Cambridge University Press, 1950).
Martin, R. C., M. R. Woodward, and D. S. Atmaja. *Defenders of Reason in Islam: Mu'tazilism from Medieval School to Modern Symbol* (Oxford: Oneworld, 1997).
Marx, K. *On the Jewish Question* (Cincinnati: Hebrew Union College, 1958).
Mathieu, S. *La transmission du judaisme dans les couples mixtes* (Paris: Les Éditions de l'Atelier, 2009).
Mautner, M. *Law and the Culture of Israel* (Oxford: Oxford University Press, 2011).
Mautner, M. "Religion in Politics: Rawls and Habermas on Deliberation and Justification," in H. Dagan, S. Lifshitz, and Y. Z. Stern, eds, *The Role of Religion in Human Rights Discourse* (expected 2014).
Mazie, S. V. *Israel's Higher Law: Religion and Liberal Democracy in the Jewish State* (Lanham: Lexington Books, 2006).
McGahern, U. *Palestinian Christians in Israel: State Attitudes towards Non-Muslim in a Jewish State* (Abingdon, Oxon; New York: Routledge, 2011).
McGarvie, M. D. *One Nation Under Law: America's Early National Struggles to Separate Church and State* (DeKalb: Northern Illinois University Press, 2004).
Menon, U. "Neither Victim Nor Rebel: Feminism and the Morality of Gender and Family Life in a Hindu Temple Town," in R. A. Shweder, M. Minow, and H. R. Markus (eds), *Engaging Cultural Differences: The Multicultural Challenge in Liberal Democracies* (New York: Russell Sage, 2002) 288.
Meyer, J. P. (ed). *Democracy in America*, translated by G. Lawrence (New York: HarperCollins, 1969).

Migdal, J. S. and B. Kimmerling. "The Odd Man Out: Arabs in Israel," in J. S. Migdal (ed), *Through the Lens of Israel: Explorations in State and Society* (Albany: State University of New York Press, 2001) 173.

Milbank, J. *Theology and Social Theory: Beyond Secular Reason* (Oxford: Blackwell, 1993).

Mill, J. S., in S. M. Okin (ed). *The Subjection of Women* (Indiana: Hackett Publishing, 1988).

Mohamed, Y. *Fitra: The Islamic Conception of Human Nature* (London: Ta-Ha, 1996).

Mohanty, C. T. "Cartographies of Struggle: Third World Women and the Politics of Feminism," in C. T. Mohanty, A. Russo, and L. Torres (eds), *Third World Women and the Politics of Feminism* (Bloomington: Indiana University Press, 1991) 1.

Mohanty, C. T. "Under Western Eyes: Feminist Scholarship and Colonial Discourse," in C. T. Mohanty, A. Russo, and L. Torres (eds), *Third World Women and Feminism and the Politics of Feminism* (Bloomington: Indiana University Press, 1991) 51.

Moors, A. *Women, Property and Islam: Palestinian Experiences, 1920–1990* (New York: Cambridge University Press, 1995).

Morlok, M. *Selbstverständnis als Rechtskriterium* (Tübingen: Mohr Siebeck, 1993).

Morris, B. "Agents or Victims of Religious Ideology? Approaches to Locating Hasidic Women in Feminist Studies," in J. S. Belcove-Shalin (ed), *New World Hasidism: Ethnographic Studies of Hasidic Jews in America* (Albany: State University of New York Press, 1995) 161.

Moses, H. "From Religious Zionism to Post-Modern Religiosity" (PhD dissertation, Department of Political Science, Bar Ilan University, 2009) (Hebrew).

Moyn, S. *The Last Utopia: Human Rights in History* (Cambridge, MA: Harvard University Press, 2012).

Muckel, S. *Religiöse Freiheit und staatliche Letztentscheidung* (Berlin: Duncker & Humblot, 1997).

Muniz-Fraticelli, V. M. *The Structure of Pluralism* (Oxford: Oxford University Press, 2014).

Nader, A. W. *Le système philosophique des Muʻtazila: premiers penseurs de l'Islam* (Beyrouth: Les Lettres Orientales, 1956).

Nagel, T. *The History of Islamic Theology: From Muhammad to the Present* (Princeton, NJ: Wiener, 2000).

Nancy, J.-L. *Dis-Enclosure: The Deconstruction of Christianity* (New York: Fordham University Press, 2008).

Naz, R. "Infidèles," in *Dictionnaire de droit canonique*, vol. 5 (Paris: Letouzey et Ané, 1953).

Nelson, B. *The Idea of Usury. From Tribal Brotherhood to Universal Otherhood* (Princeton, NJ: Princeton University Press, 1969).

Neuhaus, D. M. "Between Quiescence and Arousal: The Political Functions of Religion, A Case Study of the Arab Minority in Israel: 1948–1990" (PhD dissertation, Hebrew University of Jerusalem, 1991).

Nonet, P. and P. Selznick. *Law and Society in Transition: Toward Responsive Law* (New York: Harper, 1978).

Noreau, P. "Référents religieux et rapport à la normativité: asymétrie des rapports au droit," in J.-F. Gaudreault-Desbiens, *Le droit, la religion et le raisonnable* (Montréal: Thémis, 2009) 383–423.

Novak, D. *Natural Law in Judaism* (Cambridge: Cambridge University Press, 1998).

Novak, D. *The Image of the Non-Jew in Judaism: An Historical and Constructive Study of the Noahide Laws* (New York and Toronto: Edwin Mellen Press, 1983).

Nussbaum, M. *Liberty of Conscience* (New York: Basic Books, 2010).

Nussbaum, M. C. *The New Religious Intolerance: Overcoming the Politics of Fear in an Anxious Age* (Cambridge, MA: Belknap Press, 2012).

Oakeshott, M. *On Human Conduct* (Oxford: Oxford University Press, 1975).

Obiora, L. A. "Female Excision: Cultural Concerns," *International Encyclopedia of the Social & Behavioral Sciences* vol. 8 (Oxford: Pergamom Press, 2001) 5442–5447.

Ockham, W. *Opera Theologica* vol. 5 (New York: Franciscan Institute Press, 1967–1986).

Okin, S. M. *Is Multiculturalism Bad for Women?* (Princeton: Princeton University Press, 1999).

Okin, S. M. "Is Multiculturalism Bad for Women?," in J. Cohen, M. Howard, and M. C. Nussbaum (eds), *Is Multiculturalism Bad For Women?* (Princeton, NJ: Princeton University Press, 1999) 7.
Oomen, B. and S. Tempelman. "The Power of Definition," in Y. Donders et al. (eds), *Law and Cultural Diversity* (Utrecht: SIM, 1999) 7.
Overing, J. "Translation as a Creative Process: The Power of the Name," in L. Holy (ed), *Comparative Anthropology* (Oxford: Blackwell, 1987).
Palmer, D. and D. Perrin, *Keep Sweet: Children of Polygamy* (Lister, BC: Dave's Press, 1994).
Parekh, B. "A Varied Moral Order," in J. Cohen, M. Howard, and M. C. Nussbaum (eds), *Is Multiculturalism Bad for Women?* (Princeton, NJ: Princeton University Press, 1999) 69.
Passerin d'Entrèves, M. *The Political Philosophy of Hannah Arendt* (London and New York: Routledge, 1994).
Patterson, O. *Freedom in the Making of Western Culture* (New York: Basic Books, 1991).
Peled, A. *Debating Islam in the Jewish State: The Development of Policy Toward Islamic Institutions in Israel* (Albany: State University of New York Press, 2001).
Peleg, I. and D. Waxman, *Israel's Palestinians, The Conflict Within* (Cambridge: Cambridge University Press, 2011).
Perry, M. *Toward a Theory of Human Rights* (Cambridge: Cambridge University Press, 2007).
Pettit, P. "Groups with Minds of their Own," in F. Schmitt (eds), *Socializing Metaphysics* (New York: Rowman and Littlefield, 2004) 167–93.
Pettit, P. *Republicanism: A Theory of Freedom and Government* (Oxford: Oxford University Press, 1997).
Philips, A. *Multiculturalism without Culture* (Princeton, NJ: Princeton University Press, 2007).
Pinto, M. "Who is Afraid of Language Rights in Israel" in A. Sagi & O. Nachtomy, eds, *The Multicultural Challenge in Israel* (Boston: Academic Studies Press, 2009).
Pollack, D. *Säkularisierung—ein moderner Mythos?* (Tübingen: Mohr Siebeck, 2003).
Rabbi Sg'r, "Between Personal Perfection and Social Labeling: 'Talmud Torah' for Women According to the Rambam," in Z. Maor, ed, *The Two Great Lightings: Women's Equality in the Family from a New Jewish Point of View* ({{fix}}publication info: 2007) 35 (Hebrew).
Raday, F. "Kol ha-Isha ba-Demokratiya ha-Yisra'elit" ["The Woman's Voice in the Israeli Democracy"], in R. Cohen-Almagor, ed, *Sugiyot Yessod ba-Demokratiya ha-Yisra'elit [Basic Issues in Israeli Democracy]* (Tel-Aviv: Po'alim Library, 1999) 143.
Rakover, N. *Law and the Noahides: Law as a Universal Value* (Jerusalem: The Library of Jewish Law, 1998).
Rasch, W. *Niklas Luhmann's Modernity: The Paradoxes of Differentiation* (Stanford: Stanford University Press, 2000).
Ravitzky, A. and Y. Z. Stern, eds, *The Jewishness of Israel* (Jerusalem: The Israel Democracy Institute, 2007).
Rawls, J. *A Theory of Justice* (Cambridge, MA: Belknap Press, 1971).
Rawls, J. *Political Liberalism* (New York: Columbia University Press, 2005).
Rawls, J. *The Law of Peoples* (Cambridge, MA: Harvard University Press, 1999).
Raz, J. "How Perfect Should One Be? And Whose Culture Is It?," in J. Cohen, M. Howard, and M. C. Nussbaum (eds), *Is Multiculturalism Bad for Women?* (Princeton, NJ: Princeton University Press, 1999) 95.
Raz, J. "Multiculturalism: A Liberal Perspective," in *Ethics in the Public Domain: Essays in the Morality of Law and Politics* (Oxford: Clarendon Press, 1994) 155.
Raz, J. *Practical Reason and Norms* (New York: Oxford University Press, 1999).
J. Raz, *The Morality of Freedom* (New York: Oxford University Press, 1986).
Rebhun, U. and G. Malach, *Demographic Trends in Israel* (Jerusalem: The Metzila Center, 2009)
Reinhart, A. K. *Before Revelation: The Boundaries of Muslim Moral Thought* (Albany: State University of New York Press, 1995).
Reitman, O. "On Exit," in A. Eisenberg and J. Spinner-Halev (eds), *Minorities within Minorities: Equality, Rights and Diversity* (Cambridge: Cambridge University Press, 2005) 189–208.

Renteln, A.D. *The Cultural Defense* (Oxford: Oxford University Press, 2004).
Rivers, J. "Religious Liberty as a Collective Right," in R. O'Dair and A. Lewis (eds), *Law and Religion* (Oxford: Oxford University Press, 2001).
Rockefeller, S. C. "Comment," in A. Gutmann (ed), *Multiculturalism and "The Politics of Recognition"* (Princeton, NJ: Princeton University Press, 1992) 87.
Rohe, M. *Das islamische Recht*, 2nd edn (Munich: C.H. Beck, 2009).
Rorty, R. "Solidarity," in *Contingency, Irony, and Solidarity* (Cambridge: Cambridge University Press, 1989).
Rosen, L. *Law as Culture: An Invitation* (Princeton, NJ Princeton University Press, 2006).
Rosen-Zvi, I. "Pigs in Space: Geographic Separatism in Multicultural Societies," in M. Freeman (ed), *Law and Sociology: Current Legal Issues 2005* vol. 8 (Oxford: Oxford University Press, 2006) 225.
Rosenblum, N. *Membership and Morals* (Princeton, NJ: Princeton University Press, 1998).
Rosen-Zvi, I. *Taking Space Seriously: Law, Space and Society in Contemporary Israel* (Aldershot: Ashgate, 2004).
Ross, T. "The 'Holy Rebellion' of Religious Zionist Women as a Bridge Between Halakhah and Democracy," in A. Sagi and D. Schwartz (eds), *A Hundred Years of Religious Zionism*, vol. 3 (Ramat Gan: Bar Ilan University Press, 2003) (Hebrew).
Rubel, P. G. and A. Rosman (eds). *Translating Cultures: Perspectives on Translation and Anthropology* (Oxford and New York: Berg, 2003).
Rubin, E. *Bouquet of Memories* (Steimatzky, 1999).
Rubinstein, A. and B. Medina. *Ha-Mishpat ha-Hukati shel Medinat Yisra'el* [*The Constitutional Law of the State of Israel*], 6th edn (Jerusalem: Schocken, 2005) (Hebrew).
Ruokkannen, M. *The Catholic Doctrine of Non-Christian Religions According to the Second Vatican Council* (Leiden and New York: Köln, Brill, 1992).
Ryan, M. P. "Gender and Public Access: Women's Politics in Nineteenth-Century America," in C. Calhoun (ed), *Habermas and the Public Sphere* (Cambridge, MA: MIT Press, 2002) 259–88.
Sachedina, A. *The Islamic Roots of Democratic Pluralism* (Oxford: Oxford University Press, 2001).
Sagi, A. & O. Nachtomy. "Introduction" in A. Sagi & O. Nachtomy, eds, *Multicultural Challenge in Israel* (Boston: Academic Studies Press, 2009).
Sahlins, M. *Islands of History* (Chicago: University of Chicago Press, 1985) chapters 1, 4.
Sandel, M. J. *Democracy's Discontent* (Cambridge, MA: Belknap Press of Harvard University Press, 1996) 323.
Sandel, M. "Freedom of Conscience or Freedom of Choice," in J. D. Hunter and O. Guinness (eds), *Articles of Faith, Articles of Peace* (Washington, DC: Brookings Institution Press, 1990).
Sandel, M. *Liberalism and the Limits of Justice* (Cambridge: Cambridge University Press, 1982).
Sarles, H. B. "Cultural Relativism and Critical Naturalism," in M. Dascal (ed), *Cultural Relativism and Philosophy: North and Latin American Perspectives* (Leiden: E.J. Brill, 1991) 195–214.
Scanlon, T. M. "Rawls on Justification," in S. Freeman (ed), *The Cambridge Companion to Rawls* (Cambridge: Cambridge University Press, 2003) 139.
Scanlon, T. M. *The Difficulty of Tolerance: Essays in Political Philosophy* (Cambridge: Cambridge University Press, 2003).
Schacht, J. *An Introduction to Islamic Law* (Oxford: Clarendon Press, 1982).
Schlaich, K. *Neutralität als verfassungsrechtliches Prinzip* (Tübingen: Mohr Siebeck, 1972).
Schmitt, C. *Political Theology: Four Chapters on the Concept of Sovereignty* (Chicago: University of Chicago Press, 2006).
Schwartz, S. B. (ed). *Implicit Understandings: Observing, Reporting, and Reflecting on the Encounters between Europeans and Other Peoples in the Early Modern Era* (Cambridge: Cambridge University Press, 1994).

Schweid, E. "The Sabbath in Israel," in Uri Dromi, ed, *Brethern Dwelling Together: Orthodoxy and Non-Orthodoxy in Israel—Positions, Propositions, and Accords* (Jerusalem: The Israel Democracy Institute, 2005), 220.

Seligman, "Introduction," in A. Seligman ed, *Religion and Human Rights: Conflict or Convergence* (Hollis, NH: Hollis Publishing Company, 2005), 12.

Seligman, A., R. P. Waller, M. J. Puett, and B. Simon. *Ritual and Its Consequences: An Essay on the Limits of Sincerity* (Oxford: Oxford University Press, 2008) 103.

Sewell Jr., W. H. "The Concept(s) of Culture," in V. E. Bonnell and L. Hunt (eds), *Beyond the Cultural Turn: New Directions in the Study of Society and Culture* (Berkeley and Los Angeles: University of California Press, 1999) 35.

Shachar, A. *Multicultural Jurisdiction: Cultural Differences and Women's Rights* (Cambridge: Cambridge University Press, 2001).

Shafir, G. and Y. Peled, *Being Israeli: The Dynamics of Multiple Citizenship* (New York: Cambridge University Press, 2002).

Shell-Duncan, B. and Y. Hernlund (eds). *Female "Circumcision" in Africa: Culture, Controversy, and Change* (Boulder: Lynne Rienner, 2000).

Shifman, P. *One Language, Different Tongues* (Jerusalem: Shalom Hartman Institute, 2012) (Hebrew).

Shih, S.-M. "Toward an Ethics of Transnational Encounters, or 'When' Does a 'Chinese' Woman Become a 'Feminist'?," in M. Waller and S. Marcos (eds), *Dialogue and Difference: Feminisms Challenge Globalization* (New York: Palgrave Macmillan, 2005) 3.

Shmueli, M. "The Power to Define Tradition: Feminist Challenges to Religion and the Israeli Supreme Court" (PhD dissertation, University of Toronto, 2005).

Shweder, R. A. "Anthropology's Romantic Rebellion against the Enlightenment, or There's More to Thinking than Reason and Evidence," in R. A. Shweder and R. A. Levine (eds), *Culture Theory: Essays on Mind, Self, and Emotion* (Cambridge: Cambridge University Press, 1984) 27–66.

Shweder, R. A. *Thinking Through Cultures: Expeditions in Cultural Psychology* (Cambridge, MA: Harvard University Press, 1991).

Shweder, R. A. "'What About Female Genital Mutilation?' and Why Understanding Culture Matters in the First Place," in R. A. Shweder, M. Minow, and H. R. Markus (eds), *Engaging Cultural Differences: The Multicultural Challenge in Liberal Democracies* (New York: Russell Sage Foundation, 2002) 216.

Skinner, Q. *Foundations of Modern Political Thought* (Cambridge: Cambridge University Press, 1978).

Smith, A. *The Theory of Moral Sentiment*, 2nd edn (London: A. Millar, 1761).

Song, S. *Justice, Gender, and the Politics of Multiculturalism* (Cambridge: Cambridge University Press, 2007).

Stackhouse, M. "Why Human Rights Need God: A Christian Perspective," in B. Barnett and E. M. Bucar, eds, *Does Human Rights Need God* (Grand Rapids: Wm. B. Eerdmans Publishing Company, 2005).

Stone, J. *Human Law and Human Justice* (Stanford: Stanford University Press, 1968).

Stone, S. L. "Law Without Nation? The Ongoing Jewish Discussion," in A. Sarat, L. Douglas, and M. Merrill Umphrey (eds), *Law Without Nation* (Stanford: Stanford University Press, 2011) 101–38.

Stone, S. L. "Religion and Human Rights: Babel or Translation, Conflict or Convergence?" in *Proceedings of the Israel Democracy Institute* (forthcoming).

Strauss, L. *Natural Right and History* (Chicago: University of Chicago Press, 1953).

Sultany, N. *Citizens without Citizenship* (Haifa: Mada, Arab Center for Applied Social Research, 2003).

Swaine, L. *The Liberal Conscience* (New York: Columbia University Press, 2008).

Tabory, E. "The Israel Reform and Conservative Movements and the Market for Liberal Judaism," in U. Rebhun and C. I. Waxman (eds), *Jews in Israel: Contemporary Social and*

*Cultural Patterns* (Hanover and London: University Press of New England and Brandeis University Press, 2004).
Talmon, J. L. "National Revival," in D. Ohana, ed, *The Riddle of the Present and the Cunning of History* (Jerusalem: The Bialik Institute, 2000) 68, at 69 (Hebrew).
Tannenbaum, M. "Multiculturalism in Israel: A Linguistic Perspective" in A. Sagi & O. Nachtomy, eds, *The Multicultural Challenge in Israel* (Boston: Academic Studies Press, 2009).
Taylor, C. *A Secular Age* (Cambridge, MA: Belknap Press, 2007).
Taylor, C. *Multiculturalism* (Princeton: Princeton University Press, 1994) 44.
Taylor, C. *Philosophy and the Human Sciences* (Cambridge: Cambridge University Press, 1985).
Taylor, C. *Sources of the Self—The Making of Modern Identity* (Cambridge: Harvard University Press, 1989).
Taylor, C. "The Politics of Recognition," in A. Gutmann (ed), *Multiculturalism and "The Politics of Recognition"* (Princeton, NJ: Princeton University Press, 1992) 25.
Taylor, C. "Understanding the Other: A Gadamerian View on Conceptual Schemes," in J. Malpas, U. Arnswald, and J. Kertscher (eds), *Gadamer's Century* (Cambridge, MA: MIT Press, 2002).
Taylor, C. et al. *Multiculturalism: Examining the Politics of Recognition* (Princeton, NJ: Princeton University Press, 1994).
Tessler, M. A. "The Middle East: The Jews in Tunisia and Morocco and Arabs in Israel," in R. G. Wirsing (ed), *Protection of Ethnic Minorities: Comparative Perspectives* (New York: Pergamon Press, 1981) 245.
*The Doctrine and Covenants of the Church of Jesus Christ of Latter-day Saints.*
Thevenot, L. and M. Lamont. "Conclusion: Exploring the French and American Polity," in M. Lamont and L. Thevenot, eds, *Rethinking Comparative Cultural Sociology* (Cambridge: Cambridge University Press, 2000) 307.
Tibi, B. *Political Islam, World Politics and Europe: Democratic Peace and Euro-Islam versus Global Jihad* (Abingdon: Routledge, 2007).
Tierney, B. "Natural Law and Natural Rights," in J. Witte, Jr. and F. S. Alexander (eds), *Christianity and Law* (Cambridge: Cambridge University Press, 2008).
Tierney, B. "Religious Rights: A Historical Perspective," in N. B. Reynolds and W. Cole Durham (eds), *Religious Liberty in Western Thought* (Atlanta: Scholars Press, 1996) 29–57.
Touma-Sliman, A. "Culture, National Minority and the State: Working Against the 'Crime of Family Honour' within the Palestinian Community in Israel," in L. Welchman and S. Hossain (eds), *Honour: Crimes, Paradigms and Violence against Women* (London: Zed Books, 2005) 181.
Tuchman, B.W. *The March of Folly: From Troy to Vietnam* (New York: Ballantine Books, 1984).
Uertz, R. *Vom Gottesrecht zum Menschenrecht. Das katholische Staatsdenken in Deutschland von der Französischen Revolution bis zum II. Vatikanischen Konzil (1789–1965)* (Paderborn: Schoeningh, 2005).
Valadez, J. M. *Deliberative Democracy, Political Legitimacy, and Self-Determination in Multicultural Societies* (Boulder: Westview Press, 2001).
Vattimo, G. *After Christianity* (New York: Columbia University Press, 2002).
Vattimo, G. *Belief* (Stanford: Stanford University Press, 1999).
Vico, G. *The New Science of Giambattista Vico*, translated by T. G. Bergin and M. H. Fisch (Ithaca, NY: Cornell University Press, 1984).
Viroli, M. *Republicanism* (New York: Hill and Wang, 1999).
Vitta, E. *The Conflict of Laws in Matters of Personal Status in Palestine* (Tel Aviv: Bursi, 1947).
von Daniels, J. *Religiöses Recht als Referenz. Jüdisches Recht im rechtswissenschaftlichen Vergleich* (Tübingen: Mohr Siebeck 2009).
Von Kues, N. "De venatione sapientiae," in L. Gabriel, ed, *N. von Kues, Philosophisch-Theologische Schriften*, Vol. 1 (Wien: Herder, 1964).

Von Ungern-Sternberg, A. *Religionsfreiheit in Europa. Die Freiheit individueller Religionsausübung in Großbritannien, Frankreich und Deutschland—ein Vergleich* (Tübingen: Mohr Siebeck, 2008).
Wagner, R. *The Invention of Culture*, rev ed (Englewood Cliffs, NJ: Prentice-Hall, 1975).
Wahrhaftig, Z. "Medinat Yisra'el ke-Medina Yehudit" ["The State of Israel as a Jewish State"], in M. Rotenberg, ed, *Ha-Dat ve-ha-Medina [Religion and the State]* (Tel-Aviv: The National Religious Party Public Relations Dept., 1964) 72 (Hebrew).
Waldhoff, C. *Neue Religionskonflikte und staatliche Neutralität—Erfordern weltanschauliche und religiöse Entwicklungen Antworten des Staates?, Gutachten D für den 68. Deutschen Juristentag* (Munich: C.H. Beck, 2010).
Walzer, M. "Comment," in A. Gutmann (ed), *Multiculturalism and "The Politics of Recognition"* (Princeton, NJ: Princeton University Press, 1992) 99.
Walzer, M. *On Toleration* (New Haven, CT: Yale University Press, 1997).
Walzer, M. *Spheres of Justice* (New York: Basic Books, 1983).
Watson, A. *Legal Transplants: An Approach to Comparative Law*, 2nd edn (Athens: University of Georgia Press, 1993).
Weber, M. "Religious Rejections of the World and their Directions," in B. S. Turner (ed), *From Max Weber: Essays in Sociology* (Abingdon, Oxon: Routledge, 1991).
Weeramantry, C. G. *Islamic Jurisprudence: An International Perspective* (London: Macmillan, 1988).
Weinroth, A. *Feminism and Judaism* (Tel Aviv: Yedioth Ahronoth Publishers, 2001) (Hebrew).
Weiss, B. G. *The Spirit of Islamic Law* (Athens and London: University of Georgia Press, 1998).
Weiss, S. M. and N. C. Gross-Horowitz. *Marriage and Divorce in the Jewish State* (Lebanon, NH: Brandeis University Press, 2013).
Weizman, E. *The Least of All Possible Evils: Humanitarian Violence from Arendt to Gaza* (London: Verso, 2012).
White, J. B. "Talking about Religion in the Language of the Law" in J. B. White (ed), *From Expectation to Experience: Essays on Law and Legal Education* (Ann Arbor: University of Michigan Press, 1999).
Willke, H. *Stand und Kritik der neueren Grundrechtstheorie. Schritte zu einer normativen Systemtheorie* (Berlin: Duncker & Humblot, 1975).
Witte, J. *The Reformation of Human Rights: Law, Religion, and Human Rights in Early Modern Calvinism* (Cambridge: Cambridge University Press, 2008).
Witte Jr., J. and F. S. Alexander (eds). *Christianity and Human Rights: An Introduction* (New York: Cambridge University Press, 2010).
Wittgenstein, L. *Philosophical Investigations*, translated by G. E. M. Anscombe (New York: Macmillan, 1953).
Wolterstorff, N. *Justice: Rights and Wrongs* (Princeton, NJ: Princeton University Press, 2008).
"Women," in *Encyclopedia Judaica*, vol. 21, 2nd edn (Farmington Hills, MI: Gale, 2007).
"Women," in *Oztar Israel Encyclopedia*, vol. 7 (1924) 117 (Hebrew).
Wu, Y. "Making Sense in Chinese 'Feminism'/Women's Studies," in M. R. Waller and S. Marcos (eds), *Dialogue and Difference: Feminisms Challenge Globalization* (New York: Palgrave Macmillan, 2005) 29.
Wuthnow, R. *Meaning and Moral Order: Explorations in Cultural Analysis* (Berkeley: University in California Press, 1987).
Wuthnow, R. et al. *Cultural Analysis* (Boston: Routledge & Kegan, 1984).
Yakobson, A. and A. Rubinstein, *Yisra'el u-Mishpahat ha-Amim: Medinat Le'om Yehudit ve-Zekhuyot ha-Adam [Israel and the Family of Nations: Jewish Nation-State and Human Rights]* (London: Routledge, 2003) at 150–65 (Hebrew)
Young, I. M. *Justice and the Politics of Difference* (Princeton, NJ: Princeton University Press, 1990).
Zamir, I. and A. Zysblat. *Public Law in Israel* (Oxford: Clarendon Press, 1996).

Ziv, N. and C. Tirosh, "The Legal Battle against the Screening of Candidates to Communal Settlements: A Trap in a Pierced and Muddy Web," in A. Lehavi (ed), *Gated Communities* (Nevo Press, 2010) 311.

*Articles*

Abbas, T. "Recent Developments in British Multicultural Theory, Policy, and Practice: The Case of British Muslims" 9:2 *Citizenship Studies* (2005) 153–166.

Abizadeh, A. "'Because Baha'u'llah Said So': Dealing With a Non-starter in Moral Reasoning," 5:1 *Baha'i Studies Review* (1995) 83–85.

Achour, Y. B. "L'idea di giustizia naturale nel pensiero giuridico sunnita" 4 *Daimon. Annuario di diritto comparato delle religioni* (2004) 225–242.

Ackerman, B. "Why Dialogue?," 86 *Journal of Philosophy* (1989) 5–22.

American Anthropological Association. "Statement on Human Rights," 49 *American Anthropologist* (1947) 539–43.

Allen, C. "Down with Multiculturalism, Book-burning and Fatwas" 8:2 *Culture and Religion* (2007) 125–138.

Asad, T. "Multiculturalism and British Identity in the Wake of the Rushdie Affair" 18 *Politics & Society* (1990) 455–480.

Augsberg, I. "Die Entstehung des neutralen Staates als Vorgang der Säkularisation," 53 *Zeitschrift für evangelisches Kirchenrecht* (2008) 445–455.

Baehr, A. R. "Toward a New Feminist Liberalism: Okin, Rawls and Habermas," 11:1 *Hypatia* (1996) 49–66.

Bailey, M. et al. "Expanding Recognition of Foreign Polygamous Marriages: Implications for Canada," Queen's University Legal Studies Research Paper No. 07-12, available online (SSRN): <http://papers.ssrn.com/sol3/papers.cfm?abstract_id=1023896##>.

Barron, D. J. "The Promise of Cooley's City: Traces of Local Constitutionalism," 147 *University of Pennsylvania Law Review* (1999) 487–612.

Bartlett, K. T. "Feminist Legal Methods," 103 *Harvard Law Review* (1990) 829–88.

Batnitzky, L. "From Politics to Law: Modern Jewish Thought and the Invention of Jewish Law," 26/27 *Diné Israel: Studies in Halakhah and Jewish Law* (2009) 7–44.

Bhandar, B. "The Ties that Bind: Multiculturalism and Secularism Reconsidered," 36:3 *Journal of Law and Society* (2009) 301–326.

Billie, B. M. "The Lost Boys of Polygamy: Is Emancipation the Answer?" 12 *Journal of Gender Race & Justice* (2008–2009) 127–152.

Blank, Y. "Brown in Jerusalem: A Comparative Look on Race and Ethnicity in Public Schools," 38 *The Urban Lawyer* (2006) 367–436.

Bleich, J. D. "Judaism and Natural Law" 7 *Jewish Law Annual* (1988) 5–42.

Blidstein, G. "'Ideal' and 'Real' in Classical Jewish Political Theory," 2 *Jewish Political Studies Review* (1990) 43–66.

Blidstein, G. "On Political Structures: Four Medieval Comments," 22 *Jewish Journal of Sociology* (1980) 47–58.

Blidstein, G. "Rabbi Yohanan, Idolatry, and Public Privilege" (1974) 5:2 *Journal for the Study of Judaism* 154–61.

Brightman, R. "Forget Culture: Replacement, Transcendence, Relexification," 10 *Cultural Anthropology* (1995) 509–546.

Bunting, A. "Theorizing Women's Cultural Diversity in Feminist International Human Rights Strategies," 20 *Journal of Law and Society* 6–22 (1993).

Campbell, A. "Bountiful's Plural Marriages," 6:4 *International Journal of Law in Context* (2010) 341–61.

Campbell, A. "Bountiful Voices," 47 *Osgoode Hall Law Journal* (2009) 183–234.

Chéhata, C. "La religion et les fondements du droit en Islam," 18 *Archives de philosophie du droit* (1973) 17–26.

Chigier, M. "The Rabbinical Courts in the State of Israel" 2 *Israel Law Review* (1967) 145–166.
Cohen-Almagor, R. "Cultural Pluralism and the Israeli Nation-Building Ideology" 27 *International Journal of Middle East Studies* (1995) 461–484.
Cohn, M. "Women, Religious Law and Religious Courts in Israel—The Jewish Case" 27 *Retfærd: Nordic Journal of Law and Justice* (2004) 57–76.
Cossman, B. "Turning the Gaze Back on Itself: Comparative Law, Feminist Legal Studies, and the Postcolonial Project," 2 *Utah Law Review* (1997) 525–544.
Cover, R. "The Supreme Court, 1982 Term: Foreword: *Nomos and Narrative*," 97 *Harvard Law Review* (1983) 4–68.
Dienstag, J. I. "Natural Law in Maimonidean Thought and Scholarship" 6 *Jewish Law Annual* (1987) 64–77.
DiMaggio, P. "Culture and Cognition," 23 *Annual Review of Sociology* (1997) 263–287.
Dorff, E. "Judaism as a Religious Legal System," 29 *Hastings Law Journal* (1977–78) 1331–360.
El-Or, T. "The Length of the Slits and the Spread of Luxury: Reconstructing the Subordination of Ultra-Orthodox Jewish Women through the Patriarchy of Men Scholars," 29:9/10 *Sex Roles* (1993) 585–98.
England, I. "Law and Religion in Israel," 35 *American Journal of Comparative Law* (1987) 185–208.
Faur, J. "Understanding the Covenant," 9 *Tradition* (Spring 1968) 33–55.
Fernando, M. L. "Reconfiguring Freedom: Muslim Piety and the Limits of Secular Law and Public Discourse in France" 37:1 *American Ethnologist* (2010) 19–35.
Ferrari, S. "Adapting Divine Law to Change: The Experience of the Roman Catholic Church (With Some Reference to Jewish and Islamic Law)," 28:1 *Cardozo Law Review* (October 2006) 53–66.
Fonrobert, C. E. "Neighborhood as Ritual Space: The Case of the Rabbinic Eruv," 10 *Archiv für Religionsgeschichte* (2008) 239–58.
Ford, R. T. "Law's Territory (A History of Jurisdiction)," 97 *Michigan Law Review* (1999) 843–930.
Fox, J. "Separation of Church and State in Stable Christian Democracies: Fact or Myth?" 1 *Journal of Law, Religion & State* (2012) 60.
Fox, M. "Maimonides and Aquinas on Natural Law," 5 *Diné Israel* (1972), pp. V–XXXVI.
Frug, G. E. "The City as a Legal Concept," 93 *Harvard Law Review* (1980) 1057–1154.
Galanter, M. and J. Krishnan. "Personal Law and Human Rights in India and Israel," 34 *Israel Law Review* (2000) 101–133.
Gallie, W. B. "Essentially Contested Concepts," 56 *Proceedings of the Aristotelian Society, n.s.* (1956) 167–98.
Galston, W. A. "Two Concepts of Liberalism," 105 *Ethics* (1995) 516.
Garcea, J. "Postulations on the Fragmentary Effects of Multiculturalism in Canada" 40:1 *Canadian Ethnic Studies* (2008) 141–160.
Garcea, J. A. Kirova & L. Wong, "Introduction: Multiculturalism Discourses in Canada" 40:1 *Canadian Ethnic Studies* (2008) 1–10.
Garnett, R. "The Freedom of the Church," *Journal of Catholic Social Thought* 4 (2007) 59–86.
Gavison, R. "Feminism and the Public/Private Distinction," 45 *Stanford Law Review* (1992) 1–45.
Gavison, R. "Jewish and Democratic? A Rejoinder to the 'Ethnic Democracy' Debate," 4 *Israel Studies* (1999) 44–72.
Genut, B. E. "Competing Visions of the Jewish State: Promoting and Protecting Freedom of Religion in Israel," 19:5 *Fordham International Law Journal* (1996) 2120–2179.
Gerken, H. K. "Dissenting by Deciding," 57 *Stanford Law Review* (2005) 1745.
Ghanem, A. "State and Minority in Israel: The Case of Ethnic State and the Predicament of Its Minority" 21 *Ethnic & Racial Studies* (1998) 428–448.
Gottschalk, R. "Personal Status and Religious Law in Israel," 4 *International Law Quarterly* (1951) 454–461.

Greenberg, B. "Ultra-Orthodox Women Confront Feminism," 63 *Moment* (June 1996) 36.
Green, L. "Rights of Exit" 4 *Legal Theory* (1998) 165–185.
Greene, A. S. "Kiryas Joel and Two Mistakes about Equality," 96 *Columbia Law Review* (1996) 1–86.
Gunning, I. R. "Arrogant Perception, World-Travelling and Multicultural Feminism: The Case of Female Genital Surgeries," 23 *Columbia Human Rights Law Review* (1991–92) 189–248.
Gutmann, A. "The Challenge of Multiculturalism in Political Ethics," 22 *Philosophy & Public Affairs* (1993) 171–206.
Habermas, J. "Religion in the Public Sphere," 14:1 *European Journal of Philosophy* (2006) 1–25.
Hamilton, M. A. "*Employment Division v. Smith* at the Supreme Court: The Justices, the Litigants, and the Doctrinal Discourse" 32 *Cardozo Law Review* (2011) 1671–1699.
Harel, A. "Benign Segregation: A Case Study of the Practice of Gender Separation in Buses in the Ultra-Orthodox Community," 20 *South African Journal on Human Rights* (2004) 64–85.
Harman, G. "Moral Relativism Defended," 84 *Philosophical Review* (1975) 3–22.
Hirschmann, N. J. "Eastern Veiling, Western Freedom?," 59 *Review of Politics* (1997) 461–488.
Hoffe, O. "Human Rights in Intercultural Discourse: Cultural Concerns," 10 *International Encyclopedia of the Social & Behavioral Sciences* (2001) 7018–7025.
Horwitz, M. J. "Republicanism and Liberalism in American Constitutional Thought," 29 *William & Mary Law Review* (1987) 57–74.
Jackson, B. "The Jewish View of Natural Law," 52:1 *Journal of Jewish Studies* (Spring 2001) 136–45.
Kahn, R. A. "Are Muslims the New Catholics? Europe's Headscarf Laws in Comparative Historical Perspective," 21 *Duke Journal of Comparative & International Law* (2011) 567–94.
Kamali, M. H. "Methodological Issues in Islamic Jurisprudence," 11:1 *Arab Law Quarterly* (1996) 3–33.
Karayanni, M. M. "In the Best Interests of the Group: Religious Matching under Israeli Adoption Law," 3 *Berkeley Journal of Middle East & Islamic Law* (2010) 101–74.
Karayanni, M. M. "Living in a Group of One's Own: Normative Implications Related to the Private Nature of the Religious Accommodations for the Palestinian-Arab Minority in Israel," 6 *UCLA Journal of of Islamic & Near Eastern Law* (2007) 1–46.
Karayanni, M.M. "Multiculture Me No More! On Multicultural Qualifications and the Palestinian-Arab Minority of Israel" 54:3 *Diogenes* (2007) 39–58.
Karayanni, M. M. "The Myth and Reality of a Controversy: 'Public Factors' and the Forum Non Conveniens Doctrine," 21 *Wisconsin International Law Journal* (2003) 327.
Karayanni, M. M. "Rikoshetim Yehudi'im ve-Deimokrati'im" ["Jewish and Democratic Ricochets"] 9 *Mishpat u-Mimshal* (2006) 461.
Karayanni, M. M. "The Separate Nature of the Religious Accommodations for the Palestinian-Arab Minority in Israel," 5 *Northwestern University Journal of International Human Rights* (2006) 41–71.
Karayanni, M. M. "Two Concepts of Group Rights for the Palestinian-Arab minority under Israel's Constitutional Definition as a 'Jewish and Democratic' State" 10 *International Journal of Constitutional Law* (2012) 304–339.
Kedar, A. (Sandy), "'A First Step in a Difficult and Sensitive Road'—Preliminary Observations on Qaadan v. Katzir" 16 *Israel Studies Bulletin* (2000) 3–11.
Kimmerling, B. "Sociology, Ideology, and Nation-Building: The Palestinians and Their Meaning in Israeli Sociology" 57 *American Sociological Review* (1992) 446–460.
Kirschner, S. R. "'Then What Have I To Do with Thee?': On Identity, Fieldwork, and Ethnographic Knowledge," 2 *Cultural Anthropology* (1987) 211–234.
Kleinhans, M.-M. and R. A. Macdonald. "What Is a *Critical* Legal Pluralism?," 12 *Canadian Journal of Law & Society* (1997) 25–46.
Kronman, A. T. "Precedent and Tradition," 99 *Yale Law Journal* (1990) 1029–68.
Kukathas, C. "Are There Any Cultural Rights?" 20 *Political Theory* (1992) 105–139.

Kymlicka, W. "The Rights of Minority Cultures: Reply to Kukathas" 20 *Political Theory* (1992) 140–146.
Labelle, M. "Les intellectuels québécois face au multiculturalisme: hétérogénéité des approches et des projets politiques" 40:1 *Canadian Ethnic Studies* (2008) 33–56.
Ladeur, K.-H. "The Myth of the Neutral State and the Individualization of Religion: The Relationship Between State and Religion in the Face of Fundamentalism," 30 *Cardozo Law Review* (2009) 2445–471.
Ladeur, K.-H. and I. Augsberg. "The Myth of the Neutral State: The Relationship between State and Religion in the Face of New Challenges," 8 *German Law Journal* (2007), 143–52.
Lamm, N. and A. Kirschenbaum. "Freedom and Constraint in the Jewish Judicial Process," 1 *Cardozo Law Review* (1979), 105–20.
Legrand, P. "The Impossibility of 'Legal Transplants'" 4 *Maastricht Journal of European & Comparative Law* (1997) 111–124.
Luckman, T. "Shrinking Transcendence, Explaining Religion?" 50:2 *Sociological Analysis* (1990) 127.
Luhmann, N. "Einige Probleme mit „reflexivem Recht"," 6 *Zeitschrift für Rechtssoziologie* (1985) 1–18.
Macedo, S. "Liberal Civic Education and Religious Fundamentalism: The Case of God v. John Rawls," 105 *Ethics* (1995) 468–496.
MacIntyre, A. "Relativism, Power, Philosophy," 59 *Proceedings and Addresses of the American Philosophical Association* (1985) 5–22.
MacKinnon, C. A. "Sex Equality under the Constitution of India: Problems, Prospects, and 'Personal Laws'," 4 *International Journal of Constitutional Law* (2006) 181–202.
Madison, J. "The Federalist No. 10," an essay published 22 November 1787.
Madood, T. "Remaking Multiculturalism after 7/7" (2005), Open Democracy online: http://www.opendemocracy.net/conflict-terrorism/multiculturalism_2879.jsp
Mancini, S. "To Be or Not To Be Jewish: The UK Supreme Court Answers the Question; Judgment of 16 December 2009, R v The Governing Body of JFS, 2009 UKSC15," 6 *European Constitutional Law Review* (2010) 481–502.
Maoz, A. "Can Judaism Serve as a Source of Human Rights?" 64 *Zeitschrift für Ausländisches öffentliches Recht und Völkerrecht* (2004) n. 3, 677–722.
Maoz, A. "Enforcement of Religious Courts' Judgments under Israeli Law," 33 *Journal of Church and State* (1991) 473–494.
Marmor, A. "The Dilemma of Authority," 2 *Jurisprudence* (2011) 121, available online: http://ssrn.com/abstract=1593191.
Martinez, A. "Cultural Contact: Archaeological Approaches," 5 *International Encyclopedia of the Social & Behavioral Sciences* (2001) 3035.
Matsuda, M. J. "Pragmatism Modified and the False Consciousness Problem," 63 *Southern California Law Review* (1989–90) 1763–782.
Mautner, M. "From 'Honor' to 'Dignity': How Should a Liberal State Treat Non-Liberal Cultural Groups?," 9 *Theoretical Enquiries in Law* (2008) 609–42.
Mautner, M. "Three Approaches to Law and Culture," 96 *Cornell Law Review* (2011) 101.
McCrudden, C. "Human Dignity and Judicial Interpretation of Human Rights," 19 *European Journal of International Law* (2008) 655.
Merry, S. E. "Human Rights Law and the Demonization of Culture (And Anthropology Along the Way)," 26:1 *Political & Legal Review* (2003) 55–76.
Merry, S. E. "Legal Pluralism," 22 *Law & Society Review* (1988) 869–896.
Milbank, J. "Against Human Rights: Liberty in the Western Tradition," 1:1 *Oxford Journal of Law and Religion* (2012) 1–32.
Milbank, J. "The Invocation of Clio: A Response," 33:1 *Journal of Religious Ethics* (2005), 3–44.
Mizrachi, N. "On the Mismatch Between Multicultural Education and it Subjects in the Field" 33:2 *British Journal of Sociology of Education* (2012) 185–201.

Musschenga, A. W. "Intrinsic Value as a Reason for the Preservation of Minority Cultures," 1 *Ethical Theory & Moral Practice* (1998) 201–225.
Nagel, T., "Moral Conflict and Political Legitimacy," 16 *Philosophy & Public Affairs* (1987) 215–40.
Navon, C. "Women's Torah Study," 28 *Tchumin* (2008) 71 (Hebrew).
Nedelsky, J. "Communities of Judgment and Human Rights," 1 *Theoretical Inquiries in Law* (2000) 245–282.
Nussbaum, M.C. "Non-Relative Virtues: An Aristotelian Approach" 13 *Midwest Studies in Philosophy* (1988) 32.
Nussbaum, M. C. "Public Philosophy and International Feminism," 108 *Ethics* (1998) 762–796.
Obeyesekere, G. "Methodological and Philosophical Relativism," 1:3 MAN, n.s. (1966) 368–74.
Okin, S. M. "Feminism and Multiculturalism: Some Tensions," 108 *Ethics* (1998) 661–84.
Parekh, B. "Minority Practices and Principles of Toleration," 30 *International Migration Review* (1996) 251–284.
A. R. Peled, "Shari'a under Challenge: The Political History of Islamic Legal Institutions in Israel" 63 *Middle East Journal* (2009) 241–259.
Peled, Y. "Ethnic Democracy and the Legal Construction of Citizenship: Arab Citizens of the Jewish State" 86 *American Political Science Review* (1992) 432–443.
Pellizzoni, L. "The Myth of the Best Argument: Power, Deliberation and Reason," 52:1 *British Journal of Sociology* (2001) 59–86.
Post, R. "Prejudicial Appearances: The Logic of American Antidiscrimination Law," 88 *California Law Review* (2000) 1–41.
Raday, F. "Culture, Religion and Gender," 1 *International Journal of Constitutional Law* (2003) 663–715.
Rakover, N. "Jewish Law and the Noahide Obligation to Preserve the Social Order," 12 *Cardozo Law Review* (1991) 1076–86.
Rawls, J. "The Idea of Public Reason Revisited," 64 *University of Chicago Law Review* (1997) 765–807.
Raz, J. "Multiculturalism," 11 *Ratio Juris* (1998) 193–205.
Raz, J. "Multiculturalism: A Liberal Perspective," 41 *Dissent* (1994) 67.
Reaume, D. G. "Discrimination and Dignity," 63 *Louisiana Law Review* (2003) 645–695.
Renteln, A. D. "Relativism and the Search for Human Rights," 90 *American Anthropologist* (1988) 56–72.
Rorty, R. "Religion in the Public Square: A Reconsideration," 31:1 *Journal of Religious Ethics* (2003) 141–49.
Roth, J. "Crossing the Bridge to Secular Law: Three Models of Incorporation" 12 *Cardozo Law Review* (1991) 753.
Rubinstein, A. "Law and Religion in Israel," 2 *Israel Law Review* (1967) 380.
Rubinstein, A. "State and Religion in Israel," 2 *Journal of Contemporary History* (1967) 107–121.
Rudolph, S. H. "Presidential Address: State Formation in Asia—Prolegomenon to a Comparative Study," 46:4 *Journal of Asian Studies* 46 (1987) 731–46.
Sa'adu, H. I. "Proof of Paternity under Islamic Law" 2 *University of Ilorin Law Journal* (2005) 41, available at <www.unilorin.edu.ng/publications/proof.rtf>.
Saban, I. "Minority Rights in Deeply Divided Societies: A Framework for Analysis and the Case of the Arab-Palestinian Minority in Israel," 36 *New York University Journal of International Law & Politics* (2004) 885–1003.
Sacksofsky, U. "Religiöse Freiheit als Gefahr?" 68 *Veröffentlichungen der Vereinigung der Deutschen Staatsrechtslehrer* 7 (2009), 38.
Sa'di, A. H. "Israel as Ethnic Democracy: What Are the Implications for the Palestinian Minority?" 22 *Arab Studies Quarterly* (2000) 25–37.

Sager, L. "The Free Exercise of Culture: Some Doubts and Distinctions," 129:4 *Daedalus* (2000) 193–208.

Sandberg, H. and A. Hofri, "Arab Israeli Women's Renunciation of their Inheritance Shares: A Challenge for Israel's Courts" 8 *International Journal of Law in Context* (2012) 253–267.

Sapir, G. "How Should a Court Deal with a Primary Question that the Legislature Seeks to Avoid? The Israeli Controversy over Who Is a Jew as an Illustration," 39:4 *Vanderbilt Journal of Transnational Law* (2006) 1233–1302.

Sapir, G. "Law or Politics: Israeli Constitutional Adjudication as a Case Study," 6 *UCLA Journal of International Law & Foreign Affairs* (2001) 169.

Sapir, G. "Religion and State in Israel: The Case for Reevaluation and Constitutional Entrenchment," 22 *Hastings International & Comparative Law Review* (1999) 617.

Schachar, A. "Group Identity and Women's Rights in Family Law: The Perils of Multicultural Accommodation" 6 *Journal of Political Philosophy* (1998) 285–305.

Schachter, O. "Human Dignity as a Normative Concept," 77 *American Journal of International Law* (1983) 848–854.

Schragger, R. C. "The Role of the Local in the Doctrine and Discourse of Religious Liberty," 117 *Harvard Law Review* (2004) 1810–1892.

Seliktar, O. "Separating the Synagogue from the State: American Jews and the Struggle for Religious Pluralism in Israel" 18 *Israel Studies Forum* (2002) 57–87.

Shalev, C. "Halakha and Patriarchal Motherhood: An Anatomy of the New Israeli Surrogacy Law," 32 *Israel Law Review* (1998) 51.

Shamir, R., M. Shitrai, and N. Elias. "Religion, Feminism, and Professionalism: The Case and Cause of Women Rabbinical Advocates," 38 *Megamot* (1997) 313 (Hebrew).

Shava, M. "Comments on the Law of Return (Amendment No. 2), 5730-1970 (Who is a Jew?)," 3 *Tel-Aviv University Studies in Law* (1977) 295.

Shawa, M. "Hatsa'at Hok Beit ha-Mishpat le-Inyanei Mishpaha (Tikkun Mis. 4) (Hashva'at Samkhuyot Shipput), 5758-1998 — Ha-Omnam Brakha la-Nashim ha-Muslimiyot ve-ha-Notsriyot?" ["The Proposed Family Court Act (Amendment No. 4) (Comparing Jurisdiction), 1998 — Is It Truly a Blessing for Muslim and Christian Women?"] 44 *Ha-Praklit* (1999) 358 (Hebrew).

Simmonds, K. R. "Hugo Grotius and Alberico Gentili" 8 *Jahrbuch für Internationales Recht* (1959) 85.

Shamir, R. "Suspended in Space: Bedouins Under the Law of Israel" 30:2 *Law & Society Review* (1996) 231–258.

Shiloh, S. "Equity as a Bridge between Jewish and Secular Law" 12 *Cardozo Law Review* (1991) 737.

Smith, T. W., and S. Kim. "The Vanishing Protestant Majority," 44:2 *Journal for the Scientific Study of Religion* (2005), 211–23.

Smooha, S. "The Model of Ethnic Democracy: Israel as a Jewish and Democratic State," 8 *Nations and Nationalism* (2002) 475–503.

Smooha, S. and D. Peretz, "The Arabs in Israel" 26 *Journal of Conflict Resolution* (1982) 451–484.

Soutphommasane, T. "Grounding Multicultural Citizenship: From Minority Rights to Civic Pluralism" 26:4 *Journal of Intercultural Studies* (2005) 401–416.

Spinner-Halev, J. "Feminism, Multiculturalism, Oppression and the State" 112 *Ethics* (2001) 84–113.

Spiro, M. E. "Cultural Relativism and the Future of Anthropology," 1 *Cultural Anthropology* (1986) 259–286.

Stone, S. L. "Religion and State: Models of Separation from Within Jewish Law," 6 *International Journal of Constitutional Law* (2008) 631–61.

Stone, S. L. "Sinaitic and Noahide Law: Legal Pluralism in Jewish Law," 12 *Cardozo Law Review* (1991) 1157–214.

Stone, S. L. "The Intervention of American Law in Jewish Divorce: A Pluralist Analysis," 34 *Israel Law Review* (2000) 170–210.

Stopler, G. "The Free Exercise of Discrimination: Religious Liberty, Civic Community and Women's Equality," 10 *William & Mary Journal of Women and the Law* (2004) 459.
Taylor, C. "A World Consensus on Human Rights," *Dissent* (Summer 1996) 15.
Tessler, M. A. "The Identity of Religious Minorities in Non-Secular States: Jews in Tunisia and Morocco and Arabs in Israel" 20 *Comparative Studies in Society and History* (1978) 359–373.
Teubner, G. "Reflexives Recht. Entwicklungsmodelle des Rechts in vergleichender Perspektive," 68 *Archiv für Rechts- und Sozialphilosophie* (1982) 13–59.
Teubner, G. "Substantive and Reflexive Elements in Modern Law," 17 *Law & Society* (1983) 239–85.
Thacher, D. "The Normative Case Study," 11:6 *American Journal of Sociology* (2006) 1631–676.
Treitel, A. "Conflicting Traditions: Muslim Shari'a Courts and Marriage Age Regulation in Israel," 26 *Columbia Human Rights Law Review* (1995) 403.
Trigano, S. "The Rediscovery of Biblical Politics," 4:3 *Hebraic Political Studies* (2009) 306–307.
Troeltsch, E. "Die Bedeutung des Protestantismus für die Entstehung der modernen Welt," 97 *Historische Zeitschrift* (1906) 39.
Tsimhoni, D. "Continuity and Change in Communal Autonomy: The Christian Communal Organizations in Jerusalem, 1948–80," 22 *Middle Eastern Studies* (1986) 398–417.
Tsimhoni, D. "The Greek Orthodox Community in Jerusalem and the West Bank, 1948–1978: A Profile of a Religious Minority in a National State," 23 *Orient* (1982) 281.
Tushnet, M. "The Critique of Rights," 47 *SMU Law Review* (1993) 23–36.
Van Praagh, S. "Sharing the Sidewalk," 8:3 *Canadian Diversity* (2010) 6–9.
Van Praagh, S. "The Education of Religious Children: Families, Communities and Constitutions," 47:3 *Buffalo Law Review* (1999) 1343–1396.
Vertovec, S. "Towards Post-multiculturalism? Changing Communities, Conditions and Contexts of Diversity" 61:199 *International Social Science Journal* (2010) 83–95.
Volpp, L. "Feminism versus Multiculturalism," 101 *Columbia Law Review* (2001) 1181–218.
Volpp, L. "Talking 'Culture': Gender, Race, Nation, and the Politics of Multiculturalism," 96 *Columbia Law Review* (1996) 1573–617.
Waldron, J. "How to Argue for a Universal Claim," 30 *Columbia Human Rights Law Review* (1995) 305.
Waldron, J. "One Law for All? The Logic of Cultural Accommodation," 59 *Washington & Lee Law Review* (2002) 3.
Waldron, J. "Particular Values and Critical Morality," 77 *California Law Review* (1989) 561–89.
Waldron, J. "Public Reason and 'Justification' in the Courtroom," 1 *Journal of Law, Philosophy & Culture* (2007) 107.
Walzer, M. "Liberalism and the Art of Separation," 12 *Political Theory* (1984) 315–30.
Ward, C. V. "The Limits of 'Liberal Republicanism': Why Group-Based Remedies and Republican Citizenship Don't Mix," 91 *Columbia Law Review* (1991) 581–607.
Webber, J. "Legal Pluralism and Human Agency," 44 *Osgoode Hall Law Journal* (2006) 167–198.
Weil, P. "Why the French Laïcité Is Liberal," 30 *Cardozo Law Review* (2009) 2699–715.
White, L. E., "Subordination, Rhetorical Survival Skills, and Sunday Shoes: Notes on the Hearing of Mrs. G." 38 *Buffalo Law Review* (1990) 1.
Wong, L. "Multiculturalism and Ethnic Pluralism in Sociology: An Analysis of the Fragmentation Position Discourse" 40:1 *Canadian Ethnic Studies* (2008) 11–32.
Yadin, A. "Rabban Gamliel, Aphrodite's Bath, and the Question of Pagan Monotheism," 96:2 *Jewish Quarterly Review* (2006) 149–79.
Yiftachel, O. and A. (Sandy) Kedar. "Landed Power: The Making of the Israeli Land Regime," 16 *Theory and Criticism* (2000) 67.
Zamir, I. "Shivyon Zekhuyuot Klappey ha-Aravim be-Yisra'el" [Equality of Rights for Arabs in Israel], 9 *Mishpat U'Mimshal Law Journal* (2005) 11 (Hebrew).

Ziv, N. "An Appeal on the Rejection Decision in the Settlement of Bar Yochai" (letter to Israel's Land Authority sent by the family's lawyer, 11 April 2011) (on file with author).
Zohar, Z. "The Attitude of Rabbi Yosef Masas Towards Women's Torah Study," 82 *Pe'amim* (2000) 150–162 (Hebrew).

## Cases

### CANADA

*Blackmore v British Columbia (Attorney General)*, 2009 BCSC 1299.
*Jacobs & Jacobs and Canadian Human Rights Commission v Mohawk Council of Kahnawake* [1998] CHRD No. 2. TD 3/98.
*R v Big M Drug Mart Ltd*, [1985] 1 SCR 295.
*R v Kapp* 2008 SCC 41.
*R v Malmo-Levine* 2003 SCC 7.
*Reference re: Criminal Code*, section 293, 2010 BCSC 1351.
*Reference re: Section 293 of the Criminal Code of Canada*, 2011 BCSC 1588.
Saguenay (Ville de) c. Mouvement laïque québécois, 2013 QCCA 936.
*Syndicat Northcrest v Amselem*, [2004] 2 SCR 551.
*The Queen v Bear's Shin Bone* (1899), 3 CCC 329 (SCNWT (S Alta Jud Dist)).

### ISRAEL

*Al Sorouji v Minister of Religious Affairs*, HCJ 282/61, [1963] IsrSC 17 188.
*Am Hofshi v The Ministry of Building and Housing*, HCJ 4906/98, 2000 PD 54(2).
*Amutat No'ar Ka-Halacha v Ministry of Education*, HCJ 1067/08 (unpublished, 6 August 2009).
*Avitan v Israel Land Authority*, HCJ 528/88, 1989 PD 43(4) 297.
*Axel v Mayor, Councilors and Residents of Netanyah*, HCJ 122/54, 1954 PD 8 1524.
*Bader (Mari'ee) v Mari'ee*, HCJ 9611/00, [2004] 58(4) IsrSC 256.
*Baruch v The Tel-Aviv District Traffic Controller*, HCJ 531/77, 1978 PD 32(2) 160.
*Ben-Ari v The Registrar of Population in the Ministry of Interior*, HCJ 3045/05.
*Bethlehem Christian Fellowship Inc v Planning & Zoning Comm'n*, 807 A.2d 1089 (Conn. App. Ct. 2002.
*Edri v The Minister of Building and Housing*, AdminC (Jerusalem) 1888/09 (unpublished, 2009).
*Edri v The Minister of Building and Housing*, AdminA 68/10 (unpublished, 2011).
*Freidi v Municipality of Tel Aviv*, HCJ 72/55, 1955 PD 10 734.
*Funk Slezinger v Minister of Interior*, HCJ 143/62, 1962 PD 17 225.
*Greenberg v Local Council of Katzrin*, HCJ 2838/95, 1997 PD 53(1) 1.
*Halon v The Mayor of Local Council Ussafiyah*, HCJ 166/71, 1971 PD 25(2) 591.
HCJ 3856/1, (June 27, 2013).
*Horev v Minister of Transportation*, HCJ 5016/96, 1997 PD 51(4) 1.
*Isramax Ltd. v The State of Israel*, CrimA 217/58, 1962 PD 22 343.
*Jadday v President of the Judgments Execution Office*, HCJ 101/54, [1955] IsrSC 9, 135.
*Jerusalem Open House v The City of Jerusalem*, AdminC (Jerusalem) 219/06 (unpublished, 2006).
*Jerusalem Open House v The City of Jerusalem*, AdminC (Jerusalem) 8187/08 (unpublished, 2008).
*Jerusalem Open House v The City of Jerusalem*, AdminA 343/09 (unpublished, 2010).
*Kaadan v Israel Land Authority*, 6698/95, 2000 PD 54(1) 258.
*Lazarovitz v Food Controller*, HCJ 98/54, 1956 PD 10 40.
*Marzel v Police Chief of the District of Jerusalem*, HCJ 5277/07.
*Noar Kahalach v The Ministry of Education*, HCJ 1067/08 (unpublished, 9 August 2009).
*Ornan v. Ministry of Interior*, CA 8573/08 [2013], Nevo Legal Database (by subscription).
*Peretz v The Chairman, the Council Members and the Residents of Kfar Shemaryahu*, HCJ 262/62, 1962 PD 16 2101.
*Plonit v Druze Appellate Court in Acre*, HCJ 2829/03, [2006] IsrSC 60(4) 159.

*Plonit v Ploni*, CA 3077/90, [1995] IsrSC 49(2) 578.
*Plonit v. Ploni*, HCJ 8906/04 [2005], Nevo Legal Database (by subscription).
HCJ 8906/04 Plonit v. Ploni (July 20, 2005), Nevo Legal Database (by subscription).
*Ragan v Ministry of Transportation*, HCJ 746/07 (unpublished, 2011).
*Rodriguez Toshbeim v Minister of Interior*, HCJ 2597/99, 58(5) PD 412 (2005).
*Rufeisen v Minister of the Interior*, HCJ 72/62, 16 PD 2428 (1962).
*Saba'a v Israel Land Administration*, AdminC 2002/09 (unpublished, 2010).
*Saba'a v Israel Land Administration*, AdminA 1789/10 (unpublished, 2011).
*Sabach v The Knesset*, HCJ 2311/11 (filed 23 March 2011).
*Shakdiel v The Minister of Religious Affairs*, HCJ 153/87, [1988] IsrSC 42(2) 221.
*Shalit v Minister of the Interior*, HCJ 58/68, 23(2) PD 477 (1970).
*Solodkin v City of Beit Shemesh*, HCJ 953/01, 2004 PD 58(5) 595.
*Solodoch v Municipality of Rehoboth*, HCJ 10907/04 (unpublished, 2010).
*State of Israel v Azaizeh* CrimA 135/70, [1970] IsrSC 24(1) 417.
*Sultan v Sultan*, CA 245/81, [1984] IsrSC 38(3) 169.
*SZM Ltd v The Mayor of Jerusalem*, HCJ 230/73, 1974 PD 28(2) 113.
*The League for the Prevention of Religious Coercion v The Council of Jerusalem*, HCJ 174/62, 1966 PD 16 2665.
*The State of Israel v Kaplan*, CrimC (Jerusalem) 3471/87, PM 5748(2) 26 (1988).
*Yanovitz v Chair of the Council of Ramat Ha-Sharon*, HCJ 809/86, 1987 PD 41(4) 309.
*Yekutieli v The Minister of Interior*, HCJ 6741/99, 2001 PD 55(3) 673.

### THE EUROPEAN COURT OF HUMAN RIGHTS

*Lautsi v Italy*, Application no 30814/06, ECtHR (Grand Chamber) Judgment, 18 March 2011.

### THE UNITED KINGDOM

*R (on the application of E) v Governing Body of JFS and the Admissions Appeal Panel of JFS and others (United Synagogue)* [2009] UKSC 15.

### THE UNITED STATES

*Abortion Rights Mobilization, Inc v Regan*, 544 F Supp 471 (SDNY 1982).
*Bob Jones University v United States*, 461 US 574 (1983).
*Brown v Board of Education*, 347 US 483 (1954).
*County of Allegheny v ACLU* 492 US 573 (1989).
*McGowan v Maryland* 366 US 420 (1961).
*Plessey v Ferguson*, 163 US 537 (1896).
*Santa Clara Pueblo v Martinez* 436 US 49 (1978).
*United States Catholic Conference v Baker*, 885 F 2d 1020 (2d Cir 1989).
*Wisconsin v Yoder*, 406 US 205 (1972).

### LEGISLATION AND DOCUMENTS

*Age of Marriage Law*, 5710-1950, LSI (1950) (Israel).
*Amendment to the Collective Associations Ordinance Act* (no 8), 2011 (Israel).
*Basic Law: Freedom of Occupation*, 1994, SH 1454, 90 (Israel).
*Basic Law: Human Dignity and Liberty*, 1992, SH 1391, 150 (Israel).
*Official Report of Debates of the Legislative Assembly (Hansard)*, No 9, British Columbia, Legislative Assembly 2008.
*Business Licensing Law*, 1968 (Israel).
*Canadian Charter of Rights and Freedoms*, Part I of the Constitution Act, 1982, being Schedule B to the Canada Act 1982 (UK) 1982, c 11.
*Codex Canonum Ecclesiarum Orientalium*, cc 1–6.
*Compulsory Education Law*, 5719–1959, LSI (1959) (Israel).
Debates of the Senate, Fourth Session, Sixth Parliament (25 February 1890).

Ecclesiastical Courts in Israel: A Gender-Responsive Analysis, http://www.jadaliyya.com/pages/index/12559/ecclesiastical-courts-in-israel_a-gender-responsiv.
*Equality Act*, 2010 (UK).
Famille et Aînés Québec, "Directive: Activités ayant pour objectif l'apprentissage d'une croyance, d'un dogme ou de la pratique d'une religion spécifique dans un centre de la petite enfance ou une garderie subventionnée" (December, 2010) (Québec, Canada). "Implementation of the International Covenant on Civil and Political Rights (ICCPR): Combined Initial and First Periodic Report of the State of Israel 227," (1998) (Israel).
Israel: Law No. 5710-1950, The *Law of Return* [ ], 5 July 1950).
*Law of Return (Amendment no 2)* 5730-1970, 14 LSI 28 (1969/70) (Israel).
League of Nations, Mandate for Palestine (1922), Art. 2, available at <http://avalon.law.yale.edu/20th_century/palmanda.asp>.
*Local Authorities Act (Special Enablement)*, 1956 (Israel).
*Marriage Age Law*, 5710-1950, 4 LSI 158 (1949–50) (Israel).
Ombudsman for Complaints Against Judges Law, 5762-2002, S.H. No. 1864, p. 590.
*Order of Recognition of a Religious Community (Evangelical Episcopal Church in Israel)*, 1970, KT 2557 (Israel).
*Order of Recognition of a Religious Community (The Bahai Faith)*, 1971, KT 2673.
*Penal Law*, 5737-1977, LSI Special Volume: Penal Law (1977) (Israel).
*Prohibition of Opening of Amusement Places (Special Enablement)*, 1997 (Israel).
*Rabbinical Courts Jurisdiction (Marriage and Divorce) Law*, 1953, 7 LSI 139 (1952–53), art. 4 (Israel).
*Race Relations Act 1976* (UK).
*Succession Law*, 5725-1965, section 155(c), 19 LSI 58 (1964-65) (Israel).
*Surrogate Motherhood Agreement Law (Approval of the Agreement and Status of the Child)*, 5756-1996, SH 176 (Israel).
*The Byzantine Family Law*, Article 30(2).
*The Municipalities Act* (religious holidays and days of rest), 1964.
*The Planning and Building Law*, 1965 (Israel).
*The Water Law*, 1959 (Israel).
*The Welfare Law*, 1958 (Israel).
Women's Equal Rights Law, 5711-1951, LSI (1951) (Israel).

INTERNATIONAL DECLARATIONS, CONVENTIONS, AND RESOLUTIONS

*Declaration on Social Progress and Development* (1969), GA Res 2542 (XXIV), UN Doc A/7630 (Dec 11, 1969).
*Partition Plan with Economic Union*, annexed to Resolution Adopted on the Report of the Ad Hoc Committee on the Palestinian Question: Future Government of Palestine, GA Res 181(II), UN Doc A/RES/181(II) (Nov 29, 1947).
UNESCO, *Universal Declaration on Bioethics and Human Rights* (2005).
United Nations Congress on the Prevention of Crime and the Treatment of Offenders, *Prisons—Standard Minimum Rules for the Treatment of Prisoners* (1955).
World Food Conference (endorsed by the General Assembly), *Universal Declaration on the Eradication of Hunger and Malnutrition* (1974).

NEWS AND WEBSITES

"Anti-Polygamy Law a 'Relic': Lawyer" *The Canadian Press* (12 April 2011), available online: <http://www.cbc.ca/news/canada/british-columbia/story/2011/04/11/bc-polygamy-hearing-dickson.html>.
Arnold, J. "Anti-Veil Bill May Be Unconstitutional, Group Says," *The Canadian Jewish News* (28 October 2010), available online: <http://www.cjnews.com/index.php?option=com_content&task=view&id=20135&Itemid=86>.
Association of Religion Data Archives (ARDA), available online: <www.thearda.com>.

Bayfield, Rabbi T. "Faith Tests Do Not Fit Judaism," *Times Online* (26 October 2010).
"B.C. Polygamists Want Age of Consent Raised," *CTV News* (19 February 2005), available online: <http://www.ctv.ca/servlet/ArticleNews/story/CTVNews/1108760102803_29/?hub=CTVNewsAt11>.
"Be'emuna," available online: <http://www.bemuna.co.il/show.asp?id=5861> (Hebrew).
Blackmore, W. "Share the Light" [blog], available online: <http://sharethelight.ca/b2/>.
Bouchard, G. and C. Taylor, "Building the Future: A Time for Reconciliation," available online: http://red.pucp.edu.pe/wp-content/uploads/biblioteca/buildingthefuture-GerardBouchardycharlestaylor.pdf
Bramham, D. "Some Bountiful Brides only 15, Affidavit States; Nine of Accused Fundamentalist's 25 Wives Under 18, Document Says," *Ottawa Citizen* (1 July 2009) C10.
CanWest MediaWorks Publications (2007) "B.C. Government has a Duty to Protect Bountiful's Children while Challenging Polygamy," *Vancouver Sun* (3 August 2007) A8.
CBS Statistical Abstract of Israel 2009, available online: <http://www.cbs.gov.il/shnaton60/shnaton60_all.pdf>.
Commission de consultation sur les pratiques d'accommodement reliées aux différence culturelles, 2007. *Mandat de la commission*, available online: <http://www.accommodements.qc.ca/commission/mandat-en.html>.
*Constitution de la Commission de consultation sur les pratiques d'accommodement reliées aux différence culturelles*, 2007. D. 95-2007, GOQ 2007. IX.1372.
Dagani, A. "61% of the Ultra Orthodox Prefer to Live in Separate Settlements" (15 February 2011), available online: <http://www.relevanti.com/-אבי-פרוף/עמוד-הבית/גלובס/דגני/m7329_61-נפרדים-בישובים-לגור-מעדיפים-מהחרדים> (Hebrew).
D'Amour, M. "Sect Wives Defend Lives: Women Say Polygamy Choice Is Theirs," *Calgary Sun* (29 July 2004) A4.
"Declaration on Religious Freedom *Dignitatis Humanae*," English translation available online: <http://www.vatican.va/archive/hist_councils/ii_vatican_council/documents/vat-ii_decl_19651207_dignitatis-humanae_en.html>.
de Souza, Fr. R. J. "Religion in Retreat," *National Post* (30 December 2010).
Dougherty, K. "Yolande James Says Subsidized Daycares Can't Teach Religion: Have until June 1 to Phase Out Any Religious Teaching or Risk Losing Subsidies," *Montreal Gazette* (17 December 2010).
Ettinger, Y. "High Court: Gender Segregation Legal on Israeli Buses—But Only with Passenger Consent" *Haaretz* (6 January 2011), available online: <http://www.haaretz.com/news/national/high-court-gender-segregation-legal-on-israeli-buses-but-only-with-passenger-consent-1.335567>.
Ferretti, L. "La polygamie pour tous ou pour personne," *Le Devoir* (4 March 2009) A9.
Fish, S. "Serving Two Masters: Shariah Law and the Secular State," *New York Times* (25 October 2010).
"French MPs Vote to Ban Islamic Full Veil in Public," *BBC* (13 July 2010).
"French Senate Votes to Ban Islamic Full Veil in Public," *BBC* (14 September 2010).
Gurovich, N. and E. Cohen-Kastro. "Ultra-Orthodox Jews: Geographic Distribution and Demographic, Social and Economic Characteristics of the Ultra-Orthodox Jewish Population in Israel, 1996–2001" (July 2004), available online: <http://www.cbs.gov.il/www/publications/int_ulor.pdf> (Hebrew).
Hainsworth, J. "Canada: Leaders of Polygamist Group Arrested," *Huffington Post* (7 January 2009), available online: <http://www.huffingtonpost.com/2009/01/07/canada-leaders-of-polygam_n_156082.html>.
Hall, N. "Winston Blackmore Sues B.C. Government for Polygamy Prosecution," *Vancouver Sun* (14 January 2010), available online: <http://www.vancouversun.com/news/Winston+Blackmore+sues+government+polygamy+prosecution/2441672/story.html>.
Hamilton, G. "God Tossed from Daycare," *National Post* (18 December 2010).

"Israeli Cabinet Approves Loyalty Oath for Non-Jews," (11 October 2010) *The Independent* online: <http://www.independent.co.uk/news/world/middle-east/israeli-cabinet-approves-loyalty-oath-for-nonjews-2103194.html>.

Javed, N. "GTA's Secret World of Polygamy; A Toronto Mother Describes Her Ordeal, Imam Admits He Has 'Blessed' Over 30 Unions," *Toronto Star* (24 May 2008), available online: <http://www.thestar.com/News/GTA/article/429490>.

Kalmus, J. "Jewish Girl's King David Place Goes to Non-Jew," *The Jewish Chronicle* (11 June 2010), available online: <http://www.thejc.com/node/32947>.

Knesset Finance Committee, "Protocol of Session of the Knesset Finance Committee Concerning the Proposed Amendment to the Municipality Taxes and the Government Taxes Ordinance (Exemptions) (Synagogues), 2009 of Member of Knesset Nissim Zeev (P/662)," 2 March 2010; available online: <http://oknesset.org/committee/meeting/52/> (Hebrew).

Lapidot-Firilla, A. and R. Elhadad. *Forbidden Yet Practiced: Polygamy and the Cyclical Making of Israeli Policy* (Jerusalem: Hebrew University of Jerusalem, 2006).

*The Law of War and Peace*, Lonang Institute (2005), available online: <www.lonang.com/exlibris/grotius/gro-001.htm>.

Lewis, C. "Bountiful B.C. Case Likely to Stir Up Religious Freedoms Debate," *National Post* (6 January 2009), available online: <http://www.nationalpost.com/news/story.html?id=1152461>.

Matas, R. and W. Trueck. "Polygamy Charges in Bountiful," *Globe and Mail* (7 January 2009), available online: <http://www.theglobeandmail.com/news/national/article963758.ece>.

Mayeda, A. "Tories Prepared to Stand Ground on Polygamy: Documents," *National Post* (24 March 2009), available online: <http://www.nationalpost.com/news/story.html?id=1423616>.

Naboulsi, Z. "Civil marriage is more than just the will of two people to get legally wed. In Lebanon it is the feeling of citizenship," <http://www.yourmiddleeast.com/opinion/ziad-naboulsi-civil-marriage-in-lebanon-more-than-just-married_12,614>.

Peck, R. C. C. "Report of the Special Prosecutor for Allegations of Misconduct Associated with Bountiful, BC: Summary of Conclusions," available online (*Vancouver Sun*): <http://www.canada.com/vancouversun/news/extras/bountiful.pdf>.

Peritz, I. "Quebec Bans Religious Teaching in Publicly Subsidized Daycares," *Globe and Mail* (21 December 2010).

"Religion Ban in Quebec's Public Daycares Welcomed: Jewish Group Says Government Has Gone Too Far," *CBC* (10 March 2010).

Rotem, T. "Separate Tables" *Haaretz* (1 July 2011), available online: <http://www.haaretz.com/weekend/week-s-end/separate-tables-1.370695>.

Song, S. "Multiculturalism" in E. N. Zalta (ed), *The Stanford Encyclopedia of Philosophy* (Winter 2010 Edition), available online: <http://plato.stanford.edu/archives/win2010/entries/multiculturalism/>.

Tresniowski, A. "Castaways: In Utah and Arizona Hundreds of Teenage Boys are Being Torn from Their Families and Expelled from an Extreme Mormon Sect. Is It Because They Compete for Teen Girls that the Sect's Grown Men Want to Marry?" *People Weekly* (25 July 2005) (CPI.Q.).

"Women's Tales: Four Leading Israeli Jewelers," available online: <http://www.imj.org.il/exhibition/Israeli-Jewelers.html>.

# INDEX

Aboriginal groups, 2, 5
    identities, 2, 5
    Mohawk Nation, 124–125
    *see also* Canada; Canadian multiculturalism
*Amselem v. Syndicat Northcrest*, 125, 129
Arabic, 8
    linguistic rights in Israel, 8
Arendt, Hannah, 66–69
    compassion as pre-political, 67
    concept of judgment, 163
    critique of empathy, 66–69; *see also* politics of pity
    critique of secularism, 68
    paradox of human rights, 65–66
    politics of pity, 66–69
    stateless people, 66
Asad, Talal, 7–8, 69–71
    articulation of secularism, 86
    distinction between active and passive suffering as secular, 71
    form of cruelty, 70–71
    human rights as exclusionary of non-Christian traditions, 69
    multiculturalism as discourse, 8
    multiculturalism as normalization, 7
    *see also* Islam
Autonomy, 225–240
    jurisdictional, 225–229; *see also* Israeli multiculturalism; Palestinian-Arab religious communities

Banting, Keith, 4
Ben-Rafael, Eliezer, 3
Berger, Peter, 106
Bhandar, Brenna, 2, 8
Bouchard, Gérard, 109
    *see also* Bouchard-Taylor Commission, Interculturalism

Bouchard-Taylor Commission, 3, 109–110
    *see also* Interculturalism
Brandes, Hostovsky, 8
Britain
    Cantle Report, 6
    *Race Relations Act*, 123, 125–126, 128–129
    *see also Jewish Free School*

Canada
    aboriginal groups, 2, 5
    Citizenship and Immigration Report, 3
    *see also* Québec
Canadian multiculturalism, 3
    Distinct from interculturalism, 3; *see also* Interculturalism
    linguistic rights of French Canadians, 8
    retreat from, 6
    tool of nation-building, 3
    as unique, 2–3
Citizenship Laws
    security considerations, 6
Community
    autonomy, 179
    classification of debates of the intra-, 214
    contested terrain, 1
    linguistic, 8; *see also* Arabic, linguistic rights in Israel
    national, 3
    political, 61
    religious membership, 14–15, 42, 92–94, 124–130, 144–149
    rules, 143
    situatedness, 15
Cultural, 159–161
    categories, 159–161
    meaning, 159–161
    norms as authority-conferring, 112
Culture, 161–170
    evaluation through human rights doctrine, 164

Culture (*continued*)
  incommensurability, 161
  infrastructural categories, 161, 170
  legal, 165

Dialogue, 162–163
  cross-cultural, 162–163; *see also* Taylor, Charles
  cross-cultural evaluation, 163
  purpose, 163
  sensitive, 200

Education, 123–134, 144–145
  *see also* Jewish Free School; Religion in Daycare Directive
Empathy, 58–75
  embedded secular intolerance, 65
  history of and relationship to human right, 58–75
Equality
  empathy, 62
  human dignity, 170–178
  *see also* Gender equality
Europe
  veil controversies, 42, 64, 82–83

Freedom of conscience, 106–107
  *see also* Freedom from religion
Freedom of religion
  apostasy, 11; *see also* Islam
  autonomy from the State, 225–240
  collective rights, 104, 114, 230
  dignity, 255
  freedom from religion, 13, 56, 88, 255, 265; *see also* Freedom of conscience
  historical sources, 105–107
  individual rights, 99, 240, 253, 277
  legal recognition of, 122, 163
  legal strategy to accommodate diversity, 225–229; *see also* Canadian multiculturalism; Israeli multiculturalism; Multiculturalism
  *see also* Religious liberty

Gadamer, Hans-Georg, 156, 162–163
Garcea, Joseph, 3, 5
Gauchet, Marcel, 43
Gender equality, 134–135, 175–182, 209–216
  biases, 173
  as Canadian values, 193
  discussions around veiling practices and, 42, 64, 82–83, 134–135; *see also* Europe
  division of labor, 175–176
  exclusion from Torah study, 156, 165–182
  polygamy in relation to, 192, 209, 211, 216
  Western feminist arguments, 157–158
  *see also* Equality; Okin, Susan Moller

Gerondi, Nissim, 45–46, 48
  *see also* Medieval Jewish jurisprudence
God's law, 25–27
  Divine law, 26
  Natural law, 27
  Revealed law, 26
  *see also* Religious legal systems
Grotius, 33–34

Habermas, Jürgen, 197–200, 203
  reflexive exercise, 202–204
Hart, H.L.A., 110–111
Hebrew Bible, 45–51
  Halakha and scope in medieval period, 45–47
  political sphere, 44–51
  public and private space, 50
  public space, 50–51
  sacred and profane space, 50
Hobbes, Thomas, 107–108, 114–115
  classification of systems, 107–108
Human rights, 51–75
  discourse and Christian imagery, 51
  doctrine as evaluation of cultures, 164
  exclusionary of non-Christian traditions, 69
  history, 62–75
  history of empathy, 58–62
  limits, 57
  as non-neutral, 51–52, 173
  paradox, 65–66
  relationship with secularism, 56
  religious origins, 57
  subjective notion of, 72
  synonymous with justice, 57–58
  universality claim, 57–59
  *see also* Arendt, Hannah; Asad, Talal; Empathy; Milbank, John

Intercultural, 155–159
  communication, 156, 158–159
  encounters, 155
  Western feminist arguments, 157–158
Interculturalism
  different from multiculturalism, 3
  national minorities in Québec, 3
  *see also* Bouchard-Taylor Commission
Islam, 29–31, 81–86
  adaptation to secularization, 85–86
  association with cruelty, 69
  challenge to state neutrality, 81
  permissibility of apostasy, 11
  religious revival, 81–83
  Sunni legal system, 29–31
  *see also* Asad, Talal
Israel, 145–150, 255–256
  citizenship, 145–149, 234
  declaration of Independence, 3
  fundamental laws, 32, 255–256

immigration legislation, 146–147, 149
Jewish State, 231, 234–235, 255
Law of Return, 143, 145–149, 228
marriage, 32, 148–149
*millet* system, 32, 229, 256
nationality, 146–147
nationhood, 4, 150
non-assimilative, 233
Oath of loyalty, 4
religious feminism in, 171
*Rufeisen v. Minister of the Interior*, 145–146
*Shalit v. Minister of the Interior*, 146–147
see also Local government in Israel
Israeli multiculturalism
  absence of common Israeli identity, 233
  alignment with religion, 3
  Arabic, 8
  definition of, 4–5
  demographics, 228–229
  identity cards, 236
  Jewish identity, 5
  jurisdictional authority over family law, 229
  jurisdictional authority of rabbinical courts, 232
  jurisdictional autonomy, 225–228
  jurisdictional interventions against illiberal norms, 237–239
  multicultural entrapment of Palestinian-Arabs, 232; see also Palestinian-Arab religious communities; multiculturalism, illiberal group practices
  polygamy in Bedouin community, 239
  recognition of non-Jewish religious communities, 231
  regulation of pork selling, 256, 257, 259–260, 262–265
  see also Israel

Jewish
  cultural versus religious, 146
  legal status of the other, 28
  matrilineal lineage, 143, 147
  membership debates, 14–15, 42, 92–94, 124–130, 144–149; see also Jewish Free School
  see also Judaism
*Jewish Free School*, 92–93, 123–130, 143–151
  admissions criteria, 123, 125–128
  critical Legal Pluralism, 138
  cultural biases by judges, 145
  daily religious practices, 145
  definition of religious identity, 125, 129
  ethnic discrimination, 150–151
  internal identity rules, 124–125
  matrilineal test, 143

membership, 14–15, 42, 92–94, 124–130, 144–149
public funding, 150
racial discrimination, 123, 125, 128–129, 144–145
respect for Judaism's internal rules, 126
shared governance for religious schools, 127
shift in the focus of legal analysis, 138
test for religious identity, 129
Jewish legal system, 28–49, 171–172
  halakha, 44–47, 49, 111, 114, 148, 168, 171–172
  idea of reciprocity, 52
  legal status of the other, 28
  meta-halakhic argument, 174
  Orthodox Judaism, 28–29, 32, 34
  weakness of natural law concept in, 34–35
  see also Religious legal systems
Joppke, Christian, 2
Judaism
  membership debates, 14–15, 42, 92–94, 124–130, 144–149; see also Jewish Free School
  Orthodox Judaism, 28–29, 32, 34; see also Jewish legal system
  Ultra Orthodox culture, 163, 181
  Ultra Orthodox women, 162–163, 174–178, 277
  see also Jewish

Kymlicka, Will, 3–4, 6, 8, 17, 102, 110

Law of Return, 143, 145–149
  conversion, 148
  legal definition of Jew, 147
  see also Israel
Legal transplants, 10, 35
  danger of, 35
  Watson, Alan, 10
  see also Translation
Lerner, Hanna, 4
Liberalism, 41–43, 162–164
  art of separation, 41–42
  distinct from cultural neutrality, 162
  not exclusively Christian, 42
  illiberal citizens, 162–164
  moral critique of modern law, 49
  re-enchantment of the secular state, 51
  relationship to other cultures, 162–163
  secularization process, 43
  see also Medieval jewish jurisprudence; Taylor, Charles; Waltzer, Michael
Local government in Israel, 257–278
  closing roads during the Sabbath, 257, 260–261, 263
  decentralization as institutional safeguard, 273
  delegation of powers to, 264
  demographics, 259

Local government (*continued*)
  equal access, 267–269, 278
  gender segregation in public transportation, 277
  regulation of pork selling, 256, 257, 259–260, 262–265
  regulation of sex-oriented businesses, 261–262
  religious homogeneity of localities, 253
  religious minorities forming local majorities, 254
  religious prohibitions in cultural terms, 261
  residential patterns of segregation among Jews, 269–272
  resistance, 273–274
  risk faction, 253, 276
  segregation between religious and secular Jews, 278–279
  tax exemptions, 265–267
  *see also* Israel

Macedo, Stephen, 179
Maimonides, 45–46, 165–168
  *dinin*, 45
  teaching women Torah, 165–166, 168
  view on kinship, 45
  *see also* Medieval Jewish jurisprudence
Medieval Jewish jurisprudence, 44–46
  Gerondi, Nissim, 45–46, 48–49
  Maimonides, 45
  Rashi, 47
  Schism in Jewish thought, 48–49
  Separation of realms, 49
  universal laws, 47–48
  view on kinship, 45–48
Membership
  cultural, 145, 276
  religious, 31, 143; *see also* Jewish Free School
  *see also* Community rules; Jewish; Judaism
Milbank, John, 72–75
  critique of secular politics as absolutist, 72–75
  distinction between sympathy and *agape*, 74–75
  failure to protect human dignity, 72
  subjective notion of human rights, 72
Mill, John Stuart, 167, 170–172, 174
Minorities, 8, 225–242
  illiberal, 162–164, 225–228, 237–239
  linguistic, 8; *see also* Arabic, linguistic rights in Israel; Canadian multiculturalism; Québec
  national, 3
  permanent, 274
  religious, 225–228, 233–234, 242; *see also* Palestinian-Arab religious communities
  *see also* Canadian multiculturalism; Israeli multiculturalism; multiculturalism

Modood, Tariq, 5–6
Multicultural, 100–105, 225–228
  entrapment, 225–228, 232; *see also* Palestinian-Arab religious communities
  paradigm, 100–105
Multiculturalism, 5–7, 225–236
  attacks on, 6–7
  common markers of, 5
  identified with religious diversity, 5
  illiberal group practices, 225–228; *see also* Multicultural entrapment of Palestinian-Arabs
  in opposition with gender equality, 7; *see also* Okin, Susan Moller
  jurisdiction of religious community, 225–228
  local as privileged site, 229
  normative theory, 225
  political and philosophical dimensions of, 101–105
  right to exit, 227–228, 235–236
  *see also* Post-multiculturalism; Super-diversity

Nachtomy, Ohad, 4
Noahide law, 28, 34, 45–48
  *see also* Maimonides; Religious legal systems
Nussbaum, Martha, 62, 181
  Empathy with human experience, 62

Okin, Susan Moller, 15, 172, 175–176, 178, 253
  *see also* Gender equality; Multiculturalism

Palestinian-Arab religious communities, 229–242
  citizens, 229
  identity of, 229, 233
  increased accountability of religious community officials, 242
  jurisdictional authority over family law, 229–240
  jurisdictional interventions, 237–238
  justification of religious accommodations of, 230–231
  *millet* system, 32, 229, 231
  norms prescribed in, 230
  promoting competition between religious and civil courts, 243–244
  review of liberal family law reform, 240–242
  right to exit, 236
  transparency of judgments rendered by religious courts, 243
  women's individual rights, 240
Peres, Yochanan, 3
Pinto, Meital, 8
Political sphere in Judaism, 44–51
  Composed of distinct jurisdictions, 44–51
  distinguished from sacred space, 50–51

Halakha, 44
  profane, 48–50
  *see also* Judaism; Jewish legal system;
    Liberalism; Medieval Jewish
    jurisprudence
Polygamy, 192–195, 204–216
  Bedouin community, 239
  criminal offence in Canada, 192
  fundamentalist Mormon theology, 194
  internal conversations about, 214
  intra-community debates, 214
  legal prohibition interfered with religious
    freedom, 193–194
  lost boys, 209, 211
  Polygamy Reference, 193–194, 216
  practice of, due to community expectations,
    205
  practice of, due to economic viability, 206
  practice of, due to personal fulfillment,
    208
  practice of, due to religious teachings,
    205–206
  prohibited by Israeli Knesset, 237
  public reason, 195–199, 202, 204, 209–212,
    215–216; *see also* Rawls, John
  reflexive exercise, 202–204
  religious claims as incomplete, 194–195,
    204–216
  sanctioned by Islamic law, 230
  sister wives, 206–207
  social network, 206–208
  stigma, 212
Post-multiculturalism discourses, 5–7
  challenge to religious pluralism, 83
  fragmentation critique, 5
  post-9/11 critiques, 5–6
  *see also* Multiculturalism; Super-diversity
Public, 195–216
  discussions about polygamy, 196
  feminist revision of categories, 213
  realm, 212
  reason, 195–199, 202, 204, 209–212,
    215–216; *see also* Rawls, John
  space of governance, 122–123
  sphere as holy, 274–275
  zone, 195
  *see also* Public space in Judaism
Public space in Judaism, 50–51
  expressive, 50–51
  *see also* Liberalism; Medieval Jewish
    jurisprudence

Québec
  Bouchard-Taylor Commission, 3
  Charter of Values, 7, 134–135
  Crucifix in National Assembly, 5
  interculturalism, 3

national minorities, 3
niqab bill, 134–135
Quiet Revolution, 7
Religion in Daycare Directive, 14, 131–133
religious symbols, 5, 7, 134–135

Rawls, John, 155, 195–199
  public reason, 195–199
Raz, Joseph, 3, 112, 179
Reflexive law, 90–92
  distinguish between tolerance and
    acceptance, 91
  religious freedom reconstructed as, 90–92
  Teubner, Gunther, 90
  tolerant reflexivity, 91–92
  *see also* Religious liberty
Relativism, 162
  moral, 162
  normative, 162
Religion
  as conversation-stopper, 201, 215
  cross-pollination with the liberal state,
    136–139
  different from culture, 107; *see also*
    Reconfiguration as culture
  distinct from custom, 42
  function of, 91
  localization in Israel, 252–253
  normative system, 110
  in opposition with secularization, 90
  political, 43–44
  practical authority, 107, 113
  practical concept, 200–202
  privatization, 42
  reconfiguration as culture, 276
  Western liberalism's definition of, 42
  *see also* Art of separation; Freedom of religion;
    Religious liberty
Religion in Daycare Directive, 14, 131–133
  critical legal pluralism, 138
  *see also* Education; Québec
Religious associations, 104–111
  constituted by secondary rules, 111
  discrete boundaries, 104
  normalizing effect, 104
Religious claims, 100–104, 196–199
  distinct from multicultural claims, 100,
    103–104, 109
  exoticization of, 103
  as public reason, 196–199
  *see also* Jewish Free School; Polygamy;
    Controversies
Religious identity, 122–133
  inside out, 122–130; *see also* Jewish Free
    School
  legal recognition of, 122–129
  outside in, 131–133

Religious legal systems, 27–31
　Christian legal system, 27–28, 33–34; see also Roman Catholic Christianity
　Islamic legal system, 29–31, 35; see also Sunni Islam
　Jewish legal system, 28–29, 32, 34; see also Jewish legal system; Orthodox Judaism; Halakha
　legal status of the other, 27–32
　Noahide law, 28, 34, 45–50
　revealed law, 26
　sinaitic law, 28, 34, 85
　sound knowledge of, 36
　see also God's law
Religious liberty, 88–92, 252–273
　borrowing from multicultural paradigm, 99
　individual versus collective protection, 102–104, 225, 230, 278
　local government, 252; see also Local government in Israel
　localization, 252–253, 280
　see also Freedom of religion
Religious revival, 81–83, 263
　Islam, 81–83
　Ultra Orthodox Jews, 263
Religious wars, 32–34
　between Catholics and Protestants, 33–34, 41
Roman Catholic Christianity, 27–28, 33–34
　Aquinas, Thomas, 27, 29
　divine natural law theory, 27–29
　legal status of the other, 27
　see also Religious legal systems

Sagi, Avi, 4
Secular, 56–57, 135
　relationship with human rights, 56
　space, 135
　thematized, 56–57
　see also Secular state; Secularism; Secularization
Secular state, 32–35, 51–52
　Christian approach to, 33–34
　distinction between political and religious realms, 52
　fundamental laws, 32; see also Israel
　influenced by concept of natural law, 32
　Islamic approach to, 35

model of organizing relations, 25
not culturally neutral, 35, 42, 84
Orthodox Jewish legal approach to, 34–35
political realm, 52
preamble to constitution, 32–33
religion as a component of, 25
re-enchantment of, 51–52
see also Secular; Secularism; Secularization
Secularism, 35, 42, 56
　not culturally neutral, 35, 42, 84
　relationship with human rights, 56
　see also Secular; Secular state; Secularization
Secularization, 43, 85–88
　functional differentiation of religions, 87–88
　Islam's adaptation to, 85–86
　process, 43
Shweder, Richard, 179–180
Song, Sarah, 103, 106
Spinner-Halev, Jeff, 232
State neutrality, 84
　assumption of difference between the State and religion, 84
Sunni Islam, 29–31
　legal status of the other, 29
　weakness of natural law concept, 31
　see also Religious legal systems
Super-diversity, 6
　see also Vertovec, Steven

Taylor, Charles, 42, 162
Tradition, 167–170
　as authority in common law, 167–168
　binding force in Judaism, 168
　inactive, 170
　infrastructural category, 169–170
Translation, 92, 197–210
　between cultures, 156
　religious claims into public/secular claims, 92, 197–199, 202, 210
　see also Legal transplants

Vertovec, Steven, 6, 17
　super-diversity, 6

Waltzer, Michael, 41
　see also Liberalism
Wisconsin v. Yoder, 226
White, James Boyd, 1, 197